Language, Space, and Social Relationships

The study of the relationship between language and thought, and how this apparently differs between cultures and social groups, is a rapidly expanding area of inquiry. In this book Giovanni Bennardo discusses the relationship between language and the mental organization of knowledge, based on the results of a fieldwork project carried out in the Kingdom of Tonga in Polynesia. It challenges some existing assumptions in linguistics, cognitive anthropology and cognitive science and proposes a new foundational cultural model, 'radiality', to show how space, time, and social relationships are expressed both linguistically and cognitively. A foundational cultural model is knowledge that is repeated in several domains and shared within a culturally homogeneous group. These knowledge structures are lenses through which we interpret the world and guide our behavior. The book will be welcomed by researchers and students working within the fields of psycholinguistics, anthropological linguistics, cognitive anthropology, cognitive psychology, cross-cultural psychology, and cognitive science.

GIOVANNI BENNARDO is Associate Professor in the Department of Anthropology at Northern Illinois University.

Language, culture and cognition

Editor Stephen C. Levinson, Max Planck Institute for Psycholinguistics

This series looks at the role of language in human cognition – language in both its universal, psychological aspects and its variable, cultural aspects. Studies will focus on the relation between semantic and conceptual categories and processes, especially as these are illuminated by cross-linguistic and cross-cultural studies, the study of language acquisition and conceptual development, and the study of the relation of speech production and comprehension to other kinds of behaviour in a cultural context. Books come principally, though not exclusively, from research associated with the Max Planck Institute for Psycholinguistics in Nijmegen, and in particular the Language and Cognition Group.

Language, Space, and Social Relationships

A Foundational Cultural Model in Polynesia

Giovanni Bennardo

Northern Illinois University

CAMBRIDGE
UNIVERSITY PRESS

CAMBRIDGE UNIVERSITY PRESS
Cambridge, New York, Melbourne, Madrid, Cape Town, Singapore, São Paulo, Delhi

Cambridge University Press
The Edinburgh Building, Cambridge CB2 8RU, UK

Published in the United States of America by Cambridge University Press, New York

www.cambridge.org
Information on this title: www.cambridge.org/9780521883122

© Giovanni Bennardo 2009

First published 2009

Printed in the United Kingdom at the University Press, Cambridge

A catalogue record for this publication is available from the British Library

Library of Congress Cataloguing in Publication data
Bennardo, Giovanni.
  Language, space, and social relationships : a foundational cultural model
  in Polynesia / Giovanni Bennardo.
    p.   cm. – (Language, culture and cognition)
  Includes bibliographical references and index.
  ISBN 978-0-521-88312-2 (hardback)
  1. Sociolinguistics–Polynesia.   2. Psycholinguistics–Polynesia.   3. Tongan
  language–Social aspects.   4. Tongan language–Psychological aspects.   5. Space
  and time in language.   6. Cognition and culture–Polynesia.   I. Title.   II. Series.
  P40.45.P65B46 2009
  306.440996–dc22
  2009008253

ISBN 978-0-521-88312-2 hardback

For Katie and Maya, Lucio, Matteo

Contents

Part II: Radiality

Part III: Radiality in social relationships

Figures

Tables

Preface

This book elucidates the existence of a foundational cultural model in a Polynesian culture, the Kingdom of Tonga. In so doing, a number of central issues in anthropology, cognitive anthropology, linguistics, cognitive psychology, cognitive science, and sociology are discussed in depth. For example, regarding the nature of knowledge representation, a distinction is proposed between mental model and cultural model and how they both differ from schemas (or schemata). Regarding the relationship between language and thought, a dynamic engagement is suggested and a distinctive role for metaphors is envisaged. A clear relationship between cultural models and behavior is asserted as well as a transparent link between various cognitive modules. The role of the spatial relationships module (i.e., space) in the cognitive architecture is presented as fundamental in understanding the internal organization of other modules (or knowledge domains) with which it interacts. Finally, social network analysis is used while investigating the cognitive nature and organization of social relationships.

A mental model consists of bits of knowledge organized in such a way as to facilitate storage and/or retrieval/use of that same knowledge (Craik, 1943; Gentner and Stevens, 1983; Johnson-Laird, 1983). I propose to call "radiality" a specific type of mental model, a Tongan foundational cultural model. The choice is motivated by proposals made by Lakoff (1987), Holland and Quinn (1987) and Shore (1996). Lakoff suggested and elaborated the concept of "image-schema" defined as: a way of thinking about one's experience in the world derived from "… relatively simple structures that constantly recur in our everyday bodily experience: […] and in various orientations and relations: *UP-DOWN, FRONT-BACK, PART-WHOLE, CENTER-PERIPHERY* [my italics], etc." (1987: 267). Holland and Quinn argue that a "thematic effect arises from the availability of a small number of *very general-purpose cultural models* [my italics] that are repeatedly incorporated into other cultural models …" (1987: 11). And Shore states: "*Foundational* [my italics] schemas organize or link up a 'family' of related models" (1996: 53).

I define radiality as a 'mental' model, because in Johnson-Laird's (1999) words "A crucial feature [of mental models] is that their structure corresponds to the structure of what they represent" (p. 525). The investigation of mental models, then, is enhanced by a thorough understanding of the context (physical and human) in which they are acquired and realized. I call it a 'cultural model' because in D'Andrade's (1989) words it is "a cognitive schema that is intersubjectively shared by a social group" (p. 809). Finally, I choose to term it 'foundational' because it is shared by a number of knowledge domains in various cognitive modules (Shore, 1996). In other words, radiality is conceived as a fundamental cognitive process that is used to organize knowledge across mental modules. Its intrinsic nature is spatial and as such it belongs to the spatial representations module (see Jackendoff, 1997). Tongans, though, preferably adopt/use radiality in other domains of knowledge – exchanges, religion, kinship, social networks, political action, and social relationships – in other modules, including the action module and the conceptual structure module. The existence of radiality does not exclude the presence of other foundational cultural models.

The decision to posit radiality as a foundational model and to investigate the domain of social relationships was also influenced by two other bodies of literature: one about a number of proposals suggesting radiality in many aspects of Eastern (e.g., Nisbett, 2003), South-East Asian (e.g., Kuipers, 1998), Micronesian (e.g., Ross, 1973), and other Polynesian societies (e.g., Shore, 1996; Herdrich and Lehman, 2002); and one containing current ideas about the content of a 'cultural' component-module of the mind (e.g., Jackendoff, 1992, 1997, 2007; Pinker, 1997; Talmy, 2000a, 2000b) that is orchestrated around the mental representations of social relationships (i.e., kinship, group membership, dominance).

When representing spatial relationships in small-scale space in long-term memory, Tongans prefer the absolute frame of reference. The specific subtype of the absolute frame of reference that they use is one that I have called "radial" (Bennardo, 1996, 2002a). *A fixed point of reference in the field of the speaker is selected and objects are represented as from or toward that point.* It is this non-ego-based (other-based) mental organization of knowledge in the spatial relationships module (radiality) that is found repeated in the preferential organization of other knowledge domains in other mental modules and as such it is proposed as a foundational cultural model.

The notion of foundational cultural model I adopt needs some clarification. In cognitive psychology, Brewer defines schemata (preferred plural of schema for psychologists) as "the psychological constructs that are postulated to account for the molar forms of human generic knowledge" (1999: 729). He traces the origin of the concept back to Kant, Bartlett, Piaget, and more recently to Minsky (1975), who called these "molar" constructions frames. A subtype of schema for sequences of actions is called script by Abelson and Schank (1977).

Schemas (preferred plural of schema for anthropologists, but see Casson, 1983; Keller, 1992) are proposed as abstract mental entities whose content does not need to be completely filled before the whole structure is activated/retrieved. Thus, in talking about an 'eating at a restaurant' event, people do not need to relate all the parts of the 'eating at a restaurant' schema and at the same time expect the same/similar schema to become activated in its entirety in the other person's mind. It is this type of "cognitive schema" that D'Andrade is advocating as "shared" in his definition of cultural model given above.

I propose as a foundational cultural model a schema (or mental model) that, besides being shared by a group of individuals, is primarily shared by a number of cognitive modules and by a number of knowledge domains in each individual. Basically, I am proposing to call a foundational cultural model a homology in the organization of knowledge across mental modules and in various knowledge domains. This organization (or structure) is a set of relationships between units of knowledge that results from the generative capacity of higher-level mental processes – they derive from them. The structure itself also exhibits generative capacities and is capable of realizing a variety of instantiations – it generates a number of cultural models.

This proposal is indebted to the "image-schema" concept suggested and elaborated by Lakoff (1987) in cognitive semantics and more recently by Mandler (2004) in developmental psychology. In cognitive anthropology, I was also influenced in my thinking by the "foundational schema" concept introduced by Shore (1996). Both suggestions, though, fell short in satisfying what I needed to explain my data. Thus, the genesis of the ideas briefly introduced in the above paragraph.

The proposal is new in three ways. First, it forces one to look for similar organizations of knowledge across mental modules and knowledge domains within an individual mind, and across individuals, i.e., members of a social group/community. Second, it looks at these mental structures as a stage in the cognitive understanding and construction of meaning and behavior. Reasoning, inferences, deductions, beliefs, and behavior (including linguistic behavior) undergo this generative process and are affected/molded at this stage. Third, it dovetails with research conducted on individualism versus collectivism (Triandis, 1995; Kusserow, 2004; Greenfield, 2005). Radiality, in fact, is seen as the generative mental engine behind various forms of collectivism.

Supported by two NSF grants (no. 0349011 and no. 0650458), during my search for evidence of the hypothesized cultural model, I collected and analyzed a variety of data – ethnographic, linguistic, experimental, behavioral, social networks, and geographic (e.g., GIS and 3-D renderings) – and used a number of methodologies – participant observation, interviews, semantic analyses, analyses/parsing of texts, administration of experimental tasks (e.g., memory tasks, drawing tasks, sorting tasks, kinship tasks), administration of questionnaires, indirect observation of social networks, social network analysis – in a cross-disciplinary fashion. The motivation for such an array of data and methods is to be attributed to the cross-domain (knowledge) and cross-modular (cognition) investigation conducted.

For example, linguistic data were gathered to conduct semantic analyses of the spatial relationships domain, e.g., spatial prepositions, spatial nouns, and directionals. Some of these same data and others were also analyzed to achieve an understanding of specific linguistic practices, i.e., instances of language use. Usage patterns and preferences emerged that enhanced the supporting evidence available for the main hypothesis. Moreover, some data was analyzed in a multi-dimensional fashion. For example, some linguistic data such as interviews about social relationships (i.e., telling a story) were analyzed for linguistic reasons (e.g., frequency of use of some lexemes), for social network purposes, (e.g., influence structure of the village), and for cognitive objectives (e.g., dimensions of the group – number and type of individuals – recalled and mentioned as an indication of specific forms of mental representation of those same groups).

The following statement summarizes the major findings obtained: radial organization is pervasive in the Tongan domains of knowledge and mental modules investigated. The findings, besides supporting the hypothesis, have relevance for the way in which the human cognitive architecture can be conceptualized. Specifically, a number of domains of knowledge are shown to share a similar fundamental organization, a foundational cultural model, thus indicating a specific way in which cross-modular interactions may take place. The role of cultural models in cognition is clearly established, but many questions about the specifics of their significance still remain.

Acknowledgments

This book is the result of one and a half decades of research during which I was mentored, supported, or simply helped by a number of people, institutions, and agencies. I am deeply indebted to all of them and I am acknowledging their contribution below in some kind of chronological order. For all of those I am leaving out, I do apologize in advance and ask for their forgiveness.

Kris Lehman and Janet Keller at University of Illinois, Urbana-Champaign, Department of Anthropology, took the renegade linguist I was and made me into the linguistic and cognitive anthropologist I think I currently am. Steve Levinson, Gunter Senft, and all the other colleagues at the Max Planck Institute for Psycholinguistics, Cognitive Anthropology Research Group, Nijmegen, The Netherlands, taught me lessons about the essential value of empirical data collection. William Brewer, Department of Psychology, Jerry Morgan, Department of Linguistics, and Norman Whitten, Department of Anthropology, all at University of Illinois, Urbana-Champaign, helped me in sharpening my thinking during the first stages of the research project presented in this book.

Three parts of my research were conducted in strict collaboration with colleagues and students: the "Digitized Tonga" database, the social network analysis, and the algebraic analysis of the Tongan kinship terminology. For the "Digitized Tonga" database I want to thank the remarkable skills and patience of Kelly Hattman, a graduate assistant, of Jennifer Testa, Caroline Pempek, Naimah Ali, Suzanne Alton, Dana Cali, and Paul Herrick, all Undergraduate Research Assistantship Program (URAP) students in the Department of Anthropology at Northern Illinois University. Paul Herrick was also extremely helpful for some data analysis and data conversion (from analog to digital). Kurt Schultz, Northern Illinois University, School of Art, was essential in the conceptualization and implementation of the "Synchronized Media and Visualization Analysis Tool" (SMVAT), the 3-D part of the "Digitized Tonga" database.

Regarding social network analysis, Charles Cappell, Northern Illinois University, Department of Sociology, was the researcher and collaborator that made it possible. His contribution to the research is explicitly acknowledged in Chapter 11, but the insights into the data that he provided go well beyond the content of that chapter. I am also indebted to Jeff Wagley, Nathan Walters, and Tony Robertson, all three URAP students at Northern Illinois University, who painstakingly helped in converting raw data into sociomatrices to be later processed and analyzed.

The algebraic analysis of the Tongan kinship terminology was conducted in strict collaboration with Dwight Read, UCLA, Department of Anthropology. The project was first conceived when we met at UCLA in 1998, and it took several years to complete. I must thank Dwight for patiently working with me over these years and slowly mentoring me into the arcane world of algebraic kinship analysis. It took me a while, but I came out of this experience as a better researcher than I could ever have become all by myself. I also need to thank Sachiko Koike, a URAP student at Northern Illinois University, for processing some raw data about the kinship project.

I want to thank Nicole Simon, another URAP student at Northern Illinois University, for patiently scanning and digitizing a number of Tongan texts and readying them for analysis. It was not an easy task to work with an unfamiliar language like Tongan, but she managed perfectly. My two Tongan graduate assistants, Lisita Taufa and Siniva Samani, deserve a special mention. The linguistic analysis conducted on the Tongan data about social relationships were all conducted with their close collaboration. I want to point out especially the three year contribution provided by Lisita, who worked with me patiently and effectively, both in Tonga and in the US, while we were both discovering and learning more every day about the Tongan ways of speaking and thinking.

Most of the material presented in this book was either discussed with colleagues and with students, or presented at conferences, or published in various forms. I want to express my gratitude and appreciation to editors of journals, anonymous reviewers, participants at professional meetings, colleagues in my department and other departments at NIU, and at departments in other institutions, and students in the classes I taught at UCLA, University of Missouri, College of Charleston, and Northern Illinois University. During the production of the book, the efficient and professional contributions of Helen Barton and other staff at Cambridge University Press were invaluable. This book would not have been completed without the contributions of all these individuals. Thanks also to the various presses that gave permission to reprint material.

A number of institutions supported my research. First and foremost, the National Science Foundation honored me with two grants (BCS 0349011 and BCS 0650458) that provided fundamental support from 2004 through 2008. At the onset of the project, the University of Illinois at Urbana-Champaign, both the Department of Anthropology and the Graduate College, sponsored my initial efforts. Then, it was the Max Planck Institute for Psycholinguistics, Nijmegen, The Netherlands that provided the financial environment within which the first part of my research could be completed. Later, I received some support from the College of Charleston, both a Dean of School of Humanities and Social Sciences research grant and a Faculty Research Grant. Finally, a number of Faculty Research and Artistry Grants (2001, 2002, 2005, 2007) and two Travel Grants (2005, 2006) from the Graduate School at Northern Illinois University contributed to the continuation of the research and its final completion.

I want to thank the Government of Tonga for granting me permission to conduct the research in the Kingdom. My fieldwork experience in Tonga has not only provided the data to fill the pages of this book but mainly enriched my soul with exciting and profound human experiences. The person I must thank first is Loisi Finau, my Tongan teacher in Tonga. She introduced me to the Tongan language, but most of all to the Tongan heart. In fact, after only a few weeks of working together she asked her family in her native village, Houma, Vava'u, to host me at their house for as long as I wished. Houma eventually became my main field site and the Finau family my adoptive Tongan family.

Regarding people in Houma, I must especially thank Sione Finau and the late Mele Finau for accepting me into their family. Besides, I want to thank in particular Nunia Finau, who worked patiently with me for months as my assistant, informant, and collaborator. Her graceful explanations, her soft attitude, and her warm friendship are one of the most valuable gifts I received during my whole stay in Tonga. Thanks go to Taniela Lolohea for supervising the data collection by my collaborators in Houma in 2004, 2005, and 2007, and for spending wonderfully enlightening hours with me while we transcribed interviews. All the people of Houma deserve a special thanks because they donated to me their understanding, their patience, and above all their friendship and respect. I want to make sure that they understand that I have carved a special place for them in my heart.

I want also to thank Siaki Tokolahi, one of my collaborators, who accompanied me on my trip to Niuatoputapu, and Semisi Tokolahi in whose house I lived during my stay in the village of Hihifo, Niuatoputapu. The people of Hihifo deserve a special thanks for their joyous readiness to cooperate and comply with my requests of performing tasks, to answer my thousands of questions, and to satisfy my endless professional and personal curiosity. I devote a special thankful thought to Leo Hoponoa and his family. He was my Tongan teacher in the United States and a student colleague, but most of all by living in my house for a year we became close friends. He was my collaborator in the field and helped me greatly during my stay in Ngele'ia, Tongatapu, his native village. His family hosted me several times while visiting Nuku'alofa on my way to Houma, Vava'u or back to the United States. Above all, Leo and his family contributed greatly in making Tonga become for me a familiar, warm, and friendly place.

While in Tonga, I came into contact with several people who befriended me, helped me, talked to me, and made me feel at home in their country. I want to give my most sincere thanks to all the Tongan people not mentioned, but whose company and help I have enjoyed. Without them this book would not have been possible. I hope I am faithful to the message they have entitled me to carry outside of their wonderful world.

The writing of this book was accomplished with the essential contribution of the continuous, warm, and supporting advice of Katharine Wiegele, my wife. She listened to me when I needed to talk about my work. She pushed me along when my mental energy faulted me. She praised me when I completed a task. She took care of the millions of things I was dropping aside while intensely concentrating on my writing. She was and is my wonderful companion, she completes my life, professionally, personally, and spiritually. No words are sufficient to express what I feel, and I am forced to make a "thank you from the bottom of my heart" suffice to provide a minimal pointer towards my feelings. Maya, Lucio, and Matteo are my children and they deserve to be mentioned because they too contributed to the process. They missed me when I was not around and they wanted me, they had to bear the burden of my swinging moody days, they adjusted to a somewhat absentminded father who was not really paying attention to violin or clothing issues, Harry Potter stories, or Power Rangers adventures. They especially missed me during my fieldwork months in Tonga, and I hope that marveling their friends with their father's travels and adventures in the South Sea make up for that, even if just a little.

Finally, I take full responsibility for any mistakes, misrepresentations or fallacies that may be contained in the present book.

Abbreviations

adj	adjective
art	article
clas	classifier
conj	conjunct
dem	demonstrative
dir	direction
expr	existential preposition
interj	interjection
iposs	indefinite
N	noun
neg	negation
num	numeral
part	particle: untranslatable before numerals
poss	possessive adjective
pospr	possessive preposition
pp	personal pronoun
pr	preposition introducing subject or object
prpr	presentational preposition
sN	spatial noun
sP	spatial preposition
tns	tense
V	verb

1 A foundational cultural model in Tongan language, culture, and social relationships

1.1 Introduction

I have just finished interviewing and videotaping a minister of the Government of the Kingdom of Tonga. My Tongan assistant is slowly collecting the video-taping equipment and I am taking my leave from the minister formally thanking him for his time and patience with my non-native Tongan. When walking outside the ministry building, I ask my assistant if she had noticed an episode that took place while I was interviewing. There was a knock at the door and the minister, after interrupting his speech, allowed the person to come in. It was his secretary. She opened the door, bowed and kneeled profoundly, and then asked permission to deliver a written message. The minister told her to approach and deliver the message. She did so by keeping her kneeling position and finally exited the room still almost on her knees and continuing to bow, never turning her back to the minister.

I tell my assistant that I was a little surprised by this behavior, also because the minister is not a noble. My assistant replies that ministers are due the same respect as nobles are. First, she adds, it is only a very recent innovation that ministers are not nobles, and secondly, ministers are high dignitaries of the land and are entitled to receive the appropriate respectful behavior. Besides, she did not find the secretary's behavior odd at all. In fact, she had often used that same behavior at school with some of her teachers. Then, she goes on to tell me this story.

One day a teacher called her up to the desk. She approached the desk bowing and almost kneeling (in the same way the secretary had done). Then the teacher proceeded to pull her hair and at the same time scold her for something she had done. She adds that she felt no *mā* 'shame' because she did not have a boyfriend or a relative in the class. She continues by saying that she would have felt really *mā* had she had one of those relations witnessing the event. She also explains that she would feel *mā* because she would have brought *mā* to them by her behavior.

This episode took place during my last visit to Tonga in summer 2007. I decided to start this book by telling this story because it is illustrative of a fundamental way of thinking in Tongan. What happens to an individual's ego is not the focus of that same individual's attention. One focuses on an other-than-ego individual (or more than one individual, or a group) and the consequences of one's behavior on that other-than-ego person/s. In other words, a point, i.e., a place, a person, or event, is chosen in the field of ego, i.e., the spatial field, the social field, or the event field, and other points are put in relationship to the previously chosen one, either centripetally, i.e., toward it, or centrifugally, i.e., away from it.

The episode specifically illustrates the presence of such a mental construction in the domain of social relationships or social cognition. The nature of the mental construction, however, is inherently spatial and it is in the domain of spatial relationships that I first encountered such a Tongan preference. Besides, I found it repeated in other domains of knowledge, such as time, possession, exchanges, traditional religion, and navigation. I labeled this preferred mental organization of knowledge a foundational cultural model and named it 'radiality.' The discovery of such a mental organization of knowledge led me to reflect on the nature of cultural models and hypothesize a fundamental role they play in the overall architecture of human cognition.

1.2   Why Tonga?

The Kingdom of Tonga is a Polynesian country composed of 170 small islands, divided into three major archipelagoes and lying in a south–north direction in the South Pacific. The population, around 100,000, speaks Tongan, an Austronesian, and specifically Oceanic, Western Polynesian, Tongic language (see Chapter 2). Both cultural and linguistic reasons brought me to this tiny corner of the world to investigate characteristics of the human mind.

Tongan sociocultural organization is unique. It is a millennium-old monarchy in which the majority of the population typically resides in small villages. A recent growth of a democratic movement makes its political landscape effervescent to say the least. In November 2006, political riots broke out in Tonga's capital city, leaving widespread damage from fire and looting, and eight dead. While the debate between loyalists to the monarchy and the recently established democratic movement has deteriorated, the legitimacy of the monarchic system has largely gone unchallenged (Hoponoa, 1992; James, 1994). Among both commoners and the nation's elite, Tongans feel that their cultural history is congruent with their monarchy. The hierarchical structure is so pervasive in the society that it provides a salient variable against which other sociocultural parameters may be highlighted and measured.

There are several reasons underpinning my choice of the Tongan language as the ground for testing my theoretical approach and for comparing the results obtained by my conceptual analyses of English spatial prepositions (Lehman and Bennardo, 2003). First of all and more generally, English and Tongan belong to two different major language families, namely, Indo-European and

Austronesian, providing a minimal test of universalistic hypotheses. Second, Tongan has only three spatial prepositions, thus it provides a good comparative challenge to analyses done on a language such as English where the number of spatial prepositions is much higher (around eighty, see Jackendoff, 1992b: 107–8). Besides, since the linguistic representation of spatial relationships in Tongan is realized by different lexemes from those in English, it is relevant to find out what conceptual content the former encode.

Third, Tongan as the language of the first people to be called Polynesians shows innovations which came to characterize the Polynesian language family. This is particularly apparent in the system of directionals it currently uses. A triadic system is in place compared to a very widespread dual one (centripetal–centrifugal movement) in Melanesia (Ozanne-Rivierre, 1997), the motherland whence Polynesians sailed away more than three thousand years ago. This directional system turns out to be rooted in the foundational cultural model this book elucidates (Bennardo, 1999).

These cultural-linguistic characteristics, among others, turned my attention to Tonga. My first investigation focused on the linguistic and cognitive representations of spatial relationships. The results were very intriguing. Linguistic and cognitive preferences for the representations of spatial relationships highlighted a deep-rooted preference for a radial system of representing space. That is, a point, i.e., a place, is chosen in the field of ego, i.e., the spatial field, and other points are put in relationship to the previously chosen one either centripetally, i.e., toward it, or centrifugally, i.e., away from it.

Later, I discovered the presence of this radial system in other domains of Tongan knowledge and consequently, I continued to stay focused on Tonga. I realized that since the fundamentally spatial radial system finds its way into those other domains I could be in the presence of a foundational mental model. Moreover, this model is extensively shared within the Tongan cultural milieu and it can be labeled a foundational 'cultural' model, an essential part of what it means to be Tongan. The presence of such a preferred model has consequences in the way an individual may think and behave. Besides, the finding of such a mental organization of knowledge also has concrete implications for the way one conceives of the architecture of human cognition.

I studied Tongan language and culture for fifteen years and spent more than two years of residence in the kingdom. I collected extensive ethnographic, linguistic, and cognitive data. Most of these data found their way into this book, but much more remain at the margins, and more yet never appear. Nonetheless, all of the data and experiences gathered contribute in their own peculiar way to the emergence of the principal hypothesis for this book and to its partial resolution. It was a long journey, and the content of this book represents a stage at which the traveler regrouped and stopped to reflect on the value of the achievements obtained.

1.3   The architecture of the mind and its internal working structure

There are two hypotheses about the architecture and nature of cognition that represent the foundations of my own position. The first hypothesis is Jackendoff's (1983, 1992b, 1997, 2002, 2007) "Representational Modularity;"[1] the second hypothesis is the one advanced by Janet D. Dougherty (later J. D. Keller) with Charles M. Keller, and separately, with F. K. Lehman. They call their approach to cognition "radically intensional" (J. D. Keller and Lehman, 1991: 272, note 1).

Jackendoff defines his approach like this:

> Representational Modularity is by no means a "virtual necessity." It is a hypothesis about the overall architecture of the mind, to be verified in terms of not only the language faculty but other faculties as well. I therefore do not wish to claim for it any degree of inevitability. Nonetheless, it appears to be a plausible way of looking at how the mind is put together, with preliminary support from many different quarters. (Jackendoff, 1997: 45)

In his attempt to widen the Chomskyan research project, Jackendoff devotes extensive attention to the investigation of the semantic component of language. He reaches the conclusion that *"semantic structure* and *conceptual structure* denote the same level of representation" (Jackendoff, 1983: 95 [original italics]) and he calls this latter "conceptual structures." Furthermore, this single level of conceptual structures is the "level of mental representation onto which and from which all peripheral information is mapped" (Jackendoff, 1983: 19). In later works (1992b, 1997, 2002) he refines his proposal and suggests the overall architecture presented in Figure 1.1.

Conceptual structures remain central in this new architecture. They are propositional in nature and their modeling resembles linguistic/syntactic structures (see Jackendoff, 1983, 1990, 2002). However, three major innovations are now introduced: correspondence rules (represented by bold double-headed arrows) or "interface modules" between modules, the "spatial representation" module,[2] and the "auditory information" module which also inputs conceptual structures. An interface module provides a link between major modules by being structurally compatible with the two modules it unites. This is accomplished by a structural core of the interface module made up of correspondence rules (not directly in contact with either modules to be linked), and two peripheral structures each compatible with the structures of one of the two modules linked

---

[1] Foundational to this proposal, but not homologous, are Chomsky's (1972) and Fodor's (1983) modularity suggestions (but see others in Hirschfeld and Gelman, 1994).

[2] Jackendoff had already introduced a module called "3D model structures" in 1992b: 14, but it was at that time only related to the "visual faculty" model.

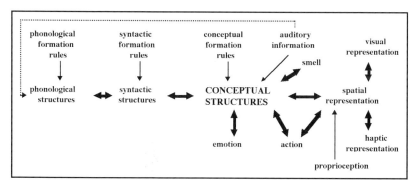

Figure 1.1 Jackendoff's architecture of cognition (from Jackendoff, 1997: 39 and 44)

(Jackendoff, 1997: 21ff; see also 2002). The advantage of this proposal is that it allows for major modules to be substantially different in their structures, while information can still move between them.

The findings of the vast literature available on the visual system convince Jackendoff to posit the module he calls "spatial representation" as separate from the central module of conceptual structures (see also Jackendoff and Landau, 1992; Landau and Jackendoff, 1993). He says, "[C]ertain types of visual/spatial information (such as details of shape) cannot be represented propositionally/ linguistically. Consequently visual/spatial representation must be encoded in one or more modules distinct from conceptual structures" (Jackendoff, 1997: 43). Furthermore, this module is also the center of reference for other modules connected exclusively and directly with conceptual structures in his previous proposals. These modules are "action," "haptic representation," and "proprio-ception." Finally, auditory information previously inputting only phonological structures is now also inputting conceptual structures. Thus, the architecture proposed has increased in complexity as a function of the increasing amount of new information about module interactions.

It is impossible in this work to summarize all the detailed linguistic analyses and literature Jackendoff brings forth in support of his proposal. One relevant feature of his architecture of the mind is that it is driven by the two largest bodies of knowledge recently accumulated about the functioning of the mind: knowledge of the linguistic system and knowledge of the visual system. In Jackendoff (1992a, 2007), a third type of knowledge, cultural knowledge, was added.[3] This led him to hypothesize another module of the mind, a social cog-nition module (Figure 1.2).

---

[3] In Jackendoff (1992a) issues related to society and culture in the mind had already been introduced.

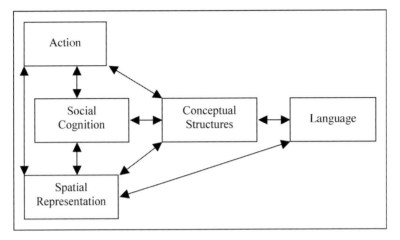

Figure 1.2 Jackendoff's revised architecture of cognition

On a very similar line of thinking, Levinson (2006) proposes that "the roots of human sociality lie in a special capacity for social interaction, which itself holds key to human evolution, the evolution of language, the nature of much of our daily concerns, the building blocks of social systems, and even the limitations of our political systems" (p. 39). He calls this system, the "interaction engine." I will restrict myself to Jackendoff's terminology for now.[4]

One problematic point in Jackendoff's overall proposal remains the collapsing of linguistic semantics with conceptual structures. Lehman and Bennardo (2003) demonstrate why this is not appropriate.[5] They argue for a conceptual content of English spatial prepositions that dictates the interpretation of their arguments as either Locus[6] or Place. An Object[7] is conceptually a Place when its geometrical characteristics count, and it is a Locus when it can be reduced to a Point because its geometric characteristics do not count. It is only when an Object (e.g., a noun like 'building') is an argument of a spatial preposition (e.g., 'to,' 'from,' 'between') that it will be considered either a Locus or a Place according to the specific preposition. The noun then acquires a specific

---

[4] Talmy (2000b) states: "Our general perspective is that there has evolved in the human species an innately determined system whose principal function is the acquisition, exercise, and imparting of culture" (p. 373). He calls this "system" the "Cognitive Culture System." In other words, Talmy too suggests that a part of our human mind is specialized for culture whose main component is the definition of the interaction between self and others or groups (pp. 378–400).

[5] See also J. D. Keller and Lehman, 1991: 281, notes 9 and 10, for a similar position.

[6] From now on a capital letter indicates a concept.

[7] The concept Object is very abstract and can be a physical object, a place, or an abstract idea (Lehman and Bennardo, 2003).

linguistic meaning that is different from its dual potential conceptual meaning (either a Locus or a Place). Similarly, Broschart (1997b) demonstrates that some Tongan lexical items are neither verbs nor nouns until they appear in a specific structural construction. That is, they acquire linguistic meaning in addition to their conceptual meaning. Thus, I will keep for now the distinction between linguistic meaning (i.e., semantics) and conceptual meaning (i.e., conceptual structures).[8]

The second hypothesis about the architecture and the nature of cognition I consider is the result of a collaboration of Janet D. Dougherty (later J. D. Keller) with Charles M. Keller, and separately, with F. K. Lehman (Dougherty and C. M. Keller, 1985; Lehman, 1985; J. D. Keller and Lehman, 1991, 1993; J. D. Keller and C. M. Keller, 1993, 1996a, 1996b). Dougherty and C. M. Keller demonstrate that it is impossible to access cognition fully by using only linguistic data. Their focus on "conceptualization" leads them to "characterize knowledge structures as constellations of conceptual units arising in response to a task at hand" (Dougherty and C. M. Keller, 1985: 165). These "constellations are ephemeral" (1985: 166), they are constructed only to tackle a "task" and do not bind the participating conceptual units beyond the duration of the task. When used repeatedly over a period of time they become "recipes," that is, habitual cognitive responses to tasks (J. D. Keller and C. M. Keller, 1996b: 91). The activated conceptual units include technical imagery, goals, and linguistic labels – that is, naming. None of these activated units, however, are independently sufficient to retrieve the conceptual constellation.

The two authors offer an anti-Whorfian argument by arguing that "the named class to which an object belongs for purposes of standard reference in general classification schemes has little influence over its occurrences in other constellations of applied knowledge" (Dougherty and C. M. Keller, 1985: 171). In other words, since cognition/thought works in task-oriented constellations that include a variety of conceptual units, it cannot be argued that language determines thought/cognition (although linguistic labels of objects are present).

This hypothesis about knowledge/cognition in action is very important, but leaves unaddressed the issue of the nature of knowledge, and unanswered the question of how it is possible for these "constellations" of units of knowledge to come together and constitute a well-connected unit eventually used in action. In other words, once it is demonstrated that knowledge is activated in bundles, the question arises about how this is possible. What is the nature of knowledge structures such that units of knowledge (i.e., concepts) can 'bundle' together?

---

[8] Recently, Jackendoff (2007) came very close to a similar position when he states "linguistics semantics per se is the study of the interface between conceptualization and linguistic form (phonology and syntax). It therefore studies the organization of conceptualization that can be expressed or invoked by language" (p. 293).

Is there a common underlying structure/nature for knowledge from different sources (e.g., perceptual, visual, emotive, etc.)?

These questions are addressed in Lehman (1985) and J. D. Keller and Lehman (1991). They state that their approach to cognition is "radically intensional" (J. D. Keller and Lehman, 1991: 272, note 1). In linguistic semantics, to adopt an 'intensional' approach means to consider meaning as the defining properties of terms (intension) and not as the set of objects in the world to which terms are applied (extension; see Frege, 1975). Consequently, Keller and Lehman look at cognition to discover its properties as mental/conceptual phenomena per se and not as defined by the external world phenomena to which they are related. They consider knowledge domains as theories, and concepts – units of knowledge – as generated within these theories (for similar positions see Murphy and Medin, 1985; Medin, 1989; Gelman, Coley, and Gottfried, 1994; but also Johnson-Laird, 1983; and Jackendoff, 1997).

They define the internal computations of these theories not as a number "of binary features in a matrix whose dimensions are nothing but such features" (1991: 288), but as a number of relations – including cause-and-effect – that are possible given the axioms of the theory. In other words, theories are computational devices; that is, given a set of axioms, a number of theorems can be obtained (generated concepts can be considered theorems). Theories are also recursive computational devices. Once theorems have been obtained, they may function as axioms for other theories. Considering knowledge domains as theories and concepts as theorems (and due to recursiveness also mini-theories) explains how they can come together to become "constellations" of knowledge. This is possible only because they share this basic intra- and inter-structure or nature.

1.4   A blended approach to cognition

I am convinced that both of these approaches to cognition and to the architecture of the mind are viable and can be combined. Then, I adopt a computational approach to cognition within a general "Representational Modularity" architecture of mind (Bennardo, 2003). My intensional analyses of both English spatial prepositions and the three Tongan spatial prepositions, five Tongan directionals (post-verbal adverbs expressing direction of movement), and Tongan spatial nouns yielded a number of axioms for a partial theory of space, that is, for a substantial part of the content of Jackendoff's spatial representation module (see Lehman and Bennardo, 2003; Bennardo, 1993, 1996, 1999, 2000b).

The major axioms of this partial theory include concepts such as Locus, Object, Vector, Path, Verticality, and Horizontality (for definitions see Chapter 6, Section 6.2.2.1). These axiomatic concepts of the partial theory of space are used to construct frames of reference (for a similar approach see Levinson, 1996a, 2003) that are part of the content of the spatial representation module (Jackendoff, 1997, 2002). In other words, frames of reference are considered theorems derived from the major axiomatic content of the partial theory of space.

For example, given the following axioms: a Locus (the speaker), a Vector – a complex concept made up of a Locus (beginning point, in this case the speaker), a Body (repeated points), and Direction – the concept of Verticality, and the concept of Horizontality, a relative frame of reference can be generated by using also the Repeat Function – to repeat the construction of vectors and obtain axes.[9] I describe a relative frame of reference as a set of coordinates – three axes: vertical, sagittal, and transversal – that create an oriented space centered on a speaker (see Chapter 3, Section 3.3.2). Once generated as theorems of the partial axiomatic content of the spatial representation module, frames of reference can function as axioms of a partial theory of space that can be used to generate specific spatial descriptions as expressed in linguistic strings (see Miller and Johnson-Laird, 1976; Levelt, 1982, 1984; Levinson, 1996b) or other behavior (see Ellen and Thinus-Blanc, 1987; for animal behavior see Gallistel, 1993).

The approach to cognition I adopt – its architecture and its computation – allows me to shed light on why my findings about the specific way of organizing spatial relationship in Tonga could be replicated in other domains of knowledge. The common generative computational nature of the content of cognition/knowledge, combined with the inevitable exchange pathway between the spatial representation and other cognitive modules, including the conceptual structures and social cognition modules, are the two explanatory landmarks. Since knowledge is structured in the same way, it can travel across modules. Since spatial representation knowledge interacts with conceptual structures, action, social cognition, and other modules, it can be replicated in other domains of knowledge.

The role that knowledge about space and the preferential way it is organized play in human cognition are of paramount importance. The vast amount of research and the numerous publications about spatial cognition clearly support this statement. I only mention here three works. First, that of Lakoff (1987) on conceptual organization in which he clearly delineates a conceptual theory in which spatial image-schemas are fundamental. Second, that of Mandler (2004) on child development in which she suggests that spatial image-schemas are pre-linguistically used and foundational to human conceptual development. Finally, Levinson (2003) poignantly shows how cross-cultural and cross-linguistic investigations of space yield findings that can illuminate our still limited understanding of the human mind.

---

[9] Please note that this process has been highly simplified for brevity and clarity of presentation.

In this book, I show how the preferred way in which Tongans organize spatial representation is reiterated in other mental modules, specifically, the conceptual structures module (several knowledge domains, e.g., possession, temporal relationships, traditional navigation, traditional religious beliefs), the action module (e.g., *fono* 'village meeting,' rituals, exchange patterns), and the social cognition module (e.g., kinship, social relationships). Thus, I argue that understanding any preference in the spatial representation module provides a unique and relevant entry into the preferred organization of other mental modules.

1.5   Cultural models

A sentence is the fundamental unit of analysis for language in mind (Chomsky, 1957, 1972, 1986, 1995; Pinker, 1994, 1997, 1999; Jackendoff, 1992, 1997, 2002; Levelt, 1989). What is the fundamental unit of analysis for culture in mind? I suggest a cultural model, specifically, a foundational cultural model. Before clarifying my position, I need to explain what I mean by culture in mind.

In 1911, Boas wrote:

Thus it appears that from practical, as well as from theoretical, points of view, the study of language must be considered as one of the most important branches of ethnological studies, because, on the one hand, a thorough insight into ethnology can not be gained without practical knowledge of language, and, on the other hand, the fundamental concepts illustrated by human languages are not distinct in kind from ethnological phenomena; and because, furthermore, the peculiar characteristics of languages are clearly reflected in the views and customs of the peoples of the world. (p. 69)

In other words, since both language and culture are mental phenomena, understanding one (language) is conducive to understanding the other (culture). Similarly, in 1952, Levi-Strauss wrote:

I would say that between culture and language there cannot be no relations at all, and there cannot be 100 per cent correlation either.
...
So the conclusion [that] seems to me the most likely is that some kind of correlation exists between certain things on certain levels, and our main task is to determine what these things are and what these levels are. This can be done only through a close cooperation between linguists and anthropologists. (p. 79)

It is well known that it was the illustration of the working of the mind underlying both culture and language that defined Levi-Strauss's life-long research enterprise (Leach, 1974). It was only with Goodenough (1957) that the locus of culture was clearly and programmatically located in the individual mind. His frequently quoted statement asserts that culture is "whatever it is one has to know or believe in order to operate in a manner acceptable to its members" (p. 36). However, since individuals all have a human mind, when they grow in the same place and have similar experiences, the content (i.e., knowledge) of their minds comes to be similar. This may have led and leads anthropologists to think of culture as external to the individual.

In summary, language and culture are related because they are both mental phenomena. Culture is located in the mind of individuals as organized knowledge that generates behavior. Thus, if we understand the content of the mind, both its working (i.e., computation) and its structure (i.e., architecture), we can possibly understand culture better (for a similar position see Strauss and Quinn, 1997). I have already outlined in the previous section my views regarding both mental computation and architecture. I am well positioned now to suggest a cultural model as a unit of analysis for culture in mind.

What is a cultural model? First and fundamentally, a cultural model is a mental model. A mental model consists of bits of knowledge organized in such a way as to facilitate storage and/or retrieval/use of that same knowledge (Craik, 1943; Gentner and Stevens, 1983; Johnson-Laird, 1983). A comparatively similar mental organization of knowledge is also called frame, or script, or schema (Bateson, 1972; Minsky, 1975; Abelson and Schank, 1977; Fillmore, 1982; Rumelhart, 1980; Brewer, 1984, 1987, 1999; Brewer and Nakamura, 1984; Keller, 1992). In Johnson-Laird's (1999) words, "A crucial feature [of mental models] is that their structure corresponds to the structure of what they represent" (p. 525). The investigation of mental models, then, is enhanced by a thorough understanding of the context (physical and human, i.e., cultural) in which they are acquired and realized.

Second, a mental model becomes a cultural model when it "is intersubjectively shared by a social group" (D'Andrade, 1989: 809). That is, a cultural model entails that the knowledge that it organizes is shared among members of a community (Holland and Quinn, 1987; Shore, 1996; Kronenfeld, 1996, 2008; Strauss and Quinn, 1997; Quinn, 2005). Third, a cultural model is used in reasoning, in planning actions, and it may motivate action as well (D'Andrade and Strauss, 1992; Holland, 1992). In other words, cultural models construct the mental context, i.e., culture in mind, within which and out of which behavior will be generated.

Where are cultural models located in the mind? Since cultural models vary in complexity and content, they can be located in possibly any major module and domain of knowledge therein of the mind. I restrict my discussion to the partial architecture of the mind introduced in Figure 1.2. Any of the five modules – action, conceptual structures, language, social cognition, and spatial representation – can host a number of cultural models. Besides, some cultural models can span over more than one of those modules and/or domains therein. That is, it may be the composite result or assemblage of some of the content, i.e., knowledge, typically found in a number of domains and sometimes also in more than one module.

These assemblages, or better cultural models, are constructed by each individual while accumulating experiences in one's life. In whatever community they grow and develop, individuals share a human mind and a similar context of experience. Again then, these individually constructed models are cultural because they are very similar and highly shared. In addition, it is not a coincidence that one of the fundamental ontological concepts, space, is assigned a mental module of its own. The representation of spatial relationships plays an essential role in highly mobile living individuals such as human beings. I suggest that a cultural model located in a spatial representation module might as well be replicated in other modules and domains simply because it is generated early in mental development and it is fundamental to subsequent bodily and mental experiences (see Strauss and Quinn, 1997; Mandler, 2004).

In other words, it is true that cultural models can be located in any of the mental modules, and it is also true that they may be firstly generated in ontological domains. However, since spatial representation is the only ontological domain with a clearly defined mental module, it is very likely that a cultural model, i.e., a foundational one, can be located in this module. The overall results of my research that I present in this book robustly confirm and definitely support this last hypothesis.

1.6   A foundational cultural model

A cultural model can exist at various levels of molarity with consequent different degrees of emergent complexity (Brewer, 1987; Shore, 1996; Kronenfeld, 2008). There exists a type of cultural model that though simple in its structure, and maybe because of its simplicity, is repeatedly used. Lakoff (1987) suggests and elaborates the concept of "image-schema" defined as: a way of thinking about one's experience in the world derived from "relatively simple structures that constantly recur in our everyday bodily experience: CONTAINERS, PATHS, LINKS, FORCES, BALANCE, and in various orientations and relations: UP-DOWN, FRONT-BACK, PART-WHOLE, **CENTER-PERIPHERY** [my bold], etc." (p. 267). Holland and Quinn (1987) argue that a "thematic effect arises from the availability of a small number of *very general-purpose cultural models* [my italics] that are repeatedly incorporated into other cultural models ..." (p. 11). And Shore (1996), after introducing a variety of types of schemas, states: "*Foundational* [my italics] schemas organize or link up a 'family' of related models" (p. 53).

I decided to combine the insights of Brewer, Lakoff, Holland, Strauss, and Shore (among others) and label my own conceptual synthesis a 'foundational cultural model.' This latter is a basic and simple structure, i.e., an assemblage of knowledge, that can generate other more complex models when used to merge a larger number of units of knowledge. I suggest in this book to compare it to a 'cognitive molecule' (see Chapter 6). I located one of these potential models in the spatial representation module of Tongans. They prefer to organize mentally spatial relationships by using a specific frame of reference, the radial subtype of the absolute frame of reference (see Chapter 3 for a typology of frames of reference). Besides, I found this preference replicated in a variety of other modules and domains. Then, I called this phenomenon a foundational cultural model and labeled it 'radiality.'

Radiality is a mental model that is specifically spatial, and since it is shared within a community, i.e., Tongans, it is also cultural. Moreover, since it is repeated in other mental modules and domains therein, it becomes a foundational cultural model. I conceive of radiality as a fundamental cognitive process that is used to organize knowledge across mental modules. Its intrinsic nature is spatial and as such it belongs to the spatial representations module. Tongans, though, preferably adopt/use radiality in other domains of knowledge – exchanges, political action, social networks, religion, kinship, and social relationships – in other modules, including the action module, the social cognition module, and the conceptual structure module. The existence of radiality does not exclude the presence of other foundational cultural models. On the contrary, it suggests the way in which other foundational cultural models could be potentially present and shared in the mind. It suggests the need to look carefully at other ontological domains and see how they are organized. It hopefully points the way to a potentially large number of possible discoveries for the overarching cross-modular and cross-domain organizations of cultural minds.

Finally, I propose here a language metaphor to illustrate culture in mind. Foundational cultural models represent for culture what sentences are for language, they are the fundamental unit of analysis. Besides, they have a syntactic structure and a phonological structure. First, they are constructed syntactically in the limited number of ontological domains (these might also be modules in themselves, e.g., only the content of the ontological domain of space is processed in the spatial representation module). Then, they are further processed and/or utilized phonologically. At this level, the interaction with other knowledge, e.g., kinship, emotions, identity, hierarchy, values, takes place and foundational cultural models become more complex cultural models with emergent properties. Eventually, performance, e.g., behavior, is generated by the 'phonological' scenarios (i.e., cultural models) mentally constructed.

1.7 Polynesian selves and cognition

Rooted in Geertz's (1973, 1980, 1984) suggestions about Balinese culture, and also in the Oceanic and Polynesian literature, "[A]nthropologists typically distinguish between two types of selves – namely, egocentric selves and sociocentric selves – that are cultivated by two types of cultures" (Mageo, 1998: 5).

The first, is a self focused on ego, and the second is a self focused on others or a group. This distinction is fundamental to many contributions to White and Kirkpatrick's (1985) volume titled *Person, Self, and Experience: Exploring Pacific Ethnopsychologies* wherein a sociocentric picture of Pacific, in general, and Polynesian, in particular, psychology emerges. Following the eastward migration of the people that colonized the Polynesian island world (Kirch, 1990), Samoans (Mageo, 1998), Tahitians (Levy, 1973), Marquesans (Kirkpatrick, 1985), and Hawaiians (Ito, 1985) all share the sociocentric self. Tongans, as the Melanesian migrating people who were the first to become Polynesian around 3,200 years ago, also show such a psychological preference (Morton, 1996; Helu, 1999; James, 2002, 2003; and also Kaeppler, 1978b; Small, 1997; Evans, 2001; van der Grijp, 2004).

A similar distinction, called collectivism versus individualism, is held in psychology. Triandis (1995) defines them in this way:

Collectivism may be initially defined as a social pattern consisting of closely linked individuals who see themselves as parts of one or more collectives (family, co-workers, tribe, nation); are primarily motivated by the norms of, and duties imposed by, those collectives; are willing to give priority to the goals of these collectives over their own personal goals; and emphasize their connectedness to members of these collectives. A preliminary definition of *individualism* is a social pattern that consists of loosely linked individuals who view themselves as independent of collectives; are primarily motivated by their own preferences, needs, rights, and the contracts they have established with others; give priority to their personal goals over the goals of others; and emphasize rational analyses of the advantages and disadvantages to associating with others. [italics in original] (p. 2)

These extensive and clear definitions can be summarized in exactly the same way as I did for sociocentric and egocentric selves: sociocentrism corresponds to "collectivism" and entails a focus on the group, while egocentrism corresponds to "individualism" and entails a focus on ego (see also Greenfield, 2005).

In 1991, Hofstede reported on a large survey of nationalities (also addressed as cultures) in regard to individualistic and collectivistic psychological posture and behavior. North Americans, Europeans, Australians, and New Zealanders display a high degree of individualistic features (with some variation within the two major groups). Latin Americans, Middle Easterns, Africans, Chinese, Japanese, South-East Asians, and Pacific Islanders instead score high on the collectivistic features (here too there is some variation within the larger groups). Both the anthropological studies and the psychological investigations, then, agree on assigning to Polynesians (a subgroup of the Pacific Islanders) a high incidence of collectivistic psychological stance and behavior.

My personal experience with Tongan and other Polynesian cultures highly resonates with those findings. I started this chapter with an episode that illustrates exactly a sociocentric/collectivistic psychological and behavioral attitude by Tongans. However, while I capitalize on the fundamental work that already exists regarding the issue of self formation and processes of socialization in Polynesia (e.g., Levy, 1973; Ochs, 1988; Morton, 1996), I decided to devote my attention to the cognitive processes that underlie the sociocentric/ collectivistic stance.

What is it that makes it possible to think and behave sociocentrically? How is knowledge organized such that reasoning with it generates collectivistic behavior? How is it possible to apply similar reasoning that generates consequent similar behavior to a variety of domains of knowledge? What makes the nature of the representation of spatial relationships dovetail with that of social relationships and that of exchange patterns? How is it possible to systematically behave in such a way as to avoid major collision with other members of the community and lead a harmonious lifestyle? In other words, what is the specific nature of Polynesian (Tongan) thought such that it realizes a sociocentric self and a collectivistic culture?

In the extensive materials I introduce in this book, I propose some answers to those questions. Foundational cultural models are generated in the basic ontological domains as a result of a collective developmental experience. These simple assemblages of knowledge are then used to structure and organize more complex cultural models in other domains of knowledge. The newly obtained models in their turn generate a cultural outlook within which specific behavior is conceived as plausible. Due to the shared nature of their internal organization, these cultural models generate types of behavior that are perceived and evaluated as consonant to the culture.

Specifically, Tongans' ontological domain of space displays a minimal organization of knowledge I call radiality, a foundational cultural model. This latter is used by Tongans when thinking and speaking about spatial relationships. In addition, radiality is employed in the generation of larger cultural models in other domains of knowledge such as religious belief systems, kinship, and exchange patterns in a number of mental modules like cognitive structures, social cognition, and action. Thus, these latter are structured homologically with the content of the spatial relationship module. Finally, these mental scenarios generate behavior considered culturally Tongan.

1.8   Methodological issues

Linguistic data are typically assigned a privileged place when inquiring into the mind, that is, mental representations (Chomsky, 1972; Miller and Johnson-Laird, 1976; Dougherty, 1985; Lakoff, 1987; Pinker, 1997; Olivier and Gapp, 1998; Bowerman and Levinson, 2001). The way in which meaning is organized and expressed linguistically is regarded as a reflection of mental organization of knowledge (see, for example, Talmy, 2000a and 2000b; Strauss and Quinn, 1997; Quinn, 2005). Since my focus was the mental organization of knowledge, I relied on a number of linguistic data acquired experimentally (e.g., space games), in semi-structured and unstructured interviews, and in available written material.

Entering into the mind via language provides a privileged but limited access to its content and internal organization. The architecture of the mind presented in Figures 1.1 and 1.2 clearly shows that connections exist between and among mental modules that make no use of language. Consequently, it was necessary to pursue a parallel methodological path to that indicated by the use of linguistic data. Then, I employed a number of methodological strategies, which I labeled cognitive or psychological tasks, that require no use of language, or a very limited and ancillary use of it. Thus, I obtained a different point of view onto the mind, quite different from that provided by linguistic data. Converging results between these two entry points into the mind provided supporting and stringent validation of the preliminary hypotheses I formulated.

Moreover, when investigating social cognition or, better, the mental representation of social relationships, a major methodological idea threaded together the data collection, i.e., linguistic and experimental. In the same way as maps of an environment drawn by subjects are compared to the geographic reality of that environment (see Gould and White, 1974; Downs and Stea, 1977; Tversky, 1981, 1993, 1996; Golledge, 1999; Bennardo, 2002a), social networks represent the (social) environment or reality against which comparisons are made. Then, I conducted a full social network survey of the village that represented my major field site. Thus, the content of the interviews about social relationships – people and groups mentioned – and the results of the analyses of the cognitive tasks (also about social relationships) were compared/correlated to the results of the analyses of the complete social network survey. Partial homologies (e.g., radial and vectorial organization with other-than-ego as center or apex) between these types of data were hypothesized and later validated as specific, i.e., 'radial,' mental representations of social relationships.

Finally, detailed ethnographic data played a crucial role in the successful completion of the whole research project. These data were acquired by more than two years of residence in Tonga over fifteen years since my first visit in 1991. It was the profound knowledge of the people involved in the research that determined the hypotheses to test. These hypotheses were conducive to the selection of the specific type of activities employed to collect data. And finally, it was again the ethnographic knowledge that allowed me to analyze the data appropriately and reach conclusions and insights otherwise unattainable. In conclusion, the linguistic, cognitive, and social network data became relevant only against the available large background of ethnographic data.

1.9   Synopsis

This book elucidates the existence of a foundational cultural model in a Polynesian culture, the Kingdom of Tonga. In so doing, a number of central issues in anthropology, cognitive anthropology, linguistics, cognitive psychology, cognitive science, and sociology are discussed in depth. For example, regarding the nature of knowledge representation, a distinction is proposed between mental model and cultural model and how they both differ from schemas (or schemata). Regarding the relationship between language and thought, a dynamic engagement is suggested and a distinctive role for metaphors is envisaged. A clear relationship between cultural models and behavior is asserted as well as a transparent link between various cognitive modules. The role of the spatial relationships module (i.e., space) in the cognitive architecture is presented as fundamental in understanding the internal organization of other modules (or knowledge domains) with which it interacts. Finally, social network analysis is extensively used while investigating the cognitive nature and organization of social relationships.

The book starts with this introductory chapter and is followed by Chapter 2 in which I orient the reader about the major coordinates to use in navigating Tongan society and culture. I also briefly outline the general characteristics of the Tongan language. Chapter 2 ends with a short description of the three major field sites where most of the data were collected. The remainder of the book is divided into three parts each containing three chapters. I close the book with a chapter in which I summarize the major findings and implications therein associated with the content of the book.

Part I, *Space in Tongan language, culture, and cognition* is dedicated to the investigation of the linguistic, mental, and cultural representations of spatial relationships in Tonga. In Chapter 3, *Space in Tongan language*, I first introduce the Tongan lexemes/words (e.g., nouns, prepositions, and directionals) used to express spatial relationships. Then, I illustrate their meaning and use. Finally, I discuss frames of reference, their typology and their preferential uses in Tongan.

When expressing spatial relationships linguistically, Tongans use prevalently the relative frame of reference (front–back and left–right axes centered on the speaker) in small-scale space (small objects very close to the speaker), but prefer the absolute frame of reference (fixed points of reference in the field of the speaker, i.e., seaward, landward) to refer to large-scale space (any size objects at some distance from the speaker) (Bennardo, 2000a). Tongan speakers are among the few documented cases – the other two are the Hausa (Hill, 1982) and the Marquesans (Cablitz, 2006) – of frequent users of the translation subtype of the relative frame of reference (an object positioned beyond a tree that is in front of the speaker is considered 'in front of' the tree) in both types of space (Bennardo, 2000a).

In Chapter 4, *Space in Tongan cognition*, I discuss the administration of a set of cognitive tasks (CARG, 1992; but see also Bennardo, 1996, and Levinson, 2003) that allowed me to detect a cognitive preference for the absolute frame of reference when Tongans represent spatial relationships in small-scale space in long-term memory. The specific subtype of the absolute frame of reference that they use I have termed 'radial' (Bennardo, 1996, 2002a, 2002b). A fixed point of reference in the field of the speaker is selected and objects are represented as from or toward that point.

In Chapter 5, *Tongan culture and space*, I introduce a clear example of the instantiation of the preferred 'radial' mental representation of spatial relationships coming from the results of drawing tasks I administered (Bennardo, 2002a). Maps of the island produced by the villagers living on it showed a radial organization with the major town at the center and their village on a radius originating from that center (neither positions correspond to their geographic reality). I also present and discuss the results of memory tasks about salient cultural events, e.g., *fono* 'village meeting,' and the analyses of significant events, such as exchange patterns.

In Part II, *Radiality*, I demonstrate how radiality is found in a variety of Tongan domains of knowledge in several mental modules. In Chapter 6, *The radiality hypothesis*, I explain what I mean by radiality and how it can be considered a Tongan foundational cultural model. I first summarize already introduced evidence, specifically from the domain of space, and then introduce new evidence from the domains of traditional Tongan religion and traditional Polynesian navigation.

In Chapter 7, *Radiality in possession and time*, I expand my investigation to two other ontological domains, possession and time. Both analyses support my hypothesis for a Tongan foundational cultural model by producing evidence for a basic radial way of structurally organizing knowledge in those domains. The semantics of Tongan possessives reveals an internal organization of the domain that is homologous with that of space. Similarly, Tongan expressions about time and temporal relationships display a preference for the same frames of reference used in expression about spatial relationships.

In Chapter 8, *Radiality and the Tongan kinship terminology*, an algebraic analysis of the Tongan kinship terminology reveals the central role played by other-than-ego terms like *tokoua* (sibling of same sex), *tuonga'ane* (brother for female), and *tuofefine* (sister for male). The non-ego perspective emerges as the crucial one for understanding the Tongan kinship terminology. The position and fundamental role of the term *tokoua* is especially discussed as supporting evidence for the main hypothesis. The findings about the Tongan kinship terminology convinced me of the necessity to devote my attention to the investigation of the mental representations of social relationships, that is, the social cognition module.

In Part III, *Radiality in social relationships*, I present my investigation of the linguistic and mental representations of social relationships, i.e., social cognition. In Chapter 9, *Radiality and speech about social relationships*, I discuss the results of three major analyses I conducted on an extensive linguistic corpus about social relationships: a lexical frequency analysis (use of the two Tongan directionals, *mai* 'towards center' and *atu* 'away from center'), a metaphor analysis, and a discourse structure analysis. The linguistic data point unequivocally toward a basic radial organization in the mental representations of social relationships expressed linguistically.

In Chapter 10, *Radiality and mental representations of social relationships*, I introduce the results of three cognitive tasks, free listing task, pile sorting task, and drawing task, administered to obtain information about specific preferences in the mental organization of social relationships. Fundamentally, I found an homology between the mental representations of spatial and social relationships centered on the shared use of radiality.

Chapter 11, *Radiality in social networks*, is dedicated to the results of the investigation of Tongan social networks. First, I present the rationale for using social network analysis. The social networks discovered are used as the territory against which the content of the linguistic production about social relationships and results of cognitive tasks about social relationships are mapped. Then, I introduce the methodology employed and the results of specific analyses like influence and social support. Finally, these results are correlated with a variety of linguistic and ethnographic data. For example, I compare the content (names and groups mentioned) of the interviews about social relationships to the results of the analyses of the complete social network survey. I found significant positive correlations; thus, I conclude with Johnson-Laird (1999) that "A crucial feature [of mental models] is that their structure corresponds to the structure of what they represent" (p. 525). Radiality, a Tongan foundational cultural model, is generated by the social networks that are characteristic of the Tongan village milieu while at the same time it contributes to generate the behavior that creates those networks.

Chapter 12, *A radial mind*, contains a summary of the findings regarding the mental organization of knowledge in four different Tongan mental modules: the spatial relationships module, the action module, the conceptual structure module, and the social cognition module. The evidence introduced throughout the book finds an integrated and coherent systematization in a clear support for the hypothesized foundational cultural model. I close the book by articulating three hypotheses: the first about the architecture of the mind; the second about a minimal typology of cultural models; and the third about a unit of analysis for culture in mind.

2 The Kingdom of Tonga: country, people, and language

2.1 Where is Tonga?

The Kingdom of Tonga lies in a south-west to north-east line in the south Pacific Ocean between 15° and 23° south latitude and 173° and 177° west longitude (Figure 2.1). The overall cultural area is best known as Western Polynesia and includes other countries such as Western Samoa, American Samoa, the Cook Islands, the Island of Niue, and New Zealand. The kingdom consists of approximately 170 islands with only 36 islands that are inhabited. The total population reached 101,134 at the last 2006 census (Kingdom of Tonga, 2007).

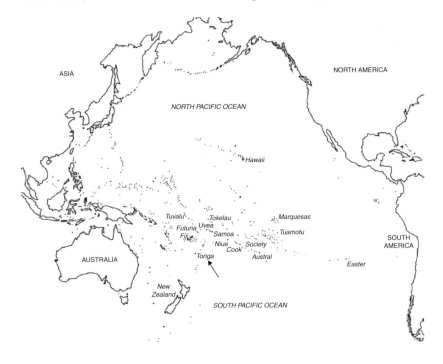

Figure 2.1 Map of the Pacific Ocean

Tonga is divided into three main island groups (Figure 2.2): Vava'u in the north (also the name of the major island in this group), Ha'apai in the center, and Tongatapu in the south (also the name of the major island in this group). To these need to be added three isolated islands situated in the far north, midway between Vava'u and Western Samoa, that is, the islands of Niuafo'ou, Niuatoputapu and Tafahi. The capital town Nuku'alofa is on the Tongatapu island, the biggest island of the southern group and of the whole kingdom.

The first human colonization of the archipelago goes back to at least 3,200 BP (Groube, 1971; Green, 1979; Kirch, 1988, Terrell, 1986). The evidence introduced by the archeological literature combined with the linguistic (Elbert, 1953; Green, 1966; Pawley, 1966, 1974; Grace, 1968; Kirk and Epling, 1973; Dyen, 1981; Besnier, 1992) and sociocultural data (Sahlins, 1958; Goldman, 1970; Kirch, 1990) clearly points to Tonga as the first place where a migrating population from the north-west (Melanesia) became Polynesian.

2.2   Tongan society and culture

The Kingdom of Tonga is a constitutional monarchy headed by King Siaosi 'George' Tupou V. He is the direct descendant of King George Tupou I who introduced the Tongan Constitution in 1875 after various wars in which he succeeded in unifying under his rule the three island group that make up the kingdom. King George Tupou I had previously converted to Christianity and opportunistically waged his expansionist war from Ha'apai on to Vava'u and then Tongatapu, also in the name of his newfound faith. Christian religious principles characterize many passages of the Constitution very likely prepared under the influence of the Wesleyan missionaries (Lātūkefu, 1974) who had first landed on the island of Tongatapu in 1797 (with very little success till the middle 1800s).

Among the many accomplishments of George Tupou I was the introduction of an hereditary title, nōpele 'noble,' that he gave to only thirty-three Tongan traditional 'eiki 'chiefs.' These nobles were the only ones, excluding the king, now entitled to own and distribute land, thus, excluding many other chiefs from extended land ownership. The Constitution also introduced a parliament with twenty[1] (later seven) members representing the thirty-three nobles, twelve members appointed by the king (ten cabinet members including the Prime Minister[2] and the two governors of Ha'apai and Vava'u), and twenty[3] (later seven) members

---

[1] Nine from Tongatapu, five from Ha'apai, four from Vava'u, one from Niuatoputapu, and one from Niuafo'ou.
[2] The Prime Minister is also the Governor of Tongatapu.
[3] Same provenance as for the nobles in note 1.

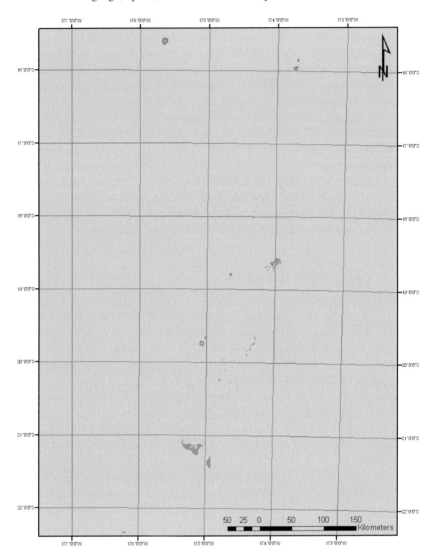

Figure 2.2 Map of the Kingdom of Tonga[4]

---

[4] This map and those in Figures 2.3, 2.4, 2.5, and 2.6 come from the Digitized Tonga database (see Chapter 5, Section 5.2.2 for a description).

elected by the Tongan people as their representatives (see Lātūkefu, 1974).

George Tupou I also actively had the last heir of the Tu'i Tonga royal line (the first Tu'i Tonga according to myth was the son of Tangaloa, the god of the sky) die without having married and having had an 'official' heir.[5] Consequently, as the head of the two other royal lines, Tu'i Ha'atakalaua (created in the fourteenth century by the twenty-fourth Tu'i Tonga who passed over to his brother the secular power and kept for himself only the religious one) and Tu'i Kanokupolu (created in the sixteenth century by the seventh Tu'i Ha'atakalaua for similar reasons as for the Tu'i Tonga), he became the only king of Tonga. The 1875 Constitution recognizes only his royal line.

In 1900 the British Government accepted the Tongan request to grant protectorate status to the kingdom. This special relationship with Britain lasted till 1970, when all powers were restored to the Tongan monarchy. However, remnants of these seventy years of protectorate status can easily be detected throughout the kingdom. For example, 'Britishism' shows in the monarchy protocol, as well as in the relevance of English in education and commerce, or in driving on the left side of the road.

The economy of traditional Tonga was based on subsistence centered around horticultural practices and fishing. So-called 'modernization' of the country in the last thirty-five years, mainly based on foreign aid and imports, has by now created the increasing presence of Western products such as cars, DVD players, and processed food. But it must be said that this process is not taking place at the same pace throughout the kingdom. In fact, village life, especially in the central and northern groups of islands, is still little affected. The life of Nuku'alofa, the capital town, instead, offers the typical picture of a small town 'bursting' with activities typical of the Western world milieu.

Typical agricultural produce are root crops such as *talo* 'taro,' *mānioke* 'tapioca,' *kumala* 'sweet potatoes,' and *'ufi* 'yams.' To these have to be added coconuts, bananas, mangoes, papayas and nowadays watermelon, peanuts and various vegetables. Pigs and fowl are abundant and are free-ranging. Cows, sheep, and goats are less predominant, but also present in the Tongan landscape. On many small islands, including Niuatoputapu, horses (introduced around one and half centuries ago by missionaries) are still used as the major means of land transportation. Intensive shell fishing and fishing with small round nets, among other systems, is conducted along the shores at low tide. Some traditional small *pōpao* 'dugout canoes with outrigger' can still be seen in use for fishing in the part of the ocean closest to the coast.

Land in Tonga is owned by the king, the nobles, and some by the government. The fact that foreigners cannot own land by constitutional decree has

---

[5] This does not mean that he did not have children, but they had no legal right to inheritance.

most likely, among other factors, saved Tonga from following the same historical pathway than that of Hawai'i and Tahiti. Each owner has the right to sublet
parts of the land to other people who will in exchange pay a tribute, usually
food. Every Tongan citizen above the age of sixteen[6] is entitled to receive from
the government a plot of 8.25 acres to cultivate for their sustenance and a town
plot of 0.4 acres to build a house. In exchange a very small monetary sum is
paid to the government every year (80 cents[7]). The increased population and
its concentration in the town of Nuku'alofa (approximately one fourth of the
population nowadays lives there) are making this right much more difficult to
be exercised with every passing year.

The contemporary distribution of the population in villages and small towns
is not the traditional Tongan way described at first contact in the late 1700s.
These first reports speak of a densely cultivated land with the population scat-
tered throughout it (Ferdon, 1987; Barrow, 1993). The only relatively high
concentration of people and houses was at a place on the island of Tongatapu
called Mu'a,[8] which was the residential compound of the Tu'i Tonga. To this
loose distribution of people on the land corresponded a very strict hierarchical social structure that is still in place in spite of very relevant changes that
occurred in the 1800s, such as the introduction of a Constitution, the abolition
of slavery, and the abolition of the absolute power of the chiefs.

Traditional Tongan society had at its top the *ha'a tu'i* 'royal line,' followed
by the *hou'eiki* 'chiefs,' *ha'a matāpule* 'talking chiefs,' *kau mu'a* 'virtual or
would-be talking chiefs,' and *kau tu'a* 'commoners' (Gifford, 1929). At times
after wars, there were also *kau pōpula* 'slaves' at the bottom of the scale.
Excluding the last two, all the titles were inheritable and mostly, but not exclusively, followed male lines of descent. The 1875 Constitution introduced the
figure of the *nōpele* 'noble' in an attempt to replace that of the chief in some
of its traditional prerogatives (such as owning land), but this latter figure still
exists. Moreover, an increasing market-oriented economy and an expanding
bureaucracy have lately added a middle class that spans some of the traditional
strata from commoners to chiefs (Gailey, 1987; Linkels, 1992; van der Grijp,
1993; James, 2003).

"Taxation [by higher classes on lower ones] took three basic forms: tribute,
so-called gifts of respect, and corvee [or enforced labor]" (Ferdon, 1987: 35).
All of the three forms have officially been abolished by the 1875 Constitution,
but it can be suggested that they have survived in 'unofficial' forms. Tribute

---

[6] While individuals are allowed to own land at the age of sixteen, they cannot marry before eighteen, and cannot vote before twenty-one. After asking many people about what age they considered a Tongan an adult, I received a variety of answers due to this tripartite system of rights. So,
   I decided to assign adulthood to individuals of eighteen and above.
[7] A Tongan *pa'anga* is worth around 50% of an American dollar.
[8] Notice that the word *mu'a* means 'front.'

was paid twice a year and one took the form of a very elaborate ceremony called *'inasi*. During this event first agricultural produce together with other gifts such as butchered animals (e.g., pigs), *ngatu* 'barkcloth,' kava roots, and various types of *fala* 'mats' were formally offered to the Tu'i Tonga and through him to the gods. Nowadays the king visits all the major islands at least once a year on an occasion that is called the *Fakatu'i Fakangaue Faka'ali'ali* 'Royal Agriculture Show.' Gift giving and formality of the types that have been described as taking place during the traditional *'inasi* ceremony (Ferdon, 1987: 82–90) take place during these events. Thus, after a detailed account of one of these events, van der Grijp (1993: 211–14) strongly suggested that it was nothing but the *'inasi* ceremony in disguise.

Kinship ties were and still are of paramount importance in Tongan society. Different names have been historically assigned to recognizable and explicitly recognized kin groups. Only two major kin groups in contemporary Tonga will be introduced here, *fāmili* and *kāinga*. A *fāmili* 'family' is made up of a married couple and their children living together in the same house and it usually includes some male and/or female collaterals and affinals (usually, son-in-law or daughter-in-law). The *'ulumotu'a* 'head' presides over this group.

The *kāinga* 'extended family' instead is a group of people living in different households, mostly in the same village, but often including residences in other villages. They are related to one another by a bilateral relationship of consanguinity (cognatic system or kindred). A specific *'ulumotu'a* 'head' presides over this group besides his own family. At marriage, a woman becomes a member of her husband's *kāinga*, but if residence is matrilocal, then, *de facto* the couple is considered part of the wife's *kāinga*. However, individuals opportunistically vary about the weight they put on their claiming membership in one of the two *kāingas*. Besides, in a changing contemporary Tongan society, membership of this kin group is not strictly following traditional guidelines and inclusion is increasingly restricted to closer relatives than in the past (van der Grijp, 1993: 135, 2004; Evans, 2001).

Four further groups are recognized at the village level: *to'u tupu* 'unmarried individuals,' *kau matu'a* 'male elders'/*fine matu'a* 'female elders,' and the *lalanga* 'weaving' group. The first one is usually composed of young individuals, but it may contain members of any age, if they never married. Interestingly, the elders group is explicitly labeled as male or female, reflecting the gender divide highlighted below. The weaving group is composed only of women of various ages with different individual skills, even though typically a minimum level of competency is expected.

The basic parameters that are applied in establishing hierarchy at any level are gender and age, with the former preceding the latter. A female is always considered higher in rank than a male. Consequently, a sister is always higher in rank than a brother even if she is younger. In the same way, if the wife is higher in rank than her husband, their children will be as high in rank as their mother. But, if the contrary is true, then their children will be as low in status as their mother. Traditionally brother–sister avoidance was strictly enforced with a complex etiquette attached to it. In contemporary Tonga the custom has become less enforceable, but it definitely still affects people's daily lives.

A certain number of events punctuate the life of Tongans. The most important are first year birthdays, weddings, and funerals. These three events are celebrated with elaborate ceremonies that may last weeks in the case of a wedding or a funeral (it depends on the status of the person), a very complex pattern of gift exchanges, and large-scale food preparation and consumption that includes the making of many speeches. These latter are characterized by an elaborate figurative language that takes years to learn and is the object of much appreciation and praise when exercised in creative, but traditional lines at the same time.

Men typically spend their days in the plantations taking care of the land and tending animals. Women make *ngatu* 'barkcloth,' weave *fala* 'mats' and do the housework (e.g., laundry). They also take care of the younger children. Food preparation is shared between male and female members of a *fāmili*. The preparation of the *'umu* 'underground oven' that is nowadays restricted to Sundays and special occasions is an almost exclusive male activity. Older children, when not at school, help in any activity that they are regarded as being able to handle.

One ritual that deeply characterizes both formal and daily events of Tongan life is that of *kava* drinking. *Kava* is prepared by grinding the dried roots of the *Piper methysticum* plant and then mixing the powder with water in a bowl. The drink obtained is non-alcoholic, but slightly narcotic. People sit cross-legged forming an elliptical shape whose long axis is headed by the bowl on one side and by the most important participant (usually a chief) on the other (see Figure 5.2 in Chapter 5). The actual preparation and serving of the drink is done by a young woman (who is usually, but not always, the only female participant).

There are different levels of formality that are followed according to the status of the people participating. The form of the *kava* ceremony that takes place when the king is present has been extensively described by Bott (1972). Drinking *kava* marks almost any event of any formality in Tongan life. More informal *kava* drinking gatherings take place almost daily in the villages. And the soft noise of the friendly chattering (usually gossip) mixed with occasional laughter and often followed by mellow chorus-like singing is a distinctive mark of Tongan village nights.

Every three years each village elects an *ofisa kolo* 'town officer.' This person is the one that goes around the village the night before a *fono* 'meeting' is to be held. He shouts the time of the meeting, making sure that every house has a chance of hearing the call. He also plays the *lali* 'wooden hollow gong' a few times before the meeting to announce its imminence and summon the villagers. Every villager above eighteen years of age is considered an adult (see footnote 6) and is entitled to participate in the *fono*. The Tongan *fono* still resembles the form and content of the traditional fono as in the words of Gifford:

Although commoners had absolutely no voice in governmental affairs they were assembled in what is called *fono*, to hear orders from the chiefs. Anciently the *fono* was employed as a means for telling the people what to do in connection with work or war. Every adult in a district had to attend. At such gatherings the chiefs and their matapules did the talking; commoners could not speak and had no representatives. Such also is the practice in modern Tonga. Chiefs and sometimes matapules had a voice in decisions, though usually it was the duty of the matapule merely to convey the chief's orders to the people. (1929: 181)

In all the *fono* I participated in, only a few questions were asked, and they were all calls for clarification since the messages that the *matāpule* 'talking chief' was delivering were regarded as somewhat complicated. No discussion or decision making stage followed the delivery of the messages by the *matāpule*.

Nobody visiting Tonga will fail to notice the overwhelming presence of Christianity throughout the kingdom. Following the first failed attempt by Wesleyan missionaries in 1797 to Christianize the islands, there was by the middle of the nineteenth century an increasing presence of Christian religions. We have already seen how the conversion to Christianity of King George Tupou I marked a new era of conquest and war, but also of unification and deep transformations for Tongan life. However, in spite of its small size, the population of Tonga did not give up their typical affiliation with a variety of gods typical of their pre-contact history by massively converting to only one newly introduced Western and Christian religion. In fact, the contemporary religious landscape of Tonga is characterized by many Churches, even if the major one still is the Free Wesleyan Church (44.1%) that is also the 'official' religion of the state and the monarchy.

Among the other Churches that are present in Tonga are the Roman Catholic Church, the Free Church of Tonga (result of a historical separation from the Wesleyan Church), the Latter Day Saints (Mormon), the Church of Tonga (also the result of a separation from the Wesleyan Church), the Seventh Day Adventists, and the Anglican. However, additional Churches are also represented, each with a very small number of affiliates.

Finally, in closing, we notice the fact that massive changes are taking place in this small corner of the world. Thus, people can drive cars on these tiny coral islands, use a cellular phone, or watch videos/DVDs, or drink and/or eat a variety of imported drinks and food. However, village life is still regulated by a different clock, one that incorporates weather phenomena (e.g., heat, tide), that adjusts to plant (and root) growth, that preserves inherited parameters for establishing one's position in the simple, but elaborated hierarchical structure they acknowledge as being their society. The new and the old, then, go together in Tongan minds, but they do not simply coexist, they are intertwined in a peculiar way that defines and models what it means to be Tongan today.

2.3   Tongan language

The Tongan language spoken in the Kingdom of Tonga is an Austronesian language of the Oceanic subgroup. Within this latter, it belongs to the Western Polynesian languages and specifically to the Tongic group, which includes only Tongan and Niuean. In linguistic, cultural and geographical terms Tongan is spoken in a country at the edge of the conventional border between Melanesia and Polynesia. On the Melanesian side we find Fiji and on the Polynesian one we have Tonga and Samoa. The major works used for the construction of this brief description of the Tongan language are Churchward (1953), Tchekhoff (1981), and Broschart (1986, 1995, 1997a, 1997b).[9] My personal knowledge of the language will also be called on when necessary.

In Tongan there are three different social dialects. One for the king, one for the chiefs and nobles, and one for the common people. The difference between these three dialects is only lexical and not syntactic. We will see shortly how this phenomenon is strictly related to a basic characteristic of the Tongan language. Tongan has two primary types of morphemes, function-markers and lexical units. The first type is a closed set and its members determine the construction of an NP (noun-phrase) or a VP (verb-phrase); as such they function as the backbone of Tongan syntactic structure. The second type is an open set and the members are not marked to be either nouns, verbs, adjectives, etc. It is their appearance after one of the function-markers that determines their grammatical role. In fact, the same lexical unit appearing after different function-markers assumes different grammatical roles.[10] However, only a closed subset of lexical units that I labeled 'spatial nouns' cannot appear after VP-markers and thus can never be considered verbs (Broschart, 1997a). The VP-markers are the following:

'oku	'present tense'
na'a or *na'e*[11]	'past tense'
te or *'e*	'future tense'
kuo	'perfect tense'

[9] Other scholars will be referred to at appropriate points.

[10] The very limited content of the first set and the massive openness of this second set partly explain the reason why the three social dialects are based on lexical and not syntactic differences. In fact, very little maneuvering is understandably allowed within the first set.

[11] *Na'a* is used if a personal pronoun follows, while *na'e* is used if a lexical unit that will be as a result considered a verb follows. This is also true for *te* and *'e*, respectively.

The NP-markers include definite and possessive markers, a subset that is usually labeled 'prepositions' (including the three 'spatial' prepositions, but see Broschart, 1995 and 1997a for extensive work on Tongan prepositions), and the peculiar NP-marker *ko* labeled 'introductive' preposition by Broschart (1986: 11) and later (1995) 'presentative.' This latter needs some discussion.

The presentative *ko* precedes an NP, that is, a lexical unit already marked to be an NP by an NP-marker. Tchekhoff (1981: 2–3) assigns to it a double function, topic-marking and predicate-forming.

(1)[12] a. *ko   e   faifekau na'a ne 'alu*
      expr art N   tns he V
      {the minister past he go}
      [the minister went]

   b. *ko   e   la'ā*
      expr art N
      {subject the sun}
      [it is sunny/there is sun]

In (1a) the presentative preposition *ko* introduces the topic of the sentence. In (1b), instead, it makes the NP '*e la'ā*' function as a predicate, that is, as a complete sentence. In agreement with both the syntactic labeling by Broschart and the functional one by Tchekhoff, *ko* could simply be labeled an 'existential' marker for both objects and/or events. Consequently, from now on I will label *ko* an 'existential' preposition (expr, for short).

"Tongan is basically a verb-central, thetic language type" (Broschart, 1986: 17) where more than selecting a subject and then making a predication about it, a state or event is first indicated and then the participants are specified. This specification is obtained by using different NP-markers (or prepositions) for the subject and the object. Tongan is also described and labeled as an ergative language (see Hohepa, 1969; Lynch 1972; Clark, 1973; Milner 1973, 1976; Tchekhoff 1973a, 1973b; Chung, 1978). In fact, the NP-marker used to indicate the subject of an intransitive verb is used to indicate the object of a transitive verb. The subject of a transitive verb is introduced by a different NP-marker. These are the two NP-markers:

'a subject of intransitive verb and object of intransitive verb
'e subject of transitive verb

Tchekhoff (1981: 8–9), however, provides a slightly different account for the Tongan verbs. He successfully argues for a basic voice-openness in the Tongan verbs that is associated with "the lack of orientation in the '*a* function-marker: this

---

[12] See List of Abbreviations p. xxiii.

means neither agent or patient [object], but merely 'first NP modifier function-marker'" (1981: 9). Then, avoiding the transitive–intransitive dichotomy, he classifies Tongan verbs as compatible with an agent-marked NP, that is, an NP introduced by *'e*, and incompatible with an agent-marked NP. Both types of verbs are compatible with the presence of another NP (either the second or the third) that is introduced by the NP-markers (or prepositions or spatial preposi-tions) *'i* 'at, by' or *ki* 'to.' Incidentally an NP introduced by *'i* or *ki* (and *mei* 'from') can be predicated. Thus, the sentence in (2),

(2) *'oku'I fale 'a e   kele*
    tns   sP N   pr art N
    {present at house subject the knife}
    [the knife is at home]

is a perfectly acceptable sentence. It must be pointed out at this juncture that there is no copula (verb 'to be') or verb 'to have' in Tongan.

The presence of the agent and first NP-markers makes the description of Tongan as a VSO or VOS language not relevant. In fact, even though it may be suggested that the first form (VSO) is the most 'typical,' it is also very common that the second (VOS) is used in normal everyday conversations. Particular interpretations of such uses may be thought of (e.g. shift of emphasis), but no systematic investigation (comparable to the one by Duranti, 1994, about the use of ergative forms in the Samoan *fono*) has been attempted so far of this issue.

Personal pronouns in Tongan are the results of the interconnection of three parameters: person (first, second, or third), number (singular, dual, and plural), and inclusion of addressee (inclusiveness or exclusiveness). They also take a different form if preposed or postposed to the verb. Table 2.1 provides all the forms of the Tongan personal pronouns. Most often the postposed pronouns are used in conjunction with the preposed ones. Incidentally, notice how 'gender' does not play any role in this personal pronoun system.

Possession in Polynesian languages is usually marked for 'alienable' and 'inalienable' things (Wilson, 1982). Tongan has two NP-markers (or preposi-tions) that express exactly this distinction,[13] namely, *'a* for alienable possession and *'o* for inalienable possession. All the possessive adjectives and pronouns are also divided along this line. Interestingly enough the forms that express alienable possession always start with *'e-* (the forms that express inalienable possession always start with *ho-*). Clearly, the alternation of *'a* as a single possessive preposition and *'e* as a morpheme for the possessive adjectives and

---

[13] In spite of being widely accepted this distinction does not capture all the nuances of the posses-sive system in Tongan. For a more extended treatment of this issue see Chapter 7.

Table 2.1 *Tongan personal pronouns*

Person	Number	Preposed			Postposed		
			Inclusion			Inclusion	
			Inclusive	Exclusive		Inclusive	Exclusive
first	singular	*ou, ku, u**			*au*		
	dual		*ta*	*ma*		*kitaua*	*kimaua*
	plural		*tau*	*mau*		*kitautolu*	*kimautolu*
second	singular	*ke*			*koe*		
	dual	*mo*			*kimoua*		
	plural	*mou*			*kimoutolu*		
third	singular	*ne*			*ia*		
	dual	*na*			*kinaua*		
	plural	*nau*			*kinautolu*		

* After the present (and perfect), past, and future tense marker, respectively.

pronouns is in a strict relationship with the two same forms introducing the agent or the 'first NP modifier function-marker.'

With very few exceptions (see Churchward, 1953: 33–6), Tongan lexical units do not have different forms for singular and plural. In order to express this concept some other lexical units or classifiers are preposed to the ones that are intended to be used with a plural meaning. There are five classifiers that perform this function. They are *ongo*, *kau*, *fanga*, *'ū*, and *ngaahi*. As must be expected from our discussion of the personal pronouns, the first classifier indicates dual forms, while the other four indicate three or more. According to Churchward (1953: 28–32), *kau* is used for persons, *fanga* for animals, *'ū* for things, while *ngaahi* can be used for almost anything. Lots of exceptions and particular cases exist regarding the use of these classifiers, but this general introduction will have to suffice for the purpose at hand.

This concludes the minimal introduction to the Tongan language attempted in this section. The description introduced has only scratched the surface of a very complex linguistic reality. However, I hope that a sufficient orientation was provided for a better understanding of the analyses of the linguistic data that will be presented and discussed in this book.

2.4   Three major field sites

I used several field sites to collect the data analyzed and presented in this book. Since the typical residential living situation for Tongans is a small village (almost 75% of the population live in villages), I collected the majority of my data in villages. The field site where I collected most of the data is the village of Houma in the northern Tongan archipelago of Vava'u (Figure 2.3). Houma's population is made up of 176 inhabitants according to the 2006 census (Kingdom of Tonga, 2007). In the early 1990s, I spent a total of twelve months in Houma with the Finau family, who still consider me an adopted member, an opinion shared by most of the villagers. I have returned to the village several time since then, but only for shorter periods of time (typically four to six weeks).[14]

Houma is composed of thirty-six houses and it is divided into three parts, *Fale Ono* (central part), *Selusalema* (south-east part), and *Holani* (north-west part) (Figure 2.4). I resided in the house that stands in front of the Wesleyan church. Notice that in spite of its small size there is also a second church in Houma and it is a Latter Day Saints (Mormon) church to which five families and eighteen people belong. The elementary school is located just outside the village on the road to Mangia. The state high school and the other private and Church-sponsored high schools are all in Neiafu, the capital town of Vava'u.

There are eighteen *kāingas* 'extended families' in Houma. Locally, though, since some men reside matrilocally, only nine are recognized as *kāinga* from Houma. This number went down to three when I tried to identify founding Houma *kāingas*. Many other *kāinga* members could easily trace their origins from the middle archipelago of Ha'apai, marrying into Houma during the last part of the eighteenth century. Coincidentally, this period roughly corresponds to the time immediately following the unification of Tonga by King George I, who was originally from Ha'apai. Thus, I gather that either by personal decision or because intentionally sent by the king, many men from Ha'apai went to marry women from the newly subjugated part of the kingdom, Vava'u. These marriages would in the future prevent the fierce opposition posed by the people of Vava'u to the conquering king by rendering a good part of the population 'king's kin.' It is in fact almost impossible not to be related to the king once tracing one's origin from Ha'apai.

While the village lacks a residing noble, the residing chief is directly descended from a well-established line of chiefs – one of his ancestors sat in the council of chiefs that approved the first set of Tongan laws (the Vava'u Code) in 1839, several years before the 1875 Constitution. However, he cannot claim full inheritance to nobility because one individual in his line of descent was conceived out of wedlock. Besides the chief, a *matāpule* 'talking chief' is also in residence, but his saliency to the life of the village seems even less recognized and very few elderly people ever mention his existing title. Much more

---

[14] I returned to Houma in 1997, 1999, 2002, 2004, 2005, and 2007.

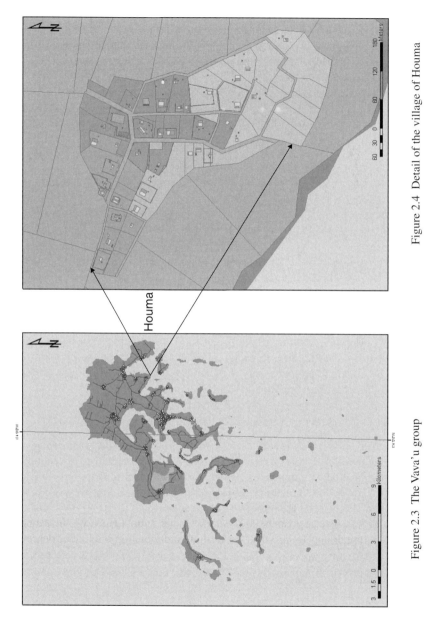

Figure 2.4 Detail of the village of Houma

Figure 2.3 The Vava'u group

Houma

33

visible is the local Wesleyan minister.[15] Ministers, however, are rotated every four years, and while they may appear very prominent during their appointment, only their office, and not them as individuals, is part of the long-lasting social fabric of the village. Another prominent figure is the *'ofisa kolo* 'town officer.' Thus, the social structure suggests three formal positions with some recognized authority: a chief with quasi-noble links, a ceremonial officer, and an elected town officer.

The main income of the villagers comes from subsistence. However, there are also a number of wage laborers earning cash and the cash economy has become more significant in the last couple of decades. Villagers can be classified into six occupational categories:

- 'subsistence workers and homemakers' (58);
- 'public employees' (2): the town officer and a police officer;
- 'professionals' (11): 3 high school teachers (commute daily to Neiafu, the main town on the island), 3 nurses (commute daily to Neiafu), 2 bank employees, 1 elementary school teacher, 1 school principal, and 1 retired minister;
- 'wage workers' (13): 2 shop assistants (commute daily to Neiafu), 2 furniture factory workers (in the capital town of Nuku'alofa), 1 security guard (commutes daily to Neiafu), 1 taxi driver (commutes daily to Neiafu), 1 at a car dealer (commutes daily to Neiafu), 1 as a cleaner at the market (commutes daily to Neiafu), 1 at the telephone office (commutes daily to Mangia, a very close neighboring village), 1 at the Ha'apai airport (in the Ha'apai archipelago, the middle archipelago of the three making up the kingdom), 1 at a gas station (commutes daily to Neiafu), 1 food distributor for *falekoloa*s throughout the island of Vava'u,[16] 1 unspecified;
- 'entrepreneur-shop owners' (4): 2 grocery store co-owners, 1 food stand owner at the market in Neiafu, 1 mechanic (commutes daily to Neiafu);
- 'not working' (5).

Several individuals (mainly men) lived abroad (either New Zealand or Australia) and came back after a few years. Other Houma-born men and women reside in other villages, in the capital town, and abroad, including New Zealand, Australia, and the United States.

Besides Houma, I also collected data for this project in two other field sites: the villages of Ngele'ia and Hihifo. The three villages represent a good sample of the variety of living conditions in Tonga. The village of Ngele'ia is located on the island of Tongatapu (Figure 2.5), the major island of the southern

---

[15] There are also some individuals of the Mormon faith in the village. However, they do not have a residing minister, probably because their number is small.
[16] This information is updated to July 2005.

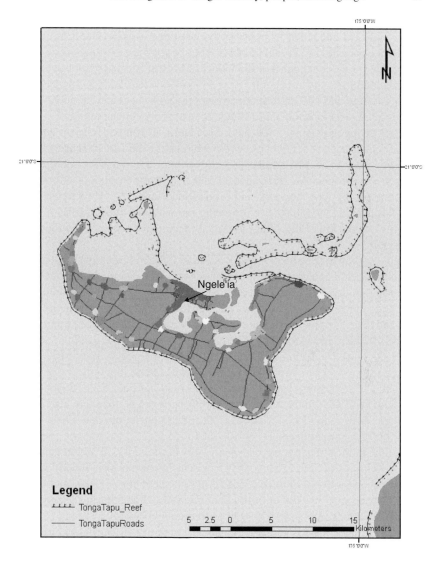

Figure 2.5 The southern archipelago of Tongatapu with the capital town of Nuku'alofa and the village of Ngele'ia (it appears on the map as the south-eastern tip of Nuku'alofa)

Tongan archipelago bearing the same name. The fast growing capital town of Nuku'alofa has expanded so much in the last three decades that it has made Ngele'ia appear to the superficial observer to be just one of its suburbs.[17] This is not true for the inhabitants of the village, who still consider themselves as a separate entity.

This village was chosen for a variety of reasons to be one of the field sites. First of all, Ngele'ia is the home village of one of my Tongan teachers, friend, and one of my assistants in the field, Leonaitasi Hoponoa. He spent an academic year as a guest in my house while teaching me the Tongan language and studying towards an MA degree in Anthropology. He was back in Ngele'ia when I resided there for three months and helped me in finding informants and transcribing long hours of audio and video tapes. My association with him was also highly valuable in providing me with precious experiences and insights into the life of the village as well as making me acquainted with many villagers.

Ngele'ia, however, was also chosen because of its close relationship with the capital town of Nuku'alofa. In fact, it shares with this latter many characteristics of its 'modern' life while keeping some of the small traditional village as well. It is situated at a walking distance from the town center and from the port. Cars and taxis are a regular feature of its landscape as well as video shops, and people can even receive on their TV sets the few hours of the daily broadcasting of the local TV station that started in 1993 and is practically restricted to the capital town. There are small grocery shops (some function also as bars at night), an elementary school, and even a couple of pool halls. Beyond the traditional hall next to the churches where *kava* is drunk, there are also some 'modern' *kava* club places. That is, a place that people join and where for a small fee they can drink *kava*.

Finally, most of the houses, with increasing exceptions, still retain the traditional 'village structure.' That is, they have a major corpus, *fale* 'house,' where bedrooms and a living room are located, a separate *peito* 'kitchen' and a *fale mālōlō* 'restroom,' usually in the back of the house. Some houses also have a vegetable or root crop garden as well as free-ranging animals, mainly fowl or pigs. In the same way as in most villages, the majority of the residents recognize themselves as relatives and strong kinship ties hold between groups of houses or subareas of the place.

The third and last field site is the village of Hihifo located on the western side of the remote island of Niuatoputapu in the north of Tonga (Figure 2.6).

---

[17] Administratively it belongs to the Kolofo'ou district, one of the seven districts in which the island of Tongatapu is divided (Kingdom of Tonga, 2007). As such there are no specific data about the population of Ngele'ia in the 2006 census, but it can be estimated at around fifteen hundred.

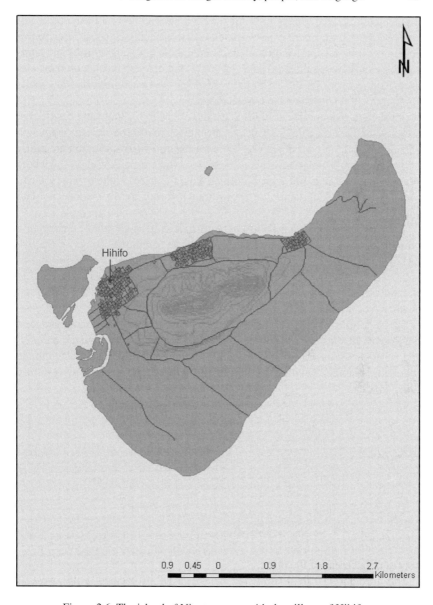

Figure 2.6 The island of Niuatoputapu with the village of Hihifo

It is a medium-sized village (683 inhabitants) and the biggest of the three villages on the island. There is no electricity on the island (except for two power generators, one for the local clinic and one for the telegraph house) and ships call there only two or three times a year in an unscheduled fashion on their way to or from Samoa. In 1992 a monthly airplane service started that has made communication with the island much easier.

Subsistence economic activities mark the life of this village and besides the presence of three pick-ups (not always usable due to long periods during which gasoline is lacking on the island) the major means of transportation are either horses or recently introduced bikes. However, you can walk around the whole island (dirt road only) in less than three hours (around eight or nine miles). Many houses are traditional *fale Tonga* 'thatched roof and woven coconut leaf wall houses.'[18]

The reason for choosing Hihifo as a third field site was that of exploring a type of village life that is the closest possible to traditional Tonga or the furthest possible from the Nuku'alofa contemporary lifestyle. Furthermore, linguistically and culturally Hihifo can stand for many other villages located in isolated islands throughout the Kingdom of Tonga, in the northern, central and southern archipelagoes.

This brief introduction to Tongan society, and to the Tongan language and the three field sites, should suffice to provide orienting geographical, cultural, and linguistic information while I discuss and analyze the data collected in the following chapters. I will add other details as necessary in the body of those same chapters.

---

[18] This information was personally collected during my visit in 1993. During my 2007 visit to Tonga, I inquired about the living conditions in Niutoputapu and I received similar information. However, the details about the number and type of houses, means of transportation, and availability of electricity (power generators) may have changed slightly in the meantime.

Part I

Space in Tongan language, culture, and cognition

3 Space in Tongan language[1]

3.1 Language for space in Tonga

In the village of Houma, on the island of Vava'u in the northern part of the
Kingdom of Tonga, Polynesia, it is Sunday. The morning sun is beaming on the
corrugated iron of the small local Wesleyan church. Most of the village people
are congregated within the freshly repainted walls of the church. The singing
of the hymns seems to linger within the building, but it is easily pouring out of
it through the numerous glass doors always left open for air circulation. The
modulated sound slowly fills the air and seems to push away the last swirls
of smoke left behind by the many fires being used for the underground ovens
where the food for the large Sunday meals is almost finished cooking.

A few youngsters hang around outside the building, occasionally peeking
in. Some of them hold babies or younger siblings in their arms; one is trying
to calm down a crying baby possibly awoken by a high-pitched note. Suddenly
one of them points towards the back of the church and starts laughing; others
join in immediately. Sunia's horse has gotten free from the tree where it had
been loosely tied up, and is taking a trot. The shadow of the building has kept
some of the morning dew on the grass behind the church. That could be what
it is after!

The episode does not go unnoticed inside the church, and feeling a certain
unrest, I ask my neighbor: *Ko e ha?* 'what?,' and he says: *Ko e hoosi 'a Sunia*
'Sunia's horse.' I continue: *'I fé?* 'where?,' and he replies: *'I mu'a, 'i mu'a 'i
he falelotu* 'at front, at the front of the church.' "Where?" I think, expecting the
horse to appear next to the officiating minister! But I don't say anything. I just
continue to look forward and finally, behind the minister, through the windows
on the wall, I see Sunia's horse raising his head with his mouth full of fresh,
green, juicy grass.

It was not the first time that the use of *mu'a* 'front' by Tongan speakers had
confused me. There are only thirty-six houses in the village of Houma and
most of them are on the two main roads of the village or on the *mala'e* 'village

---

[1] This chapter is a slightly revised version of Bennardo (2000a).

41

green.'[2] I expected that the side of the house toward the road or *mala'e* would be the front of the house as described in the literature about the neighboring Samoa (see Allen, 1993; Duranti, 1994: 60ff; and Shore, 1996: 268ff). But when I asked, the first answer I got was: *ko e mu'a fale ko é! 'oku tangutu 'a e 'eiki 'i hé* 'the front of the house is there! the chief sits there.' The side indicated for some houses was not the one I expected, and the rationale behind its being labeled as 'front' puzzled me.[3] The recurrence of this answer shows that the cultural parameter (seat of the chief) is very strongly felt and expressed. In Tongan society the figure of the chief is prominent in the daily life of villagers. But still, I thought it must be possible to understand the spatial parameter that is used. The chief knows where to sit even when he enters an unfamiliar house. He is able to determine (as are all villagers) the front of the house without being told. As a matter of fact, his choice of where to sit determines and fixes all the seating arrangements of the other participants in the event of an official visit.

It may be argued that there is no fixed front after all, and that the sitting place of the chief would simply determine the front in each event. But this is not the case. In fact, people point to a specific side of the interior of the house when asked to indicate where the front of the house is. So, even though it may change on some casual occasions,[4] there must be some spatial parameter/s that both chiefs and ordinary people apply to the house in establishing its front.

In my questioning about front assignment to cultural objects I also inquired about the possibility of a village having a front. The question itself did not cause any problems and Tongans seemed prompt and eager to answer it. However, in the same way as for houses, it was difficult for me to understand how they determine which part of the village is its front. I asked many persons in a number of villages, but could not obtain a 'typical' direction or side of the village as, probably naively, I was expecting. Every village community seems to have its own parameters for determining where the front of their village is. Is it possible that such a localized representation of space exists, or is it more likely that some general system is being used that escapes current scholarly knowledge and frustrated my understanding?

---

[2] In Polynesian villages this is a typical open space with houses around it mostly used for communal activities like formal gatherings.

[3] Tongan language distinguishes between *mu'a* 'front' and *mata* that among other meanings – 'eye,' 'face' – has that of 'façade.' By this latter they mean one of the sides of an object, including its vertical extension (that is why I glossed it 'façade'). However, while Tongans are reluctant to assign a *mata* to the house, they are eager to talk of the *mu'a* of the house. Thus, this work will deal only with *mu'a* and leave the treatment of *mata* to another occasion.

[4] I witnessed some events in which the chief did not sit in the part of the house later indicated as front. All these events where very informal. And when asked, participants stated clearly that the type of event had brought about the breaking of certain rules of which they were all perfectly aware.

In order to find an explanation for the few puzzles introduced it is necessary to look closely at the way in which spatial relationships are represented mentally and expressed linguistically in Tongan. Choosing a frame of reference, or perspective taking, is a universal prerequisite of any spatial description. A frame of reference (FoR) is a set of coordinates (three intersecting axes: vertical, sagittal, and transversal) used to construct an oriented space within which spatial relationships among objects are identified (see Brewer and Pears, 1993 for a discussion of FoR). There are three major types of FoR: relative, intrinsic, and absolute (see Levinson, 1996a; Pederson *et al.*, 1998, for a typology of FoR; and Bennardo, 1996, 2004, for a revision of that typology). A relative FoR is centered on a speaker and it remains centered on the speaker when the speaker moves, e.g., when one says, "The ball is in front of me." An intrinsic FoR is centered on an object and it remains centered on the object when the object moves, e.g., "The ball is in front of the car." An absolute FoR uses fixed points of reference, e.g., north, south, east, west, as in "The town is south of the river."

Evidence is being accumulated by research conducted in a variety of cross-linguistic and cross-cultural contexts all over the world (see Hill, 1982; Levinson, 1996b; Hill, 1997; Ozanne-Rivierre, 1997; Pederson, 1993, 1995; Pederson and Roelofs, 1995; Senft, 1997; Bennardo, 2002c; Cablitz, 2006) about the peculiar preferences of some languages and cultures to express spatial relationships in habitual modalities. In other words, some speaking communities, culturally defined, show mental and linguistic preferences for certain FoRs in describing spatial relationships.

Knowing which FoRs are preferentially used in language and in mind (independent from language) by Tongan speakers can contribute to finding an explanation of the puzzling front assignments to houses, churches, and villages. It is, in fact, only by means of one of the various FoRs universally available that any space can be constructed and oriented. Orientation of a specific space means, among other things, that a front is determined. Determining the front means that a back as well as two sides (left and right) can be assigned. If there is a preferential FoR in the language use of Tongans, this preference could be interpreted as a specific preferential organization of spatial relationships at the conceptual level. Consequently, it could be argued that the way in which Tongans assign front to houses, churches, and other entities (e.g., villages) may be influenced by this preferential mental organization of spatial relationships.

The major goal of this chapter is to describe how Tongans conceptualize and express linguistically spatial relationships, including the concept of 'front.' I first describe the methodology used for the collection of the language corpus. Second, I introduce the lexical items that are used in Tongan to express spatial relationships and discuss how these lexical items are used to realize specific

FoRs. Third, I present the results of the analyses conducted on the language corpus about both small-scale and large-scale space. The results of my study suggest that Tongans prefer different FoRs in the two contexts. Besides, their frequent use in both contexts of the 'translation' subtype of the relative FoR makes them an almost unique case in the literature about space, the only other documented cases being the Hausa speakers (Hill, 1982) and the Marquesans (Cablitz, 2006).

Finally, I close the chapter by providing an explanation for the puzzling linguistic expressions introduced. We see how the preferences of some FoRs in linguistic uses in a variety of contexts are related to the way in which front is assigned to cultural objects such as house, church, and village. I also address corollary questions such as: how much do linguistic data reveal about mental organization? That is, are data about linguistic representations of spatial relationships analyzed in isolation sufficient in clarifying habitual thought patterns? What role does culture play in such processes?

3.2   Methodology for the collection of the linguistic data

In 1953, Churchward wrote *Tongan Grammar*, a book that has since become the obligatory introduction to Tongan language. Churchward's Grammar provides very limited examples of instances of language use and even less information about the context of use of the linguistic examples presented. Most of the language examples Churchward introduced were merely intended to clarify whatever grammatical points were being described. For this reason I decided to conduct an extensive collection and elicitation of Tongan linguistic data about the representations of spatial relationships.

I collected a good part of the linguistic corpus on which I later conducted my analyses by using a number of language tasks from a set prepared by the Cognitive Anthropology Research Group at the Max Planck Institute for Psycholinguistics, Nijmegen, The Netherlands (see CARG, 1992 and Danziger, 1993). Another part was obtained by means of interviews, all conducted in Tongan. Another very relevant part consisted of my almost daily notes about conversations between Tongans and myself or between Tongan speakers. I videotaped all the language tasks and audio-recorded the interviews. I transcribed both the language tasks and the interviews *in loco* with the help of native informants. The full description and range of the language activities used to collect the Tongan data can be found in Bennardo (1996: 129ff; but see also CARG, 1992). Here I only illustrate in detail three types of language tasks.[5]

---

[5] See Pederson *et al.* (1998) for a detailed description and illustration of these three tasks.

The first type of language task involved asking two informants to take part in a game.[6] They were asked to sit next to each other, facing in the same direction with a screen between them blocking their view of one another. The two participants were then given an identical set of photographs laid out in front of them face-up. They were also told that the two sets of photographs were identical. One of the two participants was assigned the role of 'director,' that is, s/he had to choose a photograph, describe it to the best of her/his capacity, and have the other player, the 'matcher,' select the same photograph. The goal of the game was to correctly match the sequence of the oral descriptions of the photographs with the sequence of the photographs chosen and put aside. Each photograph used for this task contained two or three objects whose spatial relationship to each other varied on three axes: vertical, sagittal (front–back), and transverse (left–right). This activity was intended to elicit a maximum number of linguistic descriptions of static spatial relationships. Descriptions of motion were deliberately left out of this first type of task.

The second type of language task involved a game in which two informants sat in the same position (as above), and followed a very similar procedure. The only relevant difference between the two types of task was that this time the two participants were asked to manipulate two dissimilar types of objects. While a set of photographs containing a variety of assemblages of objects was again laid out in front of the director, the matcher was given a set of the real objects that were portrayed in the photographs. The latter had to assemble some of the objects received according to the linguistic descriptions of the director. At the end of each description of the photographs, the two players were allowed to check the results of their cooperation and make appropriate changes, if necessary.

Like the first task, this second type of task elicited many descriptions of static spatial relationships. However, this time a different discourse genre was elicited – that of 'giving instructions' – to be added to the pure and simple 'descriptions' required by the first type of task. The consequences of each instruction, or of a group of instructions, on the second informant's behavior could be checked by looking at the videotapes of the sessions. Moreover, this task was designed so that some descriptions of motion were elicited. This was especially true when the two participants were allowed to check the results of their cooperation that had clearly resulted in a wrong assemblage of the objects. But it was the third type of task that explicitly elicited linguistic expressions addressing motion events.

The third type of language task was again a kind of game involving a screen dividing two participants sitting and facing in the same direction.[7] In

[6] The instructions were given in Tongan.
[7] The name of this activity is "Route Description" and is mainly due to the work of Gunter Senft (see Brown, Senft, and Wheeldon, 1993: 92) and David Wilkins, both members of CARG (see Danziger, 1993), but based on work by Weissenborn (1986).

this game two participants have an almost identical set-up scene in front of them containing things like a Lego bridge, two Lego doors, two Lego houses, a fence, a truck, etc. The director's task is to move a little plastic human along a specified[8] route in the scene in front of him/her. In the second player's scene the route is not indicated. While the director is performing his/her task, s/he has to describe out loud what s/he is doing. In this way the partner is supposed to be able to follow exactly the same route on the scene in front of her/him with the identical plastic human s/he has available. Again, as in the second type of activity, the participants could check what they did at the end of each of the four route descriptions. The two participants took turns playing the director role.

These three language tasks were administered to eight couples for a total of sixteen individuals from three villages in Tonga, Ngele'ia on the island of Tongatapu, Hihifo on the island of Niuatoputapu, and Houma on the island of Vava'u. In choosing the individuals, an attempt was made to involve an equal number of men and women. Their ages ranged from twenty-two to seventy-three years. The level of education of the informants as well as their knowledge of English, though minimal for all, decreased with increasing age. An attempt was made to choose as many monolingual informants as possible. However, the widespread presence of English throughout the Kingdom of Tonga made this very difficult. In fact, almost all Tongans have at least a limited set of English lexical items and phrases that they manage to master and occasionally use in their lives.

The types of language tasks just described yielded language data characterized by a common denominator: they were mostly linguistic descriptions of spatial relationships in small-scale space. Regarding large-scale space, the most important tool used was the interview. Besides many topical interviews[9] (e.g., about agricultural practices, myths, rituals, etc.), I labeled one specific type of interview 'Giving Directions.' I conducted fifteen of these 'Giving Directions' interviews.

During the first part of the interview the informant was asked to provide from memory directions on how to reach by bike[10] some places, mostly villages, but also some beaches, on the island of Vava'u. The places were carefully chosen so as to lie either on the north–south or on the east–west axis. In order to avoid the use of names of landmarks and of villages, the informants

---

[8] The route was indicated by a thin metal chain laid on the scene.

[9] Again, for more detailed descriptions see Bennardo (1996: 129ff).

[10] I bought a mountain bike while residing in Vava'u, the main island of a northern homonymous archipelago in Tonga, and used it to visit many places on the island in addition to commuting from my village of residence, Houma, to town. This gave me the opportunity to ask for directions for real purposes either before or after my trips. It also provided ample opportunities to discuss lived geographical space (large-scale space).

were asked to pretend they were talking to a person with no knowledge of the island at all. After a couple of examples from memory, the informants were shown a map of the northern Tongan archipelago of Vava'u, including the homonymous island on which we were situated. They were then asked to provide directions between two new places on the island with the help of this map. The north of the map was positioned away from the informants, with the south closer to them.[11] They were free to use the map according to their felt needs. In fact, some would only look at it, others would occasionally point at it, and others would indicate the whole route on the map with either a finger or even an ad hoc pointer (e.g., a stick).

Finally, the informants were asked to give me directions on how to sail (or go on a motor boat or canoe) between two islands. As for the routes on land, the choice of the islands was intended to elicit directions of movement along both major cardinal axes. All informants were again asked first to give me directions from memory and then by looking at the map of the Vava'u archipelago. This variety of language activities was necessary in order to cover the whole range – from small-scale to large-scale space, and from static relationships to those involving motion – of linguistic descriptions of spatial relationships.[12] I now introduce and discuss relevant parts of the Tongan linguistic data that were obtained.

3.3   The Tongan linguistic data

Three types of Tongan linguistic data are introduced and discussed in the following sections. The first type consists of lexical items predominantly used by Tongans to express linguistically spatial relationships. A minimal discussion of their meaning or conceptual content is provided. The second type of data are instances of use of the lexical items presented. First, I describe how these lexemes are used to realize various FoRs. Then, I look at specific contextualized productions (i.e., in the context of language tasks) of linguistic representations (phrases and sentences) of spatial relationships. These productions highlight specific cultural preferences in realizing linguistically parts of the conceptual content of supposedly universal features of the conceptualization of space. In other words, we see if Tongans privilege any specific FoR when expressing linguistically spatial relationships. The third type of data represents an exploration of the close link between linguistic and cultural practices. In Section 3.4, I discuss how Tongans express and attribute front to cultural objects such as houses, churches, and villages. Both spatial and sociocultural parameters used by Tongans are investigated.

---

[11] Cardinal points were not indicated on the map.
[12] My personal notes about conversations with Tongans and between Tongans were also relevant.

3.3.1   Tongan lexemes expressing spatial relationships

From the analyses of these linguistic data, it appears that there are only three sets of lexical items used in the linguistic descriptions of spatial relationships in Tongan.[13] First, there are three spatial prepositions that make up a semantically defined subset of the formal closed set of Tongan prepositions (see Broschart, 1997a and 1997b). Second, there is a set of adverbs. Because of their close association with the concept of Direction, they will be referred to as 'directionals' (see also Broschart, 1995).[14] This set can be divided into two subsets, with two and three members respectively. Third, there is a formally distinct set of nouns that will be called 'spatial nouns.'

3.3.1.1   Tongan spatial prepositions
The forms and the glosses of the three Tongan spatial prepositions are the following:

(1) 'i   ki   mei
     'at' 'to' 'from'

In his grammar Churchward also indicates six other forms, 'ia, 'iate, kia, kiate, meia, meiate (1953: 109). These other forms are morphologically conditioned allomorphs of the three forms in (1). In fact, the addition of a takes place before a personal noun, while that of ate takes place before a personal pronoun. In spite of the fact that they appear in my data as well, I would still consider the three forms indicated in (1) as those that express the 'basic' forms for the three Tongan spatial prepositions. Incidentally, the two 'special' cases, that is, adding a or ate, are parallel to two ungrammatical cases in English. For example, in English the following two sentences are ungrammatical:

(2) a. *The ball was at John.[15]
     b. *The ball was at he.

The grammatical solution adopted in the English language is to disallow certain types of combinations/sequences, that is, preposition followed by proper noun or personal pronoun. In Tongan, instead, a specific affix is added to the preposition to indicate the 'special' case.

The three basic forms of the three Tongan spatial prepositions, 'i 'at,' ki 'to,' and mei 'from,' commonly appear in sentences of the following type (for the abbreviations used see List of Abbreviations, p. xxiii):

---

[13] Clearly some other lexical items have been left out of my investigation, such as the small set of Tongan dimensional adjectives and the open class of Tongan verbs expressing either state or motion.

[14] From now on, concepts will be indicated by initial capital letter.

[15] The asterisk means ungrammatical, as standard in linguistics.

(3) a. … *pea ko   e   fo'i me'a ko   é   'i   he tafa'aki to'omata'ú* …
  conj expr art clas N   prpr dem   **sP** art sN   sN
  … then ø the single thing ø there **at** the side right…[16]
  '… then, the thing there **at** the right side …'

  b. … *meimei hanga mai hono ngutú   ki he ngutu ko   é   ngata lahi* …
    adv   V   dir poss N   **sP** art N   expr dem N   adj
  … almost face to me its mouth **to** the mouth ø there snake big…
  '… almost facing me with its mouth **towards** the mouth there of the big snake …'

  c. … *'oku na tu'u **mei** 'olunga* …
    tns pp V   **sP**   sN
  …present they two stand **from** above …
  '… they (two) stand (**from**) above …'

A feature that distinguishes *'i* 'at' from *ki* 'to' and *mei* 'from' is that it always appears in conjunction with verbs of state while the other two appear in conjunction with verbs of motion (but not exclusively, i.e., *ki* 'to' appears also in conjunction with verbs of perception). Furthermore, they make clear reference to a specific part of the concept of Path.[17] Respectively, *ki* 'to' refers to the End of the Path, while *mei* 'from' refers to the Beginning of the Path.[18] Here are some illustrative sentences:

(4) a. *'oku ou nofo 'i Tonga*
    tns pp V   **sP** N
    present I live **at** Tonga
    'I live **in** Tonga'

  b. *te   u 'alu **ki** Tonga*
    tns pp V   **sP** N
    future I go **to** Tonga
    'I will go **to** Tonga'

  c. *na'a ku folau **mei** Tonga*
    tns pp V   **sP**   N
    past I travel **from** Tonga
    'I traveled **from** Tonga'

---

[16] The letter ø means untranslatable.

[17] "A PATH is an ordered collection of VECTORs in SPACE that is bounded by two VECTORs respectively lacking either left or right directionality" (Bennardo, 2000a: 7; see also Talmy, 1983). It is, in other words, a line in space with a beginning and an end.

[18] For an ample discussion of the concept of Path and all the other spatial concepts used in this work see: Bennardo (1996), Lehman and Bennardo (2003), and Bennardo (2004).

The intentions of these three Tongan spatial prepositions are the same as those of their English glosses. However, the Tongan prepositions are occasionally used in a different way from their corresponding English prepositions. For example, *'i* 'at' is used to introduce the second element of a comparison, where in English there would be 'than.' *Ki* 'to' is used after verbs of perception, where in English there would be a direct object, or in the case of 'look' the English spatial preposition 'at.' *Mei* 'from' is not used in causative expressions as in English, and it is not used with a 'stative' meaning, such as in the sentence: 'the laundry hangs from the wire.' The Tongan sentence I elicited for the same situation is: *ko e fō 'oku tautau 'i he uaia* 'the laundry hangs at the wire.' On the contrary, where Tongan uses *mei* 'from,' as in the case of *'oku ngaohi mei he 'akau* 'it is made from the wood,' in English there would be the preposition 'of.' There is no difference between the two languages in the use of *mei* or 'from' for expressions regarding space, time, or simple change of state, i.e., *te u liliu e tohi mei he lea fakatonga ki he lea fakapilitania* 'I will translate the letter from Tongan to English.'[19]

This is not the place to go any further into the comparison between the uses of the three spatial prepositions in English and Tongan, but such an undertaking would certainly yield interesting findings (see Bowerman, 1996 for a Korean–English comparison). Tongan spatial prepositions, then, represent the basic lexical forms that speakers use to encode linguistically their mental representations of spatial relationships. One of the prepositions (*'i* 'at') is used to describe relationships regarding State, and the two others (*ki* 'to' and *mei* 'from') for relationships involving Motion (real or metaphorical) – thus, including the concept of Path.

3.3.1.2 *Tongan directionals*
The members of the second set of lexical items expressing spatial relationships are labeled 'directionals.' They are found in (5) below.

(5) a. *hake   hifo*
       'up'   'down'

   b. *mai*   *atu*   *ange*
     'towards center' 'away from center'[20] 'away from center 2'[21]

The motivation for distinguishing between subsets (5a) and (5b) comes from the exclusive association of the former with the vertical axis. For the second

---

[19] I thank Jürgen Broschart for suggesting these last two examples in Tongan.
[20] This meaning includes the very common "towards addressee" meaning that is usually assigned to *atu* (see discussion in Bennardo, 1996: 186ff).
[21] "Center 2" is defined as constituted by speaker and addressee.

subset there is no exclusive association with any axis, even though a 'canonical' association with the horizontal axis may be suggested.

In Churchward's *Tongan Grammar* these five lexical items are grammatically defined as adverbs. They follow the verb directly and can be followed by a prepositional phrase. They can also be used as verbs, and there are many cases of this use in the texts I obtained.[22] Here are some sentences that contain the five Tongan directionals:

(6) a. ... *pea 'oku ne kaka **hake** ('i) he mo'unga ko   é ...*
       conj tns pp V   **dir** sP art N   expr dem
       ... then present s/he/it climb **up** at the mountain ø there ...
       '... then she climbs **up** the mountain there ...'

   b. ... *'alu **hifo** ('i) he hala fakakavakava ...*
       V   **dir** sP art N   N
       ... go **down** at the road bridge ...
       '... go **down** the bridge ...'

   c. ... *'oku ou hanga **mai** taimi ni   ki hoku to'omata'u ...*
       tns pp V   **dir** N   dem sP poss N
       ... present I turn **to me** time now to my right ...
       '... I turn **towards myself** now, to my right ...'[23]

   d. ... *na'a ku tala **atu** kia koe ...*
       tns pp V **dir** sP pp
       ... past I tell **to you** to you ...
       '... I told **you** ...'

   e. ... *toki 'alu **ange** pé 'o   fakatau ha'o lemani ...*
       adv V   **dir** adv pospr V   iposs N
       ... then go **to there** just to buy your lemon ...
       '... then go **there** to buy your lemon ...'

In sentences (6a) and (6b) the two directionals *hake* 'up' and *hifo* 'down' definitely form a subset of their own with their clear association with the vertical axis. In sentences (6c), (6d), and (6e) the three directionals *mai* 'towards center,' *atu* 'away from center,' and *ange* 'away from center constituted by speaker and addressee' suggest an association with the horizontal axis. At the same time they highlight a reference to the speaker, the addressee, and to a place that

---

[22] If not specified otherwise, all the texts referred to in this work are transcriptions of the various interviews described in Section 3.2.
[23] The speaker uses "I" in this sentence to mean "the figurine I am moving along this path" (see description of language game 'type 3').

is neither the speaker nor the addressee. However, speakers use those lexemes also in situations where reference to the vertical axis is involved, i.e., with a speaker at the bottom of a breadfruit tree, and with the addressee in the tree top directly above the speaker's head. It is apparent, then, that these three directionals are not intensionally associated with any axis, but are only canonically used with reference to the horizontal one.

3.3.1.3 Tongan spatial nouns

I have labeled the third set of lexical items used to represent spatial relationships in Tongan as 'spatial nouns.' The whole set is composed of the following members:

(7) *hahake*   'east'   *lalo*   'below'
    hihifo   'west'   *loto*   'inside'
    tokelau   'north'   *tu'a*   'outside'
    tonga   'south'   *ve'e*   'border'
    kō   'yonder'   *fukahi*   'top'
    to'omata'u   'right'   *kilisi*   'bottom'
    to'ohema   'left'   *tumu'aki* 'peak'
    mu'a   'front'   *tafa'aki* 'side'
    mui   'back'   *fa'ahi*   '(in)side'
    mua'i   'front'   *mata*   'front'
    mui'i   'back'   *tuliki*   'corner'
    'olunga   'above'   *vaha'a*   'space between'
    funga   'top'

In another work (Bennardo, 2000b) I give an extensive account of the semantics of Tongan spatial nouns, and partition the set into various subsets. Here I report only briefly the major arguments and the findings of that investigation.

The first relevant step is to distinguish Churchward's (1953) "local nouns" from the grouping I am labeling 'spatial nouns.' This step is necessary because the list of nouns I obtained from my data is different from the one available in Churchward's *Tongan Grammar*. Furthermore, the list of "local nouns" first introduced by Churchward differs from other lists of similar nouns introduced in other sections of his own work. In fact, because of their peculiar grammatical behavior, a different list of local nouns is labeled by Churchward as "preposed" nouns. He defines a preposed noun as "a noun which is placed immediately before another noun instead of being connected with it by means of a preposition" (1953: 214). Another list is introduced containing some of the preposed nouns that can be followed by *'o*, a possessive preposition that can be glossed as 'of.' Table 3.1 contains a summary of Churchward's proposals.

The content of Table 3.1 raises a set of questions. We do not know, for example, why certain nouns do not appear as local nouns but appear as preposed ones. At the same time it is unclear and not addressed why certain local

Table 3.1 *Lists of nouns found in Churchward (1953)*

'Gloss'	Noun	Local noun	Preposed/part	Followed by 'o
'Inside'	*Loto*	x	x	-
'Outside'	*Tu'a*	x	x	-
'Front'	*Mu'a*	x	x	-
'Back'	*Mui*	x	x	x
'Below'	*Lalo*	x	x	-
'Above'	*'Olunga*	x	-	-
'Right'	*To'omata'u*	x	-	-
'Left'	*To'ohema*	x	-	-
'Border'	*Ve'e*	-	x	-
'Top'	*Funga*	-	x	x
'Peak'	*Tumu'aki*	-	x	x
'Front'	*Mata*	-	x	x
'Side'	*Tafa'aki*	x	x	x
'East'	*Hahake*	x	-	-
'West'	*Hihifo*	x	-	-
'North'	*Tokelau*	x	-	-
'South'	*Tonga*	x	-	-

nouns cannot be preposed. And finally, the parameter for the possibility of a certain noun to be preposed or followed by 'o 'of' is not indicated.

The second step in the analyses of the Tongan spatial nouns was to notice that there are five structural contexts in which, differentially, they can occur (Table 3.2). The first structural context is that of a simple prepositional phrase (PP) composed of a Tongan spatial preposition and the spatial noun (Type One). The second context is a similar PP as above, but followed by another PP that is still part of the sentence containing the PP with the spatial noun (Type Two). The third one is another PP, of the same type as above, but this time the spatial noun is followed by another N (Type Three). The fourth one is another PP with an article preceding the spatial noun and an N following it (Type Four). Finally, some spatial nouns can occur preceded by an article in PPs followed by another PP whose P is a possessive P such as 'o 'of' (Type Five). Here are some examples for each structural context.

(8) a. *'i **mu'a***
         sP **sN**
         at **front**
         'in **front**'

     b. *'i **'olunga** 'i he fale*
         sP **sN**   sP art N
         at **above** at the house
         '**above** the house'

c. '*i* **loto** *fale*
 sP **sN** N
 at **inside** house
 '**in** the house'

d. '*i* *he* **lalo** *fale*
 sP art **sN** N
 at the **below** house
 '**below** the house'

e. '*i* *he* **mata** '*o*   *e* *fale*
 sP art **sN**   pospr art N
 at the **front** of the house
 '**in front** of the house'

In Table 3.2 the spatial nouns are presented with the indication of their occurrence in each structural context type. Comparing the content of Table 3.2 and that of Table 3.1 reveals that – contrary to Churchward's indications – cases of *mui* 'back' and *funga* 'top' followed by '*o* 'of' do not occur. In fact, it was not possible to elicit from any of my informants a sentence containing this construction. When such a sentence was suggested they all stated without any uncertainty that it was not correct. For the sentences proposed containing *mu'a* and *mui* followed by '*o*, all informants said that the right way to produce those sentences was by using *mua'i* and *mui'i* instead, and to use them as preposed nouns in a construction of Type Four.

It must be pointed out here that in both Churchward's *Tongan Grammar* (1953: 249–52) and in Shumway (1988: 575), an active process is indicated for Tongan that transforms phrases of the type *ko e mata '*o e helé* 'the blade of the knife,' into phrases of the type *ko e mata'i helé* 'the blade of the knife.' It is very likely, then, that the same process has been applied to *mu'a* and *mui* (with some phonological changes), thus, creating two new spatial nouns, namely, *mua'i* and *mui'i*.

It must have still been possible when Churchward wrote his grammar (1953, with data most likely collected in earlier years) to use phrases of the type '*i he mui tepilé* 'at the end of the table' or '*i he mui '*o e tepilé* 'at the back of the table,' as he himself indicates (1953: 216). In the meantime a change has occurred whose central motor must have been the process indicated above.

My analyses of the spatial nouns yielded the following results. Spatial nouns appearing in structural context Type One were shown to contain as part of their conceptual make-up the concept of Locus.[24] This feature distinguished

---

[24] "The PLACE of an object is the actual amount of space that it occupies, thus, it is equivalent to the object itself in spatial extension. It is, in other words, a relationship between the object and space (cf. Aristotle in Heelan, 1988). In more precise mathematical language a PLACE is a bounded neighborhood of interior points. That is, it is the set of all points within the boundary

Table 3.2 *Spatial nouns in five different structural contexts*

'Gloss'	Type One	Type Two	Type Three	Type Four	Type Five
	'i mu'a 'at front'	'i 'olunga 'i he fale 'at top at the house'	'i loto fale 'at inside house'	'i he lalo fale 'at the below house'	'i he mata 'o e fale 'at the front of the house'
'Yonder'	Kō				
'East'	Hahake				
'West'	Hihifo				
'North'	Tokelau				
'South'	Tonga				
'Right'	To'omata'u	To'omata'u			To'omata'u
'Left'	To'ohema	To'ohema			To'ohema
'Front'	Mu'a	Mu'a			
'Back'	Mui	Mui			
'Above'	'Olunga	'Olunga			
'Top'			Funga	Funga	
'Below'	Lalo	Lalo	Lalo	Lalo	
'Inside'	Loto		Loto	Loto	
'Outside'	Tu'a		Tu'a	Tu'a	
'Front'				Mua'i	(Mu'a)*
'Back'				Mui'i	(Mui)*
'Border'				Ve'e	
'Top'				Fukahi	
'Bottom'				Kilisi**	
'Peak'				Tumu'aki	Tumu'aki
'Side'				Tafa'aki	Tafa'aki
'(In)side'				Fa'ahi***	Fa'ahi
'Front'				Mata	Mata
'Corner'				Tuliki	Tuliki

* *Mu'a* and *Mui* used to appear in this column, but they do not any more.
** *Faliki* 'floor' and *Takele* 'curved bottom' also belong to this group.
*** Very often pronounced *Faha'i*.

them from other spatial nouns also related to the concept of Locus. These latter acquired their relationship with the concept of Locus from their appearance in a specific structural context, i.e., following a Tongan spatial preposition.

of an object (including the boundary points). The LOCUS of an object in projective geometry is defined at a more abstract level of consideration than PLACE. In fact, a LOCUS is the result of a projection or, better, a collapse of a PLACE onto any of its interior points. A LOCUS, then, is a neighborhood of possible projection points, the lower limit of which being one point. Thus, while PLACE is defined by the size, shape, and specific geometry of the object, LOCUS is not and, thus, can be arbitrarily reduced to a point by the application of the choice function for generic reference to it" (Bennardo, 1996: 28).

Spatial nouns appearing in Type Two are connected with the concept of Axis. In both subsets, spatial nouns appear that are strictly connected with frames of reference, either relative or intrinsic or absolute.

Spatial nouns appearing in Type Three, Four, and Five structural contexts were considered as separate groups of nouns whose conceptual make-up contains the concept of Part. A specific subtype of Part was indicated for each of the three subsets: 'core' parts for spatial nouns appearing in structural context Type Three; 'periphery' parts for spatial nouns appearing in Type Four; and 'secondary' parts for those in Type Five.

It seems that the object (not an animal or person) is first conceptually divided in four core parts (*funga* 'top,' *lalo* 'below,' *loto* 'inside,' and *tu'a* 'outside'). Then, peripheral parts are distinguished like *ve'e* 'border/contour,' *fa'ahi* '(in)side,' and *tuliki* 'corner' (among others). Finally, further distinctions are obtained by allowing specific features of the object to determine different lexical items. So, for example, *fukahi* 'top' indicates a 'top,' but of a non-solid object (e.g., water, grass). This type of spatial noun has been labeled 'secondary' insofar as these nouns imply an already existing division of the object as expressed by a spatial noun of the previous two types (*funga* 'top' for *fukahi*). Conceptually, the content of the two subtypes of spatial nouns referring to core and periphery parts is completely included in those of the subtype referring to secondary parts to which they are related.

In conclusion, the following definition of a Tongan spatial noun is proposed: a Tongan 'spatial noun' is a noun that is either associated with one of the three frames of reference, or that is preposed to another noun in a structural context that sees a PP headed by one of the three Tongan spatial prepositions (or lexicalizes as *vaha'a*). The parenthetical specification about *vaha'a* 'space between' is due to the fact that it appears in a structural context of its own, but one that is very close to Type Five.[25]

---

[25] The noun *vaha'a* 'space between' does not appear in any of the five constructions discussed with the exception of Type Five if we stretch its structure to incorporate a conjunction and another article-noun. This is illustrated by the following sentence:

'Oku tu'u 'a e fu'u 'akau 'i he **vaha'a** *'o   e fale mo e peito*
tns V   pr art clas N   sP art **sN**   pospr art N conj art N
present stand subject the one tree at the **space between** of the house and the kitchen
'The tree stands between the house and the kitchen'

Vaha'a describes the space between two Objects as if it were an Object itself, and as a consequence of this, the structure in which it appears has to elucidate what these two Objects are. However, the closeness of meaning with the group of nouns in Type Five becomes more evident when we think about the relationship of *vaha'a* and *loto* 'inside.' What differentiates the two nouns is only the fact that for *vaha'a* there is no Object to which something is 'inside.' But the existence and recognition of two Objects define a space separating them that, then, is treated as an Object in itself, and finally thought of as possibly containing something. In other words, we can say that the conceptual content of *vaha'a* is 'secondary' to the construction of two Objects and that of an 'inside.'

3.3.2   Linguistic realizations of frames of reference in Tongan

In Section 3.1, I defined the concept of frame of reference (FoR). I now define each of the three basic types of FoR, and describe the subtypes for relative and absolute FoR. Then, I indicate how each FoR is expressed in the Tongan language. I must stress that I have modified Levinson's (1996a, 2003) typology of FoRs, but kept his terminology. The major difference between our typologies is the way we define the conceptual content of the relative FoR.[26] Levinson (1996a: 142) states:

> The relative frame of reference presupposes a 'viewpoint' V (given by the location of a perceiver in any sensory modality), and a figure and a ground distinct from V; it thus offers a triangulation of three points and utilizes coordinates fixed on V to assign directions to figure and ground. […] the 'viewer' [V or viewpoint] need not be ego and need not be a participant in the speech event.

While it is linguistically possible to express separation between ego and V – Levinson's (1996a: 142) example is "Bill kicked the ball to the left of the goal" – both the research on the visual system (see Marr, 1982; Biederman, 1988; Hubel, 1988) and that on the developmental sequence (Clark, 1970; Moore, 1973; Liben, Patterson and Newcombe, 1981; Stiles-Davis, Kritchevsky, and Bellugi, 1983; Cohen, 1985; Pick, 1993) point towards the primacy of a stage in which viewer V and ground G are conflated on ego. As a matter of fact it is exactly the capacity to assign independent sets of coordinates to objects that marks one of the milestones of cognitive development (see also Piaget and Inhelder, 1956). Consequently, unlike Levinson, I define a relative FoR as anchored on ego.

3.3.2.1   The relative FoR

A relative FoR is a system of coordinates centered on the speaker. From the speaker three axes are constructed, one vertically and two on the horizontal plane: the front–back axis or sagittal, and the left–right axis or transverse. Any object in the space defined by these coordinates will be described in relation to the speaker. If the speaker moves in any direction, the axes will move accordingly, keeping their origin on the speaker. In other words, the speaker can be thought of as a point. As such the individual implies a field (space) around him/herself. This field will be oriented according to the three axes just mentioned. The orientation process takes into consideration several body characteristics,

---

It is, however, still not appropriate to consider *vaha'a* as part of the group of nouns that appear in Type Five construction. Further support for this decision can be found in the fact that *vaha'a* cannot appear in any other type of construction while all the other nouns appearing in Type Five construction can also appear minimally in another type of construction (typically Type Four).

[26] See Bennardo (1996: 85ff) for a discussion of this issue.

both static (orientation of face, eyes, etc.) and ambulatory (habitual direction of movement). The speaker necessarily (ontogenetically) maps these axes onto him/herself.

3.3.2.1.1 The translation and the reflection subtypes of the relative FoR   The appearance of two objects in the field of the speaker creates the double possibility of treating both objects in direct relationship with the speaker, thus, continuing to map the axes on the speaker, or to relate one object to the other object. This latter case entails the possibility of assigning orienting axes (or set of coordinates) to one object. This object assumes the same function that the speaker had performed so far (this object is called the "ground"; see Talmy, 1983: 230). In a conservative fashion the axes mapped onto this object (ground) are exactly the same as the ones that the speaker had mapped onto him/herself. In other words, the coordinates of the field – that includes both the speaker and the object – are not changed. The other object (referred to as "figure", see Talmy, 1983: 232) will then be described in relation to the by-now-oriented object.

However, something has occurred in the meantime. Namely, the front or 'away' axis has been divided in two parts by the first object or ground (Figure 3.1). At this juncture a further possibility is created. The ground's front–back axis may keep exactly the same orientation of the speaker's field, thus, we get the 'translation' subtype of the relative FoR (Figure 3.1). Or the front and back assignment can be flipped so that the front of the oriented object or ground faces the speaker, thus, yielding the 'reflection' subtype of the relative FoR (Figure 3.1).

Speech communities commonly using the relative subtype of FoR that is labeled 'translation' are extremely rare. To my knowledge the only two documented cases of such a community are the Hausa speaking people described by Hill (1982) and the Marquesans reported by Cablitz (2006). We will see later in this work that Tongan speakers represent another such community.

In both 'translation' and 'reflection' subtypes, the assignments of the left and right sides are perfectly congruent with those of the speaker. In other words, the oriented object or ground is not yet considered as a point with an oriented field of its own; rather, it is still tied to the field of the speaker. Notice, moreover, that it is not possible to arrive at the construction of the 'translation' and 'reflection' subtypes without activating (consciously or unconsciously) a 'basic' relative FoR. In fact, there would be no axis to 'translate' or 'reflect' at all without having already constructed one in advance. And this can only have happened by using a relative FoR. Figure 3.1 illustrates graphically the three FoRs discussed so far: 'basic' relative, 'translation' relative, and 'reflection' relative.

In Tongan, the linguistic realizations of these three types of relative FoR are obtained by using the following spatial nouns: *mu'a* 'front,' *mui* 'back,' *to'ohema* 'left,' and *to'omata'u* 'right.' These nouns appear in prepositional

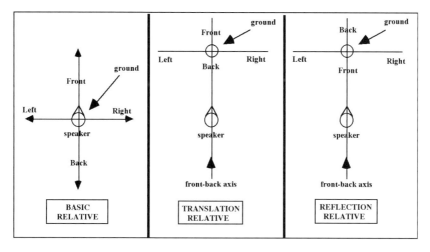

Figure 3.1 The basic relative frame of reference and its two subtypes

phrases (PP) headed by the three spatial prepositions '*i* 'at,' *ki* 'to,' and *mei* 'from.' While *to'ohema* 'left,' and *to'omata'u* 'right' may or may not be preceded by the article *he* 'the' within the PP, *mu'a* 'front,' and *mui* 'back' cannot be preceded by an article in this PP when used to realize an FoR.

3.3.2.2 The intrinsic FoR

An intrinsic FoR is a system of coordinates centered on an object that is not the speaker. In the same way as for the relative system, but this time from the object, three oriented axes are constructed, one vertically and two on the horizontal plane. Any object in the space defined by these coordinates will be described in relation to the oriented object from which the space was constructed. If the oriented object moves in any direction, the axes will move accordingly keeping their origin and assigned orientation on it. The front of a car or animal, for example, is determined and addressed independently from the speaker's and addressee's orientations.

What basically differentiates the relative and the intrinsic systems is that with intrinsic systems the axes are not centered on the speaker, but on an object. However, we have already seen that this is also the case for the 'translation' and 'reflection' subtypes of the relative FoR. What is it that distinguishes these latter two subtypes of the relative FoR from the intrinsic one just introduced?

The difference lies in the quality of the oriented field that is constructed for the oriented object or ground. This field is completely independent in orientation from the speaker. It is, in other words, a new separate field from that of the speaker. Let us be reminded that for the two subtypes of relative FoR, the

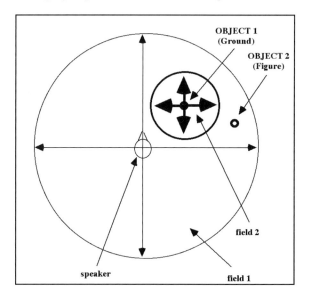

Figure 3.2 The intrinsic frame of reference

oriented field used was still that of the speaker. One major difference with the FoR we have called 'basic' relative was that the frontal axis was divided into two parts by the object addressed with either part being considered front or back. With the intrinsic FoR the field of the speaker is not addressed any more.

This difference has important consequences, the most relevant of which is that the description of the spatial relationship between two objects is freed from references to the speaker. Thus, the hearer will not need to be present in the context of language production, or better, will not need to know where the speaker was or is located at the time of language production in order to fully interpret the linguistic expression. Figure 3.2 graphically illustrates the intrinsic FoR.

In Tongan, the linguistic realizations of the intrinsic FoR are obtained by using the same spatial nouns and PPs used for the relative FoRs. The only major difference is that most of the time when realizing an intrinsic FoR these PPs are followed by another PP that specifies the ground, or oriented object, from which the front–back and left–right axes are constructed. Here is an example of the two conjoined PPs:

(9) *'i mu'a 'i he veeni*
    sP sN   sP art N
    at front at the pick-up truck
    'in front of the pick-up truck'

3.3.2.3   The absolute FoR

An absolute FoR is a system of coordinates that is centered neither on the speaker nor on an object. First, the vertical axis is constructed and kept exactly the same as for the other two FoRs. Second, on the horizontal plane one or more objects (e.g., areas, points, landmarks) in the environment (or field) of the speaker are chosen as fixed orienting points (socially agreed on). Third, either the speaker or any object in his/her field is put into relationships with these chosen objects or fixed points.

A good example of this is the system that uses cardinal points, that is, the east–west–north–south system typical[27] of many familiar Indo-European languages (also of many others). Another example is the one that uses landward–seaward directions, typical of many Oceanic languages (Bennardo, 1996; Hill, 1997; Ozanne-Rivierre, 1997; Wassmann and Dasen, 1998), and see Haugen (1957) for an Icelandic example. In many other non-Oceanic cases, the environmental features selected differ profoundly from land or sea, and may range from a mountain to a lake or from a river to a building.

In Tongan, the linguistic realizations of the various subtypes of the absolute FoR are obtained by using the following spatial nouns: *hahake* 'east,' *hihifo* 'west,' *tokelau* 'north,' *tonga* 'south,' *tahi* 'sea/ocean,' *kolo* 'town,' *lalo* 'below,' and *'uta* 'inland.' These nouns appear in PPs headed by prepositions like *'i* 'at,' *ki* 'to,' and *mei* 'from.' None of them can be preceded by an article in these PPs, when used to realize an FoR. From the short list of nouns involved it is possible to see that Tongans use both the 'cardinal directions' subtype and the 'landward–seaward' subtype of the absolute FoR. Two other absolute subtypes that Tongans use are ones in which the two poles of the absolute axis are 'town' (or village) and 'inland,' and one in which the two poles are 'below' and 'inland.'

As a matter of fact, there is also another subtype of absolute FoR that is very commonly used in Tongan and that I have labeled 'radial' (see Bennardo, 1996). When using a radial subtype of absolute FoR, a fixed point of reference is chosen and movement towards it (centripetally) or away from it (centrifugally) is expressed. The linguistic realizations of this subtype of absolute FoR is a PP in which the noun will depend on the fixed point of reference chosen, and the preposition will be either *ki* 'to' or *mei* 'from.' Here is an example:

(10) *'oku ne hanga kia Nia*
         tns   pp   V   sP   N
         present he face to   Nia
         'he faces Nia'

---

[27] This does not imply that the absolute FoR has a privileged status among these speakers in their everyday language use. According to Levelt (1982) and Levinson (1996a), it is the relative FoR that is privileged in everyday language use for this group of speakers.

In (10), Nia is the fixed point of reference chosen, and the male person considered is put in a centripetal relationship to her.

3.3.3   Uses of frames of reference in language

I now discuss the linguistic data collected, devoting my attention specifically to the linguistic realizations of FoRs. My intention is to see if there is a preferential use of any of the FoRs in linguistic production. For these analyses I use the expression 'small-scale space' when referring to language elicited within the very defined context of the linguistic tasks involving the use of miniaturized and contrived (the presence of a screen) environments (see above, Section 3.2). I use 'large-scale space' for uses elicited during language tasks about the wider geographical environment (e.g., 'giving directions' tasks), in interviews, and real-life conversations. Of course, real-life conversation can also be about 'small-scale space,' but the focus here will be specifically large-scale instead of small-scale space in this second type of data.

Before introducing the results of the analyses, I want to illustrate briefly how a particular phrase could be interpreted as the realization of a specific FoR, either relative, intrinsic, or absolute. For this purpose I am introducing two of the many photos that informants were asked to describe in the language tasks described in Section 3.2. The first photo is in Figure 3.3.

The following three descriptions of the photo in Figure 3.3 illustrate linguistic realizations of the three basic types of FoRs:

(11) a. *Ko e   tangata 'oku nofo 'i to'ohema 'i he fu'u 'akau*
         expr art N   tns V   sP sN   sP art clas N
         ø the man present stand at left at the single tree
         'the man stands at the left of the tree'

   b. *Ko e   fu'u 'akau 'oku nofo 'i he to'ohema 'o   e   tangata*
       expr art clas N   tns V   sP art sN   pospr art N
       ø the single tree present stand at the left of the man
       'the tree stands at the left of the man'

   c. *Ko e   tangata 'oku nofo 'i tokelau 'i he fu'u 'akau*
       expr art N   tns V   sP sN   sP art   clas N
       ø the man present stand at north at the single tree
       'the man stands north of the tree'

In (11a) the description of the man involves the use of a relative FoR in the mental representation of the scene later expressed linguistically. In fact, the speaker's own left coincides with the described position (also left) of the man in the photo (consider that the speaker is looking at the photo facing him/her).

Figure 3.3 Man and Tree, Set 2, photo 7, from CARG (1992)

Furthermore, trees do not usually have a left or a right side, thus, the left side that has been used must be the one that the speaker assigns to him/herself by means of a 'basic' subtype of the relative FoR. In (11b) an intrinsic FoR has been used. In fact, the left indicated is the one that is assigned to the man in the photo as an 'intrinsic' orientation of his body. The front of the man is obviously the one towards the speaker (the side of the face of the man in the photo), and the other three sides follow as default.

Finally, in (11c) an absolute FoR (cardinal points subtype) has been used. Which cardinal point is used depends on the context of production (sitting position of the speaker in relation to the local geographical cardinal points). Other typical subtypes of the absolute FoR use local landmarks such as a road, a house or building (e.g., church), or even objects in the context of the activity (e.g., videocamera, window, etc.), or people co-present during the activity. In these cases, however, prepositional phrases like the following would be used: *ki he hala* 'towards the road,' *ki he fale lotu* 'towards the church,' or *kia Mele* 'towards Mele.'

I introduce the next photo (Figure 3.4) because it elicited two specific types of description. That is, this photo can be described (among other ways) by using a 'reflection' or 'translation' subtype of the relative FoR. We will see how this is linguistically realized.

The photo in Figure 3.4 was described, among other ways, as follows:

(12) a. *Ko   e   kulo 'oku 'i mu'a 'o   e   me'a fuopotopoto*
       expr art N   tns sP sN   pospr art N   adj
       ø the pot present at front of the thing round
       'the pot is in front of the round thing'

Figure 3.4 Intrinsic relations, photo 6, from Danziger and Gaskins (1993)

b. *Ko e kulo 'oku 'i mui 'o   e me'a fuopotopoto*
   expr art N   tns sP sN pospr art N   adj
   ø the pot present at back of the thing round
   'the pot is at-the-back-of/behind the round thing'

Notice that the small round wooden wheel depicted in the photo with the pot has neither an intrinsic front nor back. Thus, any description of the pot as being 'in front of' or 'at the back of' the wheel must be associated with a set of oriented coordinates that are centered on the wheel (to be considered the ground). This is exactly what a 'reflection' and a 'translation' subtype of the relative FoR accomplish. In (12a) a 'translation' subtype of the relative FoR is used in determining the front as the part of space beyond the wheel. In contrast, (12b) shows the use of a 'reflection' subtype of the relative FoR that determines the assignment of back to that same space (see Figure 3.1 in Section 3.3.2 above for a graphic depiction of these two FoRs and their respective assignments of front and back).

It must be emphasized that each individual scene in each photo can be described linguistically in different ways depending on the FoR that is used to represent the scene mentally. In other words, informants have to make choices when describing the content of the photos. The frequent reoccurrence of one or more specific linguistic expressions – from which we can infer the use of an FoR – will be considered an indication of a preferential way in which mental representations of spatial relationships are realized linguistically in Tongan. We can now look at the linguistic corpus and see if any FoR is preferentially used. I first discuss the data about small-scale space and then the data about large-scale space.

3.3.3.1   Uses of frames of reference in small-scale space
The analyses of the linguistic corpus about small-scale space presented a time-consuming challenge due to the several hundred pages of transcriptions obtained. They represent more than fifteen hours of on-line language production by Tongan speakers. For the sake of brevity, I do not present occurrences of each use of an FoR, but discuss only percentages. The relative FoR occurs in 74% of the instances counted (1,199 out of 1,620). The occurrences of the intrinsic FoR represent 21% of the total (340 out of 1,620). And the absolute FoR was used in the remaining 5% (81 out of 1,620) of the instances of uses of FoRs.[28]

3.3.3.1.1 Uses of the absolute FoR   The minimal use of an absolute FoR is internally diversified. In fact, only one third are uses of the 'cardinal point' subtype, and the rest are of the 'ad-hoc/landmark' type. All these cases are very interesting because they are prevalently used in what I have labeled a 'repair strategy' frame. In other words, they are used when unsuccessful attempts to use other FoRs have made clear that a different approach to the content of those descriptions was needed to foster successful and quicker performing of the tasks at hand.

3.3.3.1.2 Uses of the intrinsic FoR   The limited uses of the intrinsic FoR cannot be described as occurring within any specific language frame. In other words, they do not seem to be motivated by any preceding occurrence of descriptions using another type of FoR. Their uses were all found in spatial descriptions of scenes (in photos) that contained people, animals, and vehicles. All of these contain highly oriented features like a face, or a relevant habitual direction of motion. Thus, it is their presence in the photos that triggered the uses of the intrinsic FoR.

A relevant thing I noticed is that explicit expressions, such as *'o e veeni* 'of the van,' and in many other cases the presence of possessives, seem to signal the use of an intrinsic FoR.[29] Incidentally, this supports similar findings reported by Levelt (1984: 356) for Dutch and English speakers. When this explicit signaling was omitted, misunderstandings were more likely to occur. That is, instead of communicating the use of an intrinsic FoR, usually the description was interpreted as a use of a relative FoR. Consequently, erroneous choices were made by the listener.

[28] For a more detailed numerical and statistical description of these analyses, see Bennardo (1996: 224ff).
[29] Occasionally a construction such as *'i mu'a 'i he tamasi'i* 'at front at the man' seems to perform the same function. The only difference with one of the possessive constructions is that the PP following the spatial noun is headed by a spatial preposition and not by a possessive one.

3.3.3.1.3 Uses of the relative FoR   The relative FoR was definitely the most frequently used by Tongans in the linguistic descriptions of spatial relations in small-scale space. Additionally, the analyses of the many misunderstandings that occurred during the performances of the tasks made it clear that the 'basic' relative FoR is the one used as default in both linguistic production and comprehension. In fact, misunderstandings are most likely to occur when the descriptions of the scenes in the photos or the interpretations of these descriptions do not immediately utilize the 'basic' relative FoR.

Specifically, when describing a scene in a photo with a relative FoR, the description is started with the use of a 'basic' relative FoR. If the speaker realizes that the description is unsuccessful, then s/he shifts to a 'reflection' relative FoR. Analogously, many descriptions of photos utilizing a 'reflection' relative FoR were immediately interpreted by the listener as encoded in a 'basic' relative FoR, leading to a misunderstanding. Occasionally, correct interpretations occurred due to constrained circumstances such as limited possibilities of choices because participants were already in an advanced stage of the game. That is, there were only a few photos left from which to choose.

Another noticeable phenomenon is that some descriptions utilizing the 'reflection' relative FoR were interpreted as utilizing a 'translation' relative FoR. This last phenomenon highly correlates with a specific shift in the use of these two FoRs that I noticed. At the end of the linguistic task or game, when participants were allowed to discuss the results of their efforts (usually they animatedly discussed misunderstandings), they used more often a 'translation' subtype of the relative FoR, where during the game they had used a 'basic' subtype of the relative FoR. The relevant difference in the 'playing the game' context and in the 'discussing the results' context was that the informants could see each other in the latter as in any regular, real-life conversation. In contrast, they could not see each other in the former context (playing the game) due to the presence of a screen between them. The Table 3.3 summarizes the results introduced about uses of subtypes of relative FoR in small-scale space.

Thus, it seems that the 'basic' and the 'translation' subtypes of the relative FoR are used more often in full visibility of the addressee, or better, in visibility of the whole relevant context, that is, photos and addressee. The use of the 'reflection' subtype of the relative FoR, instead, seems to be triggered by a 'lack of visibility' of the addressee. This explains why 61% (75 cases) of the uses of the relative FoR on the sagittal (front–back) axis (123 cases) are uses of the 'reflection' subtype.[30] Notice that only on the sagittal axis is it possible to distinguish between different subtypes of the relative FoR.

---

[30] These figures refer to the results of only one of the language task type 1 (see above Section 3.2) called "Man and Tree" (see Bennardo, 1996: 230).

Table 3.3 *Uses of subtypes of relative FoR in small-scale space*

When used	Basic	Translation	Reflection
By director:			
Default description	X		
In 'playing the game'	X		X
In 'discussing the results'	X	X	
By addressee:			
Default interpretation	X	X	
In 'discussing the results'	X	X	

To summarize, in linguistic description of spatial relationships in small-scale space Tongans privilege the use of the relative FoR. Generally, the 'basic' subtype of the relative FoR is used as default both in production and in comprehension of spatial descriptions. Furthermore, whenever a choice is possible between all of the three subtypes of relative FoR, that is, on the sagittal (front–back) axis, the 'reflection' subtype of the relative FoR is used more often. This happens only when a lack of visibility of the addressee characterizes the context of production.

The 'translation' subtype of the relative FoR instead is preferred in contexts where full visibility of the addressee is possible. More importantly, however, this subtype is also used by participants as a default interpretation along with the 'basic' subtype of the relative FoR. This finding is evidence of the relevance of this FoR in Tongan mental representations of spatial relationships when realized in language use.[31] The full value of this finding will be shown in the following section when uses of FoRs in large-scale space are discussed.

3.3.3.2 Uses of frames of reference in large-scale space

3.3.3.2.1 Uses of the translation subtype of the relative FoR   Part of the linguistic data examined in this section was obtained by using the elicitation task about 'giving directions' (see Section 3.2 above). However, the main portion of the data was obtained by engaging in daily conversations with Tongans during my various fieldwork residences in the kingdom. The episodes that I discuss

---

[31] This result was supported by the analyses of various videotaped sessions I ran during my third visit to Tonga. The videotaped sessions involved an informant describing to me (I was sitting in front of the informant or on his/her side) a series of scenes made up of small objects similar to the ones that were used in previous tasks (see Figures 3.3, 3.4, and 3.5). No 'reflection' subtype of the relative FoR was elicited by the task conducted in a full-visibility situation. Typically, 'basic' and 'translation' subtypes of the relative FoR were used by the informants except for a few instances in which a highly featured object with habitual direction of motion (truck) and an animate object (human being) elicited the use of an intrinsic FoR.

are taken from those that found their way into my field notes because they seemed to be good examples of patterns – and not only isolated episodes – of linguistic realizations of spatial relationships.

The first few episodes I discuss regard the use of *mu'a* 'front.' Two of them took place while I was residing in Niuatoputapu, a northern and very isolated island of the Tongan group. My assistant Siaki and I were sitting outside the house where we were staying. As we were talking (in Tongan) about people we could interview for my data collection, Siaki saw a woman in the garden outside her house at some distance from us, and he indicated this woman to me as a possible informant. At first I did not understand which house he was talking about, then he added the presence of some big banana trees in the garden and I was able to focus on the house he was referring to. He then continued his description by using this sentence:

(13) *ko   e   ta'ahaine 'i   mu'a siaine ...*
    prpr art N   sP sN N
    ...ø the woman at front banana ...
    '... the woman in front of the banana tree(s) ...'

It must be underlined that the banana trees were clearly between us and the woman, with the house behind her. I asked him about some other elements in the scene (the road and a big mango tree) and he described them as on his left (the mango tree) and on his right (the road), as I would have done. Thus, he confirmed my hypothesis that he had used in his description a 'translation' subtype of the relative FoR.

The second episode occurred while I was standing on the top of a peak that some Tongan friends and I had just climbed. From there we could see the whole of the village of Hihifo, one of the three villages on the island of Niuatoputapu, and the one in which I was residing. Somebody pointed to a house telling me that it was the one where I was staying. But, since I could not see it, I asked where it was. This friend replied by pointing to a big white house that I succeeded in focusing on. Then, he added:

(14) *ko e fale 'o   Semisi 'oku 'i mu'a 'i he fale lahi, hinehina, ko é*
    prpr art N   pospr N   tns sP sN   sP art N adj adj   expr
    dem
    ø the house of Semisi present at front at the house big, white, ø there
    'the house of Semisi is at the front of the big white house, there'

My house (that of Semisi) was in fact the one further away from us. Further exchanges that followed confirmed the fact that left and right of the 'white house' were the same as the speaker's and mine. Again, then, a 'translation' subtype of the relative FoR had been the choice of the speaker in this spatial description in a large-scale space. This use of the 'translation' subtype of the

Figure 3.5 Uses of 'in front of' and 'behind' in Tongan

relative FoR was also commonly elicited and witnessed in spatial descriptions involving houses. That is, if an object is between the speaker/viewer and the house, then, it will be described as *'i mui fale* 'at back of/behind the house.' If the object is 'yonder' the house, then it will be described as *'i mu'a fale* 'in front of the house.' Figure 3.5 illustrates this point.

A few, but important exceptions to the use of the 'translation' subtype were elicited when the object described was completely hidden by the house. In this case the 'reflection' subtype was employed.[32] Visibility of objects was also the main reason that informants most commonly provided when asked to justify their uses of a 'reflection' over a 'translation' subtype of the relative FoR in a variety of situations including the ones just indicated. It seems, then, that visibility is playing a very relevant role in determining Tongan speakers' choices of a subtype of relative FoR.

Both in small-scale and in large-scale space, the 'translation' subtype of the relative FoR is used often, though it is not the only one used in both contexts. We can suggest, then, that it plays a considerable role within Tongan linguistic realizations of spatial relationships. The relevance of this finding goes well beyond the restricted Tongan milieu; it is of primary significance for the cross-cultural literature on spatial representations. The case of the Hausa people, as reported by Hill (1982), and the Marquesans, as reported by Cablitz (2006), are the only other documented cases[33] in this literature of a speaking community commonly using such an FoR.

3.3.3.2.2 Uses of the intrinsic FoR   The uses of the intrinsic FoR in large-scale space did not differ substantially from those in small-scale space. In a way similar to the small-scale space context, animacy and objects with habitual direction of motion seem to trigger these uses. No specific preference was noticed in full, partial, or lack of visibility. In contrast, the uses of the absolute FoR are strikingly different in the large-scale context as compared to the small-scale one, both qualitatively and quantitatively.

3.3.3.2.3 Uses of the absolute FoR   One of the most common questions that Tongan people ask when meeting outdoors is the highly ritualized *'alu ki fé?* {go to where?} 'where are you going?' The answer to this question most of the time is either *ki kolo* 'to town' or *ki 'uta* 'to inland.'[34] The cardinal direction of

[32] The episode described in the introduction to this chapter, if seen from outside the church, would elicit the use of the 'reflection' subtype of the relative FoR when describing the location of the horse as in relation to the church building. That is, *'oku 'i mui fale lotu 'a e hoosi* 'the horse is behind the church.'

[33] Pederson (personal communication) reports some uses of the 'translation' subtype of the relative FoR by Tamil speakers as well.

[34] The noun *'uta* 'inland' differs from the noun *vao* 'bush.' In fact, their basic meaning is clearly distinguished as 'cultivated land' for *'uta* 'inland' and 'uncultivated land' for *vao* 'bush.'

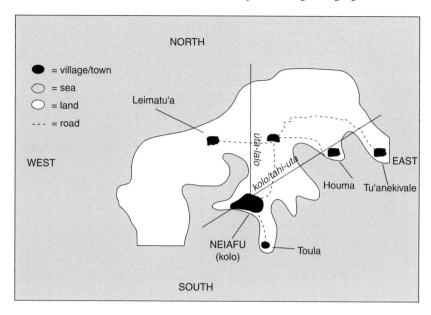

Figure 3.6 Absolute axes on the island of Vava'u

the actual motion of the person answering is disregarded, and both speaker and hearer refer to an abstract axis uniting two points, one of which is the town, and the other the origin of the movement, a village or the inland (see the sketch of the island of Vava'u in Figure 3.6). This place is unspecified, but usually highly predictable from the extensive knowledge that islanders have of each other.

This absolute axis is also used in the village to identify the positions of objects, houses, animals, or people. This is an example:

(15) *Ko e puaka ko é 'i he tafa'aki ki kolo 'o   e   fale*
     prpr art N   expr dem sP art sN   sP N   pospr art N
     ø the pig ø there at the side to town of the house
     'the pig there at the side of the house towards town'

In several exchanges I noticed that the *ki kolo* 'to town' phrase was also interpreted as meaning 'direction road-to-town.' That is, the place where the road-to-town exits the village. This dual possible interpretation of the *ki kolo* 'to town' phrase – that is, either 'to town' or 'to road-to-town' – may render ambiguous sentences like the one in (15), but this problem seems never to arise. At least, I was not able to detect such a problem during the duration of my stay. Gestures and pragmatic features of conversations certainly help to clarify what may potentially be regarded as an ambiguous phrase.

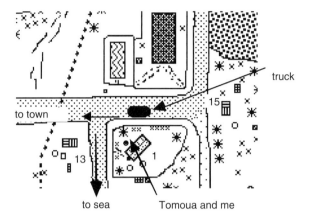

Figure 3.7 *Ki tahi* 'to sea' (from Bennardo, 1996: 127)

The two directions – 'to town' and 'road-to-town' – differ in Houma (the village on Vava'u that represents my primary field site), one being westward and the other south-eastward. Thus, it is necessary to treat the two locations – town and road-to-town – as the ends of two separate axes, one inland–town and one inland–road-to-town. Only the former is fully expressed linguistically, while the latter is only implied and never fully realized in language. To be precise, only one of the two ends of this latter axis is not commonly realized.

A different case is provided by the realization of one of the two ends of the 'town–inland' axis by the use of the word *tahi* 'sea' instead of *kolo* 'town.' Though less common, I was able to detect this use a significant number of times. However, I reached the conclusion that both words – *tahi* 'sea' and *kolo* 'town' – realize the same absolute axis. In support of my conclusion I introduce an exemplary episode which will illustrate how the two words can be used interchangeably as one of the two ends of the same axis.

I was sitting in front of house 1 (Figure 3.7),[35] that is, on its side towards the road. A pick-up truck went by heading towards town. A brief exchange took place between Tomoua, a member of the family I was living with who was sitting next to me (facing the road), and one of the passengers of the truck. Tomoua asked shouting the ritual greeting: *'alu ki fé?* 'where are you going?,' and the passenger replied shouting back: *ki tahi* 'to sea.'

House 1 is right on the corner of the road that goes to town and the road that goes to the nearby seashore. So, after the exchange described above, I expected the truck to turn to its left towards the sea, but, in fact, it continued straight on its way to town.

---

[35] For the full map see Bennardo (1996: 127).

Since I was a little puzzled, I asked Tomoua the same question he had asked the driver.[36] He replied: *'alu ki Neiafu* '(it is/they are) going to Neiafu.' Of course, he was overdoing it a little, that is, he realized I had not understood the truck direction so he stated explicitly which town the truck was heading to without even using the most common *ki kolo* 'to town' expression. Not satisfied, I investigated further into the matter and asked other informants about the possibility of substituting *tahi* 'sea' for *kolo* 'town' when making reference to that specific direction. All informants told me that both words were acceptable and that they indicated exactly the same direction. It is, then, one and the same axis that is referred to, and one of the two poles of this axis can be expressed as either *kolo* 'town' or *tahi* 'sea.'

Finally, coming to a third type of absolute axis, it is very common to hear the direction to/from town being addressed with the following phrases: *ki lalo* 'to down/below' or *mei lalo* 'from down/below.' Again, it was necessary to ask many informants about this phenomenon. Some informants told me this was perfectly acceptable for a 'to town' meaning; others said it meant something like 'to sea,' and others told me it referred to the southern islands of the Vava'u group. All agreed, though, in indicating *'uta* 'inland' as the opposite end of this absolute axis (see Figure 3.6).

Uses of this *lalo–'uta* 'below–inland' axis appeared to overlap with the north–south axis. It must be said that cardinal points are used very infrequently in daily conversations. The only time they are used is when people are talking about the directions of winds or of clouds. In order to see how uses of the *lalo–'uta* 'below–inland' absolute axis are preferred over uses of an absolute system with cardinal points, it is necessary to give detailed attention to the results of the 'giving directions' activity described in Section 3.2. Analyses of the sessions show that the absolute system characterized by cardinal points is not immediately used by the informants. It appears that they used the cardinal points sporadically only to solve specific problems. One example is the problem posed by the fact that they thought (often mistakenly) they could not count on my knowledge of the names of the places or islands they were using in giving their directions.

The accuracy of their uses of cardinal points was very high when giving directions from memory, but their uses were very inaccurate when referring to a map I provided. In fact, ten (out of fifteen) of them put a wrong cardinal point on the north side of the map (no cardinal point was indicated on the map). For north they substituted either east (seven times) or south (three times). Interestingly, the substitutions occurred on the north–south axis, and most of these substitutions coincided with the geographical direction to town

---

[36] It is very common in Tongan to drop the tense marker and the personal pronoun in this type of ritualized question; thus, the same question form can be used to refer to different subjects.

(Neiafu, see Figure 3.6). That is, most of them put south or east at the top of the map as if they had oriented the map towards that direction.

Thirteen of the fifteen informants who participated in this activity were from Houma and were interviewed in Houma, and the town (Neiafu) lies towards the south-east of this village. I interpret this latter finding as an attempt by the informants to orient the map with the absolute cardinal axis they are very familiar with: the town–inland absolute axis I have already introduced above.

Many informants (nine of fifteen) used the *lalo–'uta* 'below–inland' absolute axis in their direction-giving activity. Those who did not use it, when asked, stated that they could have used it. Peculiarly, four informants who had not used the axis, when explicitly asked about it, overlapped the *lalo* 'below' direction with the geographical 'west' direction. These same informants were those who accepted my suggestion of calling the axis *lalo–hake* 'below–above' instead of *lalo–'uta* 'below–inland.' It seems to me that once confronted with my question, they quickly thought of a solution and indicated the most semantically closed axis, such as the *hahake–hihifo* 'east–west' axis whose two forms are the result of a syllable reduplication from the two directionals *hake* 'up' and *hifo* 'down.'

One of the interviews not conducted in the village of Houma took place in the village of Toula (just south of the town of Neiafu). In this interview uses of the *lalo–'uta* 'below–inland' axis were also elicited. The directions encoded by this axis were exactly the same as the ones elicited in Houma in spite of the different location. In fact, *lalo* 'below' referred to cardinal south (towards town from Houma) and *'uta* 'inland' to cardinal north. Thus, the absolute nature of the axis received further support. It appears that the *lalo–'uta* 'below–inland' axis has to be treated as independent from the *kolo–'uta* 'town–inland' axis.

An informant interviewed on a boat at sea while going on an all-night fishing outing used the *lalo–'uta* 'below–inland' axis more frequently. He also produced and later explained to me how when describing two boats at sea, the one further away from the coast can be described as *'i lalo* 'at below,' and the one closer to the coast as *'i 'uta* 'at inland.'[37] He also added that the same description would apply if the two boats were seen from the land or from the sea (from a third boat at sea). The uses of this absolute axis, then, are clearly independent from uses of cardinal points.

The independence of the *lalo–'uta* 'below–inland' axis from cardinal points becomes clearer when we look at some data elicited during my stay in the islands of Niuatoputapu and Tongatapu. These islands have similar terrain characteristics, that is, the leeward side to the north and the windward (more

---

[37] Professor Futa Helu had already informed me about this phenomenon in a conversation we had at his home within the campus of 'Atenisi University, Nuku'alofa, Tonga, in January, 1994.

cliff-bound for Tongan islands) side to the south. In both islands uses of the *lalo–'uta* 'below–inland' axis were also elicited. But this time the *lalo* 'below' end of the axis was to the geographical north. This result is exactly the opposite of the result obtained on Vava'u, where the *lalo* 'below' end of the axis is to the south.

We can conclude, then, that the *lalo–'uta* 'below–inland' axis is an absolute axis; it is independent of the cardinal point axes and of the *kolo–'uta* 'town–inland' axis. But, whenever the geographical situation is conducive, these three axes may be used in similar contexts, thus causing the possibility of extensional overlapping.

Diachronic evidence in Tonga for the use of the *lalo–'uta* 'below–inland' absolute axis can be found in Helu (1979: 18) where he introduces a very old *fakatangi* 'chanted ballad' that goes like this:

(16) *'E Pukó mo Pukó*   'Oh Pukó and Pukó'
      Ko e fononga 'oku 'i lalo 'A visitor is below'
      Ko Sinilau mo 'ene tango 'It is Sinilau and his suit'
      Pea te u 'alu ke ma ó   'And with him I will go'

Helu goes on to say that the appropriate translation for *lalo* would be "leeward side of the island" (1979: 19) and speculates about the typology of early Tongan settlements. It is relevant that the use of such an axis has found its way into traditional oral poetry, thus pointing to deep roots in conventional language and the minds of Tongan speakers.

A final word about uses of the absolute FoR needs to be added. In both small-scale (i.e., during the linguistic tasks and in daily conversations) and large-scale space, I recorded instances of what I named the 'radial' subtype of the absolute FoR. That is, a specific point of reference is chosen in the environment of the speaker and then spatial relationships are expressed as toward or away-from it. Clear examples were collected during the performing of the language tasks, but also during speech about larger environments. I did not notice any specific preference for either environments. Similarly, no specific preference of a specific object was recorded. People, natural objects like trees or rocks, man-made objects like doors or houses were all chosen as appropriate to the specific need that had arisen during the speech event. I am not analyzing this finding any further here, but want to draw the reader's attention to it because exactly this phenomenon will assume a paramount relevance in the discussion of the mental representation of spatial relationships that follows in Chapter 4 and Chapter 5.

I now summarize the findings of the discussion about the uses of FoRs in large-scale space. The intrinsic FoR is moderately used and no specific difference is noticeable between this context and its parallel small-scale context. Uses of the relative FoR represent a more complex picture and some relevant differences between the two contexts have emerged. The incidence of use of the 'basic' subtype of the relative FoR diminishes considerably in large-scale space. Similarly, the 'reflection' subtype of the relative FoR is also used less often. The 'translation' subtype is, however, used more frequently in large-scale contexts.

The major contrastive characteristic between the small-scale and the large-scale space is the frequent use of the absolute FoR in the latter. A variety of subtypes of the absolute FoR are used including the 'cardinal points' subtype, and the 'radial' one, but the most commonly used is the 'single axis' subtype. Of this last subtype three different ones are in use, one I have labeled 'road-to-town–inland,' one 'town/sea–inland,' and finally one 'below–inland.' These three absolute axes all share the fact that they have a very clearly defined end, either 'road-to-town' or 'town/sea' or 'below,' and a more open one (inland) that is contextually defined.

In both contexts, lack of visibility or full visibility of the primary object (or figure to be described) or of the environment, or of both referred to, play a relevant role in determining choices of FoRs to be used. There is a clear shift from uses of the relative FoR to uses of the absolute FoR as appropriate perceptual visibility decreases. Uses of 'translation' subtype of the relative FoR were limited to the 'visible' environment and never extended beyond it.[38] Similarly, uses of the absolute FoR appeared almost exclusively in situations of lack of visibility.

In conclusion, there seems to be a high congruence between a relevant characteristic of the various frames of reference, that is, their relative embedding of contextual features, and a similar characteristic of the relationship between the user/s and the space referred to, that is, capacity of the user/s to perceptually share this space. In other words, the less the space referred to is perceptually accessible, the more the shift takes place from uses of the relative or intrinsic to the absolute FoR. The same has been found to be true for the differential uses of the three subtypes of the relative FoR, where decrease of visibility increases the uses of the 'reflection' subtype. A summary of these findings is presented in Table 3.4.

The two columns in Table 3.4 headed by the label 'no visibility' refer to two different phenomena. In fact, in the case of small-scale space the lack of visibility refers to the interlocutor. That is, it is the presence of a screen between the two informants during the performances of the linguistic tasks that may have caused a difference in use of FoR. In the case of large-scale space, instead, it is the lack of visibility of at least one of the elements put in spatial relationships

---

[38] The distinction I am making here between 'visible' and 'non-visible' does not include reported speech and narrative, or at least 'real' visibility in these latter events.

Table 3.4 *Uses* of FoRs in small- and large-scale space*

Frame of reference	Small-scale			Large-scale		
		Visibility			Visibility	
		Yes	No		Yes	No
'Basic' relative	xxx	xx	x	x	x	
'Translation' relative	xx	x	x	xxx	xxx	
'Reflection' relative	xxx		xxx	xx	x	x
Intrinsic	xx	x	x	xx	x	x
Absolute	x		x	xxx		xxx

* A greater number of 'x' indicates a greater incidence of use.

that is addressed. In the case of uses of single absolute axes it is the two poles of these same axes that are not perceptually accessible to the speaker. However, in spite of their differences, all the phenomena involve the perceptual accessibility of part or whole of the environment to the speaker.

The linguistic descriptions of spatial relationships by Tongan speakers have highlighted an interdependence of frames of reference with size of context and visibility. We have also emphasized that in two specific contexts, visible small-scale space and non-visible large-scale space, the linguistic production of Tongan speakers seems to privilege two different FoRs, the relative FoR in the former, and the absolute FoR in the latter, though not exclusively. I use these findings to answer the question I asked at the beginning of this chapter: How is 'front' assigned to cultural objects by Tongans? I confine the investigation to a restricted set of cultural objects, such as churches, houses, and villages.

3.4   Assigning 'front' to cultural objects

3.4.1   *Assigning front to houses*

In trying to determine the way in which front (and back, left, and right) gets assigned to the inside of Tongan houses it was necessary to go around the village of Houma and question all the residents of the thirty-three inhabited houses that actually constitute the village. The coupling of *mu'a* 'front' of the house and 'sitting place of chief' was the general answer elicited in the interviews conducted with the informants.

Since in sixteen houses (almost 45%), the *mu'a* 'front' was opposite a visibly open entrance, it seemed plausible to advance the hypothesis that the *mu'a* 'front' of a Tongan house is the part opposite the entrance. However, while interviewing one of my informants about the *mu'a* 'front' of some houses, he told me that he could not answer my question for a certain house because he had not eaten in a recent official occasion in that house – and so he could not remember where the chief sat. An open entrance of the house was clearly visible to both of us, and yet he still was not able to determine the *mu'a* 'front' of that house. It seems, then, that the perceptual accessibility to an entrance of the house is not sufficient to deduce its internal assignment of front. We need to take a look at some architectural features of Tongan houses in order to clarify this point.

There are four *fale Tonga* 'oval thatched houses' in the village of Houma,[39] and they traditionally have four entrances. One of these entrances is almost always kept closed because that side of the house is the actual sleeping place and is occupied completely by the bed (Figure 3.8). All the other houses are either *fale papa* 'European houses' that typically have three entrances on three different sides (Figure 3.8), or are more complex houses. The seven houses of the latter type still share the same features of three entrances on three sides.

This situation makes it difficult to know which of these entrances is the one used for official occasions when a chief enters the house. This 'official' entrance is not always the same one that is used daily by the people living in the house. This latter entrance is the one usually left open. This fact explains why my informant was not able to tell me about the front of that specific house in spite of his being able to see an open entrance.

For the sixteen houses in which the *mu'a* 'front' was located opposite the open used entrance, it turned out that the 'official' entrance faced the *mu'a* 'front.' That is, the entrance that was used daily and the 'official' entrance coincided. For most of the remaining houses (twelve), however, it turned out that the 'official' entrance differed from the daily one. Once the 'official' entrance was determined, also for these houses the *mu'a* 'front' was exactly the part opposite the 'official' entrance.[40] Then, my hypothesis – the *mu'a* 'front' of a Tongan house is the part opposite the entrance – seemed confirmed.

But what is the significance of this finding? Is this assignment of front to the interior of the house done by using a specific FoR? In addition, is this assignment done in congruence or contrast with common practice or habitual Tongan ways of thinking about space? Let us proceed in order, then, and try to reconstruct the process by which this assignment is made without previous

---

[39] As of summer 2007, all four *fale Tonga* were not there any more.

[40] For the remaining five houses the internal division of space was slightly more complex than in the other houses and consequently their *mu'a* 'fronts' were not opposite the 'official' entrance. However, I later discovered that the same assignment for *mu'a* 'front' was also used in these cases.

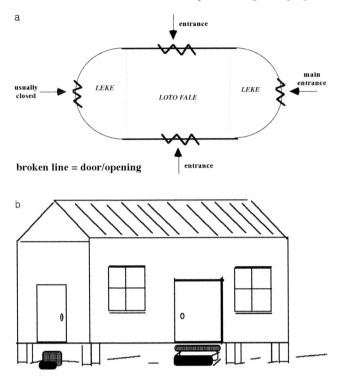

Figure 3.8 *Fale Tonga* 'Tongan house' (a) and *fale papa* 'European house' (b)

knowledge, that is, without knowing what names are assigned to the four interior sides of the house.

When a person enters the house he brings his own coordinates with him. Everything facing him, then, will be considered the *mu'a* 'front' of the house because it is 'in front of' him. By that same assignment, whatever is behind him will become the *mui* 'back' of the house. Left and right parts will be those corresponding to the left and right of this same person. In other words, a 'basic' subtype of the relative FoR is used to perform this primary assignment. This choice of FoR is in agreement with the preceding findings about preferential use of the 'basic' subtype of the relative FoR when in full visibility of the environment to be described.

However, when using a relative FoR, the coordinates move with the speaker/ viewer as he moves. Does this mean that these named parts of the house change when the person turns around and decides to leave? We know this is not the case for Tongans. Something happens that 'fixes' the orientation of the house. The house parts, in other words, have now become absolute coordinates. Every individual will move in this space and know exactly which part is which (either front or back or left or right).

That is, what was an individual assignment is now a fixed, socially agreed upon subdivision of the house in various named parts. Sociocultural parameters will determine who is to stand or sit in which part, what activities are allowed in each part, and how the relations between the parts will assume specific meanings. These sociocultural parameters exist independently from spatial parameters in the society, but they will be mapped on these spatially determined parts. One example is the chief sitting in the 'front' who will ensure that this part will be regarded as the one occupied by the most prominent person in the assembly (informal or official).

What is the process by which the interior parts of the house become fixed orientation points? It is always difficult to speculate about diachronic processes, but I feel confident in advancing the following hypothesis. I have already stated that the interior parts of the house can be determined on entering by using a 'basic' subtype of the relative FoR (in line with the linguistic preferences discovered for environments in full visibility). The chief entering houses may have preferred to choose as his seat the front established by his own use of a 'basic' subtype of the relative FoR. This historically established tradition may have contributed to 'fix' – render absolute – the otherwise relative assignment of parts to the Tongan house.

Coming back to contemporary Tonga, the only knowledge needed to deduce the interior *mu'a* 'front' of the Tongan house is to know which one (of the three) is the 'official' entrance of the house. This entrance is usually the only one kept open on such occasions. Then anybody (house occupants, villagers, or chief), even without previous knowledge, by simply using the 'basic' subtype of the relative FoR, is able to determine which part of the house is its *mu'a* 'front.' This explains the great facility with which the chief finds the appropriate place for his seat, specially when he enters houses for the first time on formal occasions where mats have been laid out fully decorated and loaded with ceremonial food.

3.4.2   Assigning front to churches

The assignment of front to the interior of churches follows a pattern similar to the one just discussed for houses. However, a distinction must be made between situations in which the speaker/s is/are inside or outside the church. Regarding the interior of a Tongan church, we have already seen in the introduction that to be *'i mu'a* 'at front' you should be in the part of the church where the minister is. This assignment will determine the internal *mui* 'back' of the church to be the opposite side, from where you usually enter. The left side and the right side of the church would be the same ones as for a person entering the church (Figure 3.9). These internal assignments along the front–back and the left–right axes do not differ from what happens in the West (Fillmore, 1975: 20, calls this assignment "user-orientation criterion"). However, Fillmore does not say how this assignment comes to be. In other words, even though these parts of the church may be common knowledge, this assignment must have been made following a procedure not in contrast with common practices or habitual Western (or Tongan, in our case) ways of thinking about space. And this would explain in part why people find it so 'natural' that these parts of the church are assigned these names.

The same mental phenomena argued for while discussing the assignment of front to the Tongan house may be called for in this case. In other words, a 'basic' subtype of the relative FoR is used to perform the assignment of front – and back, left, and right – to the church. In the same way as for the house, these named parts of the church do not change when a person turns around and decides to leave. The church parts are considered absolute coordinates. Again then, every individual moving in this space will know exactly which part is which (either front or back or left or right) by simply knowing the position of the (main) entrance.

The 'fixing' of the internal parts of the church may have followed a pattern similar to the pattern argued for in the assignments of 'fixed' parts to the house. I do not intend here to speculate about the fact that the church is not a traditional Tongan building (the introduction of Christianity to Tonga dates back only to the beginning of the nineteenth century), nor that it may resemble in structure (and parts assignment) constructions where local traditional gods were worshipped. What is relevant is the congruence of the two procedures (for the house and for the church) and of both of them with the preferential pattern – uses of the 'basic' subtype of the relative FoR – in encoding spatial relationships in language of fully visible and unobstructed environments.

Let us now consider another aspect of 'front' assignment to churches. In the West, when seen from the outside, churches trigger the use of a 'reflection' subtype of the relative FoR (called "access criterion" by Fillmore, 1975: 20). Consequently, if an object is in the area outside the church on the side where the main entrance is located, it will be described as 'in front of' the church. In Tonga, instead, the same assignments used for the interior of the church apply to its outside. On each of the four sides the interior and the exterior parts will have the same name. Figure 3.9 illustrates the point just made.

Extending the front–back–left–right assignments typical of the interior of the church to its exterior makes the Tongan church appear to acquire relevant intrinsic features. Thus, it may be the case that objects described in relation to the church would require the use of an intrinsic FoR. I checked this hypothesis with many informants and they partially confirmed it. However, I obtained

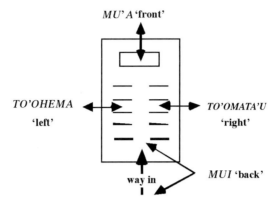

Figure 3.9 Church with front–back and left–right assignments

slightly different responses when I interviewed informants inside or outside the church.

Often they would refer to objects located outside the church on the entrance side as '*i mui* 'at back,' and on the opposite side as '*i mu'a* 'at front.' And this was true when informants were both inside and outside the church. But, at times and only when my elicitation took place outside the church, a 'reflection' subtype of the relative FoR was also used. In other words, when the exchanges were taking place outside the church, for some informants the outside area on the entrance side was considered *mu'a* 'front' and the opposite outside area *mui* 'back.'

We have already discovered that the degree of visibility of the primary object or figure can affect the choice of a subtype of the relative FoR in describing a spatial relationship. This is exactly the case for the types of descriptions involving the church and the objects outside of it. In fact, when for the speaker the object was completely or almost completely hidden from view by the church, it was described by means of the 'reflection' subtype of the relative FoR. In this case, the object (e.g., horse) was '*i mui* 'at back' of the church when it was in the space beyond the church. The object was '*i mu'a* 'at front' when it was at the entrance side of the church (outside). In case of full or partial visibility of the object, for example the top of a tree or the head of an animal (e.g., a horse), the opposite was true: the object was '*i mu'a* 'at front' when beyond the church and '*i mui* 'at back' when at the entrance side of the church. That is, the intrinsic FoR appears to be used.

This intrinsic interpretation of some of the responses, however, overlaps with another interpretation in which a use of a 'translation' subtype of the relative FoR (see Figure 3.5) can be suggested. Both are equally feasible as possible interpretations. But by looking at the linguistic forms that characterize these responses, the latter seems more plausible than the intrinsic. In fact, rarely in the responses the phrases *'i mu'a* 'at front' or *'i mui* 'at back' were followed by a prepositional phrase specifying the object (in this case 'the church'). Since this would be typical of expressions realizing an intrinsic FoR, I conclude that it is the other FoR that was used – the 'translation' subtype.

In sum, the internal front, back, and sides of a Tongan church are determined by the use of a 'basic' relative FoR. This assignment has been historically 'fixed' to make these parts of the church become absolute. This does not differ from what we know about the assignment of front, back, and sides to a church in the West (see Filmore, 1975: 20). Relevantly, a similar procedure is used by Tongans to assign the front to the house. The external front, back, and sides of the church are determined by using either a 'reflection' (as in the West) or a 'translation' subtype of the relative FoR. This latter use may lead a superficial listener to interpret certain Tongan expressions as being the instantiation of an intrinsic FoR centered on the church.

3.4.3   Assigning front to villages

A different situation arises regarding the assignment of *mu'a* 'front' to the village as a whole. In this case, the choice of front is the part where the road from town (Neiafu, site of political, administrative, and economic power) enters the village, or alternatively, where the road to town exits the village. This was true not only for Houma, the village in which I was residing, but also for other villages on the island whose geographical relations to Neiafu were of a different nature. For instance, while for the village of Houma its *mu'a* 'front' is actually to the west, it is to the north for the village of Tu'anekivale, and to the east for the village of Leimatu'a. This is because the road to town enters (or exits) these villages from these directions (see map of Vava'u in Figure 3.6).

How then is the *mu'a* 'front' assigned to a village? It cannot be in the same fashion as for the church and the house. In fact, even considering the 'road from town' as the metaphorical 'person' entering the village and still using a 'basic' or a 'translation' subtype of the relative FoR, we would end up with the opposite assignment from the one elicited from the informants. That is, what is considered *mui* 'back' of the village would end up being assigned to be *mu'a* 'front,' and the *to'omata'u* 'right' side would be considered the one elicited as the *to'ohema* 'left' side (Figure 3.10a and 3.10b).

Considering the possibility of the use of a 'reflection' subtype of the relative FoR would imply that the left side of the village is the one to the left of the road from town as it enters the village (Figure 3.10c). But, informants when asked about left and right side of the village provided exactly the opposite responses. The left side of the village is the one on the right of the road from town as it

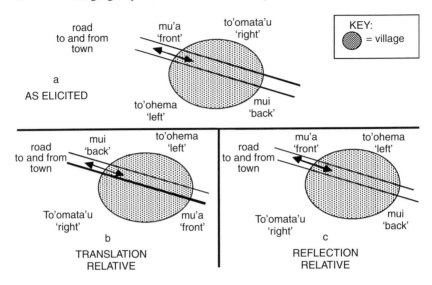

Figure 3.10 Assignment of *mu'a* 'front' to a village

enters the village. Figure 3.10 shows what was elicited from informants as well as the other two possibilities just discussed.

Another possibility would be to consider the village as metaphorically 'animate' and, thus, allowing the use of an intrinsic FoR. This hypothesis has never been confirmed by any informants and it cannot even be evinced from any ethnographic literature about traditional Tonga (see Martin, 1818; Lawry, 1852; Gifford, 1929). Nor has the village ever been indicated as possessing an habitual direction of motion!

The last hypothesis considers the use of an absolute FoR for the assignments of *mu'a* 'front' of villages. This absolute system would not use cardinal points, but a single axis. We have already seen that the use of an absolute FoR based on a single axis is not unusual for Tongans. I discussed three other similar systems when talking about uses of FoRs in large-scale space (see Section 3.3.2). This familiarity with the use of such a system makes this last hypothesis very plausible. The absolute axis used is constituted on one pole by the place where the road to/from town exits/enters the village, and the other pole would be contextually constructed, that is, it would be the place where each individual is located. Notice that this axis differs from the town/sea–inland axes introduced in Section 3.3.2. In fact, the side of the village called 'front' is not the one towards town or sea or inland, but the one at the side where the road-to-town enters/exits the village. At a more abstract level, the two axes may be related – the concrete direction to road-to-town may be the result of an analogy with the direction to town[41] – in practical terms, though, the use of these two axes gives rise to two different directions. Consequently, the axes used must be two different axes.

Furthermore, notice that the use of an absolute FoR in a large-scale context like the village is in line with the findings already introduced about a privileged use of this FoR in this same context. It seems, then, that characteristics of the context, differential levels of perceptual accessibility to this context, and preferential choices of specific types of FoR in these contexts play a fundamental role in the assignment of *mu'a* 'front' to the cultural objects discussed: house, church, and village.

3.5   Conclusion: language and space in Tonga

At the beginning of this chapter I asked how space, or better, how spatial relationships, are expressed linguistically in Tonga. Within this general question I also asked specifically how Tongans conceptualize and express linguistically the concept of 'front' and other related concepts, i.e., back. Moreover, in order to fully understand otherwise puzzling linguistic expressions regarding 'front' assignment, I had to inquire into the relationship between Tongan conceptualizations of spatial relationships (i.e., the choice and use of FoR) and their linguistic expressions. I now summarize the findings.

In English, spatial relationships are mainly expressed linguistically by means of prepositions; there are between 80 and 100 in common use (see Jackendoff, 1992b: 107–8). In Tongan, spatial relationships are mainly expressed by means of only three spatial prepositions, five directionals, and numerous spatial nouns. A grammatical-conceptual analysis of these latter reveals that for Tongans, objects are primarily divided into four parts: an inside and an outside, and along the vertical axis a top and a bottom. Further details are added later, such as contour, side, and corner. Finally, specific characteristics of the objects described determine alternative forms of the generic part already named. A good example is the three further distinctions added to *lalo* 'below,' that is, *kilisi* 'bottom,' *faliki* 'floor,' and *takele* 'curved bottom.'

Tongan provides a variety of lexemes that allow the linguistic realizations of any of the FoRs currently known in the literature about space. However, it is possible to group the linguistic uses of these FoRs according to characteristics

---

[41] On Tongatapu, the major island of the Tongan archipelago, there is a village named Mu'a 'front' that was the royal residence for several centuries till it was moved to Nuku'alofa, the current capital and royal residence. The eastern section of this island that includes the village of Mu'a is also called Mu'a. Thus, it seems that various places related to royalty or in the direction of royalty are assigned the term *m'ua* 'front' (see the discussion of the assignment of 'front' to houses in this work). I am currently investigating this fascinating aspect of the historical and cultural relationship between royalty and *mu'a* 'front.'

of the environments described and according to perceptual accessibility. The relative FoR is most frequently used in small-scale space, while the absolute FoR is most frequently used in large-scale space. In descriptions of small-scale space, full visibility of the environment correlates with a relevant preference towards the use of the 'translation' subtype of the relative FoR. A necessary condition for its use is also full or partial visibility of the primary object described. This result was coupled with an extensive use of this same FoR in a variety of large-scale contexts. In descriptions of large-scale space, Tongans use a number of single-axis subtypes of the absolute FoR. This is also found in other Oceanic communities (see Hill, 1997; Ozanne-Rivierre, 1997). Their uses increase considerably when referring to environments not accessible perceptually.

It is very interesting that all three single-axis systems share one of the two points, that is, *'uta* 'inland.' The other point is either *lalo* 'below,' *tahi* 'sea,' or *kolo* 'town.' It seems that in historically choosing these fixed points of reference – or in determining these directions – an increasing level of specificity has been used. In fact, the first represents a choice by Tongans of a side (below) of the universal vertical axis. The second represents a choice of an overwhelming presence in the Polynesian (and Oceanic) island environment such as the sea (for a similar argument see Palmer, 2002). And finally the third represents a choice of the place of human settlement (village/town) as it contrasts with the other uninhabited land.

The assignment of 'front' to cultural objects such as house, church, and village follows the preferential uses of specific FoRs already indicated. It is also strictly related to specific contexts. In the smaller, fully-visible space of the house and church the 'basic' subtype of the relative FoR is firstly used to assign a front. This primary assignment is later 'fixed' by means of sociocultural parameters such as what activity is performed in the various spaces and who is performing it. Once these names of the various parts – of house or church – are 'fixed,' these same parts become points of an absolute FoR. This allows one to make reference to them even when not sharing any perceptual accessibility to the house or church. In particular, regarding the church, this absolute assignment makes the church appear to have intrinsic features. In fact, the names assigned to the interior sides of the church are identical to the names of the same sides as seen from the outside of the church. This identical name assignment, however, takes place only when speakers are inside the church and not when they are outside of it.

Finally, the assignment of 'front' to the village is also affected by the size of the context and by the perceptual accessibility of this cultural object. Tongan villages are generally very small and range from a few hundred to a couple of thousand inhabitants. However, even in the case of very small villages like Houma, the layout is large enough that it is impossible for anybody to perceptually access the whole village. In this situation and from the findings already introduced, we would expect the use of a single-axis absolute FoR to be used for the assignment of 'front' to a village. This is exactly what I discovered Tongans do.

Before closing, I want to underline that analyses of language used by themselves could not have provided the answers presented. Often and necessarily, I had to use ethnographic data to disambiguate otherwise obscure linguistic uses. For example, only when I realized how Tongan houses are structured and used could I understand the process by which 'front' was assigned to their interiors. Levinson (1996b: 354) states that "the study of the language of space might play a fundamental role in the anthropology of space more generally." Later, he adds:

The focus has been on collective representations, on cosmologies and the symbolic uses and associations of space, with little mention of the kind of notions in daily use to solve spatial problems. (Levinson, 1996b: 354)

I regard the content of this chapter as a contribution towards filling this gap. The Tongan data I have discussed may help us understand how speakers of very different languages utilize their languages "in daily use to solve spatial problems." The unique two cases of uses of the 'translation' subtype of the relative FoR described by Hill (1982) and Cablitz (2006) have now found support in Tongan frequent uses of the same FoR. Similarly, the determining role that visibility plays in the Tongan choices of an FoR to describe their environment is of relevance to any research on space.

4   Space in Tongan cognition

4.1   Thinking about space

In the previous chapter I presented and discussed ways in which spatial relationships are expressed in the Tongan language. Clearly some other ways have been left out from my investigation, such as the small set of Tongan dimensional adjectives and the open class of Tongan verbs expressing either state or motion. Nonetheless, some salient characteristics of the language have been highlighted and their relevance to the project at hand is soon to become apparent. In the present chapter I investigate the preferred mental representations of space that generate Tongan behaviors, including language use.

Linguistic preferences may not replicate preferences in representing mentally spatial relationships. This may be more true or possible when other cognitive capacities such as long-term memory or making inferences are involved. It is for this reason that I administered a battery of tasks, named 'psychological tasks,' where individuals would provide only non-linguistic responses. The rationale being that by avoiding linguistic responses, the results would allow direct access to cognitive activities without the filtering role of language. A subset of the psychological tasks includes three activities aimed at detecting specific preferences in the use of frames of reference (FoR) for representing spatial relationships in long-term memory in small-scale space (a second subset will be discussed in Chapter 5).

The results of these activities indicate unequivocally that Tongan prefer the absolute FoR when storing spatial relationships in long-term memory and/or when engaging in making inferences.

4.2   Methodology for the collection of the cognitive data

The data about mental representations of spatial relationships were collected by means of the administration of what I named 'psychological' tasks. I describe and discuss a first subset here and a second one ('cultural tasks') in Chapter 5. This first subset is called 'frame of reference tasks,' since in each one of them a preference for a specific FoR could be elicited. In these tasks the role of language was kept to a minimum so that a serious attempt could be made to obtain insights into mental phenomena outside the linguistic realm. The possibility of linguistic coding during the tasks was not completely ruled out, but its likelihood was kept to a minimum.

4.2.1   Frame of reference (FoR) tasks

We saw in the previous chapter how FoRs, or sets of coordinates, are an essential part of spatial cognition. I also discussed there Levinson's (1996a, 2003) proposed typology and looked into the relationships between the three major types of FoR he suggested, relative, intrinsic, and absolute. The investigation of a variety of languages by members of the CARG (1992) showed that a strong preference exists among speakers of certain languages to privilege a specific type of FoR when linguistically describing spatial relationships in small-scale space (see Baayen and Danziger, 1994: 68). In order to find out if this linguistically expressed preference is congruent with the same specific way of mentally representing spatial relationships, the members of the CARG group developed a set of 'frame of reference' tasks. These latter were thought of as ways of eliciting non-linguistic responses about spatial relationships in small-scale space from speakers of those same languages in order to collect information about mental phenomena outside the linguistic realm.

Three out of the five tasks prepared by the CARG (see Baayen and Danziger, 1994: 69–75) were selected for the present project, 'Animals in a Row,' 'Red and Blue Chips,' and 'Transitivity.' The first is intended to check coding in memory of spatial relationships on the transverse (left–right) axis by means of either a relative or an absolute FoR. The second is intended to explore the same issues but on both the transverse and the sagittal (front–back) axes. Finally, the third, while keeping the capacity to check both axes, requires the addition of a logical operation to the pure memory task type of the first two, thus, providing information about uses of the same two FoRs under slightly different mental conditions.

The analysis of the linguistic data obtained about the Tongan language allowed the coding of speakers as primarily 'relative' FoR users, at least in the small-scale space. The administration of the three psychological tasks just mentioned made it possible to check the relevance of the use of this FoR at a different level of mental operations still in the small-scale space.

These three tasks were administered to twenty-seven informants in three different villages of the Kingdom of Tonga: Ngele'ia, on the island of Tongatapu, Hihifo, on the island of Niuatoputapu, and Houma, on the island of Vava'u. The reasons for choosing these three villages are those already mentioned above in Chapter 2, Section 2.4. The age of the informants ranged from seventeen to seventy-three years old. Their level of education as well as their knowledge of English varied considerably, but an attempt was made to involve informants with little or no knowledge of English. The large number of informants studied makes the interference of the data through exposure to English most unlikely.

4.2.1.1   Animals in a Row

Informants who were administered the 'Animals in a Row' task were required to stand in front of a table (in some cases, a box, a trunk, or an elevated surface). On the table they were shown a set of three small plastic farm animals, a cow, a pig, and a horse. The objects were shown standing in a row, all facing the same direction, either to the right or the left on the transverse axis in front of the informants. The informants were then asked (in Tongan) to memorize the position of the animals. When the informant declared themselves ready to go to the next step (typically, after a few seconds) the animals were taken away and a minimum of 60 seconds had to elapse in which some conversation took place between the informant and the researcher and/or assistant.

Then, the informant was directed to another table situated at some distance and right opposite the first one. Here s/he was asked to stand in front of this second table in a position that required a 180 degree rotation from the previous one. The researcher then handed the three animals to the informant and the informant had to put them on the new table in the sequence and direction they had seen earlier. This constituted the end of one trial and careful note was taken of the direction the informant chose to align the three animals. The trial was repeated five times for each informant and each time the sequence and overall direction of the three animals shown changed randomly. A training trial preceded the beginning of the five-part task to make sure that its content had been clearly understood.

The way in which the informants put down the animals provided a very clear cue towards an understanding of which FoR had been used to remember their spatial arrangement observed a few seconds before. In fact, there are only two ways (other solutions were considered mistakes) in which the informants could arrange the overall direction of the three animals (their actual sequence was also registered by the researcher and/or assistant, but had little relevance in the task). If participants used a relative FoR the overall direction of the animals would stay the same as in the way they were seen, that is, either to the informant's own left or right. If participants used an absolute FoR the direction of the animals would stay the same relative to some landmark or cardinal point, but not to the informant's left or right. Figure 4.1 illustrates the point just made.

The content of Figure 4.1a shows how the choice of one of the frames of reference, relative or absolute, for coding in memory eventually determines the responses given by the informant. Figure 4.1b illustrates the same phenomenon by showing a stylized version of the three animals involved in the task.

Beyond the understanding of the instructions in the native language, there was no other role that was overtly assigned to language in the performing of

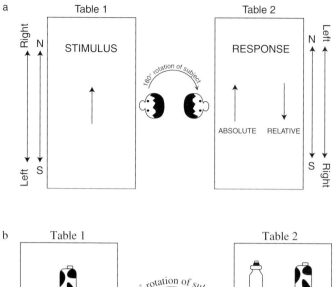

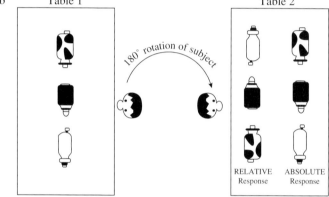

Figure 4.1 Possible responses for 'Animals in a Row' task (adapted from Levinson, 2003: 156)

this task. The stimulus involved only visual perception and the response only motor activity. Between the exposure to the stimulus situation and the response some coding of spatial relationships by means of an FoR in non-perceptual memory was involved. The nature of this coding was exactly the target of this task. In fact, the rationale behind its administration was that of investigating the possibility of a congruence between the privileged use of an FoR evinced from the linguistic data and the responses collected from this task. This latter being an attempt to obtain insights into psychological processes as distinct from language.

The content of the task makes its results highly comparable to the results obtained by the administration of the linguistic tasks insofar as both types refer to spatial relationships in a small-scale space. Furthermore, the small plastic animals involved were the same plastic animals used for the farm scenes depicted in the photographs of the linguistic tasks types one and two described in the previous chapter. Finally, most of the informants who participated in this task had also been previously administered at least one of the linguistic tasks.

4.2.1.2   Red and Blue Chips

The procedure for the administration of the 'Red and Blue Chips' task was very similar to the one for the previous task. While standing in front of a table an informant was shown and asked to remember a chip, or plastic card, lying on it. This chip contains a picture of a blue square and a red circle lined up on the transverse (left–right) or sagittal (front–back) axis. After waiting a minute the informant was asked to turn 180 degrees and brought to a second table where s/he had to recognize the same chip seen before among four of them lying in a cross on this second table.

Again, there are only two possible choices dictated by the FoR, either relative or absolute, chosen by the informant to memorize the chip seen on the first table. However, this time the task allows the investigation of these choices on two axes, that is, the transverse and the sagittal axis. Figure 4.2 illustrates this point.

Figure 4.2 demonstrate how a chip shown on the first table with the blue square and the red circle aligned along either the transverse or sagittal axis may elicit at least two types of responses, labeled relative or absolute from the fact that they indicate the use of that specific type of FoR.

The task consisted of ten trials and in each trial the choice involved one of the two axes for a total of five times per axis. The sequence of the trials was

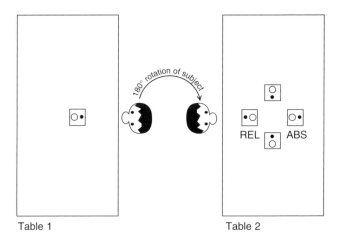

Table 1   Table 2

Figure 4.2 Possible responses for 'Red and Blue Chips' task (from Levinson, 2003: 160)

randomized. A short training session preceded the ten trials to make sure that the informant had mastered the procedure. The task involved visual perception and memory beyond perceptual input. It involved choices in small-scale space to obtain data comparable with the previously described task (as well as with some of the linguistic tasks). Also for this task almost all the informants had previously engaged in one of the linguistic tasks.

4.2.1.3   Transitivity

The two psychological tasks already described were devised in order to obtain information about mental representations of spatial relationships, specifically frames of reference, without the obvious interference of language. The stimuli used engaged first the informants' visual perception and the following part of the task asked them to use their long-term memory so that they could reproduce (by assembling three animals in a row) or simply recognize (by pointing to a chip) the content of the first stimuli. However, it became very relevant to know if the overt co-occurrence during the memorization process of other mental processes, still not language bound, would affect the type of responses elicited. The 'Transitivity' task tried to address this issue.

An informant was shown a small conical object (A) resting on a table. All objects in this task were made of plastic and their shapes were symmetrical to avoid any possible hint due to specific shape configuration. Then, a small cubic object (B) was added on either the transverse or sagittal axis. The informant was asked to remember the arrangement of the two objects and then the researcher removed them from the table.

As in the previous two tasks, the informant was now brought to a second table after a 180 degree rotation and here the same small cubic object (B) seen on the first table was shown first. A different object (C), this time cylindrical, was added on one of the two axes, but the same axis as for the two objects already seen on the first table. Again, the informant was asked to remember the arrangement of the two objects before collection.

Finally, the informant was taken back to the first table, conical object (A) was put down by the researcher and the informant was handed the cylindrical object (C) just seen on the second table. The instruction was to put the cylindrical object (C) next to the conical object (A) as it should be if the three objects seen so far were on the same table and in a straight line on the same axis, either transverse or sagittal. Figure 4.3 illustrates the sequence of the assemblages of objects on the two tables and the three parts of the task.

In Figure 4.3a the various object assemblages on the two tables are shown in the sequence as it was experienced by the informants. It can be seen that in order to perform the task the informant is required to perform a logical operation, that is, an inference. Figure 4.3b shows the three stages of the task and the positions of the informant in relationship to the two tables.

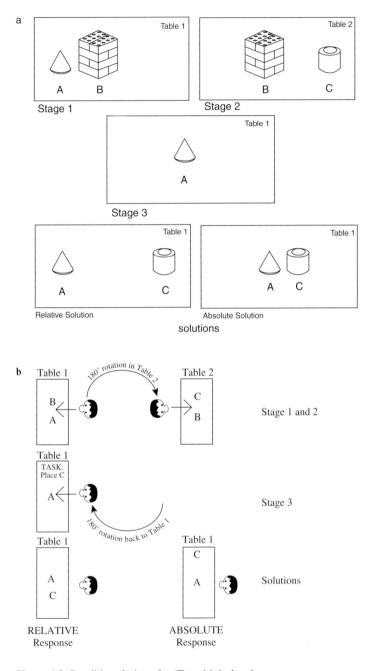

Figure 4.3 Possible solutions for 'Transitivity' task

The added complexity of this task both physical, that is, moving from table one to table two and back to table one, and mental, that is, being forced to perform an inference, made it unnecessary to include a one minute delay before asking the informant to make the final crucial choice. In fact, both moving from one table to another and performing the inference usually took up more than one minute from the first exposure to the arranging of objects on table one. The informant's choice was again of a binary nature and it may be labeled relative or absolute according to the FoR used in performing the mental coding of the spatial relationships among the objects seen on the two tables.

Before performing the task each informant went through a training session and only when they showed their understanding was the task initiated. The task as a whole consisted of ten randomized trials with objects aligned on the transverse or sagittal axis five times each. Again, the task regarded spatial relationships in the small-scale space, thus making results comparable, at least for this variable, with those obtained by some of the linguistic tasks.

4.3   Uses of frames of reference elicited by the FoR tasks

As a general working hypothesis I adopt the one put forward by Levinson (1996a, 2003; but see also Pederson, 1993, 1995, and Baayen and Danziger, 1994). Basically congruence is expected between the results of the administration of the linguistic tasks and the psychological tasks. In other words, since a privileged status has been suggested for a relative FoR during linguistic production in small-scale space, a similar result is expected for performances entailing the encoding of FoRs for non-linguistic purposes.

In Table 4.1, the information just introduced is summarized. Under the leftmost column headed by 'Task' the type of psychological task administered is indicated. The various sites in Tonga where the task was administered appear under the column labeled 'Site'. In the column headed by 'No. of infs.' the number of informants that participated in each site is indicated. It can be seen that their number is homogeneous enough among sites. In spite of the fact that their number is repeated for each task, their general total is the same as the specific total for each individual task. In fact, the three tasks were administered in a sequence to the same informants. The total distribution of males and females is fairly homogeneous, although in Ngele'ia the number of males is twice that of females.

The results for each informant in each task were coded as 'relative' or 'absolute' if all or the majority of its responses (minimum 60%) were of either specific type. This meant a cut-off point of three responses of the same type out of five possible responses for the 'Animals in a Row' task, five out of eight responses for the 'Red and Blue' task, and six out of ten responses for the 'Transitivity' task.

Table 4.1 *Number and gender of informants per task*

Task	Site	No. of infs.	Female	Male
Animals in a Row	Ngele'ia	9	3	6
	Hihifo	8	4	4
	Houma	10	6	4
Red and Blue	Ngele'ia	9	3	6
	Hihifo	8	4	4
	Houma	10	6	4
Transitivity	Ngele'ia	9	3	6
	Hihifo	8	4	4
	Houma	10	6	4
Total		**27**	**13**	**14**
		100%	48%	52%

The number of trials for each task differed and while they were an odd number in the 'Animals in a Row' task, they were an even number in the other two tasks. This fact gave rise to the possibility of an even split among the responses for each individual informant in those two tasks. Thus, raising the possibility that a specific informant could not be coded as in either of the two types.

On average, only 10% (eight cases out of eighty-one) of the whole results were of this last ambiguous type. A good portion of the remaining cases (eighteen out of seventy-three, that is, 24%) was clearly of one type or the other (all responses of the same type), and the rest had to be assigned on a 60%+ majority basis. It is relevant to underline that of the eighteen cases of homogeneous responses throughout the task, sixteen cases (89%) were of the absolute type and only two cases (11%) of the relative type. Table 4.2 summarizes the general and the specific results for each task.

In Table 4.2, in the 'Total' row of the column headed by 'No. of infs.', that is, number of informants, the informants for the three sites have been added together, even though they were the same twenty-seven for each task. In this way the total number of informants will correspond to the total number of cases. Under the column headed by '???' the ambiguous cases discussed above have been indicated. It can be easily seen that they appear only in connection with the 'Red and Blue' and the 'Transitivity' tasks, that is, in the only tasks they were possible. When one looks at the general results, one notices that the use of the absolute FoR (63%) in coding for short-term memory spatial relationships in small-scale space is significantly more common than the use of the relative FoR (27%). This is true in all the three tasks and slightly more so in the 'Animals in a Row' task as well as slightly less so in the 'Red and Blue' task.

Table 4.2 *Results for the three tasks with 60% cut-off point*[1]

Task	Site	No. of infs.	Abs	Rel	???
Animals in a Row	Ngele'ia	9	6	3	
	Hihifo	8	7	1	
	Houma	10	8	2	
Sub-total		**27**	**21**	**6**	
		100%	78%	22%	
Red and Blue	Ngele'ia	9	6	2	1
	Hihifo	8	4	4	
	Houma	10	5	2	3
Sub-total		**27**	**15**	**8**	**4**
		100%	55%	30%	15%
Transitivity	Ngele'ia	9	6	1	2
	Hihifo	8	3	3	2
	Houma	10	7	3	
Sub-total		**27**	**16**	**7**	**4**
		100%	60%	26%	14%
Total		**81**	**51**	**22**	**8**
		100%	63%	27%	10%

In order to avoid coding informants whose responses were exactly 60% and consequently close to chance, I decided to increase the cut-off point to a minimum of 70% for considering an informant as a relative or absolute encoder. This time, then, only informants with the following characteristics were coded as relative or absolute encoders: informants with four responses of the same type out of five for the 'Animals in a Row' task, six out of eight for the 'Red and Blue' task, and seven out of ten for the 'Transitivity' task. Table 4.3 summarizes the new results. The column headed by '???' in Table 4.3, contrary to the same one in Table 4.2, now contains both even responses cases and those that did not satisfy the new cut-off point.[2]

[1] Three out of four cut-off points for each axis in 'Red and Blue'; four out of five cut-off points for each axis in 'Transitivity.'
[2] For the task 'Animals in a Row' I have also checked a strategy that affected data responses by Tamil informants (Pederson, personal communication), that is, so-called 'mono-directional' responses. In this case an informant would choose a direction and use it consistently in the responses for all the five trials of the task. Of the twenty-seven informants only one could be labeled in this way, so I decided that this strategy had not had a relevant role in the performance of the task by my informants. Consequently, I have completely left out such a coding of the informants.

Table 4.3 *Results for the three tasks with 70% cut-off point*

Task	Site	No. of infs.	Abs	Rel	???
Animals in a Row	Ngele'ia	9	6	2	1
	Hihifo	8	3	0	5
	Houma	10	5	1	4
Sub-total		**27**	**14**	**3**	**10**
		100%	52%	11%	37%
Red and Blue	Ngele'ia	9	4	2	3
	Hihifo	8	1	4	3
	Houma	10	4	1	5
Sub-total		**27**	**9**	**7**	**11**
		100%	33%	26%	41%
Transitivity	Ngele'ia	9	4	1	4
	Hihifo	8	2	1	5
	Houma	10	6	0	4
Sub-total		**27**	**12**	**2**	**13**
		100%	45%	7%	48%
Total		**81**	**35**	**12**	**34**
		100%	43%	15%	42%

In spite of some changes in percentages, the general tendency previously obtained was confirmed with this new higher cut-off point. In fact, the general result is still in favor of the absolute uses (43%) over the relative ones (15%), and this is true for all the three tasks. The stronger result for the 'Animal in a Row' task is again confirmed as well as the smaller difference between the two solutions in the 'Red and Blue' task.

Both results above are in clear contradiction with that provided by the linguistic elicitation tasks in small-scale space. In fact, in the analysis of those data a privileged role was suggested for the relative FoR in that specific context. But, according to the contents of both Table 4.2 and Table 4.3 we would have to suggest the absolute FoR as having a privileged status when encoding spatial relationships for non-linguistic purposes.

Before looking at the consequences of this fact, it is appropriate to look more carefully at the results of the two tasks that allow a differentiation between the sagittal (front–back) and transverse (left–right) axes, that is, the 'Red and Blue' and the 'Transitivity' tasks. We already know from the result of the linguistic tasks that the sagittal (front–back) axis is the one associated with complex cognitive processing. In fact, we have suggested how choice

Table 4.4 *Absolute versus relative responses on the front–back (sagittal) and left–right (transverse) axes in the 'Red and Blue' task*

	Frame of reference	Front–Back axis	Left–Right axis	Total
Red and Blue				
	Absolute	[45%] **49** [42%]	[64%] **69** [58%]	[55%] **118** [100%]
	Relative	[50%] **54** [60%]	[33%] **36** [40%]	[42%] **90** [100%]
	Error	[5%] **5** [62%]	[3%] **3** [38%]	[3%] **8** [100%]
Possible cases		[100%] **108** [50%]	[100%] **108** [50%]	[100%] **216** [100%]

is exercised between a 'translation' and a 'reflection' relative FoR, that is, a different assignment of sides on the sagittal axis, on the basis of the presence or absence of some form of visibility. The latter, however, does not affect the assignment of left and right on the transverse axis. Consequently, we may expect variation in the results regarding the two axes, specifically, more homogeneity in the responses connected with the transverse axis and more variety in those connected with the sagittal axis. Let us now look at the results of the two tasks in more detail.

As regards the 'Red and Blue' task, considering twenty-seven informants from the three sites and eight trials for the tasks that each informant was asked to perform, it can be derived that the total number of trials for all the informants was of 216. Of these latter, 118 (55%) involved choices of the absolute FoR, while 90 (42%) choices of the relative one. The overall result is confirmed with decreased percentage differences compared to percentages in both Table 4.2 and Table 4.3. However, if we look at the incidence of absolute versus relative choices within and across the two axes, we get a slightly different picture. Across axes there are more absolute responses in the left–right axis (58%) than in the front–back one (42%). And the opposite is true for relative responses; in fact, there are more of them in the front–back axis (60%) than in the left–right one (40%). Within the left–right axis sixty-nine (64%) choices are absolute, thirty-six (33%) are relative and three (3%) are errors made. Here again the general tendency seems confirmed. Within the front–back axis forty-nine (45%) choices are absolute, fifty-four (50%) are relative, and five (5%) are errors made. Here, instead, the choices of the relative FoR are slightly more than the absolute ones, thus posing a problem of how to interpret this particular result as distinguished from the general one. Before attempting an interpretation, I introduce Table 4.4 where the results just discussed are summarized. The percentages in Table 4.4 refer to the same column when on the left of the bold number, and across columns when on the right of the bold number.

Pederson (1995) discusses the results from the administration of the same three tasks to two Tamil speaking subpopulations. In that discussion he points out what he defines as an 'axis bias' (pp. 50–1), that is, a tendency (for almost any population) to make more relative choices on the sagittal axis than on the transverse one. And he justifies this phenomenon in the following way:

On the sagittal axis, when two objects are placed before the speaker and are relatively closer to or further from the subject, they are distinguishable in terms of presumably universal human proximal deixis ("here" versus "there") and by perceptual size. (Pederson, 1995: 51)

In other words, the relative choice can be the result of a 'bias,' not because of a privileged status of the relative FoR, but because of the proximity and perceptual input of the stimulus. This observation would be in line with what was already stated within this discussion. That is, the small-scale space fosters uses of the relative FoR. The latest findings oblige us to qualify this statement as true on the sagittal axis, but not on the transverse one.

Pederson's observation explains very well the data obtained across axes, that is, more relative responses in the sagittal axis than in the transverse one. However, there are two more issues related to his proposal. The first is that it does not help us to explain the observed phenomenon within the two axes. The second is that it was generated by the analysis of the 'Transitivity' task and not of the 'Red and Blue' one. It is appropriate, then, to see whether my specific data about the 'Transitivity' task are providing further support for Pederson's proposal. Table 4.5 summarizes the results for the 'Transitivity' task. The content of Table 4.5 is organized in the same way as Table 4.4, thus, providing within and across axes percentage information.

The total number of trials for all the informants in the 'Transitivity' task, considering twenty-seven informants from the three sites and ten trials for the task that each informant was asked to perform, is 270. Of these latter, 169 (63%) were absolute choices, while 87 (32%) relative choices. The overall result is confirmed again, but we have to look more carefully at the incidence of absolute versus relative choices within and across the two axes.

Across the two axes Pederson's 'axis bias' is confirmed, that is, more relative choices are made in the sagittal axis (57%) than in the transverse axis (43%) and vice versa for the absolute choices. The only salient difference this time is the difference in percentages, which is definitely lower (ranking between 6% and 14%) than the 20% indicated by Pederson (1995: 50).

Within the left–right axis eighty-nine (66%) choices are absolute, thirty-seven (27%) are relative and nine (7%) are errors made. These data confirm the general tendency. Within the front–back axis eighty (60%) choices are absolute, fifty (37%) are relative, and five (3%) are errors made. These latter results too are congruent with the general tendency, but the data for the front–back

Table 4.5 *Absolute versus relative responses on the front–back (sagittal) and left–right (transverse) axes in the 'Transitivity' task*

	Frame of reference	Front–Back axis	Left–Right axis	Total
Transitivity				
	Absolute	[60%] **80** [47%]	[66%] **89** [53%]	[63%] **169** [100%]
	Relative	[37%] **50** [57%]	[27%] **37** [43%]	[32%] **87** [100%]
	Error	[3%] **5** [36%]	[7%] **9** [64%]	[5%] **14** [100%]
Possible cases		[100%] **135** [50%]	[100%] **135** [50%]	[100%] **270** [100%]

axis are in contrast with the same ones obtained by the administration of the 'Red and Blue' task. Thus, we are still obliged to try to find an explanation for this phenomenon.

At this juncture it is relevant to know how each individual informant performed on the two axes in the two tasks. In fact, the results in Table 4.4 and Table 4.5 that we have discussed refer to responses by all informants and we do not know if they are affected by clusters of responses by individual informants instead of representing a genuine tendency of all informants. Table 4.6 shows the distribution of responses by informants on each axis.

For ease of comparison, I repeated the results for the two tasks by informants with both axes combined (these results appeared in Table 4.3) in the three rightmost columns of Table 4.6. The three columns headed by L–R represent results on the left–right (transverse) axis and the three columns headed by F–B those on the front–back (sagittal) axis.

Very robustly informants privileged absolute responses over relative ones on the transverse axis in both tasks. That is, 63% over 22% in the 'Red and Blue' task, and 52% over 4% in the 'Transitivity' one. But, by looking at the data referring to the sagittal axis we obtain again a difference in the quality of the responses in the two tasks. In fact, whereas in the 'Transitivity' task the informants giving absolute responses are within the general tendency (37% absolute over 19% relative), in the 'Red and Blue' task informants giving relative responses are slightly higher (41% relative over 37% absolute). In other words, at least five informants in the 'Red and Blue' task switched from an absolute strategy to a relative one when giving responses on the sagittal axis, and at least four informants did the same in the 'Transitivity' task.[3] A variety of responses in the sagittal axis were predicted from the results of the linguistic tasks, but the specificity of the phenomenon, alternation between an absolute and a relative FoR on the two axes, had been left underspecified. It is

---

[3] The three tasks were always administered in the following sequence: first the 'Animals in a Row,' second the 'Red and Blue,' and finally, the 'Transitivity' task.

Table 4.6 *Absolute versus relative responses on the front–back (sagittal) and left–right (transverse) axes by individual informants in the 'Red and Blue' and the 'Transitivity' tasks*

Task	Site	No. of infs.	L–R			F–B					
			Abs	Rel	???	Abs	Rel	???	Abs	Rel	???
Red and	Ngele'ia	9	7	1	1	4	4	1	4	2	3
Blue	Hihifo	8	3	4	1	2	3	3	1	4	3
	Houma	10	7	1	2	4	4	2	4	1	5
Sub-total		**27**	**17**	**6**	**4**	**10**	**11**	**6**	**9**	**7**	**11**
		100%	63%	22%	15%	37%	41%	22%	33%	26%	41%
Transitivity	Ngele'ia	9	7	1	1	3	3	3	4	1	4
	Hihifo	8	1	0	7	2	1	5	2	1	5
	Houma	10	6	0	4	5	1	4	6	0	4
Sub-total		**27**	**14**	**1**	**12**	**10**	**5**	**12**	**12**	**2**	**13**
		100%	52%	4%	44%	37%	19%	44%	45%	7%	48%
Total		**54**	**31**	**7**	**16**	**20**	**16**	**18**	**21**	**9**	**24**
		100%	57%	13%	30%	37%	30%	33%	39%	17%	44%

appropriate at this point to try to find an explanation for the behavior of these informants.

We know that the nature of the two tasks is different. In fact, the 'Red and Blue' task is more 'bounded' to perception, that is, it requires a perceptual input to be stored in memory and then the matching of that memory with another visual perception. The 'Transitivity' task, instead, requires informants to perform a logical inference on the two stored perceptual inputs, thus making them still use visual memory, but only as a means to a logical operation. It was for this reason that no memory constraint (waiting a minute before producing a response) was put on the performing of the task. We know that the informants privileged consistently absolute responses in the three tasks administered, with the exception of their choices within the front–back axis in the 'Red and Blue' task where a very slight preference was given to relative responses. We also know from the results and analyses of the linguistic tasks that certain preferences have been expressed in specific contextual instances, such as privileging the absolute FoR in non-visible large-scale environments or the relative one in visible small-scale space. From these three pieces of knowledge we may advance a suggestion towards the explanation of the phenomenon observed, namely, not privileging the absolute FoR within the front–back axis in the 'Red and Blue' task.

When representing in short-term memory highly visible spatial relation-ships both in the small-scale and large-scale space, informants privilege the relative FoR. When similar perceptual input is used for higher psychological processes, like inference, the FoR privileged is the absolute one. This includes also reconstruction from memory of large-scale environments non-visible at the moment of production, either linguistic or non-linguistic. Regarding the 'Red and Blue' task, its small-scale space context created a strong tendency towards the relative choice, but also the type of task may have conditioned choices towards the relative FoR. In fact, since no particular logical operation had to be applied to the mental representations of perceived spatial relation-ship, 'visibility' (straight perceptual input) may have played a major role in those memories. As a result we have a higher incidence of relative choices in this task when compared to the 'Transitivity' task and more relative choices within at least one axis, exactly the axis towards which a 'relative bias' had been indicated, the sagittal (front–back) axis.

An interesting question to ask now would be why this double push towards a relative choice did not succeed in overcoming the privileging of absolute choices as a whole. It could be suggested that the fact that informants were asked to wait sixty seconds before providing their responses (the actual time between seeing the first scene and making the choice was even longer) may have played a major role. In fact, in this time gap most of them might have transformed relative mental representations into absolute ones by using the now intervening necessity of the absolute FoR, thus possibly indicating a privi-leged status for the absolute FoR within a specific stage of mental operations, more independent from perceptual input.

That which was just suggested relates very well to the fact that in the linguis-tic tasks informants made more use of the relative FoR. Linguistic production does not allow the kind of time that is needed to reveal the privileged status of the absolute FoR within the mental representation of spatial relationship in Tongan speakers. The informants' attempts at describing the photos they were seeing were immediate and fast, thus very close to perceptual input, and con-sequently more consistently coded in relative terms.

Another suggestion that can be made from the results of this discussion is the fact that these data seem to support the proposed 'basic' status (closer to perceptual input) of the relative FoR among the three suggested (Bennardo, 1996, 2002b, 2004). But for now I will just note this fact down and propose to discuss this issue at a later stage in the present work. Finally, it must be noted that the way in which the three tasks were conceived and administered does not allow the results to disambiguate a differential use of any subtype of the abso-lute FoR, namely, a cardinal points type, a single axis type, or a radial type. This fact makes more relevant the attempt to investigate Tongan spatial cogni-tion by means of the 'cultural tasks' that will be discussed in Chapter 5.

4.4   Conclusion: Tongan spatial cognition

The results of the analyses of the data obtained by the administration of the 'frame of reference tasks,' a subset of the 'psychological' tasks, indicate that Tongans prefer the absolute FoR[4] when storing spatial relationships in long-term memory and/or when engaging in making inferences on spatial relationships. Some evidence was also provided of a close relationship between a higher use of the absolute FoR and the presence of a logical operation, inference, to be applied to perceptual input. It appears as if the further away the spatial information gets from the perceptual stage, the more frequently the choice of the individuals performing the tasks moves toward the absolute FoR.

   No significant congruence was found between the results of the linguistic elicitation tasks and the psychological tasks. The only exception to this latter finding is the predicted more varied behavior of informants on the sagittal (front–back) axis. It seems, then, that we need to look in a different direction, thus formulating a different hypothesis, in order to be able to obtain more appropriate insights into Tongan spatial cognition. The administration of the second subset of the 'psychological' tasks obtained exactly the needed and sought-for different perspective on Tongan spatial cognition.

---

[4] It was impossible to induce which subtype of the absolute FoR was being used.

5 Tongan culture and space

5.1 Culture and space

In the previous two chapters, I suggested how a number of factors such as complexity of mental operations, perceptual input versus short-term memory, and small-scale versus large-scale space play a relevant role in affecting choices of specific frames of reference for Tongan speakers. In addition, I introduced a clear tendency to privilege different FoRs in linguistic production in small-scale space (relative) and performance in the three psychological 'frame of reference' tasks in the same space (absolute). In other communities (i.e., Guugu Yimithirr, Australia; Kilivila, Trobriand Islands; and Tamil, India),[1] Levinson (1996a, 2003), Senft (1994), and Pederson (1993, 1995) administered the same tasks (linguistic and psychological) and obtained very different results.

In speakers of Guugu Yimithirr, a high congruence between the use of the absolute FoR in the language tasks and the psychological tasks was found (Levinson, 1996a). In the second group, Kilivila, no specific preference was detected in either group of tasks (Senft, 1994). And finally, two different groups of Tamil speakers, one urban and one rural, were found to privilege either a relative or an absolute FoR, respectively. Both groups were consistent in both type of tasks (Pederson, 1993, 1995).

Contrasting results within one language, Tongan, and across several languages, Tongan, Guugu Yimithirr, Kilivila, and Tamil, require an explanation. Thus, I hypothesized the peculiarity of the Tongan cultural milieu as a possible salient factor in determining the privileged use of specific FoRs. The linguistic practices of favoring the relative FoR (and specifically, the translation subtype of the relative) in small-scale space and the absolute in large-scale space may be the results of a close relationship between Tongan cognition and cultural experiences. Similarly, the discovered preference afforded to the absolute FoR in long-term memory may stand in a significant relationship with the cultural behavior it may generate and/or from which it may be molded.

---

[1] See Baayen and Danziger (1994: 89–91) for results concerning other languages.

What is a cultural milieu? And what does it mean to explore the relationships between a cultural milieu and linguistic and cognitive representations of spatial relationships, i.e., preferred uses of FoRs? What type of data is it necessary to collect and how? In answering the first question, I offer only my personal solution to an issue that requires the whole history of anthropology to be properly assessed. A cultural milieu for me entails a physical place with its geographic and spatial characteristics, a human place with its various sets of social relationships, and a behavioral place with its sequence of instantiated behaviors (including linguistic ones) ranging from daily routines to occasional rituals. In addition, it entails also a mental place with sets of emotions, beliefs, and various knowledge structures that contribute to the generation of all three other spaces just mentioned. Linguistic and cognitive data have already been collected, presented, and discussed. Once the focus of the research shifted onto the cultural milieu, it became apparent that physical, social, and behavioral (not linguistic) data also needed to be collected.

The fundamental assumption behind the collection of these data was that the same linguistic and mental preferences about FoRs would be found in the physical and sociocultural environment, parts/aspects of the cultural milieu. Thus, the physical layout of a village may reveal a specific cognitive preference for spatial relationships. The organization of social relationships too may be informative about those same preferences. Similarly, the organized behavior in and about frequent or rare ritual events may expose hidden-to-consciousness patterns of preferences for representing spatial relationships. The focus of the analyses, though, was principally on the mental realm. Cognitive preferences were sought in order to discover wider applications of those same preferences in domains of knowledge that are typically labeled as 'cultural.' If such a positive relationship is found to be in place, it would be appropriate to talk of a cultural milieu participating – and at the same time being the place where they are realized – to the already indicated linguistic and cognitive preferences in representing spatial relationships.

5.2   The Tongan cultural milieu

The collection of the linguistic and psychological data required a minimum sampling of the population in order to avoid individual idiosyncrasies and/or local peculiarities. In contrast, I chose the in-depth and long-term acquaintance with a specific community – a representative locus of main cultural traits – as the most appropriate way to arrive at the gathering of relevant cultural data. The community chosen was that of the Tongan population living in the village of Houma, Vava'u. My extensive residence, a total of more than a year and a half in the last decade, in the village provided me with the rich and precious experience of a full immersion in contemporary Tongan life as lived by contemporary historical beings.

5.2.1   A physical and human place

The first type of data collected about the village of Houma were of a general geographic nature, that is, its position within the Kingdom of Tonga, the northern Tongan archipelago of Vava'u, and the homonymous island of Vava'u. Most of this information was acquired by the acquisition of maps and from existing geographical literature (see Crane, 1991; Christopher, 1994). The map of the village itself that was obtained from the *Ofisi Savea Mo e Fonua* 'Survey and Land Office.' This map did not show any houses, but only indicated the division of the land into village and subsistence lots. It also showed a road network that was later found to be quite different from reality. Thus, it was necessary to draw a personal map of Houma. The general orientation and the interior subdivision of each house was also sketched as well as some of their relevant and culturally determined spatial features such as 'front' and 'back.'

The second type of data collected were about the social nature of the village population. A personal census of the population was conducted. Minimally information about gender, age, religious affiliation, literacy, social status, and occupation was collected about all the inhabitants. The census contained also information about the people living in each house of the village, their relationships among themselves, with the occupants of other houses, and at times with people living in other villages. Family trees that spanned several generations were also obtained about almost all the villagers.

A relevant part of the human place data collected is the social network data. A survey of the whole village adult population was conducted and salient information about the social network structures in the village was obtained. The role and use of these data within the general structure of the research project about which this book reports is extensively dealt with in Chapters 6, 10, and 11. It is sufficient to say for now that the collection of these social network data was an integral part of the attempt to obtain a satisfactory clear picture of the human place, part of the Tongan cultural milieu.

5.2.2   The Digitized Tonga database

Over several years, in my linguistic and cognitive laboratory with the support and collaboration of staff, students, and colleagues in various departments at Northern Illinois University, all the information about the physical and human place of Houma was entered in the Digitized Tonga database.[2] The information

[2] This work was supported at Northern Illinois University by the College of Liberal Arts and Sciences, which provided the funds to set up an audio/video/digital lab, an undergraduate research apprentice from the Department of Geography in spring 2001, and one from the Department of Anthropology in fall 2001, in spring and fall 2002, in spring and fall 2003, and in spring 2004; by the Department of Anthropology, which provided a research assistant in fall 2000 and in spring

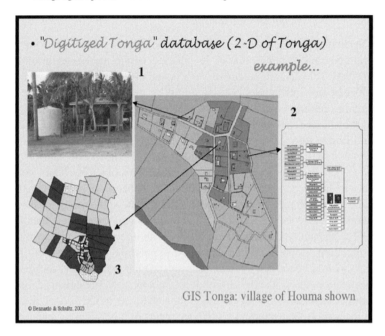

Figure 5.1 The digitized village of Houma (from Bennardo and Schultz, 2003: 103)

for this database is updated every time I go back to the field. The database was built by entering in the computer – using the application ArcView GIS – the map of Tonga, detailed maps of specific archipelagoes and islands, detailed maps of specific villages (including Houma), and a map of the capital town. The web page containing the first draft of the project is: http://atlas.lib.niu.edu/tongalayer1.html.[3]

The layout of the village of Houma and its surrounding subsistence plots were digitized (Figure 5.1). Each house on the map I had drawn (Bennardo, 1996: 127) was linked to its photo, to a family tree of its residents, to the other houses where the relatives of the residents live, and to the plots cultivated by the house residents and their relatives (Bennardo, Hattman, and Testa, 2001; Bennardo and Schultz, 2003). Some preliminary information (clique analyses) about social networks was also entered. In 2003, the GIS accurate 2-D world of

2001; and by the Graduate School, which provided a Research and Artistry Grant in summer 2001 and summer 2002.
[3] This web page has not been updated since 2002, but the database is available in my laboratory with information updated till summer 2007, my last visit to the village.

the northern island of Vava'u and of the village of Houma were 3-D rendered (Bennardo and Schultz, 2003, 2004).

This database offers a unique and unprecedented opportunity to store together all these diverse types of information. It also allowed me to digitally access both real and imagined social and geographic spaces. In doing so, it offers a distinctive and unparalleled occasion to analyze ongoing speech events as they occur in social and cultural contexts. Linguistic representations of those contexts can be compared to the digitized reality (see Bennardo and Schultz, 2003: 119). Ethnographic, demographic, geographic, and perceptual information can be brought to bear during the analyses of linguistic data (interviews) and social network data. For example, the houses of the cliques' members can be color coded and their distribution in the village can be displayed. This distribution can be compared with the distribution of kinship groups, cultural groups, and religious affiliation groups. Thus, the relationship between distribution in space, sociocultural grouping, and social networks can be explored.

Furthermore, the database allows digitized clips of the interviews (with English and Tongan subtitles) to be displayed and synchronized with related 3-D views of the village (this part of the database is called "Synchronized Media and Visualization Analysis Tool," SMVAT). The central visual fields (around 30°) for specific visual takes made by the interviewees are indicated by white semi-transparent cones that extend over the territory for around 150 yards. While running the video clip in SMVAT, at selected points corresponding to a specific linguistic production and a visual take by the interviewee, the cones appear to highlight the extension of the visual take. Thus, a relationship can be established between a visual take and the content of a linguistic expression (see Bennardo and Schultz, 2004, for an example of analysis). Finally, the database was used at home to decide which new data to collect, it was used while in the field to help collect new data, and it was used extensively during the analyses of linguistic data and of the social network data.

5.2.3   A behavioral place

During my extensive residence in the village of Houma I had the opportunity to experience a good portion of the people's yearly life-cycle. Since my first trip to Tonga in summer 1991, whenever I visited the village, I lived with the same family and was fortunate to establish a very close connection with them. This allowed me to witness village life from an insider's point of view. The content, intensity, and novelty of the daily experiences were carefully noted down and later more formally recorded.

In addition to the taped interviews, I devoted keen attention to the content of everyday conversations either between myself and a/some villager/s, or between villagers themselves. Linguistic, mental, and cultural representations of spatial relationships find their most frequent instantiations in such a large portion of the villagers' lives. Participating in *kava* drinking sessions was also a very important part of the cultural experience necessary for an understanding of certain general features of Tongan life as well as an essential step in the direction of an understanding of formal and informal use of space.

I also observed seating arrangements of people in several situations, either formal or informal, but mostly of the former type. Every formal gathering in Tonga, mainly for food consumption, but also for other occasions, is a good opportunity for what is thought of as a required speech-giving chance on the part of the culturally designated speech givers within that specific occasion. Often the sequence of the speakers as well as some of the content of their speeches were recorded. This information too provided good material that was used to elucidate the range of representations of spatial relationships peculiar to the Tongan milieu.

Finally, it became apparent to me that a variety of exchanges within and between villages, as well as between islands, are a very salient aspect of Tongan life. Then, I collected data about exchanges. Some of the exchanges have already been widely and excellently described in the existing ethnographies, such as those regarding events pinpointing the individual and communal life-cycle, i.e., exchanges of goods at marriage, birth of a child, and funerals (Evans, 2001; Gifford, 1929; Kaeppler, 1978b; van der Grijp, 1993, 2004), or more mundane social life, such as *fono* 'village meeting.' Great relevance is also given in this literature to other types of exchanges such as those that take place for a visit of the king or in other special yearly events, e.g., *misinale*, in which goods, especially money now, are donated to the church.

All the events just indicated (except for the marriage) took place during my residence in Tonga and information was collected about them. However, my extended period of residence also allowed me to collect information about two other types of exchange that were not as extensively examined in the existing literature. One is the *fakaafe* 'invitation' that consists of a meal offered to a variety of people in connection with some church-related events.[4] The other is what I have labeled *fetongi* 'exchange' (see Evans, 2001). This latter is carried out between women from villages on the islands of Vava'u and Tongatapu (in my experience, but I know of similar exchanges taking place between different islands). Typically, women from Vava'u give out woven goods such as mats, and receive from the women from Tongatapu *ngatu* 'tapa, bark cloth' goods. Informants of advanced age confirmed in several interviews the existence of such types of exchange for at least three or four generations.

In summary, the data about the village as a physical place, a human place, and a behavioral place participate in the construction of a sufficiently detailed

---

[4] In Evans (2001: 137ff) a very similar event is described.

picture of the Tongan cultural milieu. This information provided the background for further data acquisition about mental representations of spatial relationships. This time the activities used for the acquisition of the data were generated by parameters dictated by the cultural milieu. In fact, psychological tasks such as drawing tasks and memory tasks, for example, while commonly used in the investigation of mental phenomena, were administered about topics, activities, and rituals regarded as salient in the cultural milieu obtained. I regarded this dual source for the next set of data-gathering activities the appropriate step for a successful attempt to investigate the close relationship between cultural milieu and mental representations.

5.3   The cultural root of the new psychological tasks

Besides rank, i.e., king, royal family, noble, chief, and commoner, two fundamental social axes contribute to the constitution of hierarchy in Tonga, that is, gender (man–woman) and age (older–younger). Women are superior to men and older people are superior to younger ones. The use of these two axes and rank, both diachronically and synchronically, determines a social stratification in which each individual occupies a unique place. In highly salient social events in contemporary Tonga this hierarchy is spatially instantiated, that is, the place that each individual occupies during these events is determined by their rank in the social hierarchy. Clear examples are the *kava* drinking ceremony, the village or district *fono* 'meeting,' and the *misinale*, a ceremony in which church members donate money[5] to their church. The latter event represents a relatively recent (middle 1800s) innovation in the Tongan cultural milieu. Nonetheless, it would be a great mistake not to consider it as a very important event in the lives of contemporary Tongans.

What is relevant here is to see how these events provide an 'absolute' orientation to the participants, observers, and possibly, after the events, to the people talking about them. First, in the *kava* ceremony participants sit in a circle or some kind of ellipse whose longer axis is determined by the *kava* bowl, at one pole, and by the person who is the highest in social status (the king, the noble, the chief) of the participants, at the other pole. The latter will sit in front of the bowl, at some distance, facing it. All the other participants will sit in a decreasing order towards the bowl on both sides of the chief (Bott, 1972). So, in order to know where to sit, first, you have to know where the chief is sitting, knowledge you can infer from knowing the chief, and if one does not know the chief

---

[5] The choice of donating money is a relatively new introduction. In fact, during the first stage of the missionary presence in Tonga, the donations consisted of various kind of produce and livestock. It is only in the last forty to fifty years that money has been substituted for those type of donations all over the country.

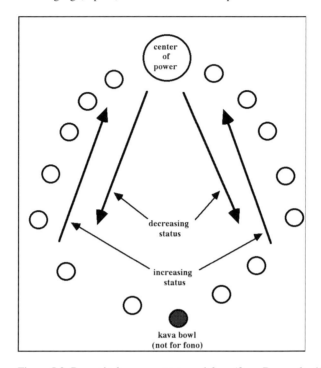

Figure 5.2 Power in *kava* ceremony and *fono* (from Bennardo, 1996: 278)

or the chief has not arrived yet, from the position of the bowl; and second, who will eventually be sitting to your right and left next to you, because this will exactly display your status.

The *kava* ceremony has a variety of formality levels that change according to specific events, e.g., funeral versus mid-week village gathering, and/or participants, e.g., noble versus local chief. The spatial parameters used, though, are always the same, even if they may be handled loosely in very informal situations. In fact, as a *pālangi* 'white person,' I was assigned almost the same rank as a chief; consequently, any time I participated in an informal *kava* drinking gathering I was always offered first the 'chief's place' in front of the bowl. Politely declining this offer most of the time made these events retain their informal atmosphere.

The sitting arrangement in the *fono* 'village meeting' is exactly the same as in the formal *kava* ceremony and in the past usually included the presence of the *kava* bowl and the drinking of *kava*. In contemporary Tonga the drinking of *kava* has been dropped, but the sitting arrangement has been preserved. So, the high status person will sit at one end of the axis defined by the elliptical shape (at times it is a circular or a rectangular or a square one) formed by the participants. Again, the distance on both sides from the high status person will display the hierarchy among the participants, thus, making the people sitting next to you very significant.

The content of Figure 5.2 represents the sitting arrangement of people during the *kava* ceremony and the *fono* as seen from above. The presence of the *kava* bowl is optional nowadays in the *fono*, at least as far as my experience goes. Sitting closer to the 'center of power' displays a higher degree of social status (centripetal movement of power), while sitting further away displays a lower degree of social status (centrifugal movement of power).[6]

The participants in the *misinale* 'donation to church' follow a pattern of sitting arrangement that does not belong to the Tongan 'traditional' culture, but it will become evident below that it bears its influence. I introduce in Figure 5.3 a map of the church and of the areas into which it is divided.[7] In assigning names to the different areas of the church shown in the figure, I use the exact terminology proposed by my informants and on which they all agreed.

Number 1 is the place for *hou'eiki* 'chiefs'; number 2 is that for *faifekau* 'minister,' but it is also used for *kau malanga* 'speakers,' that is, those people that on that particular day will deliver a short sermon or speech; number 3 is the place for *fānau iiki* 'small kids'; right behind them in number 4 sit *talavou mo finemui* 'young boys and girls'; in number 5 sit *tangata mali 'ikai motu'a lahi* 'married men not very old';[8] in numbers 7 and 8 sit *finematu'a* 'older women' and *matua'a* 'older men,' respectively; number 6 is the place for *faihiva fefine* 'female director of chorus' and number 9 for *faihiva tangata* 'male director of chorus' (this person is also the *'eiki* 'chief' of the village, but he usually sits here instead of in place number one); in number 10 sit *kau fine'eiki* 'chiefly older women' and, finally, in number 11 sits *le'o matapā* 'door voice,' who is the person that repeats aloud for people outside the church the important events taking place inside.[9]

Within three areas of the church, namely numbers 7, 8, and 10, there is a further hierarchy that is spatially expressed by sitting closer to the front if of higher status. Area numbers 3, 4, and 5, instead, are strictly arranged according

---

[6] In spite of the fact that there are only two lines coming in and out of the established center, we can still refer to this movement of power as centripetally and/or centrifugally constituted. In fact, we have to think of the 'real' world situation (the two lines coming out of the center and later forming an elliptical shape) as a unique possible instantiation (pragmatically determined) of a potential number of instantiations in which closeness to the center would still determine differential amount of power. Ample support for this comes from the rich literature on the concept of *mana* 'power' in Polynesia (see Shore, 1989).

[7] I already mentioned in Chapter 3 how the inside of the church is divided into *mu'a* 'front,' *mui* 'back,' *to'ohema* 'left,' and *to'omata'u* 'right.'

[8] 'Married women not very old' were not mentioned by my informants as occupying a specific area of the church. From my personal experience I can state that they were sitting either in area number seven or in area number ten.

[9] A kind of human loudspeaker!

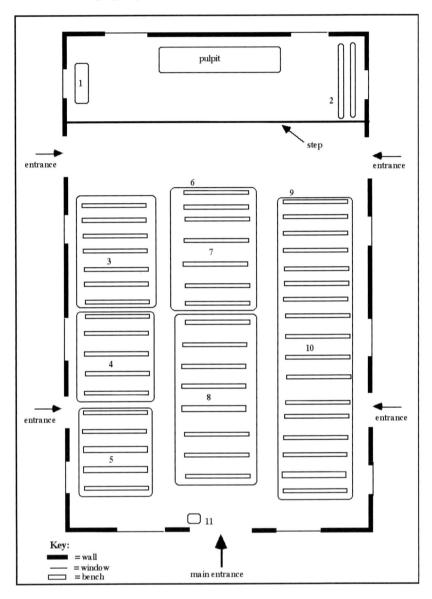

Figure 5.3 Map of church in Houma, Vava'u

to age and centrifugally[10] from the front. This may seem to contradict a possible interpretation of the *mu'a* 'front' of the church as the center of the movement of power determining increasing or decreasing amount. In fact, both movements would have to be of the same type ('towards center' meaning more power, 'away from center' meaning less power). However, if we consider the fact that this distribution of people in the church is the result of two worldviews, the Wesleyan and the Tongan, a different conclusion may be reached. In fact, the internal hierarchy of sections 7, 8, and 10 may be seen as a Tongan 'intrusion' undermining the 'block' division imposed by the Wesleyan organization of the internal space of the church. Thus, it may be argued that one important feature, centripetal and/or centrifugal movement of power, typical of the sitting arrangement of both the *kava* ceremony and the *fono* is clearly employed in this case as well.

It is interesting to notice that the two powers, the secular and the religious, are kept neatly separated in the *mu'a* 'front' part of the church (see numbers 1 and 2 on map of church in Figure 5.3). But, the internal hierarchy within the mentioned subdivisions (7, 8, and 10) of the church space receives a centripetal or centrifugal (it all depends on the point of view) organizing force that treats both powers as a unified 'center' of attraction.

From this brief description of these three Tongan cultural events I can propose a new hypothesis regarding the already introduced preference for the absolute frame of reference in mentally representing spatial relationships. It appears that a specific subtype of the absolute frame of reference is being used, that is, the 'radial' subtype. Its presence and use is detected in the centripetal and centrifugal spatial arrangements described. Fundamentally, a 'center' is chosen in one's environment and then relationships between objects in that environment are expressed toward or away from that center. This is detectable in the spatial arrangements described in the kava ceremony, the *fono* 'village meeting,' and the *misinale* 'yearly donation to church.'

I have, however, only introduced 'external,' i.e., observable, partial evidence that such a type of spatial representation underlies the spatial arrangements of people in those public events. I thought that it would be valuable to have evidence coming from 'internal,' i.e., 'mental' activities of individuals who live with those specific spatial arrangements, and who actively participate in creating them. To this end, I prepared a set of tasks that I labeled the 'culture' subset of the psychological tasks. The first type of task, two 'drawing' tasks, was intended to collect information about mental representations of familiar physical space. The second type, a 'memory' task, had a similar goal, and focused on familiar events within what I labeled the human space. In addition,

---

[10] Here again the term 'centrifugally' is used given the caveat introduced in note 6.

the results of these tasks led to an insightful interpretation of salient events in the likewise very familiar behavioral space.

5.4   The 'culture' subset of the psychological tasks

The 'culture' subset of the 'psychological' tasks comprises 'drawing' tasks and 'memory' tasks. In the first 'drawing' task, a number of villagers were asked to draw a map of their village and allowed to look around them as much as they pleased before starting their drawings. In a second task of the same type, they were asked to draw a map of their island from memory. The rationale behind this task was that of eliciting non-linguistic instantiations of mental representations of spatial relationships in their closer (the village) and larger (the island) geographical environments with a differential incidence of perceptual input (a good portion of the village, but no sizable part of the island was visible to the drawer). The hypothesis was that in both drawings the villagers would focus on an other-than-ego place, from this place they would start their drawing, and then they would draw other physical salient features of the environment as lying away from that place. Thus, a radial subtype of the absolute frame of reference would underlie their mental representations of the environment and it would show in the nature of their drawings.

No specific time limit was imposed on the performance of these two tasks. Consequently, effects due to fast encoding such as in language production could not play a role. The transfer of the representations from both visual and memory mode to the drawings implied some higher level of psychological processing to be performed over both types of input, that is, from perception and from memory. In these tasks, mental representations only available through long and repeated experiences of the environment would be used in order to perform the task (drawing the map). In fact, neither the whole village nor the whole island (or archipelago) were perceptually available during the task, thus further mental representations had to be activated in order to complete the map.

In the 'memory' task, I asked villagers who had participated the day preceding the interview in a culturally salient event to list as many people as they could remember who were at the event. The events chosen were two village *fono* 'meetings' and a *misinale* 'yearly donation to church.' Then, I asked each one of them to draw the positions of those people they had remembered, in the same sequence they were listed, on a sketchy map of the place that I provided. Both the lists and the drawings produced were later compared to the 'real' list of the participants and the 'real' map of their locations obtained by using a videotape I had made of the event.

The rationale behind this task was to elicit mental representations in long-term memory of spatial arrangements of co-villagers – part of their human place – in salient cultural events. The hypothesis was that the villagers' memories of these arrangements, both composition and relationships between parts, would be skewed in a 'radial' fashion. That is, an other-than-ego individual point would be chosen, most likely one or more authoritative figures, and memory would be organized as radiating out of that point. Thus, further supporting evidence would be gathered toward clarifying the mental preference for the absolute frame of reference as a special preference for the radial subtype, and not for the cardinal direction subtype nor the single-axis subtype.

5.5   Map drawing tasks: the Tongan 'radial' representation of space

In Bennardo (2002a), I extensively reported on the results of the drawing tasks. I include here only the main points of that article relevant to the present discussion. The map drawing task consisted of asking the informant to draw a map of a specific environment on a provided sheet of paper. The instructions were given in Tongan and kept to a minimum such as "Please draw a map of X."[11] Basically, the language of instruction was kept to a minimum (i.e., "Do this," to avoid any linguistic interference on the output of the activity).[12] I administered two different types of tasks: one in which I asked the informants to draw their village from memory, and one in which I asked them to draw their island, also from memory. Due to the nature of the Tongan village – a small number of houses (thirty-six in this case) and the majority of activities conducted outdoors – the perceptual access to at least part of the village while drawing was unavoidable (i.e., part of the village could be seen). This may have affected the nature of the drawing and must be remembered when analyzing the results of the task. Regarding the second task, the size of the island – several miles in extension – rendered the perceptual access to a relevant section of the environment while drawing much more limited and thus less likely to be conducive to distortions. Quality and quantity of perceptual availability, however, must be noted down and considered when analyzing the results. I discuss now the context in which the tasks were administered and the results yielded.

I administered the map drawing tasks to eight men and eight women in the village of Houma, Vava'u, in January 1995. According to my personal census, there were 172 people in the village of Houma during my stay there,[13] so I could not vary the sample systematically by age. Even villagers who had

---

[11] Another example of the instruction used is: "This is the village X, can you draw a map of it on this sheet of paper?"

[12] As I will discuss later, informants had little familiarity with maps and map drawing. This, however, does not mean that they did not know what a map was and what it entailed to draw one on a piece of paper.

[13] The official census figure from the 2006 census is 180 (Kingdom of Tonga, 2007).

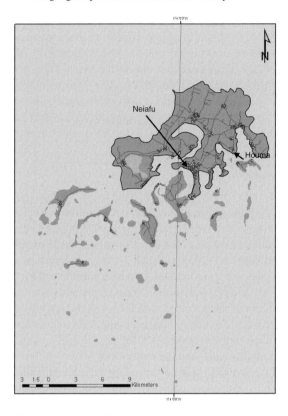

Figure 5.4 Island of Vava'u

attended school for several years were unfamiliar with maps.[14] Furthermore, drawing ability turned out to be poor in most of the informants. However, I did not consider this factor to affect the ability of externalizing in a drawing a point of view or frame of reference of the environment. The type of maps produced confirmed such an assumption.

---

[14] I have visited several Tongan schools, both elementary school and high school, and have seen no map on the walls except in very few cases. There is an elementary school in the village of Houma, and I did not see any map on the walls there either. Familiarity with maps, however, does not prevent the administering of this task (see Gould and White 1974). Polynesians have a long history of the use of complex charts for their navigation, so it may be surprising that my informants had little familiarity with maps. I am well read about Polynesian navigation and have also written about it (Bennardo 1998). It seems to me that a few facts need to be taken into consideration: (1) The art of Polynesian navigation was restricted to few masters and not available to the population at large; (2) this art has completely disappeared in Polynesia and survives only with a few individuals in Micronesia; (3) contemporary Tongan villagers are mainly subsistence farmers like the majority of their ancestors. Thus, their unfamiliarity with maps could simply be a result of the deficiencies of their education system, or more likely, a reflection of their lifestyle.

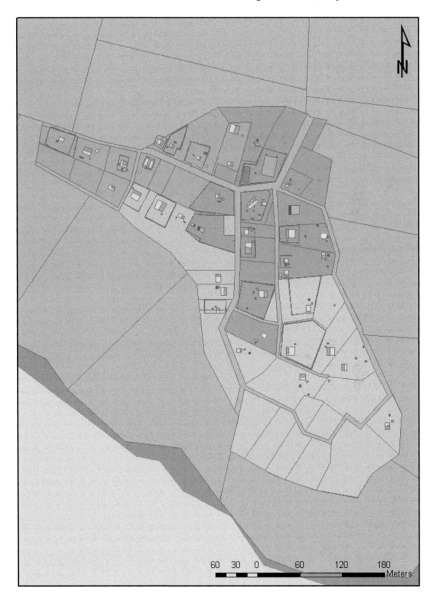

Figure 5.5 Village of Houma, Vava'u

With the exception of two pairs of informants, the sessions took place with one informant at a time and all in different parts of the village. The sessions were conducted either inside (56%) or just outside (or very close to) (44%) the informant's residence, as indicated in Table 5.1 under the columns labeled "In"

Table 5.1 *Gender, place, and orientation of informants for Task 1*

Subject	Male	Female	House no.	In	Out	Facing	Top 1
1	X		13		X	W	W
2		X	34		X	S	S
3		X	11		X	W	S
4	X		1	X		S	N
5	X		14	X		S*	S
6	X		14		X	S*	S
7	X		35		X	S	S
8	X		30	X		N	N
9		X	19		X	N	N
10		X	23		X	W	N
11		X	2	X		N*	N
12		X	2	X		W	S
13		X	3	X		S	S
14	X		10	X		N	N
15		X	18	X		W	N
16	X		5	X		W	S
Total	8	8		9	7		
%	50%	50%		56%	44%		

* Asterisk indicates a deliberate choice on the part of the informant.
Shading indicates same cardinal point in the 'Facing' and 'Top 1' columns.

(inside) and "Out" (outside). Informants could choose the place in which they felt more comfortable.[15] The informants could also decide the direction they faced during the task. Only three of them deliberately chose a specific direction when starting the drawing (indicated by an asterisk in Table 5.1), changing their position from the previous one they occupied while the task was explained to them. Had I asked informants to sit facing a specific direction, such relevant information about a preferred direction would not have been available.

5.5.1 Results and analysis of map drawing 1 (the village)

The analyses of the results relate to two types of data: (1) the content and characteristics of the maps drawn by the informants; and (2) the notes taken

[15] Both entering a Tongan house or asking a resident to come outside call for a series of ritualized behaviors that I did not want to initiate by asking my informants either to come outside or to go inside. The impact of this uncontrolled variable on the results of the activity is less salient than the impact that unwanted social obligation could have on the disposition of the informant who performs it (i.e., she or he did not want to invite me in because of a temporary lack of necessary food to offer).

during the task about specific features of the individual's drawing activity. The first characteristic of the drawings I considered was the cardinal orientation of the map. In other words, I checked which cardinal point in real space had been put at the top of the paper, that is, the side where cartographers usually put north.[16] The assumption is that the cardinal point put on the "top" of the map is the most salient for the informant. The universality of the saliency of the vertical axis with "up" considered positive and "down" either neutral or negative is widely accepted (see Miller and Johnson-Laird 1976; Lakoff 1987; Carlson-Radvansky and Irwin 1993). The results are indicated in the column headed by "Top 1" in the rightmost column of Table 5.1. In this column, eight informants (50%) chose south, seven (44%) chose north, and one (6%) chose west. It is important to note that the cardinal direction going from Houma to Neiafu – the main town on the island of Vava'u – is southwest, but Houma villagers always indicate it as south. The road to Neiafu – the major road crossing almost the entire length of the village – exits (or enters) Houma on the west side (see Figure 5.5). Further, for all those informants that put north at the top, the road to Neiafu was to their geographical north (also shown clearly in their drawings).

Next, I compared the direction the informants faced while drawing with the choice of cardinal direction they had made in orienting the map in their drawings. The majority of the informants (ten out of sixteen, or 63%) paired their facing direction and the cardinal point they put on the top side (cartographer's standard north) of the map. This pairing is indicated by shading in Table 5.1.[17] The pairing was more likely when the session took place outdoors (five out of seven times, or 71%), than when indoors (five out of nine times, or 55%). It seems that the orientation of the environment faced by the informants is reproduced in the orientation of their maps. In fact, they drew with the sheet of paper in the horizontal plane, thus the so-called top is nothing but the part of the environment in front of them. This may lead to the conclusion that they used a relative FoR to orient the maps drawn. However, informants who oriented their maps in a different way from their facing direction give an important clue about a phenomenon that might have been obscured otherwise.

The remaining informants paired either their west-facing direction to an orientation of the map toward south (three cases) or toward north (two cases), and there was only one case with a pairing of a south-facing direction to an orientation of the map toward north. Their pairings can be interpreted as a

---

[16] No informants wrote the cardinal points on the maps they drew, but the orientation of the contents of their drawings indicated which arrangement of the cardinal points they had implicitly used.

[17] Chi-square result for "Facing" matching "Top 1" is very significant even with χ^2 at 0.001.

movement from a drawing orientation toward the *mu'a* 'front' of the village where the road from/to Neiafu enters/exits (see Bennardo 1996) to either real cardinal directions to Neiafu (the three cases of a shift from west to south) or toward the road (the whole road and not just the entering/exiting direction) to Neiafu (the two cases of a shift from west to north). This latter interpretation is also possible for the only case of a shift from south to north. In other words, the direction to Neiafu (south) or the direction to the road to Neiafu (north) account for fifteen cases (94%) of the directions chosen. The only exception is informant 1, who oriented the map toward the west, that is, toward the *mu'a* 'front' of the village. Below we see how this is a salient landmark in the village.

5.5.1.1   Analysis of the drawing activities

While the drawings were being produced, I took notes about some specific characteristics of the events. For example, I wrote down from which side of their sheet of paper they started to draw the map of their village and which side of the village they drew first. I also noted how often they looked at their surroundings. Although difficult to evaluate in isolation, all of this information becomes meaningful when analyzed jointly.[18] In fact, after carefully going through these notes and comparing them with the actual drawings, I was able to highlight three "strategies" adopted by the informants in the production of the drawings.

The first strategy is to start from the self, or better, the area close to and containing the self, and continue with what is present in the environment in front of the informant (for a good example see Figure 5.6). Later adjustments are made to complete the map. A second strategy is to start the drawing from what is visible in the environment in front of the speaker and finish by later adding what is not visible and finally the person's own location/house or self. The self is at times added before other non-visible parts. These non-visible parts of the village are usually drawn smaller than the visible parts and they appear more crowded on the page than the other parts of the drawing (for a good example see Figure 5.7).

A third strategy is to start the drawing from the road to Neiafu, actually from that part of the road that enters/exits the village, in other words, from the *mu'a* 'front' of the village (for a good example see Figure 5.8). I have indicated the first strategy with the word 'Self,' the second as 'See,' and the third as '*Mu'a*' in Table 5.2.

---

[18] I am aware of the difficulty in assigning specific meaning to a temporal precedence (i.e., one place drawn before another). However, in line with Romney's (1989) suggestions, and the just-stated step of considering all this information jointly, I feel confident about my analyses.

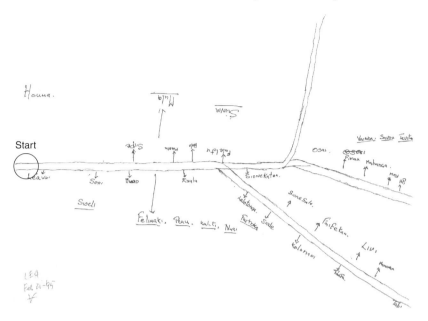

Figure 5.6 Map of Houma by no. 8 ('Self' strategy)

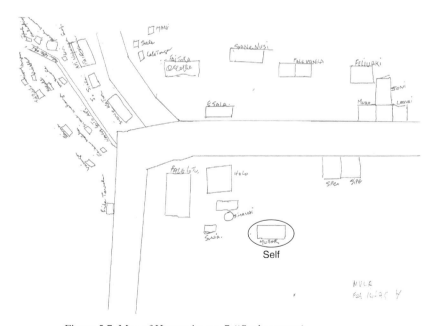

Figure 5.7 Map of Houma by no. 7 ('See' strategy)

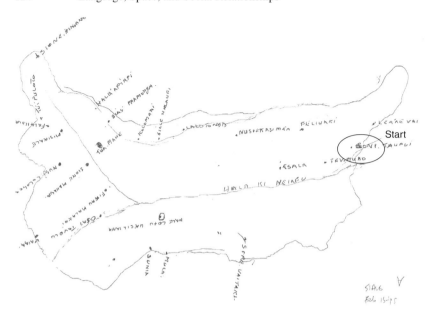

Figure 5.8 Map of Houma by no. 3 ('*Mu'a*' strategy)

A dash (−) in Table 5.2 indicates the presence in some drawings of the salient participation of a secondary strategy to the production of the map in addition to the primary one. In the three cases indicated, the major strategy used was *Mu'a* and the secondary one was See. It can also be seen how the simultaneous use of more than one strategy never involves an overlap between the strategies Self and *Mu'a*, but only the *Mu'a* and the See strategies. It seems that after deciding whether to start from the self or from the environment (not-self), informants made another choice between giving precedence to the perceivable environment or to the culturally relevant (and seldom perceivable) one of *mu'a* 'front (of village).'

The tension between self and other (i.e., *mu'a* 'front [of village]') is solved in favor of the latter, 75% of choices. The cultural salience of this village landmark shows its potency in participating in the construction of mental representations of spatial relationships regarding one's village. It functions as an anchoring point for the various maps drawn. Either visible or not visible, it is the place from which maps of the village are initiated. It is an absolute point of reference that indicates a preference for the absolute frame of reference, but specifically for the subtype I called 'radial' (Bennardo, 1996). It is the starting point from which and toward which spatial relationships are constructed and expressed both linguistically and otherwise, in this case, graphically.

Table 5.2 *Drawing strategies for Task 1*

Name	'Self'	'See'	'Mu'a'
1		–	X
2		X	
3			X
4			X
5		–	X
6		–	X
7		X	
8	X		
9	X		
10			X
11			X
12			X
13			X
14			X
15			X
16			X
Total	2	2	12
%	12.5%	12.5%	75%

A capital X indicates a primary choice.
A dash (–) indicates a secondary choice.

5.5.2 Results and analysis of map drawing 2 (the island)

The second task administered involved drawing a map of the island of Vava'u, that is, the island where the village of Houma is located (see Figure 5.4). The contexts in which these drawings were produced were exactly the same as in the first task. In fact, this second task was administered to the informants a few minutes after they had finished drawing the map of their village. The cardinal point they put on the top of their second map was again mainly south (nine cases, or 56%) as compared to north (two cases, or 12.5%) and west (one case, or 6%). However, in some cases (four, or 25%) it was impossible to determine the exact cardinal point they had used. In fact, these maps have representations of places that do not correspond to their real geographical locations. Further, the spatial relationships among these dislocated places do not provide any clues as to the orientation used in creating the maps (see Table 5.3).

Without considering the ambiguous maps, the number of drawings showing congruence between the facing direction of the informants and the cardinal point they chose to anchor the map is 50%, the same percentage as in the previous task. Again, there are more cases among informants who were sitting outdoors. Regarding the remaining informants, four shifted from a real

Table 5.3 *Gender, place, and orientation of informants for Task 2*

Name	Male	Female	House no.	Inside	Outside	Facing	Top 2
1	X		13		X	W	S
2		X	34		X	S	S
3		X	11		X	W	S
4	X		1	X		S	S
5	X		14	X		S*	S
6	X		14		X	S*	N
7	X		35		X	S	S
8	X		30	X		N	N
9		X	19		X	N	?
10		X	23		X	W	?
11		X	2	X		N*	?
12		X	2	X		W	S
13		X	3	X		S	?
14	X		10	X		N	S
15		X	18	X		W	S
16	X		5	X		W	W
Total	8	8		9	7		
%	50%	50%		56%	44%		

* Asterisk indicates a deliberate choice on the part of the informant.
Shading indicates same cardinal point in the 'Facing' and 'Top 2' columns.

facing direction toward the west to an anchoring point on the map toward the south. One informant shifted from facing the north to anchoring point toward the south and one from the south to the north. The tendency was to orient the map toward the south,[19] an orientation that corresponds to the cardinal direction toward Neiafu (the main town on the island) as perceived by the people of Houma.

Three major strategies were used to produce the drawings. The first, which I labeled 'Village,' uses the village of Houma as a starting point (for a good example see Figure 5.9). The second I labeled 'From Neiafu,' that is, the starting point of the drawing is the town of Neiafu, the main town on the island (for a good example see Figure 5.10). In the third case, 'Center,' the center of the drawing and of the island is the town of Neiafu. Figures 5.11 and 5.12 contain drawings in which this strategy is used (the drawing in Figure 5.10 is also an example of this strategy).

The central position of Neiafu in the maps in Figures 5.10, 5.11, and 5.12 does not correspond to its real geographic position on the island. In real

---

[19] Chi-square result for south in both tasks combined is very significant even with χ^2 at 0.001.

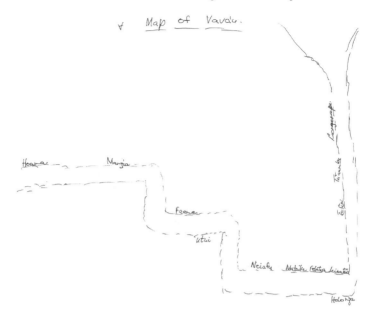

Figure 5.9 Map of the island of Vava'u by no. 11

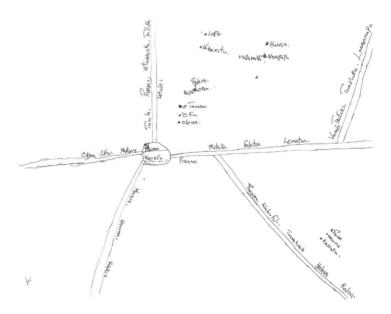

Figure 5.10 Map of the island of Vava'u by no. 14

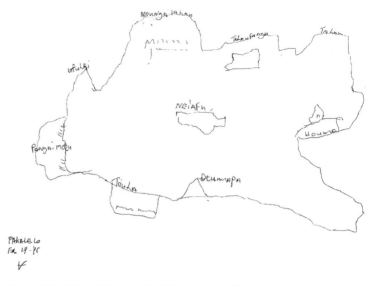

Figure 5.11 Map of the island of Vava'u by no. 10

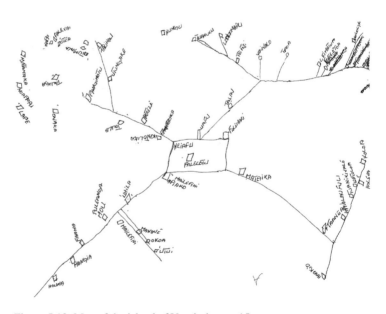

Figure 5.12 Map of the island of Vava'u by no. 15

Table 5.4 *Drawing strategies for Task 2*[20]

Name	'Village'	'From Neiafu'	'Center'
1		X	X?*
2		X	X
3		X	X
4		X	X
5		X	
6		X	
7		X	X
8		X	
9	? †	?	
10		X	X
11	X		
12		X	
13		X	X
14		X	X
15		X	X
16		X	X?*
Total	1	14	10
%	6%	87.5%	62.5%

* Neiafu is on the coast, but at the center of the sheet of paper.
† No information available.

geographic terms, Neiafu is on the coast and in the south part of the island (see Figure 5.4).

The results in Table 5.4 show a clear privileging of the 'From Neiafu' strategy (fourteen cases, or 87.5%). This strategy is often but not always combined with the 'Center' strategy, which by itself has a high incidence (ten cases, or 62.5%). On the other hand, the 'Center' strategy is always used with the 'From Neiafu' strategy. Finally, the 'Village' strategy is used in only one case. It seems, then, that Neiafu plays a very primary role in Houma villagers' mental representations of their island. They orient their drawings toward it, start their drawings from it, and locate it in the center of their drawings. In other

[20] The percentages for each column represent the total sample of informants. The question marks in the row headed by no. 9 are due to the fact that there is not enough information in the field notes to fill either box. The only thing that can be indicated for certain is the fact that she did not put Neiafu in the center of her map. The two question marks in the 'Center' column refer to the fact that these two informants did not put Neiafu in the center of the island, but they put it correctly on the coast as it is in real geographical space. However, they still put it in the center of their drawing space (the sheet of paper). All the remaining informants (eight) drew Neiafu inland, in the middle of the island. Drawings in which Neiafu appears more schematically as a central box from which lines depart, are interpreted in the same fashion. On these lines, other locations on the island are indicated.

words, it is a cultural landmark that induces a systematic distortion (see Lloyd 1997: 59) of the cognitive map of their island. Moreover, by looking at the explicit characteristics of their drawings (see Figures 5.10, 5.11, and 5.12), their mental representations of space have a specific, salient, and notable feature: radiality. A large non-perceivable environment, like the island they live on, is represented with a central point (Neiafu), and all the other places are represented as radiating from it, that is, put in relationship with the center of the representation as points on rays.

How does this finding relate to the previous ones? The absolute FoR is constructed mentally by choosing a set of fixed points of reference – four in the cardinal-points subtype and two in the single-axis subtype. These fixed points and relative axes (one or two) are later used to locate objects in the environment. The procedure used by Houma villagers to draw maps of Vava'u is similar: choose a fixed point of reference (only one) and then draw others radiating out from it (see Figure 5.12). I have called this FoR a radial subtype of the absolute FoR. The radial subtype of the absolute FoR does not use axes as the other two subtypes, but only points and vectors. It is, however, as absolute and efficient in obtaining appropriate descriptions of spatial relationships as all the other subtypes of the absolute FoR.

"The idea of 'center' and 'periphery' in spatial organization is perhaps universal" says Tuan (1974). Moreover, in discussing the use of landmarks in cognitive maps, Golledge (1999: 16) says: "Landmarks may be defined in a number of ways, such as strategic foci toward or away from which one travels." Later, he adds: "[T]hey [landmarks] may be used as a centroid for spatially partitioning a region" (1999: 17). Similarly, Lloyd (1997: 69) says: "Reference points on cognitive maps apparently have a special significance. Some have argued that special landmarks in environment serve as anchor points for encoding other information."

These extremely brief excerpts from the vast literature about cognitive maps and the environment support my findings. However, there is a novelty in my proposal that needs to be pointed out. I consider the choice and use of a landmark evidence for the choice and use of a radial FoR, a subtype of the absolute FoR. This suggestion clarifies what is left unsaid in the literature about landmark use where the consequences of choosing one are examined – distortion of the cognitive map – but not what the choice of a landmark or a sequence of landmarks implies as a mental activity, that is, the use of an FoR (see also Bennardo, 2004).

In conclusion, the analyses of the results of both map drawing tasks provide supporting evidence about the preference for the absolute FoR indicated by the results of the FoR 'psychological' tasks. In addition, the hypothesized use of the radial subtype of the absolute FoR – reached after the analyses of three salient Tongan cultural events in Section 5.3 – was supported by these findings about mental representations of familiar physical space. Consequently, the radial subtype can be proposed as a relevant aspect of Tongan mental representations of spatial relationships. Finally, the spatial choice of using a radial FoR is combined with cultural choices such as using the *mu'a* 'front' of the village (in the first task) and Neiafu (in the second task), the major town on the island and site of economic and sociopolitical power, as the center of their attention and subsequently, of their drawings.

5.6   Memory tasks: a 'cultural' absolute frame of reference

The hypothesis of a salient presence of the radial subtype of the absolute FoR in Tongan spatial cognition was also tested by the second subset of the 'cultural' psychological tasks, namely, the 'memory' tasks about human space. In a memory task, I asked people who had participated in a culturally salient event to try to remember as many participants as possible. Then, I asked them to use the list obtained from memory to position the people contained in it by drawing them (using simple symbols and in the same sequence they were listed) on a sketchy map I provided of the place where the event occurred.

The rationale behind the activity was the consequence of three facts. First, the preference assigned to the absolute frame of reference elicited by the 'frame of reference' subset of the psychological tasks. Second, the discovered use of the radial subtype of the absolute FoR elicited from the results of the 'drawing' tasks. Third, the observable way in which the use of space in these events provides a cultural 'absolute' frame of reference (see Section 5.3). Given these three facts, it was possible to predict certain features of their memory recall activity. In other words, I expected the lists of people they remembered to be skewed towards the pole of the axis representing power as a consequence of a plausible activated strategy that can be labeled 'powerful people first.' At the same time it was expected people in the proximity of the informant would be remembered better than people far away. The former individuals, in fact, do define the social status of the person participating in the task.

Because of their cultural saliency, I chose to conduct the memory task on the village *fono* 'meeting' and the *misinale* 'donation to church.' I conducted a pilot run of the task during my one month period of residence on the remote island of Niuatoputapu, Kingdom of Tonga. A village *fono* 'meeting' was announced to take place in the village of Hihifo towards the end of my residence there. After obtaining permission from the local authorities, I videotaped the meeting. The day following the event eight participants in the *fono* were contacted and interviewed. The informants were selected on the basis of their status in the community, from Representative to the Parliament to farmer, their knowledge of English (monolingual individuals were preferred), their sex and age.

The participants were four males and four females and ranged from thirty to seventy-three years old. With the help of some assistants as much information as possible was also collected about the kinship ties among the participants, but especially those regarding the persons interviewed. It was possible to collect information of this type for only four of the informants. Piloting the task, however, made possible later a much smoother administering in the main field site, the village of Houma, as well as providing great introductory insights into the potentiality of the activity itself.

In the village of Houma, I administered the task on two occasions. The first, after a *fono* and the second after a *misinale* 'donation to church.' The latter consists of a once (sometimes twice) a year day celebration in which almost the whole village[21] gathers in the local Wesleyan chapel and makes a monetary donation to the church. The celebration also includes food preparation and consumption for all the participants. It represents one of the most important events in the contemporary life of the village and it is one of those significant occasions in which its hierarchical structure is basically reiterated by the different amounts of money offered.

Owing to the limited number of people that participated in the *fono*, seventeen persons, the task was administered to only six informants. Ten informants were interviewed instead for the *misinale* event. All the informants were again chosen on the basis of their status, their knowledge of English, their sex and age. They were three males and three females for the *fono* event and five males and five females for the *misinale* event. Their ages ranged from twenty-six to seventy-four years.

5.6.1   A village fono 'meeting' in Hihifo, Niuatoputapu

In November 1993, during my fourth and last week of residence in the village of Hihifo, Niuatoputapu, I witnessed the announcement of a *fono*. I asked and obtained the *ofisa kolo* 'town officer' permission to participate and videotape the meeting. In the day following the meeting I administered the 'memory' task described in the previous section to some of the participants (eight out of forty-three participants, that is, almost 20%). With the help of my Tongan assistant Siaki and other informants I obtained the names of all the participants and their relationships to one another. Then, I drew a map of the hall where the event took place and I marked the specific places each participant occupied as they appeared on the video. The map in Figure 5.13 reflects as closely as possible the places occupied by the various participants in the event. The

---

[21] In Houma, there only three families with a total of sixteen persons that are members of the Latter Day Saints (Mormon).

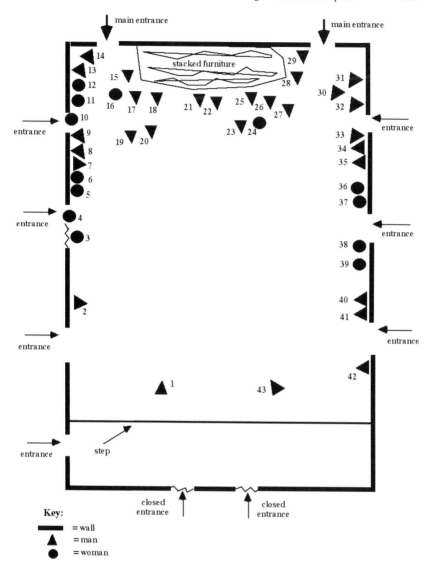

Figure 5.13 Map of *fono* at Hihifo, Niuatoputapu

standardized map obtained was used to trace onto it the participants in the various lists of the people remembered by the informants. But, before looking at an example of this procedure, it is relevant to look at the memory lists elicited from the informants.

Table 5.5 *Presence of powerful people in memory lists of* fono *in Hihifo*

Informant	Ofisa kolo			Matāpule			People's representative		
	Part 1	Part 2	Part 3	Part 1	Part 2	Part 3	Part 1	Part 2	Part 3
1	–	–	–	–	–	–	–	–	–
2		x			x		–	–	–
3		x		x			–	–	–
4	x			x			na	na	na
5	–	–	–		x		–	–	–
6			x	–	–	–	x		
7		x		x			–	–	–
8			x			x	–	–	–
Total	1	3	2	3	2	1	1	0	0

The memory lists show a range of four to twenty participants remembered (not counting mistakes[22]) out of forty-two actual ones (not counting the informant), that is a 9.5–48% range of the total. The average number of participants remembered is 10.1, that is, 24% or almost one out of four. These numbers were a little lower than expected. But considering that I did not count people they remembered only by gender (and not by name) or that were not inside the hall where the event took place or were obtained with the help of bystanders, they may be considered a representative range of possibilities.

I first checked the position that the three people embodying authority, that is, the *ofisa kolo* 'town officer,' the *matāpule* 'talking chief,' and informant number 4, the people's representative, occupied in these lists. The guiding criterion was 'first remembered, more salient.' But, since lists of different lengths were elicited, a straightforward comparison of the positions of these three people in the various lists was not possible. In fact, a fifth place in a list of ten is not the same as a fifth place in a list of twenty. In order to minimize this problem I divided each list, irrespective of length, into three parts, and then assigned the appearance of each person to one of these parts. Table 5.5 shows the result of this count. Sometimes my informants inserted people only by gender in their lists and not by name, or people that were not present in the event, or people that they remembered only after being helped by bystanders during the interview. I only counted as part of their lists those people whose names they

---

[22] For an interesting study of mistakes on list of people elicited from memory see Williams and Hollan (1981).

remembered (not only gender), that were really present in the event, and those that they had mentioned without any help.

Table 5.5 shows that the *ofisa kolo* 'town officer' and the *matāpule* 'talking chief' are better remembered than the people's representative. Furthermore, the talking chief is remembered at an earlier stage more often than the town officer. A possible explanation for the first phenomenon is the fact that the talking chief and the town officer are not only embodiments of authority, but also sit in the places where authority is traditionally and usually mapped onto the space of such type of meetings (see Figure 5.13, number 1 for town officer and 43 for the talking chief). The people's representative (number 37), instead, is sitting in a place relatively low in the traditional ranking system as mapped onto space. Of course, it must also be pointed out that her role was minimal in the meeting and that most of the talking was conducted by either the town officer or the talking chief, as is typical of such meetings in Tongan contemporary and traditional cultural settings (Gifford, 1929: 181; Howe, 1984: 231; van der Grijp, 1993: 21).

A second factor that I regard as relevant in both phenomena indicated above is the difference between traditional authoritative figures and new ones introduced by the Tongan Constitution in 1875, namely, the *matāpule* inheritable title versus the *ofisa kolo* and people's representative, both new and elective titles. It is significant, then, that a slight preference is highlighted by these memory lists towards the person embodying a more traditional title than towards those other two titles relatively more recently introduced. It appears as if traditional titles still hold their influence both in Tongans' imagination and in their cognition (memory).

Later I compared the features of the drawings of the *fono* that the informants produced by mapping onto them the content of their lists of participants from memory and the standardized map of the event previously obtained (Figure 5.13). This procedure yielded another way of obtaining information about some parameters that affected the performance of the informants in the memory recall task. I illustrate below the procedure by discussing it for one informant step by step. The results of the procedure for all the informants are in Table 5.7.

In Table 5.6 I present the memory list obtained from a male informant indicated by the number 14 on the map in Figure 5.13. The first column headed by 'memory sequence' contains the number sequence that the informant used in providing me with the list. The column headed by 'No. on map' contains the number on the map in Figure 5.13. Finally, the column headed by 'No. in drawing' contains the number that the informant used in positioning the participants on the map. The groupings obtained by mapping the list in Table 5.6 onto the map of the event are shown in Figure 5.14.

Table 5.6 *Memory list about* fono *from an individual in Hihifo*

Memory sequence	Name	Gender	No. on map	No. in drawing	Status
1	Kiko	m	13	2	
2	Kiko T	m	15	3	
3	Sione Holi	m	20	4	
4	Lemoto	m	22	5	
5	(Ta)Paita	f	10	6	
6	Saane	f	16	7	
7	Fehi'a	f	18	8	
8	Peata	f	6	9	
9	'Uluaki	f	5	10	
10	Tafea	m	35	11	
11	Mosese	m	23	12	
12	Heneli	m	?	13	
13	Sione Pauli	m	42	14	
14	Hu'aki	m	40	15	
15	Talanoa	m	?	16	
16	Apolo	m	?	17	
17	Solo Lahi	m	31	18	
18	Sione Vea	m	2	19	
19	Kalo	f	3	20	
20	Kelemete	m	1	21	*Ofisa kolo*
21	Vivili	m	43	22	*Matāpule*
22	Salote	f	12	23	
23	Taufa	m	9	24	
24	Isileli	m	?	25	

The members of group A (13, 15, 20, 22, 10, 16, and 18)[23] were determined not only by the obvious increased distance from 14 to the members of group B (6 and 5), but also from the explicit content of the drawing that he produced. In his drawing, in fact, he grouped what I have indicated as members of group A much closer to himself than in reality and slightly detached from the two members of group B. In Figure 5.15, I introduce the drawing produced by participant 14. I obtained group C (members 35, 23, 42, 40, and 31) by collapsing what on the drawing appear as three smaller subgroups, the first made up of members 35 and 23, the second of 42 and 40, and the third by member 31. The decision was based on the fact that the informant seems to be scanning his left, and relatively far, side by picking persons he can remember sitting on that side.

[23] An arrow indicates the sequence in which the members of each group were remembered and also delimits the extension of the group.

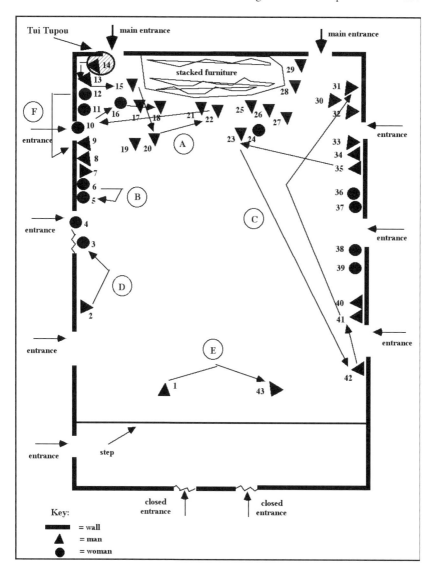

Figure 5.14 Memory route for participant 14 in *fono* at Hihifo

He switches back to his right side for group D (members 2 and 3) and he finally arrives at the authority group, that is, letter E (members 1 and 43). He completes his memory search by adding two persons that in reality were close to him on his right side, but that in his drawing appear in the space between the previous two groups (B and D) he had already remembered and indicated as

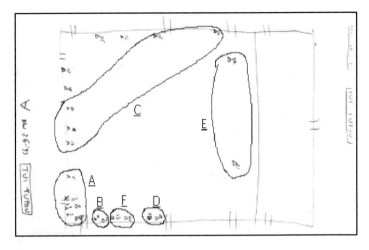

Figure 5.15 Drawing of *fono* by participant 14

sitting on his right side. I tend to believe that the gap in the drawing created by the two previous insertions might have caused such a distortion.

A similar procedure was adopted in forming groups for the data elicited from the other informants. A summary of the results for all eight informants is produced in Table 5.7. The various groups in the table have been labeled under the following common headings: proximity, authority (abbreviated as auth), front (abbreviated as F), side (abbreviated as S). The latter group was also qualified as left (abbreviated as L) and right (abbreviated as R). Two or more categories at times overlap and are indicated accordingly.

The data collected for informants 1 and 2 in Table 5.7 need some clarifying comments. In fact, while I was interviewing informant 2 (a man in his late seventies) outside his house, informant 1, a relative, was inside the house and most likely listening to the conversation from an open window. When informant 2 stopped (very early) naming people he could remember, from inside the house informant 1 started suggesting some names and informant 2 confirmed them. I wrote them down, but they were not counted because of the way they had been elicited. This explains the reason behind the very short list indicated as produced by him.

When I had finished with informant 2, I also interviewed informant 1, now standing outside the house and overtly showing her willingness to be interviewed. Her list is complementary to the one produced by informant 2, thus, lacking what I would call all her 'left side' (people sitting on her left side), including the 'authority' group, already mentioned by informant 2. Finally, informant 1 does not appear on the general list of participants because she was not in the hall, but standing outside behind numbers 37 and 38 on the map. In

Table 5.7 *Grouping of content of memory lists from* fono *in Hihifo*

Informant	1	2	3	4	5	6	7	8	9	10
1*	1–5 side R	6 proximity	7–8 side R							
2*	1 proximity	2–3 S L-auth	4 proximity							
3	1 proximity	2–3 F-auth	4 side L	5–6 side R						
4	1–3 S L-auth	4–5 front	6 proximity	7 side R	8–9 front	10–14 side R	15 side L	16 side R	17 front	18 proximity
5	1 proximity	2 side L	3 F-auth	4–7 side R						
6	1–2 prox-auth	3–5 front	6–7 side R	8 front	9 S L-auth	10–12 side R				
7	1 F-auth	2 proximity	3 F- auth	4–5 front						
8	1–7 proximity	8–9 side R	10–14 side L	15–16 side R	17–18 F-auth	19–20 proximity				

* See text for comments on the data of these two informants.

Table 5.8 *Frequency of category in subparts of memory lists from* fono *in Hihifo*

Category	1	2	3	4	5	6	7	8	9	10
Proximity	5	2	2	–	–	1	–	–	–	1
Authority	3	2	2	–	2	–	–	–	–	–
Front	1	3	2	2	2	–	–	–	1	–
Side left	1	2	2	–	1	–	1	–	–	–
Side right	1	1	2	4	–	2	–	1	–	–

fact, she was remembered by informant 4 in Table 5.7, specifically, in group number two that I labeled as 'proximity.' But this occurrence (of informant 1 in the memory list of informant 4) was not counted in order to be consistent with the procedure used with the other informants. To see the frequency of occurrence of each category in each memory list, I introduce a general count in Table 5.8.

In Table 5.8, the most salient category, as a consequence of being very frequently used (but see 'front' and 'side right' each used eleven times), and mostly applied (five times) to the first group of people remembered and drawn, is that of 'proximity.' But, there are some considerations to be made. First, for informant 6 'proximity' co-occurs with 'authority.' Second, for informant 1 'authority' does not appear for the reasons discussed above. Third, and very importantly, I have not counted as 'authority' four *faifekau* 'minister' that represent very 'authoritative' figures in the community. We may, then, be led to think that the difference between the two categories is not as large as it appears, notwithstanding a slight preference for the 'proximity' category.

However, what is extremely interesting is the fact that these results had been predicted and expected. In fact, externally observable cultural parameters, such as relevance of authority and proximity in determining status, had been hypothesized as possibly affecting mental representations of spatial relationships for certain types of events (including the *fono*). Thus, these results support the possibility of a privileged status of a culturally induced absolute frame of reference for Tongan speakers. Furthermore, with the exception of informants 1, 4, and 7 (where 'front,' 'authority,' and 'proximity' almost overlap), there is a clear trend to start from 'proximity' and then slowly move away from self. A good example of this trend is participant 14 who was discussed above (see Table 5.6 and Figures 5.14 and 5.15).

Relevantly, though, where the movement away from the self is abruptly broken, it is connected with skewing towards authority (e.g., informant 3). In other words, not only are informants making use of some type of absolute frame of reference, but they are also showing a preference towards a spatial representation that moving away from their selves is later 'centered' on the authority figures, that is, an instantiation of a radial representation. Since a radial representation, a subtype of the absolute frame of reference, was also suggested at the end of the analyses of the two drawing tasks, some relevant congruency was found between these two types of data.

5.6.2   A village fono 'meeting' in Houma, Vava'u

During my various periods of residence in the village of Houma, there were three *fono* called by the *ofisa kolo* 'town officer' in the traditional manner. In fact, it is part of the duties of his office to announce the next morning (day) event by shouting (literally) it while walking around the village at dusk so that everybody, by now back home from any working duty, has a chance to hear the announcement and be informed.

The first time, I missed the meeting in spite of the fact that I had received permission to videotape it. In fact, the *ofisa kolo* had given me a specific time when the meeting was supposed to take place. But the following morning he decided to proceed earlier since everybody had already assembled at the end of the early morning service and an hour before the appointed schedule. The second time, only a few people showed up and the meeting was cancelled. Finally, the third time, I was able to videotape the *fono* and it is during the day following this event that I was able to administer my 'memory' task to some of the participants.

Houma is a very small village (172 inhabitants) and the number of participants was limited, only seventeen. For this reason only six participants were interviewed, three men and three women, representing 35% of the total. To the 'memory' lists elicited from the informants I applied the same procedures that have been used with the lists discussed in the previous section. Thus, the range of people remembered goes from eleven to fifteen, that is, from 69% to 94%. The average number of participants remembered is 13.2, that is, 82.5%. It is immediately evident that these percentages are much higher than the ones obtained for the *fono* in Hihifo. But we have to consider the fact that there were many fewer participants (only seventeen and not forty-three), and the village of Houma is a tighter, smaller community than Hihifo (683 inhabitants, Kingdom of Tonga, 2007).

The *fono* to which these lists refer was held because of the upcoming visit of the king to the island. In fact, the burden of supplying food for the big feast that this event demands is divided among the various villages. A *faifekau pule* 'chief minister' who is at the head of the district to which Houma belongs visited the village to inform its inhabitants about the amount of food preparation assigned to them. The only context in which this could take place is within a

Table 5.9 *Presence of powerful people in memory lists of* fono *in Houma*

Informant	'Eiki			Ofisa kolo			Faifekau pule			Faifekau		
	1	2	3	1	2	3	1	2	3	1	2	3
1	x				x		x			–	–	–
2		x		x			x			–	–	–
3	x			na	na	na	–	–	–		x	
4	x				x		x			x		
5		x		x			x			x		
6	x			x			x			x		
Total	4	2	0	3	2	0	5	0	0	3	1	0

fono. There were, then, four people embodying authority in this meeting: the local *'eiki* 'chief,' the *ofisa kolo* 'town officer,' the district *faifekau pule* 'chief minister,' and the village *faifekau* 'minister.' Again I employed the same procedure as for the previous case in determining the relevance of each person embodying authority within the lists elicited and obtained the data in Table 5.9. All four 'authority' persons are well remembered, and the local chief and town officer are remembered by all the informants interviewed (the town officer was one of the informants, then, being remembered by five persons is the totality of the informants). However, the one who was remembered most in the first part of the lists is the guest district minister.

At this juncture it is important to briefly discuss the sitting arrangement of the people during the event. Reference will be made to the standardized map (Figure 5.16) of the event that I was able to draw out of my notes and sketches taken during the meeting and by viewing the video made of the event. The hall in which the *fono* was held has a canonical assigned *mu'a* 'front' and *mui* 'back' as shown in Figure 5.16 by the long thin double-arrowed axis running through the middle of the hall. The chief is supposed to sit in that area of the hall defined as *mu'a* if a public meeting is held. Usually, however, in informal *kava* drinking circles with a relatively smaller number of participants, the kava bowl is put between the two side entrances and the chief, if present, or any 'authority' figure, will sit in front of the bowl, at some distance. In this case the *mu'a* and the *mui* of the event are indicated as constituted in this different way by the double-arrowed axis in bold on the map.

On the morning of the event described the local chief on entering the hall realized that a small number of people had turned up to participate. Then, once inside the place he decided that it was not necessary to use the more formal *mu'a* part of the hall, and he opted for the 'informal' one. Consequently, he sat on the mat on his left (he had entered through the main entrance). The guest, district minister, was invited to sit next to the chief and the same happened for

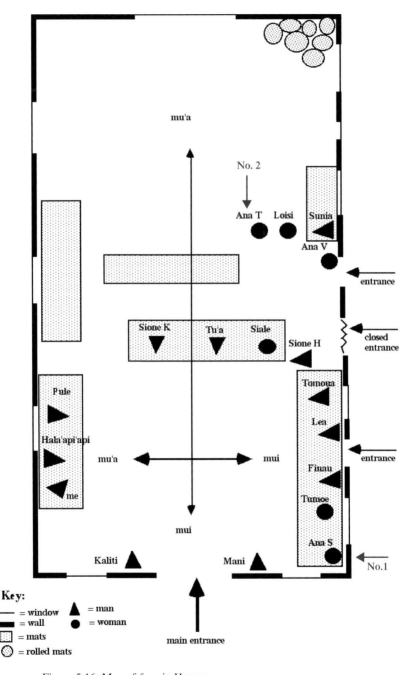

Figure 5.16 Map of *fono* in Houma

me, even though we had agreed beforehand that I needed to be going around freely in trying to videotape the event. After the semi-formal invitation to sit in a specific place, out of due politeness, I complied with the formality of the event and could not leave my assigned place anymore. When town officer entered the hall a minute later, he sat right in front of the chief, thus, creating an absolute axis in which traditional and non-traditional authority made up its polarity. The local minister arrived a little late and sat as close as possible to the 'authority' space as he could, but on the canonical *mu'a* side of the hall.[24]

Looking back to Table 5.9 we can now try to find some further meaning in its content. The fact that the local minister was the least remembered among the authority figures may be explained by the fact that he was sitting 'outside' the absolute axis of the event that had the chief–chief minister at one pole and the town officer at the other pole. It is relevant to point out that the two informants that left him out from their memory lists (1 and 2) are sitting in two diametrically opposed places (see Figure 5.16), then, their memory gap cannot be assigned to occupying a specific location in the event (i.e., not being able to see him very well). Furthermore, the two local authority figures (local chief and town officer) are only once remembered in the same part of the lists, that is, they are usually remembered with a consistent gap between them, thus indicating a slight privilege assigned to spatial collocations over social categories. However, the fact that they were both remembered by all the informants indicates that the spatial–cultural axis provided by the two figures played a role in the performing of the 'memory' task.

When comparing the content of Table 5.5 (*fono* in Hihifo) with the content of Table 5.9 (*fono* in Houma) – both tables refer to the precedence and presence of 'authority' figures in the memory lists elicited after a *fono* – participants in the *fono* in Houma, remembered more saliently (first part of their lists) and more often (twenty times out of twenty-three, instead of thirteen times out of twenty-three) these authority figures. Two plausible factors that may help in explaining these differences could be the size of the events considered and the number of authority figures within the general number of participants. In fact, we have already seen how there were forty-three participants for the event in Hihifo and only seventeen in Houma. Furthermore, in Hihifo there were three authority figures out of the forty-three participants (one for every fourteen participants, excluding the informant), while in Houma there were four authority figures out of the seventeen participants (one for every four participants, excluding the informant).

---

[24] The layout of the mats (see Figure 5.16) and the space available constrained his choice. He could not sit on the mats where the chief and the guest Pule (and me) were sitting, he most likely did not want to sit on the mat in front of the chief where the *ofisa kolo* was sitting, so he had to choose a side. One of the two sides already had a mat, while the other did not have any, so he decided to sit on the mat where Sione K was already sitting.

Table 5.10 *Grouping of content of memory lists from* fono *in Houma*

Informant	1	2	3	4	5	6	7
1	1–2	3–9	10–11	12–15			
	F-auth	side R	side L	S R-far			
2	1	2–5	6	7	8–9	10–13	
	S R-auth	front	authority	proximity	far-front	gender	
3	1	2	3–5	6	9–12	16	18
	F-auth	proximity	side R	S R-auth	gender	side L	side R
4	1–2	3–6	7–11	12	13–15		
	S R-auth	front	side L	far-front	proximity		
5	1	2–3	4–5	6	7–8	9–10	11
	S L-auth	front-auth	S R-auth	authority	F-gender	far-S R	proximity
6	1–4	5–7	8	9–10	11–13		
	S R-auth	side L	front	side L	gender		

In the same fashion as for the data collected in Hihifo, I mapped onto the standardized map of the meeting the lists of participants elicited. The division in groups was done using the same 'categories,' such as proximity, authority, front, side, left and right. The different sitting arrangements of the participants, a closed circle with an 'outer' group (see Figure 5.16, and compare with Figure 5.13), seems to have affected the memory recall of the informants and compelled me to introduce a new category like 'far.' Furthermore, I also felt obliged to introduce the category 'gender' because some informants (numbers 2, 3, and 6) clearly used it in a salient way in the performance of the task. Evidence for this latter phenomenon was evinced from the content of their lists, especially the bottom parts (of the lists), and from their drawings, in which they mapped some people far away from their real locations, but grouped them according to their 'gender.' I do not repeat here the details of the procedure as I did for the *fono* in Hihifo, and introduce directly the results of the application of the procedure to the new data in Table 5.10.

In group numbers two and three for informant 5, a double-category has been indicated. In this case the two categories do not overlap, but represent two persons. In fact, he put the two persons very close together in his drawing and they are actually very close in real space. At the same time, one of the two is an 'authority' person; thus, I felt almost compelled to separate the two pairs. The final decision was to leave them together since both 'real' and 'drawn' space were giving clear indications to do so.

In Table 5.11 the incidences for each category in the various subgroups of the memory lists are summarized. It appears that the subjects assigned a privilege to the 'authority' category over all the others. And this is even more evident when we realize that only twice the 'front' category overlaps with the

Table 5.11 *Frequency of category in subparts of memory lists from* fono *in Houma*

Category	1	2	3	4	5	6	7
Proximity	–	1	–	1	1	–	1
Authority	6	1	2	2	–	–	–
Front	2	3	1	1	2	–	–
Side left	1	1	2	1	–	1	–
Side right	3	1	2	2	–	1	1
Far	–	–	–	2	1	1	–
Gender	–	–	–	–	3	1	–

'authority' one. This result is also more apparent than the one we already discussed about the *fono* in Hihifo. The difference in the incidence of the 'proximity' category can be attributed to the smaller environment, both physical and human, that characterized the event just discussed.

The discovered preference for 'authority' (most first-used strategy) in performing the task suggests a specific organization of memory about the event. A cultural 'center' is chosen as anchor, e.g., chief, and is followed by other individuals grouped spatially. Gender also appears to play a role in organizing information in long-term memory. The preference for the radial subtype of the absolute FoR finds further support from these findings. Meshed with cultural parameters such as status and gender, individuals do organize their memories about this salient event radially, that is, they choose a culturally skewed other-than-ego point of departure (authority) toward and from which other information, i.e., individuals, is added.

5.6.3   A misinale *'donation to church' in Houma, Vava'u*

While residing in the village of Houma, I witnessed one of the most important church-related events of the year, the *misinale*. This word, the Tongan version of the English word 'missionary,' stands nowadays for offerings to the church during a day-long celebration that includes the preparation and consumption of large amounts of food. This event is clearly related to the years of the coming of missionaries to Tonga in the early 1800s (Lātūkefu, 1974) but it also has deep-seated roots in the large offerings of goods to the now largely forgotten traditional Tongan deities (Ferdon, 1987).

The offerings that once consisted mainly of agricultural produce are nowadays only monetary. The amount offered may vary from a few Tongan *pa'anga* (the local currency unit is worth around $0.50) to a few hundred and even thousands. These sums represent a huge amount of money for Tongans (especially for the people from small villages) and in order to collect them they often have to undergo long-term planning and constant attention to income and expenditures in their daily lives. However, when the day of the *misinale* comes and their contributions are loudly announced in the church by the *ofisa kolo*, repeated for the people outdoors by the *le'o matapā* 'door voice,' and that same evening broadcast throughout the kingdom by radio, the only thing that counts is the pride of having been able to match or even outdo one's social status.

The actual offering takes place within the confines of the church build-ing. A chief minister from the main town of the island (in this case, Neiafu) supervised the donation ceremony that was actually chaired by the local chief. The *ofisa kolo* collected the offerings and repeated them aloud with the exact amount and the name of the donor, while the *le'o matapā* 'door voice' repeated all this information for the benefit of the people assembled outside the church. The local minister was also present and sat in the front of the church with the chair (chief) and the chief minister. Still in the front, but on the left side below the step that delimits the pulpit area (see map of event in Figure 5.17), the sec-retary sat at a table with two helpers writing down all the offerings in a register. People sat in the benches and in turn got up to meet the town officer with their donations. The whole festive mood was underlined by humorous comments by the town officer. At times, moments of deep sorrow followed donations in memory of recently deceased persons.

The part of the day-long celebration that was videotaped was the one that took place in the church. Later, in the same way as for the two events dis-cussed in the previous two sections, a map was drawn of the event with the help of my assistants. The numbers next to the symbols for men and women in the map in Figure 5.17 refer to adult inhabitants of Houma. The only few exceptions are person number 2, that is, the *faifekau sea* 'chair minister' who was from Neiafu, number 16 (American), numbers 35 through 38, numbers 40 through 42, and numbers 44 and 45. All of these participants (except number 2) were included because relevantly related to families in Houma, even though not residing there anymore. Other participants from the neighboring villages of Mangia and Ha'akio were not considered and informants were asked not to mention them when producing their memory lists. This solution was adopted in order to limit the investigation to the village of Houma, about which suffi-cient ethnographic information had been collected.

The total number of participants was forty-six, with sixteen males and thirty females. Twelve participants were not Houma residents, ten females and two males, and this brought down the total of participants resident in Houma to thirty-four, fourteen males and twenty females. The content of the memory lists collected ranges from a minimum of seventeen (37%) to a maximum of thirty (65%) with an average length of 25.6 (56%). It has to be pointed out that in all the lists the informants included as participants some persons that were

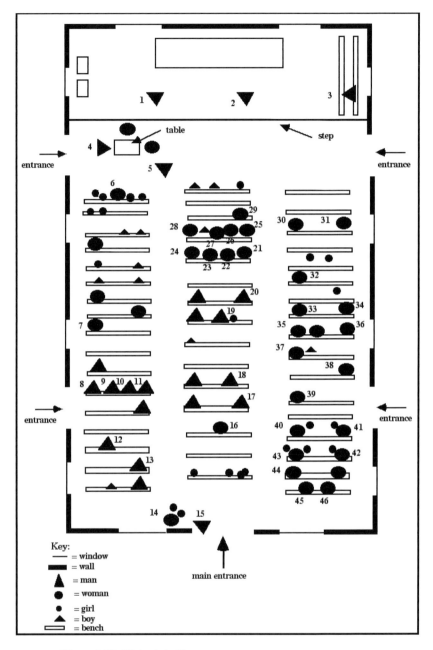

Figure 5.17 *Misinale* in Houma

not present in the church. Their names were not counted in determining the length of the lists.

Following the same procedure used for the memory lists obtained after the two *fono*, each list was divided into three parts and the appearance in each part of a so-called authority figure was marked. The authority figures taken into consideration are the local chief, *'eiki sea* 'chair chief,' the district minister, *faifekau sea* 'chair minister,' the local minister, *faifekau* 'minister,' the *ofisa kolo* 'town officer,' the *sekelitali* 'secretary,' and the *le'o matapā* 'door voice.' Compared to the two previous events analyzed, the list of people under the authority heading is slightly longer. Two further persons were included (the secretary and the door voice) because the higher complexity of the event as well as the relatively prominent roles they played in it demanded such an extension. Table 5.12 summarizes the place occupied by the authority figures in each of the three subparts of the memory lists.

It is relevant to notice in Table 5.12 that the most powerful and authoritative figure (the district minister) is also the least remembered (two times). However, since informants were explicitly asked to mention only participants from Houma, this instruction may have played a major role in causing such a result. In fact, after all, the district minister is not from Houma! The local chief is the only one among the authority persons remembered by everybody (nine times represents the totality because the local chief is also one of the ten informants) and also the one that most frequently appears in the first part of the list. The town officer (nine times out of ten and four times in the first part), and the 'door voice' (nine times and three times in the first part) follow. The local minister is remembered well in the first part of the lists (five times), but the total is lower than the other persons just mentioned. The secretary closes the list, whose presence in the event must have passed by almost unnoticed (four times).

The most 'active' roles in this event were actually played by the town officer (collecting money) and by the 'door voice' (repeating aloud the amount and provenance of the donations). They were the ones who can be regarded as running the 'show,' almost entertaining the audience. However, in spite of a presence in the event that could be defined as 'silent' or 'in the background,' the local chief pole is the one that affects memory recall most effectively. It seems that this person may be providing a very important fixed point of reference used by the villagers to orient themselves socially, spatially, and in their memory retrieval tasks.

In the same way as was shown for the task administered after the *fono* in Hihifo, I grouped the contents of the memory lists into parts. This grouping was arrived at also by considering the positions the informants drew on the map of the event for each of the persons they remembered. The grouping in Table 5.13 contains three new memory 'strategies.' The first strategy had

Table 5.12 *Presence of powerful people in memory lists of misinale in Houma*

Informant*	'Eiki sea			Faifekau sea			Faifekau			Ofisa kolo			Sekelitali			Le'o matapā		
	1	2	3	1	2	3	1	2	3	1	2	3	1	2	3	1	2	3
1	x			–	–	–	x	–	–				–	–	–	x		
2	x			–	–	–	–	–	–		x		–	–	–			x
3	na	na	na	–	–	–	–	–	–	x			x	–	–	x		
4			x	–	–	–			x	x		x	–	–	–			x
5	x			x	–	–	x					x	–	–	–			
6	x			x	–	–	x			–	–	–					x	
7	x			–	–	–	x			x			x	–	–	x		
8	x			–	–	–	–	–	–	x				x			x	
9	x			–			x				x			x				
10			x						x		x			x				x
Total	7	0	2	2	0	0	5	0	2	4	3	2	2	2	0	3	3	3

*Subject 3 is the same person as the authority figure indicated by 'Eiki sea.

Table 5.13 *Grouping of content of memory lists from* misinale *in Houma*

Informant	1	2	3	4	5	6	7	8
1	authority	women front L	men side L	women side R	w&m FL prox			
2	men proximity	men authority	men front R	women front R	women side R			
3	authority proximity	men front	men front R	women front	women front L			
4	women side L	women proximity	women front L	men side L	authority	men side L		
5	authority	women proximity	women side BR	men behind	women side BR			
6	authority	women proximity	men behind	women side BR	men side BL			
7	authority	men side R	women front R	women side R	men proximity		women front	men proximity
8	men side R	authority	women front R	authority	men side R	women front R		
9	authority	women front	men proximity	women side R	women front R	women side L		
10	women proximity	men behind	men side BL	authority	women side R			

already become evident in the analysis of the data about the *fono* in Houma in Section 5.6.2, that is, remembering by one's 'gender.' In fact, the majority of the lists are clearly divided into two parts where usually, but not always, the first part includes people of the same gender, women remembering women first or men doing the same with other men. The second very prominent strategy is that of remembering people by grouping them according to their canonical sitting place. That is, for instance, remembering a group of men not because they were sitting close to each other on the specific event (the *misinale*) to which the memory list was supposed to refer, but on the basis of a specific area where they would usually sit on any other church-related event. The third strategy was that of remembering by associating a very close kin, a husband/wife, a mother/father or a daughter/son, to each individual person remembered.

The use of any of the three strategies did not exclude the use of the other two. In fact, often two or more strategies were used at the same time. However, while the use of the first (gender) and the third (close kin) overlapped only in two cases, the overlap of the first (gender) with the second (canonical place) was common. To be more precise, all the informants used the first and the second strategy in their recall task both in providing the memory lists and in drawing the positions of the participants on the map of the event. It seems, then, that this fact alone is already supplying some supporting evidence towards a privileged use of an absolute FoR culturally and experientially constructed (canonical position of people in church, see map of church in Figure 5.3). Such a phenomenon was predicted and hypothesized as an active parameter affecting retrieval from memory in performing the task.

After highlighting the strategies used, I divided the lists into subparts. Seven lists were divided into five subparts, two into six subparts, and only one into eight subparts as shown in Table 5.13. Each subpart was labeled by a category such as proximity, authority, front, side, behind, men, and women. There is only one category that did not appear in the analyses of the two previous sets of data, 'behind.' This had to be added since it clearly characterized some subparts. The specific physical setting and people distribution for this event may have caused the use of this category. Finally, the 'gender' category introduced for the *fono* in Houma, was here divided into its two subcomponents, men and women.

The results in Table 5.14 show that the category 'authority' is the one mostly employed (six times) in the first subpart of the memory lists. Since in the analysis of these lists the 'first remembered, more salient' parameter was employed, I suggest for this group of data that the authority category is to be considered the most salient factor used to organize memory data while performing the task. The second most salient factor is the 'proximity' category (three times). Its saliency is very similar to the two 'gender' ones when we look at the first two subparts of the lists instead of at the first subpart only (six times

Table 5.14 *Frequency of category in subparts of memory lists from* misinale *in Houma*

Category	1	2	3	4	5	6	7	8
Proximity	3	3	1	–	2	–	–	1
Authority	6	2	–	2	1	–	–	–
Front (R or L)	–	3	5	2	3	–	–	–
Side (R or L)	2	1	3	5	5	3	1	–
Behind	–	1	3	2	2	–	–	–
Men	2	4	6	2	5	1	–	1
Women	2	5	4	6	6	2	1	–

for 'proximity,' six times for 'men,' and seven times for 'women'). However, I conclude that the predicted salient role played by 'proximity' in the memory task is again supported by these findings.

To summarize, at the end of the discussion of the first group of data collected after a *fono* in Hihifo, two strategies were highlighted as saliently used by informants to retrieve data from their memory, that is, proximity and authority. They were ranked first and second, respectively, but reasons were suggested that made the difference in rank between the two categories appear very small. The analysis of the data obtained after the *fono* in Houma yielded different results. While authority was the most salient strategy used by the informants, it seemed that proximity played a lesser role. The human size of the event (only seventeen participants) and the physical size of the space in which the event took place (a section of a small hall) may have contributed to the lesser role played by the proximity factor in these data. The analysis of the data obtained after the *misinale* in the village of Houma yielded a primary status for the authority strategy, and a moderate but interesting one for the proximity strategy. The predicted activation of the church map with canonical sitting arrangements was also found to be used by the informants.

The culturally constituted and spatially instantiated radial subtype of the absolute FoR centered on the authority pole appears to have an active role in shaping and informing memory retrieval of data for Tongan informants. Thus, the major hypothesis suggested by the knowledge and personal experience of Tongan culture – *villagers' memory of cultural salient events, both composition and relationships between parts, would be skewed in a 'radial' fashion, that is, an other-than-ego individual point would be chosen, most likely one or more authoritative figures, and memory would be organized as radiating out of that point* – found supporting evidence. The secondary hypothesis – *saliency of proximity because of its role in displaying status* – is found to have a differential status in the three memory tasks administered. Various reasons for such a phenomenon were suggested during the analyses. Another suggestion could be that of looking at the proximity strategy as one in which the absolute and the relative FoR overlap, resulting in inconsistent behavior. The importance of proximity, however, in two of the tasks – *fono* in Hihifo and *misinale* in Houma – makes the prediction a sound one. Finally, the hypothesized use of a specific subtype of the absolute FoR instantiated in the 'map' of the church also found some supporting evidence.

A pattern that can be elicited from these results is of a privileged status for the use of the radial subtype of the absolute FoR in memory storage and retrieval. This finding contributes towards a clarification of the discovered incongruence between results obtained by the language tasks and those by the psychological tasks in Chapter 3 and Chapter 4, respectively. In other words, it can be suggested that culturally provided parameters, specifically a radial FoR socially constituted, affects the use of specific thought patterns. In fact, where spatial cognition makes available any of the three FoRs and their subtypes, cultural beings may be assigning any of them a privileged status because they find themselves using that specific one not only more often, but more saliently in highly marked cultural events.

Some congruence was found between ethnographic observations and psychological data. In order to accept the privileged status of the absolute FoR (radially instantiated) in Tongan cognition it is necessary to introduce further evidence from ethnographic data. In fact, it is clear that a privileged status of the absolute FoR in Tongan spatial cognition would have consequences over a wider array of cultural behaviors than those already discussed. It is highly likely, then, that other patterns of behavior can be organized according to similar parameters. Specific ethnographic data, such as patterns of exchange that are frequent and salient in Tongan life (Evans, 2001), are now introduced and analyzed.

5.7   Exchange patterns: spatial cognition in the behavioral place

During my residence in Tonga, I witnessed and participated in several celebrations and festivities. All of these events were characterized by a large preparation and consumption of food. The quantity, type, and arrangement of food varied according to the level of formality, i.e., more formality, more food. The specific type of event determines the number of people involved in the preparation of the food as well as who is going to eat first and who is entitled to a share of the leftovers. Food is not the only element that enters into the complex pattern of exchange that these events punctuate. Often live or butchered animals are donated, but most importantly *tapa* 'bark cloth,' *fala* 'mat,' *kava* (root of the *Piper methysticum* plant), and sometimes money. These exchange items are very salient in Tongan culture. They constitute traditional wealth (i.e., *tapa* and *fala*), they mark formal events (i.e., *kava* drinking), and they acknowledge the new parameters of the contemporary Tongan milieu (i.e., money).

I chose to analyze three events in which I participated: the *fakaafe* 'invitation,' the *kātoanga maka fakamanatu* 'commemorative stone feast,' and the *fetongi* 'exchange.'[25] These events represent exchanges in which people of different social status participate. Also a different number of people are involved in each individual event and in a variety of different locations within the Kingdom of Tonga. The first event is a relatively common occurrence in the yearly life-cycle of any Tongan village. The second is a rare occasion, but it stands for a class of events that occur minimally once a year. The third is even rarer, and its occurrence does not fit the constraint of a yearly cycle, but it follows the whims of the people that organize it. It may typically be regarded as an event taking place within the boundary of a two-year period, but with no necessary specific interval between two occurrences.

I introduce the three descriptions according to socio-geographic parameters. I start with the *fakaafe* because it took place within the boundary of a village and involved only one (rarely more than one) guest from outside the village. The description and analysis of the *kātoanga maka fakamanatu* follows since it involved people from the whole archipelago of Vava'u. Finally, the *fetongi* event is described because participation in it included people from the northern archipelago of Vava'u and the southern archipelago of Tongatapu, thus, geographically spanning almost the whole Kingdom of Tonga.

5.7.1   The fakaafe *'invitation'*

The description of the *fakaafe* 'invitation' that follows is not an account of a specific one, but the results of a range of experiences I had in participating in many such events. Although I was in a number of *fakaafe* in at least three locations during my fieldwork, the place to which I refer here is the village of Houma, Vava'u, this being my main field site and the place where I spent the longest section of my fieldwork. The *fakaafe* I was able to observe more closely are the ones that took place in the household I was living and to which I belonged in a form close to a temporary 'adoption.'

In the yearly life of the contemporary village of Houma there are several occasions in which a *fakaafe* takes place. Typically, these occasions are related to Church (Wesleyan[26]) activities. In fact, whenever a speaker (or more than one) from another village comes to deliver a sermon during the Sunday services (either early morning, middle morning, or afternoon), a *fakaafe* is held. The most intense periods of such activities usually overlap with the most typical Church holidays like Christmas, Easter, and other similar occasions. The first week of the year is celebrated with a series of guest speakers delivering

---

[25] These three descriptions come from Bennardo (1996).
[26] I must remind the reader that 91% of the village population belongs to this Church.

sermons every day and consequently every day a *fakaafe* takes place in the village. When planning the Church activities, usually at the beginning of the year, the whole congregation gathers in the church and people volunteer to give a *fakaafe* on a specific date or dates of the year. The most prominent persons in the village are expected to and usually do offer to give more than one *fakaafe*. Circumstances may vary and when asked, informants told me that nobody is really obligated to volunteer, especially if it is known that a specific year may have brought some financial constraints onto a household.

I reintroduce here the two concepts of *fāmili* 'family, household' and *kāinga* 'extended family' because they are actively used to organize, prepare, and give a *fakaafe*. A *fāmili* is made up of a married couple and their children living together in the same house and it usually includes some male and/or female collaterals and affinals (usually, son- or daughter-in-law). The *'ulumotu'a* 'head of family' presides over this group. The *kāinga* 'extended family' instead is a group of people living in different households, mostly in the same village, but often including residences in other villages. They are related to one another consanguineally, but all the affinal and collateral relatives are also included. These latter are both maternally and paternally acquired. Also for this group an *'ulumotu'a* presides over the affairs of its members (of course, he also presides over the affairs of his own *fāmili*).

When the date of the *fakaafe* is approaching, an informal meeting of the household to which the person giving it belongs is held. In this meeting several things are discussed and decided. First, the quantity of food to be prepared. This involves deciding about number and size of pigs and/or goats and/or chickens (sometimes also sheep meat is acquired from stores); number and size of fish and quantity of shellfish; number and size of root crops like taro, yams, and tapioca; fruit like bananas, pineapples, watermelons; quantity of coconuts to be used for cooking and as drink; beverages like lemon water, sodas, and most importantly *kava*; type and quantity of desserts like pies, cookies, ice-cream; and finally, all sorts of other complementary, but necessary things like dishes, pans, silverware, banana leaves for cooking, palm leaves for decoration, sweets, chips, and even balloons. It is obvious from this list that no individual person could possibly put together all that food without going through a draining financial experience. This is exactly the second important issue discussed at the meeting. The members of the *fāmili* are asked to pool together their individual resources and contribute in a differentiated manner to the accomplishment of the task at hand. Typically, however, also members of the *kāinga* are contacted and required to contribute to the event in a variety of ways that range from bringing live animals, and/or harvesting root crops, to providing manual labor.

Finally, the meeting closes with the assignment of specific tasks to each individual or group of individuals. However, most of these tasks are so traditionally intertwined with daily gender-related tasks that they almost go unmentioned if not for any special, specific one that may occur out of unforeseen circumstances. Consequently, men will, among other things, harvest root crops and slaughter animals as well as prepare the underground oven and gather a sufficient amount of coconuts and fruit. Women will, among other things, collect shellfish on the nearby reef and prepare the non-meat food to be put in the underground oven as well as bake pies and clean and decorate the house and the area around it. Young boys and girls (and children) will also take part in the preparation, but their tasks may vary according to need.

By the following Saturday evening all the food to be cooked has already been gathered within the premises of the household involved. The whole day has been marked by young boys chasing and seizing free-ranging animals such as pigs or fowl, or the arrival of men from their garden with a variety of crops and/or fruit, and the feverish cleaning activity of the house and its surroundings. The day closes with the usual *kava* drinking by the men in the hall next to the church. Very early on Sunday morning, between three and four o'clock, muffled noises of people getting up and starting a variety of activities can be perceived in the household still embraced by a thick, humid dark blanket. The first light of dawn sees an underground oven already full of burning wood filling the air with its pungent smell. The bell calling people for the five o'clock early morning service has no job to do since everybody is already up by this time and fulfilling their tasks. Everything will be ready by approximately twelve o'clock when after the end of a slightly longer ten o'clock second morning service the *'ulumotu'a* 'head of family' will come back home with his guests. In fact, not only the person giving the sermon is invited for lunch, but also the *'eiki* 'chief,' the *ofisa kolo* 'town officer,' the *faifekau* 'minister,' and any other person, man or woman, that has accepted the repeated invitation made to people (not from his *kāinga*) at the end of the service in front of the church. Usually, however, almost everybody declines the invitation, with the exception of a few persons who may be part of another long-term exchange not specifically related to the present event.

Meanwhile the food has been laid out on the best mats in the main room of the house. When everybody arrives in the room they sit on the floor crossed-legged and their location is determined in a fashion similar to the *fono* and formal *kava* ceremony described in Section 5.3. This time, however, the arrangement of the people follows the rectangular shape of the tablecloth on the mats. The chief sits at the *mu'a* 'front' of the house and so do the guest and the *ofisa kolo* with any other relevant person participating. Other persons sit in decreasing ranking away from the chief with the children closing the group. The consumption of the food is preceded by a brief prayer and punctuated by a number of speeches that are started by the *'ulumotu'a*, followed by the guest and the chief, and also include anybody who feels his/her speech is due on that specific occasion.

When everybody has finished eating the gathering is called off, and this usually takes place when the chief (in agreement with the guest) decides to stand up and leave. Soon after everybody has left, all the people that prepared the food, both men and women, have a chance to come in and have their turn.

The quantity of food prepared exceeds so much the needs of both turns of eaters that a great amount of leftovers will be available when everybody has finished eating. Then, typically, the women of the house divide up this food in such a way as to make as many portions as the number of *fāmili* from the *kāinga* that participated in the event preparation. The distribution of these portions follows immediately after the dividing up and before people leave to go back to their houses. If no person is present from a specific *fāmili*, usually a youngster is sent with a portion of food to the house of that specific *fāmili*. This distribution of food closes the event and all the persons that contributed to it hurry home to a deserved rest. After all it is Sunday, and no working activity is legally permitted on Sundays in Tonga, not even car driving![27]

I now present a short analysis of the *fakaafe* as an instantiation of a variety of movements in space within locations that stand among themselves in specific relationships in order to highlight the use of specific FoRs. First, an individual establishes her/himself as a 'center' by volunteering to give a *fakaafe*. Second, a specific fixed point of reference is chosen by deciding the specific person (on a specific date) that is the recipient of such an event. Pooling of a variety of resources from a culturally circumscribed number of people, i.e., *kāinga*, follows. The movement of these resources is definitely centripetal, that is, they are all directed towards the already established 'center.' Then, during the first eating episode, the spatially instantiated relevance of a fixed point of reference, i.e., the guest speaker, is further stressed by adding to it other very familiar fixed points of reference such as the chief, the town officer, and the minister. Finally, the event is closed by a centrifugal movement of the leftover food back towards the same periphery (and only to that one) that had participated in centripetally constructing the 'center.' The whole event and the movements involved in it are schematically represented in Figure 5.18.

In part (a) of Figure 5.18 two moments preliminary to the actual *fakaafe* are shown together, the establishing of a 'center' and the pooling of resources from the *fāmili* and the *kāinga*. Part (b) of the same figure shows the part of the event in which resources gathered in the 'center' are donated to a fixed point of reference, that is, the guest speaker. Considering that this latter has already provided what we called the constituted 'center' (as a member of the congregation) with the gift of her/his sermon, we may also interpret this part as a centripetal movement towards another 'center' embodied this time by the guest speaker (or fixed point of reference). Finally, in part (c) the centrifugal

---

[27] Since 1994 this ban has been lifted, but generally, people still comply with it.

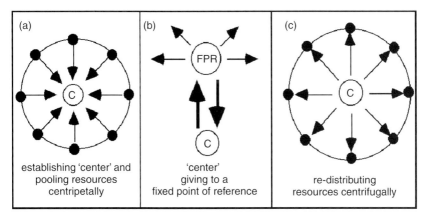

Figure 5.18 Exchanges in the *fakaafe*

movement of the leftover resources returning to the periphery, i.e., members of the *kāinga*, is shown.

This schematic description of the event allows one to realize how certain elements of spatial cognition already highlighted in Chapters 3, and 4, are here reiterated in the behavior people display in planning, preparing, and performing a *fakaafe*. In fact, centripetal and centrifugal movements of objects towards a fixed center (in the preparation and the performing of the *fakaafe* by the giver and the guest speaker, respectively) are possible only within a representation of spatial relationships that uses a specific type of absolute FoR, a radial representation. I want to highlight that both movements of objects, e.g., food/resources, sermon, are underscored by a similar thought pattern. The thinking pattern that must be activated to centripetally pool the resources for the *fakaafe* from the *fāmili* and the *kāinga* is 'radial.' Similarly, the thinking pattern behind the centrifugal distribution of the food back to the *kāinga* is 'radial.' And the thinking pattern activated in performing the exchange of the sermon to the congregation for food from one of its members is also radial (but with the two moments reversed, that is, first centrifugal and then centripetal movement). We may conclude this very brief discussion about the *fakaafe*, then, suggesting that this Tongan event, culturally constructed, entails the use of a radial representation of spatial relationships, that is, a subtype of the absolute FoR.

5.7.2   *The* kātoanga maka fakamanatu *'commemorative stone feast'*

On December 3, 1995, during a *kātoanga maka fakamanatu* 'commemorative stone feast,' an engraved stone was uncovered by King Taufa'ahau Tupou IV in Neiafu, Vava'u, to commemorate the first written code of law in Tonga, the Vava'u Law. King George Taufa'ahau Tupou I officially promulgated these laws in a *fono* held in the same town on November 20, 1839 (Lātūkefu, 1974: 121). The names of five people who collaborated in the writing and first implementation (usually referred to as 'first government') of this code were also engraved on the stone. The preparation for this event deeply affected the life of this northern Tongan archipelago as any very rare visit of the king could be expected to do in such a small kingdom.

The first news about the upcoming visit of the king to the island of Vava'u was heard after a meeting held in Neiafu of the *pule fakavahe* 'head of district' in August, 1995. However, few people still completely understood the meaning of the work that had started in Neiafu to build a small tree and flower garden in the place where the stone had to be erected. When a couple of weeks later also the *ofisa kolo* 'town officer' of each individual village were summoned by their respective *pule fakavahe* to be informed about the upcoming event, more people came to know about the *kātoanga*[28] and the reason behind the event. In the meantime, the local (Tongan) weekly newspapers had already started to report on the event. The teachers and students of two high schools (Government and Wesleyan) in Neiafu were also informed and both were asked to prepare a *lakalaka* 'Tongan dance' to be performed during the event in front of the king. Finally, a *fono* was held in all the villages of Vava'u at the very beginning of November and specific duties regarding the event were assigned to each of them.

The people of Houma were asked to provide two *pola* 'tray between twelve and fifteen feet by three feet full of food' and two *kato* 'tray between three and five feet by two feet full of food' for the *kātoanga;* the former to be used by the people of Houma during the celebration and the latter to be used by the king and the *kakai ma'olunga* 'important people' that would be present. During the *fono* it was also decided to divide the village into three parts along traditional lines (*Faleono*, *Selusalema*, and *Holani*; see map of Houma in Figure 5.1) and the residents of each section would supply either a *pola* or two *kato*.[29] Interestingly, *Selusalema* and *Faleono* were referred to as "*kolo ko é, 'eiki*" 'village there, chief' (chief's village) and "*kolo ko é, ofisa kolo*" 'village there, town officer' (town officer's village), respectively, because the *'eiki* and the then elected *ofisa kolo* resided in those two parts of Houma.

In the person of the *'eiki* the village of Houma still had more to contribute to the *kātoanga*. In fact, since the local *'eiki* is a direct descendant of one of the five men who belonged to the 'first government' and whose names are engraved on the stone, he had to provide a *koloa* 'precious things' to be donated directly to the king. This *koloa* consisted of a *puaka toho* 'very big pig,' *fala*

---

[28] From now on I will indicate the event only by this word.
[29] A *kato* is approximately half the size of a *pola*.

'mat,' *ngatu* 'barkcloth,' *kava*, and agricultural produce. Contributions to fulfill this duty came from all the prominent *kāinga* of Houma, but the main burden remained with the *kāinga* of the *'eiki*.

In the weeks that followed some kind of excitement could be felt throughout the island. Two weeks before the date of the celebration the engraved stone arrived and was put in the still unfinished square garden and covered with *ngatu* 'tapa, barkcloth.' Then, arches clothed with woven palm tree leaves and adorned with all sorts of colorful and sweetly scented flowers started to be erected in the main streets of Neiafu leading to the little square garden where the stone had to be uncovered. School final exams were administered earlier and schools closed a week earlier to allow students and teachers to conclude their preparation and rehearsal of their welcoming dances and official protocol for the *kātoanga*. The few high school students and teachers (two) of the village of Houma could be seen leaving in the morning with their costume apparel on and coming back in the afternoon later than usual, but happily and loudly rehearsing their songs on the pick-up truck from town. Finally on the evening of the Friday preceding the day of the *kātoanga*, the same scenes like the ones already described for the *fakaafe* characterized the village landscape. This time, however, there were more households involved and consequently more activities going on.

Again, earlier than dawn on Saturday morning, the day of the *kātoanga*, the whole village seemed to burst with quiet but steady activities. The still dark air was filled with smoke from several underground ovens and many *haka* 'boiling pots on open fire.' Three different groups of people were in the meantime finishing weaving the two *pola* and *kato* from freshly cut palm tree leaves and branches, banana leaves, and several types of flower (i.e., hibiscus, frangipani, pandanus). By seven o'clock, in spite of a gray sky that at times let down some light rain, three pick-up trucks were loaded with the two *pola* and two *kato* among the happy shrills of onlookers and the majority of the village headed for the town. The four trays were brought to a covered hall in the Government High School in Neiafu where the actual feast would be held after the official uncovering of the stone. The ceremony at the small square garden prepared to host the commemorative stone was attended by relatively fewer people. The king and part of his entourage were located on a platform erected for this purpose. After the conventional introductory speeches, the king read his brief speech and uncovered the stone. Soon after he left the scene in his car, thus allowing everybody else to leave the square garden and reach the hall in the Government High School. He reappeared at the hall after more than an hour.

In the hall the real bulk of the *kātoanga* took place. First, the presentation of the *koloa* by the chiefs of the villages related to the five men of the 'first government,' including the *'eiki* from Houma. Then, the welcoming dances were performed, including a *ta'olunga* 'solo dance' by one of the king's nieces. The whole ceremony was punctuated by several speeches. Finally, food was served to the king, the nobles, and other important persons. As soon as they had started their meal, everybody else started to eat from the *pola* lying in front of them. When the king finished his meal and left the scene accompanied by most of the nobles and important people, all the people from the various villages started to prepare to go back home. All the leftovers from each village *pola* were carefully packed and divided into small portions to be distributed to all the *kāinga* and *fāmili* who had contributed to their preparation. During the trip back home on the pick-up trucks not much was said and everybody looked and certainly was really tired, but the first succulent pieces of gossip started to be exchanged as far as the situation allowed. They had definitely been part of an event that would fill their conversations for a long time to come.

The official festivities did not end with the *kātoanga* just described. In fact, the following day, Sunday, all the various Ministers of the Government of Tonga officially presented a *pola* each to the king. Their contents were consumed in a less crowded, but no less long ceremony in which a strict protocol was observed including formal offerings, speeches, and dances. The following Monday an official *coktele* 'cocktail party' given by the king and held at the best resort hotel in Neiafu closed the three day celebration. Only officially invited guests participated including nobles, the Prime Minister and his family, various ministers and their families, the Head of the Wesleyan Church, and many members of the royal family.

The brief description of the *kātoanga* provided made clear the relevance of an established 'center' for all the activities that fundamentally constituted it. This 'center' is embodied in the person of the king who has historical (he is the direct descendant of King George Taufa'ahau Tupou I) and contemporary reasons (he is the Head of the Nation) to assert himself to be the 'center.' Furthermore, the actual location of the event is taking place in what is the 'center' of the island, the town of Neiafu (we have already seen how this was even empirically elicited in the 'map drawing' tasks). In other words, the 'center,' historically, politically, and geographically defined, coincides with the king.

The primary movement of objects (food, wealth items) was from the periphery, the whole of the Vava'u archipelago, to the 'center,' the king. However, the *pola* went from the villages to the location of the *kātoanga* and, then, after being used by the villagers to celebrate the event, the leftovers came back to the periphery. The *kato* also came from the villages to the 'center' and were used by some people (king and important people) participating in the event to celebrate, but remained within the 'center.' The *koloa* moved from a section of the periphery (five villages) towards the 'center' (the king) and remained there as well (the king usually distributes most of the *koloa* among the members of the royal family).

Whatever goods arrived at the *kātoanga* they were the results of smaller movements within the villages. We have seen, in fact, how in Houma three centers were established and used to pool resources and prepare the required two *pola* and two *kato*. It must be stressed again how in Houma two of the 'centers' were the *'eiki* and the *ofisa kolo*. The *'eiki* himself also pooled resources centripetally (towards himself) from the village at large to satisfy his duty towards the king (i.e., preparing the *koloa*). It can be strongly suggested that most of the behaviors that characterized the preparation and realization of the *kātoanga* have been the consequence of a specific pattern of thought. This can be described as a first moment in which a 'center' is established, followed by either centripetal or centrifugal movements of goods between the periphery and that 'center.' In other words, a radial representation of spatial relationships is needed to conceive, represent, and realize the behavior described.

5.7.3   The fetongi *'exchange'*

In January 1994 a group of women in Neiafu, capital of Vava'u, was contacted by another group of women in Nuku'alofa, Tongatapu, to exchange *ngatu* 'bark-cloth' for *fala* 'mats.' One of the women in Nuku'alofa belonged to the same *kāinga* 'extended family' as one of the women in Vava'u. In June of the same year a woman who lives in Houma heard about the exchange from a woman of the exchanging group who belongs to her *kāinga*. Immediately, she went to ask the group if she could participate in the exchange. Once consent was given, in spite of the very short time left till November, only five months, she started to prepare all the mats needed with the help of the *lālanga* 'weaving' group[30] in Houma.

This type of exchange immediately attracted my attention because as far as my knowledge goes it had never been reported in the existing literature on Tonga, even though it was widely described in a variety of forms as occurring in many Melanesian and Western Polynesian areas (Malinowski, 1922; Weiner, 1976; Kaeppler, 1978c).[31] The information I was able to collect from informants in their eighties dates this type of exchange to at least a century back, but I would not be surprised if further research would push back its occurrence well before that time. I can think of two reasons why this exchange may have failed to attract the attention of the many ethnographers who worked in

---

[30] This group is made up of all the adult women of the village. They typically get together in the hall next to the church almost every morning except on Sundays and on those days in which other collective activities take priority. Not everybody shows up all the time, but whenever individual needs require differently, each woman freely attends to those. The projects they work on are of two types, either individual mats for their own need or mats for any member needing them at that specific time, like somebody who is going to marry or has a child who will marry, somebody whose number of mats has recently been depleted by the occurrence of an event like a funeral, or somebody who has a specific need like participating in an exchange for *ngatu* like Tupou. According to the size of the mat to be weaved, one, two, or three women work at it. But it must be considered that the actual weaving is the last stage of a long preparation that starts with collecting the pandanus leaves, continues with their cleaning, washing and drying in the sun, and finishes with rolling them up in neat bundles of at least two different colors, a darker brown and a lighter cream. All these activities may be carried out individually or with the help of other women, usually from their own *kāinga* though.

[31] A good description of such an event is included in Evans (2001), but at the time I wrote this piece it had not been published.

Tonga. First, researchers preoccupied mainly with the chiefly traditions might not have noticed this exchange going on at the commoners' level of Tongan society. And second, this exchange is really irregular in its occurrence and long periods may pass before it can take place again; consequently, it may very well not take place even during a prolonged residence in Tonga. This last situation has recently been affected by the improved transportation links between the islands that have made movement of people, regardless of social level, possible, faster and definitely more frequent.[32]

The women who took part in the exchange did not know about the history of this event or the reason behind it. When asked, the only reason they suggested is that some groups of women are 'lazy' and do not like to make *ngatu* 'barkcloth,' but prefer to make *fala* 'mat' (all Tongan women know how to make both). It must be said that some kind of specialization in the production of these two valuable goods was always present among the various island groups. In fact, it was well known that *kie Tonga* 'fine mat' from Ha'apai and Niuatoputapu were the most valuable, the *ngatu* from Tongatapu were the most beautiful, and the *fala* from Vava'u were the most well crafted. Whatever the reason, it is significant to report the modality that this exchange takes and to see how it follows specific patterns of Tongan thinking.

Once the names of the women in Tongatapu who were participating in the exchange were known, the group of women in Vava'u drew names so that specific exchanging partners could be established. The woman from Houma was coupled with two women who belonged to the same family and counted as one exchanging partner (the two women were sisters and had married two brothers). The group also let her know about the quantity and types of mats she had to prepare for the various stages of the exchange. On November 22 the group of women from Tongatapu arrived at the wharf in Neiafu, major town of Vava'u, on board the *Loto Ha'angana*, a privately owned ship that travels on a weekly basis between Tongatapu and Vava'u. They were welcomed by the local group of women and the first exchange of goods called *tu'uta* 'landing' occurred. The woman from Houma gave a *kie Tonga* 'fine mat' of 10 ft. and received a *fuatanga toko hongofulu*[33] 'royal barkcloth.' The women from Tongatapu

---

[32] The navigational skills of Polynesians have already been well established and it is an indisputable fact about Tongans as well. Sione, my adoptive father and *'ulumotu'a* of the family I lived with while in Houma, told me that when he was attending high school in the 1940s he was traveling two or three times a year from Vava'u to Tongatapu, around three hundred kilometers, with a sailing boat in the company of a few other people. The trip was undertaken only by a few privileged individuals, and was still dangerous, unpleasant and unavoidable. The point that I am trying to make is that traveling nowadays is not confined to a specific high stratum of Tongan society neither is it considered a difficult and dangerous enterprise; thus, the frequency of the type of exchange under discussion may have increased in more recent times.

[33] *Fuatanga* are royal *ngatu*, square in form and could be *toko valu* (8 ft.) or *toko hongofulu* (10 ft.) They are now also used by commoners in a changing Tongan society.

spent the night under a tent prepared for the occasion right next to the Catholic cathedral of Neiafu. The place was chosen because it belonged to some of the women from Neiafu participating in the exchange.

The following day, the tent was used to shelter people and partners from the glaring sun and the various partners started the second part of the exchange. The whole procedure was supervised by the *fefine sea* 'chair woman' from Vava'u[34] who also helped to organize the sequence of displays. A group of men played guitars and accompanied the various stages of the event. The first ones to exchange goods were the two *fefine sea*, with the woman from Tongatapu starting first. After two couples had exchanged their goods and finished folding up their goods, the woman from Houma's turn came to show hers. Accompanied by the music and in an atmosphere of intense joy and happiness, the mats and the various presents were exhibited. She also improvised a *ta'olunga* 'solo dance' that pleased the audience so much that they started to *fakapale'i*[35] her and she collected around twenty *pa'anga* 'Tongan dollars.' Her goods were divided into four groups and consisted of the following:

A new *Tu'uta*	2 *fala tekumi manima*	[mat of 15 ft.]
Sino'i katoanga[36]	2 *fala tekumi maua*	[mat of 12 ft.]
'body of feast'	3 *fala tekumi*	[mat of 10 ft.]
	both in exchange for one *launima*[37]	[barkcloth]
	1 *fala uangokumi*	[mat of 20 ft.]
	2 *fala tekumi maua*	[mat of 12 ft.]
	both in exchange for one *launima*	[barkcloth]
Mafana[38]	1 *fala lotaha*	[mat of 15 ft.]
'warming'	1 *ta'ovala putu*	[dark mat for funeral]
	2 *ta'ovala kiekie*	[very fine mat]
	1 *fala lotaha*	[mat of 10 ft.]
	1 sack of mango	(40 kilos)
	1 sack of pineapple	(25 kilos)
	4 pillows *fakatonga*	(made from Tongan cotton[39])
Mavae[40] 'separation'	2 *fala tekumi manima*	[mat of 15 ft.]

[34] This woman was aided by a second *fefine sea* and by a treasurer; this latter looked after financial problems like buying the tent, buying food (i.e., a pig) for the women from Tongatapu to eat during their stay in Vava'u. The group of women from Tongatapu also had their *fefine sea*.

[35] A traditional way of donating money to performers as a sign of appreciation by attaching banknotes to their well-oiled bodies.

[36] This is the real corpus of the exchange, all the others parts are just embellishments.

[37] A 50 ft. long *ngatu*, beautifully decorated with natural dyes. Its length is actually 52 ft. because there are two edges of one foot each.

[38] These are items given out in a sign of friendship and are not 'assigned' by the committee, but are used to please the partner/s in view of a possible future exchange.

[39] This 'cotton' comes from the fruits of the kapok tree (*Ceiba pentandra*), called *vavae tonga* in Tongan.

[40] This is a farewell present.

When the woman from Houma finished with her display, the goods were folded and put aside by her partners, who started their own display. During their presentation the music was playing and the women were dancing on their *ngatu* and accompanying their dance with high thrills and various expressions of joy. Their goods consisted of the following:

A new *tu'uta*	2 *ngatu fualanga toko hongofulu*	[barkcloth of 10 ft.]
Sino'i katoanga	2 *ngatu launima*	[barkcloth of 50 ft.]
Mafana	1 sack of sugar	(30 kilos)
	1 sack of rice	(30 kilos)
	1 sack of flour	(30 kilos)
	1 bag of laundry detergent	
	chocolate powder	(a dozen boxes)
	1 box of biscuits	(20 kilos)
	1 small piece of *ngatu*	(to show the above on)
Mavae	2 *ngatu fualanga toko hongofulu*	[barkcloth of 10 ft.]

When the partners finished their exchanges, it was time to eat. The woman from Houma had been asked by the group to prepare a small *pola* and she received in exchange from the two women a *vala kie kai kie tonga* 'fabric' and fifty *pa'anga*. After eating and having had a little rest, everybody went to the wharf where the *'Olovaha*, a government boat sailing between Tongatapu and Vava'u, was to take the women from Tongatapu back home. On the wharf a final exchange took place during which the woman from Houma gave the following goods:

kape[41]	(3 pieces)	coconuts	(7 pieces)
kumala	(10 pieces)	melons	(2 big ones)
a roasted pig	pineapple	(10 pieces)	corned beef (1 tin of 2 kilos)
otai[42]	(1 bucket)		

and received back the following:

a piece of fabric
fifty *pa'anga*.

The exchange was over, the celebration had been consumed and people were happy but tired after the long day of singing, dancing, and entertaining. Back in the village, I heard at the usual evening talks, that this time the beauty and worth of the *ngatu* from Tongatapu had surpassed the value of the local *fala*. Not only that, but the *mafana* was also greater on the part of the women from Tongatapu than on those from Vava'u. From the lists above, these comments

---

[41] *Alocasia macrorrhiza*, a local aroid plant. A root crop less esteemed than *talo*.
[42] A traditional fruit beverage.

do not seem to be justified, but beyond the actual size of *ngatu* and *fala* (this is one of the few things that is fixed in advance) many other factors have to be considered such as precision of craftsmanship, creativity of design, quality of material used (i.e., dark colors for *ngatu* or *fala*). However, the only exception was the exchange of the woman from Houma whose mats were highly appreciated. Of course, I thought that this was the usual over-appreciation of what is local and known best! But, I must say that by February 1995, a new exchange had been planned for June of the following year and this time only between women from Houma, excluding those from Neiafu, and the same group from Tongatapu. This was the consequence of an explicit request from the group of women from Tongatapu, clear sign that the 'village talk' had been true this time.

Two days after the exchange, the woman from Houma put out to dry in the sun the *ngatu* obtained. It was also a way of showing to the village what she had gotten and how much the value of her *koloa*[43] 'wealth' had increased in the meantime. While I was paying my compliments to the beauty of her newly acquired precious items, she was thinking about the new exchange to be held in June 1996 and maybe of the worth of those *ngatu* that might definitely increase the chances of her daughter Fane getting married. She is the only daughter who is not married yet out of the eight she had (and one son). Then, she called her daughter to come in a hurry and meet me. I felt her thoughts of a Tongan mother linger in the air, "Who knows what this *pālangi* 'white person' may have in his mind when he says that these *ngatu* are extremely beautiful?"

There is a major difference between this event and the two previous ones. The movement of goods from the woman from Houma is not directed towards a common 'center' where other similar movements converge, but is limited to a singular specific 'fixed point,' i.e., drawn partner/s. Without the selection of such a referent point, i.e., drawn partner/s, the actual exchange cannot even take place. It can be argued that such a need for a 'fixed referent point' is more supporting evidence towards a privileged status of the absolute frame of reference in Tongan cultural representation of spatial relationships. After all, using one or more conventional fixed points of reference is the basic characteristic of an absolute frame of reference.

The way in which the goods for the exchange were prepared clearly shows another instance at the village level of the radial arrangements of activities towards a specified 'center' (centripetal), that is, towards the woman from Houma in this case. It was only this type of organization of specific activities within the *lālanga* group that made it possible for her to think of arranging and participating in the exchange. She explicitly told me that since the beginning

---

[43] Tongan word for 'precious things,' but it is also used to indicate 'wealth' and 'dowry.'

she knew that without the help of the *lālanga* group she could not even start to think of being able to prepare all the *fala* she needed. But she was also certain that that support would have come and it turned out to be as she expected. This specific radial representation of cultural relationships is, then, not only informing activities, but also actively participating in their inception, planning, and implementation.

I would like to point out that the three events described are not unique instances of patterns in Tongan behavior. In fact, a pattern similar to the one elicited from the analysis of the *fakaafe* is also present within other events like the feast for a first birthday of a child (Bennardo and Read, 2007). In the same fashion, the visit of the king to Vava'u during the yearly Royal Agricultural Show displays similar patterns for movements of goods as the ones elicited from the description of the *kātoanga* (van der Grijp, 1993). And finally, the beautiful patterns of exchange that take place at the time of Tongan weddings between the two *kāinga* involved clearly resemble those highlighted for the *fetongi* (Evans, 2001). The brief analyses of the three events provided us with some constant thought patterns evinced from specific behavior acted out within the events.

The first and foremost pattern was the establishing of a fixed point of reference other-than-ego, in other words, the identification of a 'center.' The second most relevant factor I highlighted was the consequent centripetal and/or centrifugal flow of goods that follows the first moment in which the 'center'[44] is identified. Finally, I already pointed out that both the establishing of a fixed point of reference and radial relationships among points are strictly related to the absolute FoR, the former as a constituting element (finding one or more fixed points of reference is fundamental for the genesis of an absolute FoR), the latter an instantiation of a specific type of it, that is, the radial subtype. I suggest, then, that this latter subtype of the absolute FoR plays a fundamental role in the generation, i.e., conceptualization and planning, of the very salient Tongan patterns of behavior realized in the three events introduced, the *fakaafe*, the *kātoanga*, and the *fetongi*.

5.8   Conclusion: Tongan culture and spatial cognition

All the analyses conducted in this chapter were about data collected because of the need to find a plausible explanation for the contradictory results of the linguistic investigation (Chapter 3), i.e., preference for the relative FoR, and the cognitive investigation (Chapter 4), preference for the absolute FoR. The

---

[44] The parameters that regulate the eligibility of any individual as 'center' have not been discussed at all. In fact, such a discussion would entail a description of the ethnographic data that goes well beyond the scope of the present work.

ethnographic data presented and the tasks administered provided a wider context, the Tongan cultural milieu, within which that explanation could emerge. A cultural milieu was defined as the merging of three cultural spaces, a physical place, a human place, and a behavioral place. Ethnographic data yielded specific arrangements of objects and people in space that were interpreted as generated by the use of an absolute system of orientation. Specifically, the *kava* ceremony, the *fono* 'village meeting,' and the *misinale* 'donation to church' were the three events in which fixed points of reference (objects and people) were found to be distinctively realized. In addition, movements away from (centrifugal) and/or toward (centripetal) these points/centers were highlighted.

Inspired by these findings, I administered a set of 'cultural' psychological tasks, that is, drawing (about the physical place) and memory (about the human place) tasks. The results of the drawing tasks, village and island, provided a relevant clue towards the discovery of an important aspect of Tongan spatial cognition. Specific drawing strategies, orientation of the maps, and organization of the various landmarks introduced in the maps drawn, all participated in shaping a strong argument on which to suggest that Tongan representations of spatial relationships privilege a radial representation. That is, a specific form of an absolute FoR. The fixed points of reference used were provided by cultural parameters.

I administered 'memory' tasks about salient cultural events, i.e., *fono* 'village meeting' and *misinale* 'donation to church,' to see if that finding would be replicated in the human place. The preference for the radial subtype of the absolute FoR was replicated. Thus, a close relationship between spatial cognition and cultural milieu emerged. Where, in the former, a point in the field of the speaker/cognizer is chosen to be the center of centripetal and centrifugal movements, in the latter culturally salient other-than-ego places (in the drawing tasks) and/or individuals (in the memory tasks) are chosen to be the 'centers' out of/toward which memory of places and/or participants to events are anchored.

Finally, in the behavioral place, I used ethnographic data about three salient exchanges, the *fakaafe*, the *kātoanga*, and the *fetongi*, to see if the found preference for the radial subtype of the absolute FoR could possibly be participating in the generation of those events. I showed in the analyses positive results in this direction, that is, the preference for the radial FoR was seen as necessary in explaining how those events were conceptualized, planned, and implemented. In fact, the three events analyzed show specific characteristics like the establishing of a fixed point of reference and/or 'center' as well as centripetal and centrifugal movement of goods and resources from those 'centers.'

From my ethnography of Tongan space, I was led to administer tasks (drawing/memory), and the results of these tasks led me later to more ethnographic data. A constant finding characterizes this itinerary, the use of the radial subtype of the absolute FoR. That is, I was able to show that radiality is a central aspect of Tongan spatial cognition. This was possible only because fundamental aspects of the Tongan cultural milieu were examined and made an integral part of the administered tasks. In conclusion, then, I can answer positively one of the questions posed at the beginning of the chapter: does Tongan culture lie behind the preference for the absolute FoR elicited in the cognitive tasks? Yes, it does, and it also provides the specific physical-human-behavioral context within which learning the preference can take place.

Part II

Radiality

6   The radiality hypothesis

6.1   Radiality

What is radiality? In its most abstract form, radiality is a structural organization in which a number of vectors share a common origin that may also function as an ending point for all these vectors. In spatial relationships, radiality is the relationship between two points where one of them functions as the origin or goal of the vector that signals the relationship. This origin/goal remains constant over a number of relationships with any number of points. The origin/goal can be ego, i.e., cognizer, viewer, and/or speaker, or a point in the field of ego. I decided to label 'radiality' this latter specific case; that is, a point in the field of ego, i.e., other-than-ego, is chosen to function as the source/goal of a number of relationships with other points in the same field, including ego. Essentially, this type of radiality stands for a foregrounding of other-than-ego while at the same time ego is relegated to the background (Figure 6.1).

This minimal structural organization, a cognitive 'molecule,'[1] is fundamental to human cognition and can be found in a variety of knowledge domains within and across linguistic and cultural boundaries. Why, then, focus on it? Because, I am convinced that in Tongan cognition this 'molecule' plays a fundamental role in the generation and organization of a variety of knowledge domains. It is, in other words, a cultural primitive, i.e., a distinctive feature of Tongan culture. Thus, the privileged role assigned to this cognitive molecule makes Tongans think – and eventually act – in a specific manner about the physical, human, and social world in which they live and which they help to create.

A knowledge structure like the one I just named a cognitive 'molecule' is variously called a frame (Bateson, 1972; Minsky, 1975; Rumelhart, 1980; Fillmore, 1982), a script (Abelson and Schank, 1977), a schema (Bartlett, 1932; Casson; 1983; Brewer, 1984; Mandler, 1984; Lakoff, 1987), a mental model (Craik, 1943; Johnson-Laird, 1983, 1999; Gentner and Stevens, 1983; Shore, 1996), or a

---

[1] For the 'atoms' of this molecule see Section 6.2.2.1 and Lehman and Bennardo (2003), and Bennardo (2004). In brief, they are: ego, ego's field, a vector from ego to a point in ego's field, vectors away from this point to other points in ego's field (one of these points can be ego itself), vectors toward the chosen point in ego's field.

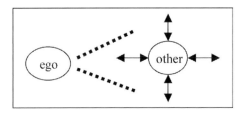

Figure 6.1 Radiality

cultural model (Holland and Quinn, 1987; D'Andrade and Strauss, 1992; Strauss and Quinn, 1997; Quinn, 2005). All of these terms commonly point toward a cognitive structure in which knowledge is organized in such a way as to simplify and interpret the overwhelming synchronic sensorial input and the always growing, diachronic experiential input. These structures operate at various levels, from the simplest, e.g., seeing the contour of an object, understanding the meaning of a word, or interpreting a configuration of facial parts as a smile, to the most complex, e.g., seeing the complexity of a busy street, understanding a lengthy speech, or evaluating the behavior of self and/or others. Once in place, these cognitive structures are used to reason about the world and eventually motivate action/s in it (Johnson-Laird, 1980; D'Andrade and Strauss, 1992).

In D'Andrade's (1989) words, "a cognitive schema that is intersubjectively shared by a social group" (p. 809) is called a cultural model. A relevant feature of cultural models "is that their structure corresponds to the structure of what they represent" (Johnson-Laird, 1999: 525). Besides, cultural models can be nested into each other, that is, "a given schema may serve as a piece of another schema" (Holland and Quinn, 1987: 33). The first feature informs the relevance attributed in this work to the investigation of the Tongan cultural milieu. This milieu is what is being learned and represented; thus it needs to be extensively and appropriately known if we want to investigate and highlight salient characteristics of its representation. The second feature makes possible the existence of 'special' models that participate in the construction of a number of other models, some kind of building blocks for a few/many other models (D'Andrade, 1987). Borrowing from Shore (1996: 53), I call the suggested cognitive molecule named radiality, a 'foundational' cultural model.

My proposal for radiality as a Tongan foundational cultural model entails that a number of knowledge domains are organized in a similar way: a point is chosen in the field (i.e., domain of knowledge) of an individual and relationships are expressed as toward or away from that point. The 'cultural' part of the foundational model entails that the cross-domain organization is shared among members of a community (see Holland and Quinn, 1987; D'Andrade, 1989; D'Andrade and Strauss, 1992; Shore, 1996; Kronenfeld, 1996, 2008; Strauss and Quinn, 1997; Quinn, 2005), in this case, Tongans. Sharing a foundational cultural model does not make a description of Tongan culture homogeneous.

On the contrary, it points toward a generative process that makes possible uniformity and/or variety of cultural instantiations in individuals.

I discuss now some data about Tongan language and the Tongan cultural milieu which corroborate my claim. The data about the representations of spatial relationships were already introduced in the preceding chapters and I only summarize them. The data about other domains of knowledge, i.e., religion and navigation, are introduced for the first time. At the end of the discussion, I delineate a picture of Tongan radiality that informs the remaining parts of the book.

6.2   Radial organizations in the representations of spatial relationships

In Chapters 3–5, I introduced ways in which spatial relationships are represented linguistically, cognitively, and in memory of culturally salient physical spaces and human events. Radial organizations emerged from the way in which Tongan language represents spatial relationships, and specifically, in the meaning and use of directionals and frames of reference. When spatial relationships are represented mentally in long-term memory, a preference for the absolute frame of reference was detected, and in particular, a preference for the radial subtype of the absolute frame of reference. Similarly, when physical, human, and behavioral places are stored in memory, Tongans organize relationships in a radial manner.

6.2.1   Radial organizations of spatial relationships represented linguistically (directionals, translation FoR, and absolute FoR)

In Bennardo (1999) I discussed in detail the conceptual content of Tongan directionals and their relationship to an ancestral Melanesian system of directionals. All five Tongan directionals are found in a post-verbal position and are very frequently used in any type of discourse. I focus here on only two of the Tongan directionals, *mai* and *atu*. These are the core meanings I proposed for them: *mai* 'towards center,' and *atu* 'away from center' (Figure 6.2). Both *mai* and *atu* are used with two meanings: *mai 1* as 'toward speaker' or *mai 2* 'toward other,' and *atu 1* as 'away from speaker toward addressee' or *atu 2* 'away from other' (Figure 6.3).

In Figure 6.3, I indicate that the conceptual spatial organizations of *mai 2* and *atu 2* represent a close replication of what I called 'radiality.' In other words, a point in the field of ego is chosen as a reference point out of which and toward which relationships are established. The intentional content of *mai* and *atu* appears to be structured by the cognitive 'molecule' I labeled radiality.[2]

---

[2] My argument here resembles very closely that of a lexical 'frame' as introduced by Fillmore (1982).

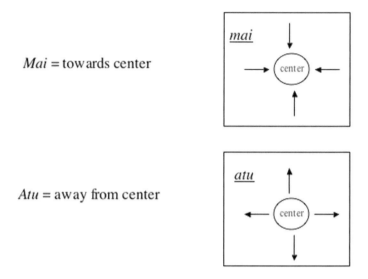

Mai = towards center

Atu = away from center

Figure 6.2 Basic meanings of *mai* and *atu*

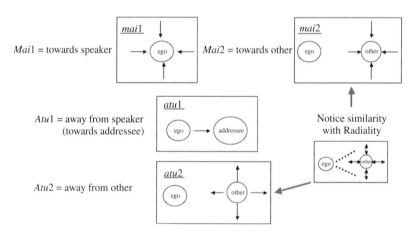

*Mai*1 = towards speaker

*Mai*2 = towards other

*Atu*1 = away from speaker
(towards addressee)

Notice similarity
with Radiality

*Atu*2 = away from other

Figure 6.3 Two meanings for *mai* and *atu*

In Chapter 3, I presented evidence for a Tongan preferential use of the translation subtype of the relative FoR. This FoR entails the appearance of an object
(typically without an intrinsic orientation, e.g., a tree) in the 'front' part of the
oriented field of ego. The front axis of the relative FoR built on ego is thus split
into two parts, and the part beyond the object is described by using the term
'front,' while the part toward ego is described by using the word 'back.' The
left and right side are the same as those for ego (Figure 6.4).

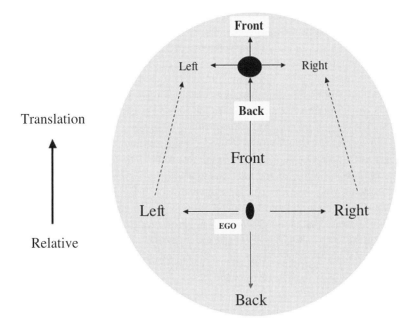

Figure 6.4 The translation subtype of the relative FoR

In the same chapter, I discussed the frequent use of the absolute FoR in large-scale space. The two most frequent subtypes are the one-axis *'uta–tahi* 'land–sea' and *kolo–'uta* 'town–inland.' That is, two points are chosen in the field of ego and the consequent axis joining them is used to establish spatial relationships. I also reported uses of the four cardinal points subtype, as well as the use of the one-point subtype (later named 'radial'). This latter, choosing only one point in the field of ego, is used in both large-scale and small-scale space. Also used in both types of space is the intrinsic FoR (axes centered on an object – with its own oriented field – in the field of ego).

In summary, while both the intrinsic FoR and the translation subtype of the relative FoR are used without any specific preference for type of space, the relative FoR is preferred in small-scale space, while the absolute is preferred in large-scale space. What can we conclude? Overall it appears that the focus on an other-than-ego object in the field of ego (translation subtype of the relative FoR, intrinsic FoR, and subtypes of the absolute FoR) is privileged over the focus on ego (relative FoR). In terms of overall frequencies of use in language, what really tilts the balance toward the focus on an object in the field of ego is the frequent use of the translation subtype of the relative FoR. This FoR shares features with the relative FoR – rooted on ego, same transverse axis (left–right) – and with the intrinsic FoR – focus on other-than-ego object, sagittal axis different from ego's one. In other words, unlike the intrinsic FoR, the translation FoR does not have an oriented field completely independent from ego's field. Similarly, contrary to the relative FoR, the translation FoR does not depend completely on the axes centered on ego. Halfway between the relative FoR and the intrinsic FoR, the translation FoR demonstrates the saliency of other-than-ego, oriented and not-oriented objects in the field of ego.

Finally, and similar to the suggestion in Figure 6.3, essential radiality features are shared between the translation subtype of the relative FoR and the radial subtype of the absolute FoR. They both share ego's field without having one of their own, they both are focused on an other-than-ego not-oriented object in the field of ego, they both establish spatial relationships with ego or a second object in the field of ego as toward or away from the focus object. In other words, it appears that, when expressed linguistically, spatial knowledge is organized preferentially in a radial fashion. That is, an other-than-ego point is chosen in the field of ego and relationships are established towards and away from this point.

6.2.2   *Radial organizations of spatial relationships represented mentally (absolute FoR, map drawing, and radial FoR)*

In Chapter 4, I presented and discussed the results of a number of cognitive tasks intended to collect information about a preference for a specific FoR in the mental representations of spatial relationships. The results pointed unequivocally towards a preference for the absolute FoR. Since the tasks were about small-scale space, they contrasted with the preference for the relative FoR detected in the same type of space for the linguistic representations of spatial relationships. Besides, because of the way the tasks were conceived and conducted, the results could not distinguish between subtypes (i.e., four cardinal points, one axis, one point) of the absolute FoR. A clear indication of which subtype of the absolute FoR is privileged in the Tongan mind was provided by the results of the drawing tasks introduced in Chapter 5. The organization of the drawings of the village and of the island, together with the strategies used demonstrate how the radial (one point) subtype of the absolute FoR is privileged by Tongans to represent geographical space.

In Bennardo (2004), I conducted a conceptual analysis of the various frames of reference that led to the suggestion of a typology. The occasion that motivated the analysis was a proposal advanced by Levinson (1996a, 2003) that suggests the untranslatability of information between frames. When an FoR is realized linguistically, the information coded in one FoR (e.g., relative FoR: 'the ball is behind me') is not translatable into another (e.g., absolute FoR: 'the ball is south of me'). My conclusion, instead, was that untranslatability only holds between linguistically instantiated FoRs, while at the conceptual level FoRs are nested into each other.

6.2.2.1   The conceptual apparatus

A computational approach to the general architecture of cognition was adopted to arrive at the set of spatial concepts suggested by Lehman and Bennardo (2003). Within this approach, cognition is conceived as computational (cf. Ballim and Wilks, 1992), thus generatively 'abstract.' Only the characteristics of the computational, or, relational spaces that make up what we call 'cognition' are reiterated in each cognitive module and not the specific characteristics of the substantive content that instantiate these 'abstract' relationships.[3] A computational approach to cognition can be proposed by accepting compositionality without embracing a Fregean (logico-positivist) point of view and by turning to the domain of mathematics (e.g., algebra and geometry). In mathematics the primitives of a system are a set of axioms. These axioms generate indefinitely many theorems and each theorem can establish a foundation for yet another theorem. Furthermore, theorems may share parts with other theorems in a redundant manner. The set of relational properties of any cognitive system could be, then, nothing but a theorem derived from a set/s of other theorems. Such a system is compositional by definition.

The linguistic analyses conducted on English spatial prepositions, and languages like Burmese, Thai, Italian, and Tongan (Polynesian) in Lehman and Bennardo (2003) yielded the following set of spatial concepts:[4]

State: Object; Place or Locus; Neighborhood: Vicinity, Contact, Interiority;
Motion: Time; Direction; Path: Beginning*, Body*, End, (Direction)*;
Verticality: Angle: Unit, Quantity (+ or –);
Horizontality: Visibility, Left or Right;
Centre;
Part.
(*all conceptual content of Vector)

Some concepts are not primitives, but rely on other concepts of the same group to function as their axioms. This is the minimal set of axioms that is necessary to account for the theorems (e.g., prepositions, directionals, spatial nouns) that make up the representations of spatial relationships in the languages analyzed.

The concept of Object is used with the meaning of any entity existing in a possible world, either concrete or abstract, e.g., table, idea. The place of an Object is the actual amount of Space that it occupies. In other words, a Place is the set of all points within the boundary of an Object (including the boundary points). The Locus of an Object in projective geometry is defined as the collapse of a Place onto any of its interior points. Then, a Locus is a neighborhood

[3] Hirschfeld and Gelman (1994) draw a similar distinction between 'module' and 'domain.'
[4] From now on a concept is indicated by initial capital letter.

of possible projection points, the lower limit being one point. Thus, while a Place is defined by the size, shape, and specific geometry of the Object, a Locus is not and can be arbitrarily reduced to a point.

The concept of Neighborhood includes the concept of Vicinity (more than zero distance) between two Objects, the concept of Contact (zero distance) between them, and the concept of Interiority, or one Object in the interior of another. The Neighborhood's border is pragmatically determined. These three concepts (Object, Place or Locus, and Neighborhood) make up the concept of State.

The concept of Motion is an ordered sequence (consequently, with a Direction) of Places (of an Object) in Time, bounded by two Places without either left or right directionality in a disjunctive fashion and never missing both. The concept of Path, instead, is a geometrical (purely spatial) description of motion 'abstracted' from Motion. The focus is not on the moving Object, but on the ordered sequence of Places, now considered as Loci. The concept of Motion is inextricably tied to Time, but the concept of Path is partially free from it. In fact, we can indicate a Path at $Time_1$ and then indicate another Path at $Time_2$ and state that they are the same without incurring a contradiction as would happen if the two parts of the comparison were two instances of Motion. The instances of time used in the construction of a Path are not unique, but they are repeatable.

Two features that Path also shares with Motion are ordered sequence and boundedness. The interior points of a Path are an ordered sequence of Loci with a Direction, that is, they are Vectors with a finite magnitude. This magnitude we call its Body and consists of a set of Loci whose members may at a limit be one, thus overlapping with the first constitutive Locus. The boundary of a Path consists of two Loci, a Vector that lacks left directionality (Beginning), and one that lacks right directionality (End). Object and Place (axioms of State) participate in the construction of Motion. Locus, instead, participates only in the construction of Path. Thus, the difference between Place and Locus is used to separate the temporally bound Motion from the spatially bound Path.

Verticality and Horizontality were not analyzed in as much detail as State and Motion, and only some conceptual components are indicated. First, Object, Locus, and Vector (a Beginning, a Body or magnitude, and a Direction) participate in their composition. The concepts indicated for Verticality are Angle and Quantity (Increasing or Decreasing). The instantiation of one or other type of Quantity will determine the 'up' or 'down' Direction of a Vector. Angle and Quantity are also part of the concept of Horizontality together with those of Visibility and Left or Right. Visibility contributes to the construction of a 'front–back axis.' After this, Left or Right can be constructed. Finally, the two concepts of Center and Part were added after the analyses of Tongan directionals and spatial nouns (Bennardo, 1999, 2000b).

Table 6.1 *The conceptual content of FoRs (from Bennardo, 2004: 105)*

Concept/Axiom	Relative			Intrinsic	Absolute
	Basic	Translation	Reflection		
Locus	X	X	X	X	X
Object	1 + V*	2 + V	2 + V	2 + V	1/2+2/4+V
Path	1	2	2	2	3/5 or 4/6
Vector	6	6	6	10	6
Verticality	X	X	X	X	X
Horizontality	X	X	X	X	X
Orthogonality	X	X	X	X	X
Visibility			X		
Part				X	
Animacy***				X***	
Habitual Direction of Motion***				X***	
Habitual Use***				X***	
Choice Function**	X	X	X	X	X
Repeat Function**		X	X	X	X

* V is the viewer or cognizer or speaker.
** These two are cognitive processes.
*** Only one is necessary.

6.2.2.2 The conceptual content of the various FoRs

The conceptual apparatus just delineated was used to determine the conceptual content of the various FoRs. I am not replicating here the discussion in Bennardo (2004), and I am only introducing Table 6.1, in which I summarize these conceptual contents. A capital X indicates the presence of a concept in the construction of an FoR. For the concepts of Object, Path and Vector a number indicates how many times the concept is minimally used.

The content of Table 6.1 shows how the conceptual axiomatic content of the basic relative FoR is properly contained in its entirety in all the others, both subtypes (translation and reflection) and types (intrinsic and absolute). The intrinsic and the absolute are both derived from the relative, although not in an ordered sequence. The relative FoR, then, is suggested as an axiom for both the intrinsic and the absolute ones. The intrinsic and absolute FoRs are made of two different sets of concepts. The intrinsic FoR expresses more attention to the nature of the Object functioning as ground (see the participation of the concepts of Part, Animacy, Habitual Direction of Motion, Habitual Use in Table 6.1). The absolute FoR, instead, expresses greater attention to the nature of the field (see the participation of a greater number of Objects and Paths in Table 6.1).

These findings are perfectly congruent with those of Baayen and Danziger (1994) and Levinson (2003) regarding a preferred use of the intrinsic FoR by speakers of Mayan languages, where an extremely elaborate vocabulary also exists for describing parts of objects. Similar congruency can be highlighted with the findings of Levinson (2003) concerning the preferred use of the absolute FoR by speakers of Australian Aboriginal languages where a very elaborate system of naming landmarks in one's environment has also been reported.

Finally, I looked closely at the issue of 'untranslatability' among the various FoRs suggested in Levinson (2003: 57–9). When we consider FoRs as instantiated into linguistic expressions, it is true that in principle only two cases of translation are possible from one FoR to another (i.e., from either absolute or relative to intrinsic). Do we deduce that there is 'untranslatability' among FoRs at the conceptual level? The results of our brief discussion point towards a negative answer. In fact, the conceptual content of the relative FoR was suggested as an axiom for the intrinsic and the absolute ones. Thus, if at the linguistic level we find 'untranslatability' between FoRs, at the conceptual level we find 'nesting.' Besides, the direction of the translatability from relative and absolute to intrinsic correlates with one independent field contained in the former versus two independent fields contained in the latter.

6.2.2.3 *Subtypes of the absolute FoR and a new typology of FoRs*

In Table 6.1, I did not include the conceptual content of the radial subtype of the absolute FoR (Bennardo, 1996). The discovery of this FoR led me to a reexamination of the typology of FoRs. In particular, I took a closer look at all three subtypes of the absolute FoR: the cardinal points, the single axis, and the radial. For each of the three subtypes there are two cases to be considered. The first is when the ground is the viewer, e.g., "X is north of me." The second is when the ground is an Object different from the viewer, e.g., "X is north of Y." Each case yields a different conceptual content.

In radial 1, we need a Center that is the viewer and an Object (figure). A Path from the viewer to the Object is also required as well as (minimally) a Vector made up of the Body of a Path and its End (centrifugal movement) or Beginning (centripetal movement). Either the End or the Beginning of this Path would be co-indexed with the Center. In radial 2, we must add a second Object, which will function as Center, and a Path that is used to determine this Center (or second Object). The difference between the two cases is crucial. Choosing a Center different from viewer makes possible the construction of a second field different from the one constructed around the viewer.

The conceptual content for the single axis subtype consists, in the first case, of one Object (Figure) plus two Objects (the two ends of the axis), the viewer, three Paths (from the viewer to the three Objects), and six Vectors (up, down,

Table 6.2 *Conceptual content for types of absolute FoR (from Bennardo, 2004: 106)*

Subtype of absolute FoR	Concept		
	Object	Path	Vector
Radial 1*	1 + V**	1	1
Radial 2*	2 + V	2	1
Single axis 1	1 + 2 + V	3	6
Single axis 2	2 + 2 + V	4	6
Cardinal points 1	1+ 4 + V	5	6
Cardinal points 2	2 + 4 + V	6	6

* Notice that this FoR does not have an up–down axis.

** V is the viewer or cognizer or speaker.

front, back, left, and right). In the second case, an Object for the new ground Object and a Path for its construction are added. A new field different from the viewer's is not constructed. The conceptual content for a cardinal points subtype consists, in the first case, of one Object (Figure) plus four Objects (the cardinal points), the viewer, five Paths (from the viewer to the five Objects), and six Vectors (up, down, front, back, left, and right). An Object is added for the new ground Object and a Path for its construction. A new field different from the viewer's is not constructed.

In Table 6.2, the conceptual content of the radial subtype is the simplest. The contents of the two radial subtypes are also simpler than the content of the basic subtype of the relative FoR in Table 6.1. Consequently, the axiomatic relation between the relative, the intrinsic, and the absolute FoRs needs some further attention.

In discussing the relationships between the types and subtypes of FoR, three parameters are considered. The first is the magnitude of the conceptual content, that is, the number of concepts necessary to derive each theorem. The second is the reference that will be made to axiomatic relationships. When the content of an FoR is completely contained in another, then the former will be considered an axiom of the latter. The third is the emergent properties that each FoR displays. Namely, it must be considered if an FoR is based on the construction of one or two fields.

The minimal conceptual content and the construction of only one field associated with the radial 1 subtype of the absolute FoR make it the choice as the most basic. This FoR, then, is an axiom for all the other types and subtypes. Its great simplicity makes it highly context-bound and hence very unlikely to be the only one that any individual/culture will have. Nonetheless, it represents a minimal stage of spatial organization assigned to the external world. Evidence from languages around the world suggests that this system is always used, i.e., in demonstrative systems.

Looking for an FoR at the second stage of complexity, or more precisely, the first theorem derived from a set of axioms whose content is at a limit only the radial 1 axiom, we are faced with two options. The first is to choose the radial 2 subtype of the absolute FoR, simple in conceptual content, though it uses two fields. The second is the basic relative FoR that is more complex conceptually (it needs six Vectors instead of one), but uses only one field. A decision is not strictly necessary at this juncture; both options are viable. Empirically, there are language speakers that choose to use prevalently one option only (e.g., English speakers choose a basic relative FoR), and others that choose both (e.g., Tongan speakers).

I stated that the relative FoR functions as an axiom for the absolute and the intrinsic FoR, and for two subtypes of the relative FoR. These latter keep the single field feature, but increase their conceptual content because of their complex treatment of the front–back axis. The single axis and cardinal points subtypes of the absolute FoR and the intrinsic FoR are obtained in substantially different ways. The two absolute FoRs represent an increased conceptual content from the relative FoR and use a single field. This is confirmed by the fact that they both use the vertical axis. The radial 1 and 2 subtypes did not have it in their conceptual content.

The intrinsic FoR is obtained by an increased conceptual complexity due to two other factors (besides the addition of the vertical axis). The first is a closer attention devoted to the Object that functions as figure (this Object is oriented). The second is the construction of two fields (the viewer's and the figure's). We have seen that the construction of two fields is part of the conceptual content of the radial 2 subtype of the absolute FoR. Then I suggest that the conceptual content of the intrinsic FoR is derived in a complex way from the basic subtype of the relative FoR, from the radial 2 subtype of the absolute FoR, and from conceptual characteristics of the Object.

The arrows in Figure 6.5 indicate that the FoR receiving the content of another FoR treats this latter as an axiom of its conceptual content. Further conceptual material is added at each stage, hence the necessity of a new label for that particular type of FoR.

The new typology of FoRs in Figure 6.5 assigns a central role to the relative FoR, that is, it plays an axiomatic role in respect to the intrinsic and the absolute FoRs. The radial 1 and radial 2 represent another novelty for the typology. The appearance of radial 1 basically indicates that a further level of abstraction is needed to account for a fundamental stage in the construction of FoRs. Ego starts by conceptualizing the world as centered on itself and vectorially coming out of itself, thus creating a field that surrounds ego (the boundary of this field is provided by the capacity of the sensorial input, e.g., how far one

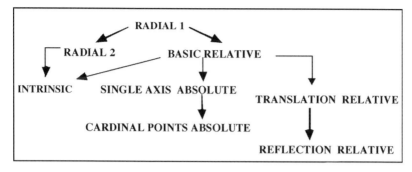

Figure 6.5 A typology of frames of reference (from Bennardo, 2004: 107)

can see, hear, smell). In this field, other independent Objects appear and are recognized. Some display movement not related to ego, thus possessing their own fields (see Mandler, 2004). This realization is conducive to the construction of the radial 2 FoR. Simultaneously, ego's field is constructed as oriented by the incoming perceptual direction dependent on the 'oriented' body humans possess (e.g., direction of face, locomotion). Thus, the basic relative FoR is constructed. This new typology, in other words, is also a representation of a developmental process that reaches its end when all FoRs are made available to human cognition. Which one is chosen to be preferentially used either for linguistic or mental representations of spatial relationships is a matter confined to specific cultural and/or linguistic groups.

Why do I still call radial 1 and radial 2 subtypes of the absolute FoR when the former actually appears to precede developmentally the construction of the latter? Because they all provide an 'absolute' orientation independent of the context of speaking. That is, they organize spatial relationships in a way that can be understood without being in the place where these relationships exist. "X's house is *toward the church*" (radial 1 FoR), "X's house is *away from town*" (radial 2 FoR), "X's house is *south of the city*" (absolute FoR) are three clarifying linguistic realizations in English. And because all three imply the choice of a point/s (i.e., Object/s) in the field of ego (only one for radial 1 and radial 2 subtypes, two points for the single axis subtype, and four points for the cardinal points subtype) and the establishing of relationships either toward or away from that/those point/s. However, the radial 2 subtype is the only one that uses two fields (ego's and Object's). Thus, the fact that it is a preferred way by Tongans to organize spatial relationships becomes even more salient, i.e., this preference points toward a continuous acknowledgment of other-than-ego, namely, the Object in ego's field.

Why is this new typology of FoRs relevant to the present discussion? Because it highlights the fundamental role played by the two radial organizations of spatial relationships in the construction of the three major types of FoRs, relative, intrinsic, and absolute. Besides, radiality, especially as exemplified by the radial 2 FoR, appears to be a step, a potential one, in the developmental sequence that characterizes human learning to represent space. Thus, it is extremely likely that it represents a mental organization of spatial relationships universally available. Nonetheless, possibly, not typically though, few cultural/linguistic groups make it the system to privilege over the others available (see Hill, 1982; Bennardo, 1996; Cablitz, 2006). In other words, radiality is a universally available cognitive knowledge structure (system/FoR), but it is preferred in representing spatial relationships only by a few languages and cultures, including Tongan.

6.2.3   Radial organizations of spatial relationships in memory (fono, misinale, and exchanges)

The Tongan cultural milieu was investigated in Chapter 5 in an attempt to see if it played a role in the detected preference for the radial subtype of the absolute FoR in representing spatial relationships mentally. I defined a cultural milieu as a physical, human, and behavioral place. Specific strategies to remember features of these three types of place were detected. All involved the establishing of a focal other-than-ego point, and subsequent relationships expressed either away from or toward this point.

The Tongan physical place is typically organized radially as exemplified in the spatial arrangements of people in the *kava* drinking ceremony and the *fono* 'village meeting.' The highest ranking individual sits 'in front of' the *kava* bowl or 'at the front' of the meeting space and everybody else sits away from him/her in a descending ranking order. Similarly, people's memory of formal events of this type (e.g., *fono, misinale*) – both people's presence and their spatial arrangement – is skewed toward the higher status individual present. This latter represents the focal point chosen in ego's field toward which and away from which all other participants are remembered.

In memory for culturally salient behavior as that instantiated in a variety of exchanges e.g., *fakaafe, kātoanga,* and *fetongi*, the same radial pattern clearly emerged as the fundamental principle informing a number of behaviors essential to the realization of those events. In these exchanges as well, focusing on other-than-ego is the basic characteristic of the complex thought patterns employed in the realizations of those events. Thus, I posited a mental representation in a radial manner of the events as they transpired from the way they are remembered. In sum, the Tongan cultural milieu is shaped by the form of these representations. But, at the same time, it contributes in a relevant way to the construction of these representations in that fashion. The cultural milieu, in other words, contributes to the context out of which representations of that same context are constructed. In a circular fashion, these representations in their turn contribute to the shaping of the context.

6.3   Radial organizations and traditional knowledge domains

Thus far, I have argued that radiality represents a preferred fundamental organizational principle in the Tongan domain of space, and specifically, spatial relationships. I was also able to demonstrate how the Tongan cultural milieu – conceived as geographical, human, and behavioral places – provides the essential context for the acquisition of such a preference. This latter fact led me to inquire about other domains of knowledge. Basically, I asked, is radiality also present in the organization of other domains of knowledge or is it restricted only to space? If radiality in the representation of spatial relationships is strictly linked to the Tongan cultural milieu, is it possible that other domains of knowledge are affected in a similar way?

In order to answer these questions, I had to decide which other Tongan domains of knowledge to investigate. First, I focused on two domains of knowledge such as traditional religious beliefs and navigational practices. Both represent knowledge that is either not believed or not practiced any more. Nonetheless, traditional knowledge, especially of the saliency of navigation for Polynesians and religion for any culture, is not simply erased from the mind (or collective memory) of a community in one or even more than one generation. Thus, I concluded that it would be relevant if radial organizations were to be detected in these two domains as well. Second, my attention fell on the ontological domain of possession because Polynesian languages express it in a dual manner. That is, all possessives have two forms with a focus on either the possessor or the possessed object. However, other proposals also exist about the interpretation of these two forms. Consequently, I chose to investigate this domain convinced that I could find some evidence for radiality. I report about this investigation in Chapter 7.

Third, it is well known that in many languages lexemes realizing spatial relationships are also used for temporal relationships. It was then apparent to me that I had to investigate the ontological domain of time to see if the preference elicited for the representation of spatial relationships would be also found in the representation of temporal relationships. I report about this investigation also in Chapter 7. Fourth, in any cultural milieu, the role of kinship is always of paramount significance. Thus, the mentioned relationship between radiality and the Tongan cultural milieu should have a similar relevance in the domain of kinship relationships. Therefore, in collaboration with Dwight Read, I conducted an algebraic investigation of Tongan kinship terminology. The intention was to highlight the inherent logic of the system so that a specific – we hypothesized radial – cognitive organization could be detected as underlying the kinship terminology system. I report on this investigation in Chapter 8.

Finally, a substantial part of any cultural milieu is represented by a large variety of social relationships. Which ones characterize the Tongan milieu and how are those relationships mentally represented? The decision to answer these questions led me to the adoption of a multidisciplinary methodological strategy that employed protocols and analyses from linguistics, cognitive science, and social network analysis. I devote the third part of this book (Part III) to my investigation of the domain of social relationships. In the remainder of this chapter, I briefly report on the findings of the first two domains investigated: religion and navigation.

6.3.1   Radial organizations and traditional religious beliefs

At the core of traditional Polynesian and Tongan religious belief systems is the concept of *mana* 'power' (Handy, 1927; Gifford, 1929; Williamson, 1933). Described either as substance or process (Keesing, 1984; Valeri, 1985), as cause or effect (Hogbin, 1936; Firth, 1940), *mana* always implies coming into contact with supernatural forces by means of another human being – usually a chief – who acts as mediator. The supernatural 'power' radiates out of this person and brings good to individuals, to the land, and to crops if a number of procedures are followed, otherwise misfortune results. Thus, the practice of 'binding' and its relationship with the concept of *tapu* 'taboo' can be understood (see Gifford, 1929; but also Shore, 1989).

I suggest, then, that radiality – in this case, radiating power from other-than-ego – is an essential and pervasive concept in the traditional (i.e., pre-contact) Tongan domain of religion. It may be argued that since Christian religions have by now replaced the local religious belief systems in Tonga,[5] this fact does not provide any further support to my hypothesis. On the contrary, I believe that this fundamental way of conceptualizing the religious domain is still in place. Witness to this is a variety of stories and events I collected in my field notes, and in particular the one that I am reporting here.

In March 1995, after a long period of residence in Tonga, I left the village where I had resided for almost a year (over three separate periods). A new Wesleyan minister had just arrived to take care of the village spiritual life and church and he too joined the farewell. In January 1997, I returned to Tonga and again spent several weeks in 'my' village. I was surprised to find that a new minister was in charge of the community and asked about the one I had left

---

[5] The conversion to Christianity started at the beginning of the nineteenth century and was completed by the end of that same century (Lātūkefu, 1974).

behind less than two years before (Wesleyan ministers are usually appointed for four years to a community and sometimes their appointment is renewed). The first type of answers I received were vague enough to trigger my curiosity.

After many questions and a lot of patience over several weeks, I found out that the minister had been removed from his position and transferred to another village. The request for such an unusual event came from some members of the village who believed that the minister had brought bad 'luck' to the community; "he lacked *mana*," I was told. This episode principally bears witness to the astute management of the Wesleyan Church in Tonga, which acknowledges local complaints even if based on 'traditional' belief. At the same time, it supports my claim that belief systems are not easily erased within a few generations, even if conversion to Christianity appears on the surface to have transformed people's way of life and thinking.

In conclusion, the complex belief system that characterized pre-contact Tonga was based on the concept of *mana*, "precontact Polynesia religion was an economy of *mana* in which generative powers were appropriated, channeled, transformed, and bound" (Shore, 1989: 143). A fundamental part of the conceptual content of *mana* overlaps completely with that of radiality. In other words, the concept of *mana* entails that of radiality in which power radiates out of other-than-ego. This way of conceptualizing essential religious ideas is still found in contemporary Tongan spiritual life, at least conceptually, and in some cases it even generates behavior.

6.3.2   Radial organizations and traditional navigation

Polynesian navigation has been described at length (Buck, 1938; Golson, 1963; Lewis, 1964, 1972, 1974; Sharp, 1964a, 1964b; Hilder, 1965; Gladwin, 1970; Finney, 1976; Hutchins, 1983; Kyselka, 1987; Feinberg, 1988; Turnbull, 1994). Hutchins (1995), after a review of various interpretations, states:

All navigation computations make use of frames of reference … Here there are three elements to be related to one another: the vessel, the islands, and the directional frame … one can have the vessel and the direction frame move while the islands stay stationary (the Western solution) or one can have the vessel and the directional frame stationary while the islands move (the Micronesian solution) … In the Micronesian case, the directional frame is defined by the star points of the sidereal compass, and the star points are fixed. (1995: 92)

The imaginary island used in navigational practices, or what Hutchins is referring to as "moving island," had been called a "phantom island" by Gladwin (1970). Hutchins (1995) also shows that such a point (not ego, but in its field) is a necessary computational mental device to assure successful navigation. This imagined fixed point of reference combines with the other fixed points of reference provided by the sidereal compass, i.e., the star points, to allow the navigator to compute the necessary positioning of the vessel along the journey, both in direction, distance from origin, and time passed. In other words, fixed points of reference, e.g., star points and a "phantom island," chosen in the field of the navigator are used to compute movement to and away from them.

Hutchins is describing Micronesian navigation, but it is well accepted in the literature that Micronesian and Polynesian navigation were very similar (Lewis, 1964, 1972, 1974: 134; Turnbull, 1994: 133). Consequently, I use Hutchins' conclusions to argue for a further presence of radiality in a knowledge domain that is one of the most salient in the recent past – the last Tongan navigator died around forty years ago (Hilder, 1965) – and the distant past of Polynesians.

6.4   Conclusion

Traditional religious beliefs, and navigation are certainly salient domains of knowledge for Tongans. The fact that I found radial organizations in the representations of these types of knowledge is important. It makes me feel even more confident that my hypothesis of radiality as a foundational cultural model organizing several domains of knowledge is appropriate. Based on preferential organization of knowledge in the spatial domain, homologies can be found in other domains, even in some not necessarily linked to space.

However, I did not feel satisfied with the amount of support collected, due also to the nature of my hypothesis/claim. Claiming that a specific organizing of knowledge in the spatial domain is replicated, thus assuming generative power, in many other domains needs more than the evidence I have presented so far. Minimally, other fundamental ontological domains besides space need to be found in line with the claim, for example possession, and more necessarily, time, which is typically linguistically realized in the same way. Furthermore, since I demonstrated that the Tongan cultural milieu provides the context within which the radiality preference is experienced, acquired, and implemented, other types of critical knowledge acquired in the same context, e.g., kinship relationships and social relationships, need also to be found in line with my claim.

In the following two chapters, I introduce the extensive research I conducted in three domains of Tongan knowledge: possession, time, and kinship terminology. I devote a whole section of this book, Part III, to the investigation of the domain of social relationships. This latter is an extremely complex domain and it required the acquisition of a substantial quantity of linguistic, cognitive, and social network data. It was only when this data was analyzed that a clear picture emerged about the generative process at the root of the domain. Thus, I could draw some conclusion about the common foundation for the various domains of knowledge investigated.

7   Radiality in possession and time

7.1   Radiality and possession

In Bennardo (2000c), I reported on a conceptual analysis of Tongan possession that I am summarizing here. Analyses of Oceanic (and Polynesian) A- and O-possession[1] typically distinguish between the two types by making reference to the nature of the relationship between possessor and possessed: dominant and subordinate possession (Biggs, 1969; Pawley, 1973; Lynch, 1982), or control and not-control possession (Wilson, 1976, 1982), or alienable and inalienable possession (Lichtenberk, 1985). In 1996, Taumoefolau proposed a fascinating analysis of Tongan possessives in which she rejected the validity of these analyses and approached the Tongan A/O-possessive dichotomy by using metaphor and prototype theory.

There are two types of possessives in Tongan, those that precede the noun and those that follow it (this is true for personal pronouns as well) (see Churchward, 1953: chapters 13 and 20; and Shumway, 1988: 441–4). For each type there are A-forms and O-forms. I limit my discussion only to the preposed possessives. The A- and O-forms for the preposed possessives in Tongan are listed in Table 7.1.

The morphological structure of the possessives in Table 7.1 comprises *'e* followed by the various forms of the personal pronouns for the A-forms and *ho* followed by the same personal pronouns for O-forms. Regarding the second person forms, Churchward (1953: 137) gives the derivations in Table 7.2.

The initial structural form of the possessive is hypothesized as being composed of three parts: the article *he*, the possessive marker (either *'a* or *'o*), and the personal pronoun (Churchward, 1953: 135). Various phonological processes – such as elision and assimilation – occurred later to arrive at the current forms (see Churchward, 1953: 136). The apparent contrast between the initial

---

[1] Oceanic (and Polynesian) possession is characterized by the so-called A- and O-forms. That is, each possessive (e.g., 'my') has two forms (one called 'A-form-my' and one called 'O-form-my') that are used in conjunction with the nominal (either preceding or following). These two forms convey different meanings. This section is about the meaning to be attributed to these two forms in Tongan.

Table 7.1 *Preposed possessives in Tongan*

A-possession	O-possession	Gloss
'e-ku	ho-ku	my
ho'o	ho	your
'e-ne	ho-no	his/her/its
'e-ta	ho-ta	our (dual, yours and mine)
'e-tau	ho-tau	our (inclusive, plural)
'e-ma	ho-ma	our (dual, his/her/its and mine)
'e-mau	ho-mau	our (exclusive, plural)
ho'o-mo	ho-mo	your (dual, his/her/its and yours)
ho'o-mou	ho-mou	your (plural)
'e-na	ho-na	their (his/her/its and his/her/its)
'e-nau	ho-nau	their
'a	'o	of

Table 7.2 *Derivation of second person forms*

A-possession	O-possession
he 'a o → he'o → ho'o	he 'o o → heoo → ho
he 'a mo → he'omo → ho'omo	he 'o mo → heomo → homo
he 'a mou → he'omou → ho'omou	he 'o mou → heomou → homou

'e of the A-possessives and the A-possessive marker *'a* may be explained by reference to similar phonological processes.

These are examples of phrases containing preposed possessives:

(1) a. *ko e hele 'a Sione*   *ko 'ene helé*
        'the knife of Sione' 'his knife'
    b. *ko e huo 'o Sione*   *ko hono huó*
        'the hoe of Sione'   'his hoe'

To explain the variety of uses of these possessives, Taumoefolau argues in this way: first, she says that it is useless to group words in semantic domains and then expect all members for each domain to be possessed in the same way (1996: 297). In fact, this approach inevitably leads to 'exceptions.' Then, she defines two metaphorical functions: A-possession pronouns have 'verbal function' (activity-oriented) and O-possession pronouns have 'part-function' (part-oriented). Each function has a prototypical application and three other areas of metaphorical extension (Figures 7.1 and 7.2).

The prototypical A-possession is an activity such as 'going' conducted by a subject/agent. This is metaphorically extended (step 2) to an 'activity' such as

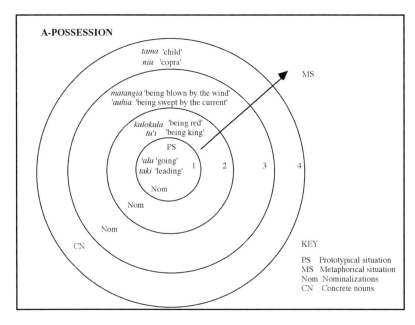

Figure 7.1 A-possession in Tongan (from Taumoefolau, 1996: 298)

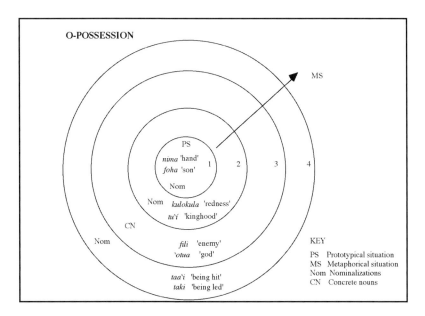

Figure 7.2 O-possession in Tongan (from Taumoefolau, 1996: 299)

'being of a specific type,' for example, 'being red.' I must point out that two
typically distinct semantic properties like 'state' and 'activity' have been col-
lapsed. I find difficult to accept this step because of the inherent distinction
commonly drawn between the two meanings (see Lyons, 1977).

The second metaphorical extension of prototypical A-possession (step 3)
regards an activity in which the subject is the recipient of the action. Is this fundamental shift in meaning[2] simply due to a metaphorical extension? And why
is this same meaning then found again as a metaphorical extension (step 4)
from prototypical O-possession (Figure 7.2)? Why is this complex metaphorical machinery working to produce two instances of the same meaning by such
different routes? These questions are not answered in Taumoefolau's analysis.

Finally, both the third metaphorical extension of A-possession (step 4 in
Figure 7.1) and the second of O-possession (step 3 in Figure 7.2) deal with
concrete nouns. A noun is A-possessed if it is considered an activity, and it is
O-possessed if it considered a part. The plausibility for this suggestion is found
by Taumoefolau in her very interesting suggestion that Tongan lexical items
are "multifunctional," that is, they can all be either verbs or nouns depending
on the syntactic context in which they appear (1996: 303; see also Broschart,
1997b). Taumoefolau concludes like this:

What appear to be quite disparate uses of each A and O are really metaphorical extensions of only one basic, prototypical function the specification of which, therefore,
requires only one rule. For A, the function is to mark a possessive relationship as one of
agentivity in which the possessor 'carries out' the possessed. For O, the function is to
mark a possessive relationship as of partitiveness in which the possessed 'characterises'
the possessor. (Taumoefolau, 1996: 305)

I regard Taumoefolau's characterization of Tongan possession as an important
step towards an adequate treatment of the various phenomena involved. She
moves beyond attempts to explain possession based on semantic domains, and
identifies the conceptual realm as the one where an appropriate description can
be found. She formulates a systematic description of the phenomena involved
in a clear and easy binary manner based on one "simple rule." Her analysis,
however, needs further explanation and possibly a different, but complementary approach to the whole conceptual treatment of Tongan possession.

Both metaphor and prototype theory have limitations in the way in which
they address conceptual content (see Lehman, 1985; Fodor, 1998: chapter 5).
One major problem is the fact that they leave unexplained the nature of the
prototype or the source of the metaphorical extension. I do not deny the psychological reality of both prototypical and metaphorical phenomena. However,
these phenomena are not enough to give us an adequate description of our

---

[2] Theta theory (assignment of theta-roles to arguments) is part of universal grammar (Chomsky,
1986: 93ff).

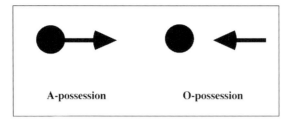

Figure 7.3 The conceptual content of Tongan possession (from Bennardo, 2000c: 276)

conceptual realm. It is necessary to use an approach to conceptualization that accounts for what prototype and metaphor theories leave unexplained, and that at the same time does not undermine the correctness of the metaphorical/prototypical phenomena they describe.

In Section 6.2.2.1, I introduced the computational approach to cognition I adopted that looks at conceptual content as organized in theories (Murphy and Medin, 1985; Gopnik, 1988; Keller and Lehman, 1991; Gelman, Coley, and Gottfried, 1994). In a theory, a set of axioms (binary in nature) is considered given, and a number of theorems are derived from them. These theorems are thus composed of a number of axioms – this conceptual feature makes my proposal agree with others that regard meaning as compositional (see Jackendoff, 1990, 1997, 2002; Pinker, 1994, 1997, 1999) – and can be recursively used as axioms themselves from which further theorems can be derived, and so on. Thus, any concept is considered either an axiom (binary), or a theorem (not binary, compositional, and derived). For space, a number of axioms and derived theorems were identified (see Section 6.2.2.1).

I propose two types of vectors as the minimal conceptual content of the A-possession and O-possession in Tongan (and possibly in other Polynesian/ Oceanic languages). A-possession is a Vector whose origin is specified, while O-possession is an inverted Vector whose direction is specified (Figure 7.3). Activities, that is verbs, can be both A-possessed or O-possessed. The meaning of the phrase/sentence, however, shifts precisely according to the conceptual meanings proposed for the two types of possessions.

Let us consider the following well-known Tongan examples (Churchward, 1953: 78):

(2) a. *'ene taki*
        'his leading'
     b. *hono taki*
        'his being led'

In (2a), the A-possessive indicates a relationship of the possessor with an activity whose origin is specified, i.e., the possessor. In (2b), the O-possessive indicates a relationship of the possessor with an activity whose recipient/direction is specified, i.e., the possessor. This is exactly what the two proposed conceptual meanings for A- and O-possession predict.

Further support for my proposal came when I looked at a group of nouns, concrete nouns, that pose some problems for Taumoefolau's metaphorical approach, specifically in area 4 of A-possession and area 3 of O-possession. She says:

> Given human or personified possessors, these concrete possessions could conceivably be viewed as 'parts' or 'properties,' thus attracting O, but could also conceivably be viewed as 'activities,' thus attracting A. (1996: 304)

Thus, tools can be possessed as A if conceived as 'activities,' and as O if conceived as "members of a set of partnership in which the possessor is a focal point" (1996: 304).

Two very common tools are used with two different possessives: a knife for which one uses *'eke* 'my' (A-possession), and a hoe for which one uses *hoku* 'my' (O-possession). Both tools can be considered as members of a set with the possessor in a focal point, and they both can be considered related to activities. Why then choose A-possession for knife and not for hoe? To explain one choice over the other (because both are in theory possible), Taumoefolau uses the idea of "conventionalization," that is, in a novel situation, the choice follows established patterns. This approach, however, begs further explanations. How did the "established pattern" come about? Or better, how did conventions come about? I think that we need to go a little further than metaphor and prototypes and look at the two Tongan (and Polynesian/Oceanic) possessions in the spatial terms I have indicated.

From the brief history of the two tools that an informant gave to me, I deduce that the traditional knife was, as the contemporary iron knife is, a personal possession, probably made with ease from largely available bamboo. Thus, the A-possession is used with knife because the origin of the possession is easily specified (origin + Vector). The traditional hoe, instead, made of limited available stone, was not a personal possession. It was a social object whose possession was assigned only temporarily to various people. Thus, the O-possession is used with hoe because not the origin, but the direction/recipient of the (temporary) possession is indicated (inverted Vector + direction).

Other examples that support my suggestion are provided by the different use of A-possession and O-possession with *foha* 'man's son' or 'productivity,' and its contrast with *tama* 'woman's child.'

(3) a. *hono foha*
        'his son'

b. *'ene fohá*
   'its productivity'
c. *'ene tama*
   'her child'

The metaphorical 'activity' or 'part' function is not applicable in these cases either. O-possession is used in (3)a not because the 'son' is considered metaphorically a 'part' of the father. What is relevant is the direction/recipient of the possessive relationship. The son belongs to the father. Notice that stating that something belongs to something else implies a part-to-whole relationship (i.e., the father and the son are parts, but the two make up a whole). The O-possession is then indicating a possessive relationship that can be represented as an inverted Vector with a specified direction/recipient: son towards father.

In (3)b, it is not an 'activity' that is metaphorically expressed. Instead, the 'productivity' of the plot is possessed by the plot itself, hence the use of A-possession that specifies a vector with a clear origin (in this case, the plot). In (3)c, not only does the child of a woman have a different lexical term, but when possession is expressed, A-possession is used to refer to the mother. And, again, not because an 'activity' is referred to. The mother is simply the origin of the Vector along which children come into the world, clearly justifying the use of A-possession.

It has been suggested (Joseph Finney, personal communication) that any adequate proposal about Polynesian possession should be able to explain the controversial treatment of body parts as O-possessed. According to my proposal, O-possession implies a specified end of the vector (ego/possessor), but not its origin. While this may seem odd when used with body parts, it makes much sense when we consider the 'theory' out of which possession of the body comes. We do not have control over the body that we 'receive' at birth; in other words, it is something we are born with, it is 'given' to us. I suggest that Tongan O-possession of body parts is the result of the interaction between this 'theory' of body provenance (part of the 'conceptual structures' module) and the concept of inverted Vector (part of the spatial 'representation module').

7.1.1   Radiality 'in' possession

How does the vectorial conceptual nature of Polynesian/Tongan possession become relevant to the present discussion? The answer lies within the following two points: (1) when interpreting possession in spatial terms, i.e., vectorially, clarity was achieved in the disambiguation of the puzzling use of the two types of possessives with similar arguments, e.g., concrete objects; (2) conceptualizing possession in vectorial terms repeats almost exactly the conceptual theme of radiality. Away-from-an-origin and toward-a-goal-from-an-unknown-origin are the two most salient concepts utilized. The linguistic forms used to express possession include those for ego (first person singular). Thus, conceptually, both radial form 1 (away from – from ego) and radial form 2 (away from – from other-than-ego) are used to realize linguistically the domain of possession. However, it remains relevant that conceptual spatial 'radiality' is extensively replicated in the domain of possession.

7.2   Radiality and time

It appears that we think about time in the same way we think about space. After all, the only difference between the two domains is in the number of dimensions, three for space and one for time. Besides, we typically use the same lexemes to talk about both space and time. For example, in English, the term 'before' can be used to talk about both spatial relationships and temporal relationships. This is not completely true in all languages of the world where a variety of situations are recorded. Nonetheless, the lexical overlap between the two domains is consistently of a large size in many languages (e.g., Boroditsky, 2000; Gentner, 2001; Gentner, Imai, and Boroditsky, 2002; Kita, Danziger, and Stolz, 2001; McGlone and Harding, 1998; and references cited there).

The ever-growing literature about the linguistic and cognitive representations of spatial relationships clearly indicates that languages and cultures all over the world show a preference in their use of a specific spatial frame of reference (FoR) over a number of possible ones (e.g., Bennardo, 2002c; Haviland, 2000; Levinson, 2003; Senft, 1997; Wassmann, 1994). Owing to the just mentioned lexical overlap between space and time, it is conceivable that preferences similar to those in the domain of space could also be found in the domain of time. Some positive evidence regarding the overlap in the use of FoR between space and time has already appeared (e.g., Boroditsky, 2001; Boroditsky and Ramscar, 2002; Casasanto and Boroditsky, 2003; McGlone and Harding, 1998).

In a couple of recent publications (Bender, Bennardo, and Beller, 2005; Bender, Beller, and Bennardo, forthcoming), data from Tongan figure prominently in putting forward the argument that indeed preferences for a specific FoR in representing spatial relationships are replicated in temporal relationships. I will summarize below their hypothesis, argument, methodology, and findings. My ultimate intention is to show how the hypothesized foundational cultural model of radiality is shared between the domains of space and time. I can only achieve my goal if a relationship can be proven between the two domains, if the nature of this relationship is proven to be structural, and if the type of structural organization is proven to be the same, i.e., radial.

7.2.1   *Temporal perspectives and frames of reference*

There are two fundamental ways of conceiving time, either Moving-Ego (ME) or Moving-Time (MT). Adopting the first perspective, we conceptualize ego moving along the stationary time 'highway' and thus we can say: "We have passed Wednesday, but Friday is still to come." In the same fashion, "the future is in front of us" and "the past is behind us." Basically, we move towards events yet to happen. Adopting the second perspective, we conceptualize time as moving while ego is stationary and thus we can say: "Wednesday has passed, but Friday is yet to come." In the same fashion, "the future is in front" and "the past is in the back (of the future)." Basically, events move towards us.

These two perspectives, however, differ substantially insofar as the ME perspective is deictic and it necessarily and explicitly involves an ego. The back of ego corresponds to past and the front corresponds to future. The MT perspective, on the other hand, while implicitly requiring an ego, does not explicitly involve one. In fact, the relationship expressed is between two points on the moving time line that ego observes. Past will be the point positioned in front and is typically but not necessarily closer (away from) to ego. Besides, it can be either in front of or behind ego. Future will be the second point that lies behind the first point and thus, typically but not necessarily, further away from ego. This point too can be either in front of or behind ego.

What is becoming apparent from this very brief discussion is that considering time as moving or not moving does not bring clarity to the various issues and linguistic expressions used to talk about time. Thus, recently there has been a shift from classifying time expressions as referring to movement to a classification based on referencing (Bender, Bennardo, and Beller, 2005; Kranjec, 2006; Núñez, Motz, and Teuscher, 2006; Núñez and Sweetser, 2006).

Núñez and colleagues, for instance, consider both the MT and ME perspective as subclasses of an Ego-Reference-Point (Ego-RP) metaphor, as they appear to require the Ego's subjective now as a reference point. In addition, they argue for a Time-Reference-Point (Time-RP) metaphor that does not require the Ego, as it is defined by virtue of an intrinsic direction derived from a perceived motion of events (for a detailed metaphorical mapping as well as an overview of the metaphor literature, see Núñez and Sweetser, 2006). (Bender, Beller, and Bennardo, forthcoming: 5)

Essentially, what is at stake here is the direct involvement of ego as reference-point or the choice by ego of the line of time as the reference-point. Individuals easily shift between the two perspectives, thus contributing to the ambiguity of specific expressions used to refer to time. For example, when McGlone and Harding (1998) asked US individuals to answer the following question: "Next Wednesday's meeting has been moved forward two days.

What day is the meeting now that it has been rescheduled?" half of the people answered Monday and half answered Friday.

Bender, Bennardo, and Beller (2005; Bender, Beller, and Bennardo, forthcoming) continue by hypothesizing that spatial FoRs are mapped onto temporal cognition. Thus, if a preference is detected and documented in a population regarding a specific spatial FoR, it is conceivable that that same preference will be apparent in expressions about temporal relationships. Space and time, however, are different – minimally, they differ in dimensionality, three for space and one for time – how do we conceive of spatial FoR being transferred onto temporal relationships?

A spatial absolute FoR localizes an object without reference to the observer (see discussion of FoR in Chapter 3, Section 3.3.2); how can this be done in temporal relationships? The solution offered by Bender, Beller, and Bennardo is the following:

An equivalent absolute determination in the temporal domain may be provided by the "arrow of time" (Evans, 2003; Mackey, 2003; Magnon, 1997). According to the arrow of time – manifested, for instance, in the second law of thermodynamics, in the direction of evolution, or in radioactive decay – the future is what lies ahead. (forthcoming: 13)

The use of the spatial intrinsic FoR requires the internally determined orientation of an object. For temporal relationships, the intrinsic FoR will be grounded in the fact that events have an internally determined orientation that corresponds to their beginning and end.

Finally, the spatial relative FoR requires an ego-observer and this is obtained for temporal relationships by the subjective present. Besides, by exploiting the unidimensionality of the time line, one can distinguish between the use of the translation and the reflection subtypes of the relative FoR.

In a translation subtype, we expect the observer to transfer his or her own position to the point of reference. Accordingly, "after" should be used for events that fall between the speaker and the point of reference (irrespective of where in time the point of reference itself is), while "before" should refer to events beyond. When applying the reflection subtype, the observer's perspective is reflected in G [ground] and the prepositions are swapped. In this case, "before" should be used for events that fall between the speaker and the point of reference, while "after" should refer to events beyond. (Bender, Beller, and Bennardo, forthcoming: 15)

A consequence of the transfer of the relative FoR on the temporal time line is that events will be localized symmetrically in one's past and future, with diverging fronts and backs. That is, the pattern in the past will mirror the one for the future and vice versa.

The hypothesized transfer of spatial FoR onto the temporal time line gave rise to the construction and administering of two related experiments by Bender, Beller, and Bennardo (forthcoming) to speakers of English, German, and Tongan. Both experiments represent a variation on the one originally used by Boroditsky and Ramscar (2002). In the first experiment, participants were asked to solve a spatial problem that would prime them toward a specific FoR and then asked some questions to solve some temporal problems, e.g., "The meeting that was supposed to happen on Wednesday next week will be moved forward 2 days. On which day of the week will it now take place?" The second experiment, administered only to US subjects, omitted the spatial priming and repeated the requiring of the solution of spatial problems.

The results for the three groups of speakers differ regarding the FoR preferences they employ in solving the temporal tasks. German speakers privilege the intrinsic FoR, Americans split between the absolute and the intrinsic, while Tongans show no specific preference, except for a very low use of the reflection subtype of the relative FoR. In comparison, though, to a very low frequency of use by the German and American speakers, Tongans are the only group that uses the translation subtype of the relative FoR at least a third of the time. In addition, in the elder and less educated section of the Tongan sample, the percentage of use of the translation FoR reaches 49.2% (p. 26). A clear explanation for this phenomenon is provided in the following:

Following the introduction of an English school curriculum and of English as school language, the frames of reference were deliberately changed a few decades ago. Some Tongans still remember this change, as one of our research assistants stated: "The Tongan system was changed when I was still in school, because everybody else in the world did it the other way around." (Bender, Beller, and Bennardo, forthcoming: 20)

The conscious effort to change the FoR used to express time relationships in Tongan schools that are officially supposed to be using only English (not in practice) is giving its results. Nonetheless, the fact remains that the older and less educated population still makes ample use of, showing a very marked preference for, the traditional linguistic convention of employing the translation subtype of the relative FoR in expressing temporal relations.

7.2.2   Radiality 'in' time

How does this preference for the translation subtype of the relative FoR in temporal expressions relate to the hypothesized radiality? First, it establishes a strong link between preferences in the linguistic and mental representations of spatial and temporal relationships. Second, the shared preference between the representations of temporal and spatial relationships is located specifically on the use of the translation subtype of the relative FoR. Third, we have already seen in the preceding chapter (Sections 6.2.1 and 6.2.2) that the translation subtype of the relative FoR shares fundamental characteristics with the radial subtype of the absolute FoR. Thus, we may conclude that radiality itself is replicated in the temporal domain.

The co-presence of other FoRs as also used in the temporal domain should not discourage one from reaching this conclusion. Let me repeat here the argument about the relationship between focus on ego and focus on other-than-ego as realized in the use of the various FoRs. The relative FoR typically realizes a focus on ego. The intrinsic FoR focuses on an oriented object in the field of ego, thus, on other-than-ego. The absolute FoR definitely focuses on points/landmarks in the field of ego, thus on other-than-ego. The translation subtype of the relative FoR shares features with the relative FoR since it is rooted on ego and it has the same transverse axis (left–right). It also shares features with the intrinsic FoR since it focuses on an other-than-ego object (oriented for the intrinsic FoR) and its sagittal axis is different from ego's one. In other words, in contrast to the intrinsic FoR, the translation FoR does not have an oriented field completely independent from ego's field. At the same time, in contrast to the relative FoR, the translation FoR does not depend completely on the axes centered on ego. Halfway between the relative FoR and the intrinsic FoR, the translation FoR demonstrates the saliency of other-than-ego objects, either oriented or not oriented, in the field of ego.

7.3   Conclusion

In this chapter I briefly presented the results of the analyses of two Tongan domains, possession and time. In both domains I was able to show that a specific spatial configuration, the cognitive molecule I labeled 'radiality,' is essentially present in the organization of the knowledge they contain. Thus, a relationship was established between the domain of space and those of possession and time. This relationship appears to be structural in nature. That is, the spatial molecule of radiality that represents a minimal organization of objects[3] in space, is replicated in the other two domains.

Possession is conceptualized as objects moving from out there and coming in close vicinity, hence possession, of an individual or as objects (and/or properties) generated by an individual and thus moving away from it. This gives rise to a dual grammaticalization of possessive terms in Tongan, each form labeling either type of the two possessive configurations. The emphasis on other-than-ego and on centripetal and centrifugal movement out of it shows the use of a specific modality of thinking (organizing knowledge) that is structurally a replication of spatial radiality.

Similarly, temporal relationships are preferentially expressed by using the translation subtype of the relative FoR that reveals the underlying emphasis on

---

[3] By 'object' I mean any entity, either concrete or abstract, that may enter into a spatial configuration either in the outside world or in the mental world of an individual.

other-than-ego. I take this emphasis as an indicator of the structural presence of spatial radiality. While this is not the exclusive way of thinking about time, the significant preference found points toward a substantial structural homology between the domain of space and that of time. The homology is rooted in the common use of radiality.

8   Radiality and the Tongan kinship terminology[1]

8.1   Introduction

Tongan social events such as first birthday, marriage, and funerals are deeply intertwined with one's world of kin. The persons central to these events are kin of various kinds and the events serve to define and redefine core kin relations and relations between kin such as the *fahu* relationship. This chapter begins with the ethnographic account of a first birthday in Tonga. The events of that day highlight the interplay between the formal properties of kinship expressed through a kinship terminology and how the meaning of those kin relations are played out and reconstructed in the context of a family celebrating the first birthday of a daughter.

The ethnographic account provides us with the activities of that day and the centrality of kin relations in those events, but it does not inform us of the conceptual system that the participants bring with them as culture bearers to this event. Rather, it is a slice in time of an ongoing, dynamic process linking behavior with a conceptual system for kin relations and a conceptual system for kin relations with behavior. The events of the day are a co-production of the dynamic and the static; of kinship as it is lived and kinship as it is conceptualized. To understand this interplay we need not only the ethnographic account but also an account of the underlying conceptual system that is being activated during this event.

We argue that the genealogical framework in which kinship analyses have generally been implemented is inadequate for this task and instead needs to be embedded within a more encompassing framework. The genealogical framework assumes that genealogical categorizations are primary to understanding a kinship system, yet it does not account for these categorizations. What does account for these categorizations is the underlying generative logic of a kinship terminology. That logic is made evident through commonly reported ethnographic observations regarding the way kinship terminologies are used directly to compute and thereby determine kin relations even when the genealogical

---

[1] This chapter is a slightly revised version of Bennardo and Read (2007).

connection between the persons in question is unknown. The underlying, generative logic of the terminology can be made explicit through formal, algebraic modeling of the logic of kin term computations. In addition, and important for our accounts of Tongan social life and kinship, the algebraic modeling makes it possible to determine those terminological features that do not derive from the underlying, generative logic and thus must have been adjoined to the terminology through cultural intervention. What is activated in social life, we argue, is a conceptual system relating how kin and kin relations are constituted.

8.2   Tongan social life and kinship

I begin the argument with an episode (a child's first birthday) that occurred during my residence in Tonga. Through this event I introduce the specific ways in which the Tongan kinship system shapes social events such as children's first birthdays, marriages, and funerals and the kinship issues that these events pose.

It is a special day today in the village of Ngele'ia, Tonga. Manu[2] and Mele's daughter Loisi,[3] their third child, is one year old. Traditionally in Tonga, the celebration of a child's first birthday is one of the few, major social landmarks in a person's life – the other two being a wedding celebration and one's funeral. Manu and Mele are living with Manu's parents and their house is not big enough to host the celebratory gathering and consumption of food. The celebration takes place in the hall next to the church located right in front of Manu's parents' house.

As I approach the hall, I see people carrying large pieces of *ngatu* 'tapa/barkcloth' or mats being met at the door by Mele. I get a glimpse of Manu, still in the backyard of his parents' house, cheerfully chatting with other men while finishing the roasting of a few small pigs over a hot fire. My attempt to move in his direction is interrupted by his clear invitation to proceed to the hall. When I enter the hall, to my right stands Manu's sister Nunia (she is much younger than Manu) holding Manu's daughter, Loisi. Of course, they are dressed up for the occasion wearing their best *ta'ovala* 'mat worn around waist,' as are all the guests either sitting on the numerous chairs available or just standing and chatting in small groups. Behind and next to Nunia and Loisi, a pile of pieces of *ngatu* and mats with other presents like pieces of fabric, canned food, meat, and money is slowly forming.

One side of the hall is occupied by a few tables with tablecloths, on which many plates full of food have already been put on display. After a few celebratory speeches performed by the minister and a few elders, and after roasted

---

[2] Names have been changed as common practice in anthropology to maintain privacy of participants.
[3] The sex of the child would not bring any change in the episode I am about to narrate.

pigs have been put on the large empty dishes on the table, guests are invited to help themselves to the food.

The celebration closes with Nunia choosing and keeping some of the presents for herself and with the remaining presents being distributed by her to some of the guests. After this distribution, almost all the guests leave. Then, finally Manu enters the hall and has some food while gleaming with happiness about the successful completion of the celebration. During the whole celebration Manu was nowhere to be seen. The focus of attention during the whole event was either Loisi or Nunia (Loisi's *mehekitanga*) or Mele (Loisi's mother).

I must admit that I was already aware of the special role that the father's sister, called *mehekitanga*, plays in the life of Tongans, but witnessing its instantiation was quite a different experience. The *mehekitanga* of the celebrated child was the center of the whole ceremony. Presents were piled at her side, she chose how many to keep, and she decided which ones had to be given to the various departing guests. In the coming years, she would actively participate in the raising of the child, but exercise especially her privilege (called *fahu*) to ask and receive material objects and services from her brother's children. All sisters of a Tongan male will be *mehekitanga* to his children, but the eldest sister would be the only one exercising the privilege of her position.[4] The same *fahu* relationship exercised by one's father's sister (*mehekitanga*) over her brother's children (*fakafotu*, both male and female) is also exercised by any individual over their mother's brothers (*fa'e tangata*).[5]

A Tongan female sibling is always higher in rank than her brother, and an older same sex sibling (*ta'okete*) is always higher in status than a younger one (*tehina*) (Gifford, 1929; Tupouniua, 1977; Bott, 1981, 1982; Gailey, 1987; van der Grijp, 1993). The gender hierarchy is further stressed by the brother/sister or *tuonga'ane* 'male sibling for a female'/*tuofefine* 'female sibling for a male' avoidance practice (Gifford, 1929; Tupouniua, 1977; Helu, 1999). Siblings of different sex are moved into separate sleeping quarters around the age of ten. Specific linguistic (e.g., topics such as sex) and behavioral restrictions (e.g., dancing, watching a movie) are also part of this avoidance system that continues throughout one's life.[6] This partly explains Manu's behavior and his late entrance into the hall.[7]

---

[4] In traditional Tonga this privilege was exercised by all *mehekitanga*. In contemporary Tonga this privilege is often contested, especially when it is exercised in ways that tend to clash with the principles of a newly introduced market economy in a rapidly Westernizing population (see Small, 1997; Morton, 1996; 2003).

[5] This type of *fahu* is also limited nowadays to "the eldest female child of the father's eldest sister" (Tupouniua, 1977: 24).

[6] Many contemporary Tongans do away with separate sleeping quarters or avoiding the same dance floor with one's opposite sex sibling, but the taboo is still very much in their consciousness and can still be a cause of social embarrassment if broken.

[7] Traditionally cooks were also considered as the bottom of the society's ladder (see Martin, 1818) and this sentiment may have had a part in motivating Manu's behavior. After all, he had been preparing food all day up to the time of the birthday celebration.

The birthday celebration already highlights the complex and fundamental interaction between kinship and social life. This interaction is even more apparent in funerals. The death of an individual triggers a series of events that constitute the mold into which kinship relationships are poured in order to establish the social position of that individual for the last time and serves as one of the main occasions wherein "much of the enculturation of the young in Tongan tradition takes places" (Kaeppler, 1978b: 174). The reiterative enactment of these events with culturally constituted kin sets forth the conditions for the continuation of the form of praxis often referred to as 'tradition' (extensive accounts of Tongan funerals are found in Kaeppler, 1978b and van der Grijp, 1993).

The participants in a funeral all belong to the same *kāinga* (bilateral kindred) and are constrained in their behavior by their kinship relationship to the deceased: "[F]unerals are the occasions *par excellence* when status and rank prescribe the actions of all concerned" (Kaeppler, 1978b: 174). Ranking in Tonga establishes who is high (*'eiki*)[8] and who is low (*tu'a*)[9] (Kaeppler, 1971; James, 1991; van der Grijp, 1993). In the generation above ego, the father side is *'eiki* and the mother side is *tu'a*. However, rank acquired through the mother is more important than rank acquired through the father. In the generation below ego, children are *tu'a* if the deceased is male and *'eiki* if the deceased is female (Kaeppler, 1971).

Only relatives that are *'eiki* to the deceased (ego) are allowed to touch the body and prepare it for the burial. The person who sits at the head of the corpse during the wake is the *fahu*. In the case of a dead woman, typically the child of her 'father's sister' is the *fahu*. In the case of a dead man, a child of his 'sister' or grandchild of his 'father's sister' would be the *fahu*. All the relatives that are *tu'a* to the deceased belong to the *liongi* or group of people responsible for bringing presents that will later be distributed by the *fahu* after choosing some for personal use. The *liongi* are not allowed to enter the wake room where the corpse is lying and they must wear enormous mats around their waists (at times covering even the backs of their heads) as an overt sign of their sorrow and status.

It is important to notice that the conceptual content of the various kinship terms used in defining the *fahu* in a funeral (see Bennardo and Read, 2005: 6) is more complex than suggested by simply referring to the positions in a genealogical space referenced by the transliteration of a kin term. In the genealogical space, for example, an ego is not marked with gender, but in Tongan kinship there is no ungendered ego and when calculating who is the appropriate *fahu* at a funeral, the calculations are based on gender marked terms (see Biersack,

---

[8] *'Eiki* also means 'chief.'
[9] *Tu'a* also means 'common people' and 'outside.'

1982: 184). This seemingly small, yet substantial, difference between features of kin terms and features of the genealogical space – another one being relative age – has important consequences when we consider how the Tongan kinship terminology is constituted.

8.3   The Tongan kinship terminology

The Tongan kinship terminology (TKT from now on) spans over five generations with generation 2 up and 2 down containing only a closure term, *kui* 'grandparent' and *mokopuna* 'grandchild,' respectively (information about TKT comes from Aoyagi, 1966; Beaglehole and Beaglehole, 1941; Biersack, 1982; Bott, 1982; Collocott, 1924, 1927; Gailey, 1987; Gifford, 1929; Helu, 1999; Kaeppler, 1971; Korn, 1974, 1978; Marcus, 1977, 1978, 1980; Martin, 1818; Morton, H., 1996, 2003; Morton, K., 1972; Rivers, 1916; Rogers, 1977; Tupouniua, 1977; van der Grijp, 1993; and from my fieldwork in 1993–95). Table 8.1 contains the whole set of Tongan kin terms with partial genealogical descriptions – partial since the TKT is a classificatory terminology with terms that are not easily defined just using genealogical relations – for each kin term along with its closest transliteration. The three major generations (zero, 1 up, and 1 down) covered by the terminology contain between five and six terms each.

All the terms in generation zero (*tokoua, tuofefine, tuonga'ane, ta'okete*, and *tehina*) are also used for genealogical parallel cousins and cross-cousins, without regard to linking relative. Nonetheless there is a behavioral distinction between genealogical parallel cousins and cross-cousins (Biersack, 1982: 184; Kaeppler, 1971: 177). In fact, individuals would behave towards the two types of genealogical cousins in the same way as their parents do, and these latter distinguish them terminologically (i.e., using either *fakafotu* 'child of *tuonga'ane*' or *'ilamutu* 'child of *tuofefine'*).

The behavior that distinguishes between genealogical parallel and cross-cousins is part of the *fahu* system discussed above. One is *'eiki* 'high' to one's mother's brother's children and *tu'a* 'low' to one's father's sister's children. Why this shift from labeling persons by kinship terms to labeling the relationship between persons without simultaneously labeling the persons involved in different relationships? Is this to be considered a gap in the terminology? Or is there enough computational power in the terminology already to make the addition of further terms unnecessary? Furthermore, why distinguish between siblings only according to gender and age (but only in some cases)? And finally, why only one term for same sex sibling? None of these questions are answered by mapping kin terms to a genealogical space but are answered through the more encompassing framework we present below.

The term *motu'a* 'parent' in the generation 1 up is very rarely used with the glossed meaning. Only a few people ever accept it as a cover term for

Table 8.1 *Tongan kinship terminology*

Generation	Term	Partial genealogical description	Transliteration
2 up	*Kui*	(FF, FM, MM, MF)	'Grandparent'
1 up	*Motu'a*	(M, F)	'Parent'
	Fa'e	(M, MZ)	'Mother'
	Fa'e tangata	(MB)	'Maternal uncle'
	Tu'asina	(younger MB)	'Younger maternal uncle'
	Mehekitanga	(FZ)	'Paternal aunt'
Zero	*Tokoua*	(same sex B, Z)	'Same sex sibling'
	Tuofefine	(Z of male)	'Sister of male'
	Tuonga'ane	(B of female)	'Brother of female'
	Ta'okete	(older B, Z)	'Older same sex sibling'
	Tehina	(younger B, Z)	'Younger same sex sibling'
1 down	*Tama*	(S, D of female)	'Child of female'
	Foha	(S of male)	'Son of male'
	'Ofefine	(D of male)	'Daughter of male'
	Fakafotu	(BS, BD of female)	'Child of *tuonga'ane* (brother of female)'
	'Ilamutu	(ZS, ZD of male)	'Child of *tuofefine* (sister of male)'
2 down	*Mokopuna*	(SS, SD, DS, DD)	'Grandchild'

both parents, and if so, they preferentially use it for father rather than mother. The four main terms in generation 1 up are, then, *tamai* 'father' and 'father's brother,' *fa'é* 'mother' and 'mother's sister,' *mehekitanga* 'father's sister,' and *fa'é tangata* 'mother's brother,' and are constituted by gender and siblinghood. The gendered terms *tamai* and *fa'é* are also applied to the same sex siblings of father and mother (and other genealogical relations), respectively. This highlights the saliency of the relationship between same sex siblings expressed in generation zero by the single term *tokoua*. Cross-siblings (parent's) are named in the same way as in generation zero by two different terms. But while on the father's side the term *mehekitanga* 'father's sister' stays the same irrespective of sister's age, on the mother's side the term *fa'é tangata* 'mother's brother' is replaced by the term *tu'asina* when referring to the mother's younger brother.

What are the regularities and repetitions of conceptual content (e.g., same sex siblings indicated by same term) in generation zero terms and in generation 1 up terms indicating about the underlying logic of the TKT? Is the basic logic for generation 1 up terms already present in generation zero terms? Why are there more terms on the mother's side (*fa'é tangata*, *tu'asina*) than on the father's side (*mehekitanga*)? Again, these questions are not answered through reference to a genealogical space.

Finally, the five terms in generation 1 down display conceptual content partly similar to the terms in generation zero, but with a different combination than those in generation 1 up. *Tama* 'child of female' is not marked for sex, but the node by which it is reached must be female. On the other hand, both *foha* 'son of male' and *'ofefine* 'daughter of male' are marked for sex and need to be reached through a male node. These three terms are also applied to children of one's same sex siblings or *tokoua*. Both *fakafotu* 'child' of *tuonga'ane* and *'ilamutu* 'child' of *tuofefine* are not marked for sex, but they need to be reached by two nodes marked for sex (e.g., female → male sibling → child for *fakafotu* or male → female sibling → child for *'ilamutu*). These last two terms are also used for children of genealogical parallel cousins and cross-cousins in accordance with the fact that genealogical parallel and cross-cousins are addressed as *tuonga'ane* and *tuofefine*, depending on gender.

It seems as if gender has salience only when reference is made to a male's offspring (*foha* or *'ofefine*). The general tendency of the terminology at this generation level is not to mark for gender (see *tama, fakafotu, 'ilamutu*). Why? Is this part of the internal logic of the TKT? Or is this the result of cultural interventions that are skewing the otherwise lack of gender marking in the generation 1 down terms? I will address all the these questions in my analysis of Tongan kinship space.

8.4   Conceptual basis for kinship space

One widely accepted view of kinship systems presumes that kin terms are labels for categorizations made of kin type products in a genealogical space. But this leaves unanswered the criteria upon which the presumed categorizations are based. Ethnographic evidence implies, instead, that there are, conceptually, two ways we consider individuals to be our kin. One is through tracing genealogical connections and the other is by using the computational logic through which the kin terms form a system of kin relations and thus is not simply a list of semantic labels for categories of kin types. Correspondingly, Bennardo and Read (2007) argue that kinship space is composed of two conceptual systems. One conceptual system is based on the logic underlying the structural form of the genealogical space (see Lehman and Witz, 1974, 1979). The other conceptual system relates to the logic underlying the structural form of the terminological space determined from the way kin terms constitute a computational system and from which the genealogical categorizations may be deduced (Read 1984, 2001a, 2001b, 2005; Read and Behrens 1990). Together, these two conceptual systems form the kinship space (Figure 8.1).

8.4.1   *Distinction between genealogical space and terminological space*

Lack of a clear distinction between the genealogical space and the terminological space is conducive to unavoidable misrepresentations of both. Here are two examples illustrating the problem with restricting analysis of a kinship terminology just to features derived from a genealogical framework.

In Biersack (1982), the author presents an analysis of Tongan exchange structures by referring to the people involved as occupants of nodes in a genealogical space. In her exercise, though, she is obliged to introduce variants of the typical symbols used in representing a genealogical space. In fact, because she has the TKT in mind, and because she is centering the genealogical space on ego without sex marking, she cannot express the terms *tuonga'ane* (male sibling for a female) and *tuofefine* (female sibling for a male) with the symbols used to represent the genealogical space. Consequently she introduces the unconventional solution of labeling a node in a genealogical space with a linguistic expression such as 'opposite-sexed sibling.' But 'opposite-sexed sibling' is not a feature of the genealogical space and instead refers to a transliteration of the kin term *tuofefine* whose meaning is best understood by its relation to other terms through a kin term product (defined below). Thus she is conflating information about the two domains of genealogical space and kinship terminology space.

Similarly, when trying to represent the TKT, van der Grijp (1993) maps it onto a genealogical space centered on a male-gendered ego and is obliged to omit some of the kin terms such as *tuonga'ane* ('brother of female'), *tama* ('son, daughter of female'), *ta'okete* ('older brother, sister'), *tehina* ('younger brother, sister'), *fakafotu* ('brother's son, brother's daughter of female'), and also *motu'a* ('mother, father'). The author is aware of the omissions, but regards them as unavoidable and irrelevant for his purposes. Nonetheless, if we want to consider the totality of the terminological space in order to find its constitutive properties and generative logic, it is a conspicuous deficiency.

These two examples highlight the difficulty in faithfully embedding the Tongan terminology in a genealogical space centered on a hypothetical ego. In addition, the respective authors do not elucidate the underlying logic that leads to the distinctions considered by them and so their respective discussions remain at the level of a description of whatever pattern is made evident by a partial mapping of the terminological space onto the genealogical space. The mapping is partial as the logic of the Tongan terminology (and other classificatory terminologies) does not permit a faithful mapping of kin terms onto an ego-centered genealogical space.

The difficulty with mapping the Tongan kinship terminology onto an ego-centered genealogical space does not imply that the terminology is not "egocentric" since in this analysis the "ego-centeredness" of a kinship terminology arises from its structural form and what Read (1997) has defined to be a focal term for a terminology. A focal term is a term mapped to the individual identified as the reference self in the domain of discourse when the terminology is instantiated in usage. A focal term will be an identity element for the kin term product (defined below), either for the terminology as a whole, or for the terms having a single sex marking, depending on the particular terminology. In the

American kinship terminology (and other descriptive terminologies) the focal "term" is the Self concept; in the TKT, as it will be demonstrated, there are two, gendered focal terms, namely *tuonga'ane* ('brother (f.s.)') and *tuofefine* ('sister (m.s.)'), hence from a genealogical perspective an ego is necessarily gendered. The reason why these are the focal terms arises from the very core of the logic underlying the structural form of the TKT.

8.4.2   Kinship terminology structural form (kin term products and kin term maps)

The structural form of a kinship terminology can be expressed visually by constructing a kin term map (Leaf, 1971; modified by Read (Read and Behrens, 1990); see Figure 8.2 for an example using the male terms of the TKT) based on referential usage of kin terms as described in ethnographic observations about kin calculations, such as the comment made by Marshall Sahlins:

> ... [kin] terms permit comparative strangers to fix kinship rapidly without the necessity of elaborate genealogical reckoning – *reckoning that typically would be impossible.* With mutual relationship terms all that is required is the discovery of one common relative. Thus, if A is related to B as child to mother, *veitanani*, while C is related to B as *veitacini*, sibling of the same sex, then it follows that A is related to C as child to mother although they never before met or knew it. *Kin terms are predictable. If two people are each related to a third, then they are related to each other.* (Sahlins, 1962: 155, emphasis added)

And in a review of Scheffler's book *Australian Kin Classification*, Shapiro observes that his (Shapiro's) informants "were generally more comfortable operating through the relationship terminology; it made little or no personal or social difference to them whether (say) an alleged brother of the MM was in fact an MMB or a more remote 'brother' of the MM ...[they] easily decode the messages 'aunt's children' and 'X's children' *but not the message 'father's sister's children'* ..." (Shapiro, 1982: 275, 274, emphasis added). Similar comments disconfirming the priority of genealogy in calculations of kin relationships can be found in Behrens (1984) for the Shipibo of Peru, Marshall (1976) for the !Kung san, and Goodale (1971) for the Tiwi, among others. These ethnographic examples highlight the fact that kin relations are determined directly from the way in which kin terms form an internally organized structure of concepts through which kin relations expressed using kin terms can be computed without first referring to a supposedly universal set of genealogical relations.

We can express kin term computations in the form of a kin term product described as follows. Consider three individuals labeled ego, alter and alter*. If K and L are two kin terms from a kinship terminology, the kin term product of K and L, denoted K o L, is the kin term that ego would (properly) use (if any) to refer to alter* when K is the kin term that ego (properly) uses to refer to alter and L is the kin term that alter (properly) uses to refer to alter*. For example, for the American kinship terminology, if ego refers to alter by the kin term Uncle and alter refers to alter* by the kin term Daughter, then ego properly refers to alter* by the kin term Cousin. The calculation may be made without knowing or tracing the genealogical connection between ego and alter, between alter and alter*, and between ego and alter*.

Once we have constructed a kin term map using kin term products, we next determine whether or not the kin term map structure, unlike a structure formed on an ad hoc basis, has an underlying generative logic. In our analysis we infer from the kin term map what appear to be the primary/generating kin terms and the underlying kin term equations for generating the structure displayed in the kin term map. We validate the claim that the kin term map has an underlying generative logic by constructively determining if it is possible to generate the kin term map exactly (i.e., isomorphically) from products of the primary kin terms simplified by the inferred equations (Read and Behrens, 1990; Read, 1997, 2000, 2001a, 2001b). Failure to isomorphically generate the kin term map would constitute falsification of the claim that the kin term map has an underlying generative logic.

The claim of a generative logic for a kin term map has already been validated for the American kinship terminology, the Shipibo kinship terminology, and the Trobriand kinship terminology (Read, 1984; Read and Behrens, 1990), among others. If the claim is validated for the TKT, delineation of the details of the generative logic will help answer the questions raised above. Our core analytical task, then, is to make evident the generative logic for a kin term map of the Tongan terminology by determining the primitive terms and structural equations that account for its structure. To do so, we first need to identify more precisely some of the salient features of a terminological space and its relationship to the kinship space.

8.4.3   Terminological space

For the terminological space (see right side of Figure 8.1) the objects making up the space are the kin terms from a kinship terminology viewed as a set of (abstract) symbols, along with a symbol, Self, serving as a label for the concept of self.[10] For a terminology such as the TKT, Self is a gendered concept. The entries in the middle right box in Figure 8.1 are transliterations of the generating kin terms for the Tongan kinship terminology. The kin term symbols are linked and form a structure through taking kin term products of the generating

---

[10] By "concept of self" is meant the conscious awareness of one's own existence, in contrast to the existence of others, as a sentient being (see Mead 1967[1934]: 135–226).

kin terms for the terminology. The form of a kinship terminology is specified through structural equations and structural rules (to be discussed below).

The kinship space is constructed through instantiation of the symbol combinations comprising the terminological space based on relations and symbols from the genealogical space (see bottom box, Figure 8.1). The last entry in the bottom box in Figure 8.1 connects the construction procedure for the terminological space with the prevalent assumption made in kinship studies that genealogical definitions of kin terms are the primitives of kinship terminologies. (Instantiation is not limited to genealogical relations; e.g., kin terms are also instantiated via adoption (Read, 2001b), among other possibilities.) These definitions are, in fact, predictable and derivable from the terminological space (middle right box in Figure 8.1) through instantiation of the generating terms for the terminological space with the generating genealogical relations for the genealogical space (middle left box in Figure 8.1) (Read, 2001a) and then using the generative logic of the terminological space to predict the genealogical definitions for all of the other kin terms.

The instantiation of the generating terms via genealogical primitives for genealogical tracing also provides a way to link an abstract, conceptual system

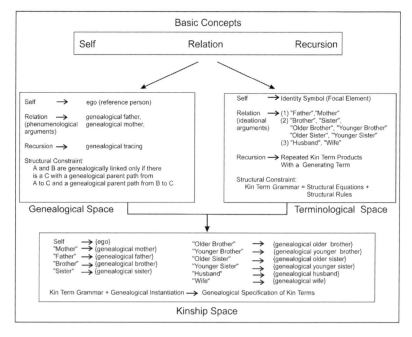

Figure 8.1 Concepts underlying genealogical space, kin term space and kinship space

(the terminological space) to concrete individuals when genealogical ego is identified with a specific individual. In other words, Figure 8.1 provides the conceptual basis for going from concepts fundamental to any account of culturally constructed kinship, namely the concepts of self, relation and recursion, to the way in which a specific individual implements the conceptual structures (the genealogical space and the terminological space) that constitute the kinship space through the actual usage of kin terms.

For the Tongan terminology we now have two analytical goals. The first is to sketch out the algebraic argument that the terminology has a structure based on the concepts identified in the box labeled Terminological Space in Figure 8.1. (A more detailed argument can be found in Bennardo and Read, 2005.) The second is to identify the structural and conceptual location of the kin terms *tokoua*, *tuofefine* and *tuonga'ane* in the terminological space and to clarify the manner in which they are concepts fundamental to the generation of the terminological space. The conceptual embedding of these terms in the terminological space, we argue, is not only central to the production of the structure of the Tongan terminology, but provides a "cultural model" for many other domains in Tongan cultural conceptualizations.

8.5   Algebraic analysis of the generative logic for the Tongan kinship terminology

8.5.1   *Kin term products and Cayley tables*

As discussed above, when Tongans (and others) determine kin relations they need not first refer to a genealogical space and then to kin terms but can determine kin relations directly through kin term calculations such as "older brother" of "father" is "father." We may express the results of these calculations through what mathematicians call a Cayley product table (named after the nineteenth-century mathematician Arthur Cayley; see Kronenfeld, 1973, for an example of a kin product table for the Fanti terminology). We will use an abbreviated table (Table 8.2) in which the generating terms for the Tongan terminology are listed as column headings. The generating terms for a terminology are a minimal set of kin terms from which every other term can be expressed as a product.

We initially adjoin a MaleSelf and a FemaleSelf symbol to the kinship terminology. As the argument proceeds, we will see that these symbols correspond to the kin terms *tuonga'ane* and *tuofefine*, respectively. We extend the kin term product to the symbol MaleSelf by defining MaleSelf o K = K o MaleSelf = K in the Cayley table for a kin term marked as male. Under this product definition, MaleSelf becomes the identity element for kin term products with male marked kin terms. Analogous comments apply to the FemaleSelf symbol.

Table 8.2 *Tongan kin terms products and kin term structure predicted from products of algebraic symbols*

Algebraic symbols	Transliteration Terms	C "Y Brother" *Tehina*-M	P "Father" *Tamai*	I MaleSelf *Tuonga'ane*	A "Son" *Foha*
H	*Tehina*-F	0	P = *Tamai*	I = *Tuonga'ane*	Ei&Ai = *Tama*
G	*Fa'e*	0	PP = *Kui*	IG = *Fa'etangata*	I = *Tuonga'ane*
i	*Tuofefine*	0	P = *Tamai*	Ii = ♀*Tuonga'ane*	Ei&Ai = *Tama*
Ei&Ai	*Tama*	Ei&Ai = *Tama*	0	Ei&Ai = *Tama*	AA&EE = *Mokopuna*
D	*Ta'okete*-F	0	P = *Tamai*	I = *Tuonga'ane*	Ei&Ai = *Tama*
B	*Ta'okete*-M	I = *Tuonga'ane*	P = *Tamai*	B = *Ta'okete*-M	A = *Foha*
A (= AI)	*Foha*	A = *Foha*	I = *Tuonga'ane*	A = *Foha*	AA&EE = *Mokopuna*
I	*Tuonga'ane*	C = *Tehina*-M	P = *Tamai*	I = *Tuonga'ane*	EI = '*Ofefine*
P	*Tamai*	P = *Tamai*	PP = *Kui*	P = *Tamai*	I = *Tuonga'ane*
C PP&GG	*Tehina*-M *Kui*	C = *Tehina*-M PP = *Kui*	P = *Tamai* PP = *Kui*	C = *Tehina*-M PP = *Kui*	A = *Foha* P = *Tamai*
IG	*Fa'etangata*	IG = *Fa'etangata*	PP = *Kui*	IG = *Fa'etangata*	I = *Tuonga'ane*
Ii	*Tuonga'ane*	Ii = ♀*Tuonga'ane*	P = *Tamai*	Ii = ♀*Tuonga'ane*	AIi&EIi = *Fakafotu*
AA&EE	*Mokopuna*	AA&EE = *Mokopuna*	Ei&Ai/A = *Tama/Foha*	AA&EE = *Mokopuna*	AA&EE = *Mokopuna*
EI	'*Ofefine*	0	I = *Tuonga'ane*	A = *Foha*	AA&EE = *Mokopuna*
iI	*Tuofefine*	0	P = *Tamai*	I = *Tuonga'ane*	EiI&AiI = '*Ilamutu*
iP	*Mehekitanga*	0	PP = *Kui*	P = *Tamai*	I = *Tuonga'ane*
AIi&EIi	*Fakafotu*	Aii&EIi = *Fakafotu*	Ii = *Tuonga'ane*	AIi&EIi = *Fakafotu*	AA&EE = *Mokopuna*
EiI&AiI	'*Ilamutu*	EiI&AiI = '*Ilamutu*	0	EiI&AiI = '*Ilamutu*	AA&EE = *Mokopuna*

Table 8.2 *(cont.)*

B	D	i	G	H	E
"O Brother"	"O Sister"	FemaleSelf	"Mother"	"Y Sister"	"Daughter"
Ta'okete-M	**Ta'okete-F**	**Tuofefine**	**Fa'e**	**Tehina-F**	**'Ofefine**
0	i = *Tuofefine*	H = *Tehina*-F	G = *Fa'e*	H = *Tehina*-F	Ei&Ai = *Tama*
0	G = *Fa'e*	G = *Fa'e*	PP = *Kui*	G = *Fa'e*	i = *Tuofefine*
0	D = *Ta'okete*-F	i = *Tuofefine*	G = *Fa'e*	H = *Tehina*-F	Ei&Ai = *Tama*
Ei&Ai = *Tama*	Ei&Ai = *Tama*	Ei&Ai = *Tama*	i = *Tuofefine*	Ei&Ai= *Tama*	AA&EE = *Mokopuna*
0	D = *Ta'okete*-F	D = *Ta'okete*-F	G = *Fa'e*	i = *Tuofefine*	Ei&Ai = *Tama*
B = *Ta'okete*-M	0	i = *Tuofefine*	G = *Fa'e*	0	EI = *'Ofefine*
A = *Foha*	0	EI = *'Ofefine*	0	0	AA&EE = *Mokopuna*
B = *Ta'okete*-M	0	Ii = *Tuofefine*	G = *Fa'e*	0	EI = *'Ofefine*
P = *Tamai*	0	iP = *Mehekitanga*	PP = *Kui*	0	i = *Tuofefine*
I = *Tuonga'ane*	0	i = *Tuofefine*	G = *Fa'e*	0	EI = *'Ofefine*
PP = *Kui*	PP = *Kui*	PP = *Kui*	PP = *Kui*	PP = *Kui*	iP = *Mehekitanga*
IG = *Fa'etangata*	0	G = *Fa'e*	PP = *Kui*	0	i = *Tuofefine*
Ii = ♀*Tuonga'ane*	0	i = *Tuofefine*	G = *Fa'e*	0	Ali&Eli = *Fakafotu*
AA&EE = *Mokopuna*	AA&EE = *Mokopuna*	AA&EE = *Mokopuna*	Ei&Ai/A = *Tama/Foha*	AA&EE = *Mokopuna*	AA&EE = *Mokopuna*
0	EI = *'Ofefine*	EI = *'Ofefine*	0	EI = *'Ofefine*	AA&EE = *Mokopuna*
0	iI = ♂*Tuofefine*	iI = ♂*Tuofefine*	G = *Fa'e*	iI = *Tuofefine*	Eil&Ail = *'Ilamutu*
0	iP = *Mehekitanga*	iP = *Mehekitanga*	PP = *Kui*	iP = *Mehekitanga*	i = *Tuofefine*
Ali&Eli = *Fakafotu*	Ali&Eli = *Fakafotu*	Ali&Eli = *Fakafotu*	0	Ali&Eli = *Fakafotu*	AA&EE = *Mokopuna*
Eil&Ail = *'Ilamutu*	Eil&Ail = *'Ilamutu*	Eil&Ail = *'Ilamutu*	Eil&Ail = *'Ilamutu*	Eil&Ail = *'Ilamutu*	AA&EE = *Mokopuna*

Note 1: first row: algebraic generators; second row: transliteration; third row: kin term isomorphic to a generator. First column: algebraic symbol products; second column: isomorphic kin terms. Body of table: kin terms isomorphic to the algebraic product of column headings × row headings. Body of table is the predicted kin term for the corresponding column and row algebraic product; e.g., P ($\cong$ *Tamai*) × G ($\cong$ *Fa'e*) = PP and *Kui* corresponds to PP. Thus *Kui* is the predicted kin term for the kin term product: *Tamai* of *Fa'e*. In fact, *Tamai* of *Fa'e* is *Kui* as a kin term product.

Note 2: -M and -F are added to kin terms when the kin term depends on sex of speaker; e.g., *Ta'okete* is "O brother" only for a male speaker so the table lists the term *Ta'okete*-M.

Note 3: A kin term begins with a sex symbol to indicate when the sex of the speaker is necessary; e.g., ♂*Tuofefine* is "Sister" (m.s.).

We can display the kin term map as a graph by letting the graph nodes be the kin terms listed as row headings in the Cayley table and then using an arrow to represent the result of taking the product of a kin term with one of the generating terms listed in the column headings. The tip of the arrow points to the kin term resulting from that kin term product. We use distinctive arrows, one for each generating term, to identify what kin term product is represented by which arrow.

A kin term map for Table 8.2 is quite complicated as ten kinds of arrows are needed. Alternatively, we can graph one portion of the kin term map at a time by using a more restricted map such as male marked terms (Figure 8.2) or female marked terms (not shown, but structurally identical to Figure 8.2). Note that the kin term *tuonga'ane*, which has transliteration 'brother (f.s.),' is not included in Figure 8.2 as it is properly used by a female speaker, hence is not a term from the viewpoint of a male speaker. Similarly, the male term, *fa'etangata* 'older brother' of 'mother,' is excluded at this stage in the analysis since it is isolated from the male marked kin terms in Figure 8.2 and so is not part of the structure shown in Figure 8.2. This term will be introduced into the structure as the analysis proceeds.

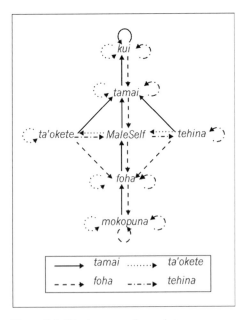

Figure 8.2 Kin term map for male terms

8.5.2   Construction of an algebraic model

The goal of the algebraic analysis is to determine whether or not the collection of kin terms making up the Tongan terminology has a structure that can be generated from a small set of atomic kin terms and structural equations relating to the products of kin terms; that is, it has the form of an algebraic structure. The algebraic analysis proceeds by first simplifying the kin term map, next finding an algebraic representation of the simplified kin term map, and then adding to the algebraic representation the structural aspects of the full kin term map removed through the simplification. Isomorphism between the kin term map and the resulting algebraic structure demonstrates that the kinship term structure has the form of an algebraic structure. But not all empirical structures can be represented in this manner, hence our claim that the kin term map for the Tongan terminology can be represented isomorphically as an algebraic structure would be falsified if there is no algebraic structure isomorphic to the Tongan kin term map. From the perspective of the genealogical "received view" that kin terms are added to a terminology for reasons exogenous to the terminology per se, there is no reason to expect that the collection of kin terms will have an algebraic structure.[11]

From the algebraic representation of the structure of the kin term map, a set of predicted genealogical definitions of kin terms can then be constructed. The predicted definitions are formed by first mapping the generating kin terms onto the genealogical space and secondly by determining the portion of the genealogical space that would be covered by a kin term based upon mapping the generating kin terms onto the genealogical space using the algebraic representation of the kin term map structure (Read, 2005). Being able to generate genealogical definitions for kin terms falsifies the fundamental assumption of the "received view" that genealogical definitions of kin terms are the primitive kinship concepts upon which kinship structural analysis should be based.

The analysis proceeds by first simplifying a kin term to a core structure and then constructing (if possible) an algebra isomorphic to this core structure. Next the structural properties removed during the simplification of the kin term map are introduced into the algebraic structure.

8.5.2.1 Simplification of a kin term map
A kin term map for the Tongan terminology can be simplified by first restricting the map to consanguineal terms of a single sex (including relevant neutral terms) (Figure 8.2).[12] Next, we remove reciprocal terms. For the TKT, we first

---

[11] The falsifiability of the claim that the kin term map has an algebraic structure contrasts sharply with descriptive methods such as componential analysis and rewrite rules as the latter simply provide descriptions, hence there is nothing to be falsified.

[12] Some terminologies are simplified by considering neutral, "covering" kin terms; e.g., the terms Parent, Child, Grandparent, Grandchild, etc. in the American kinship terminology.

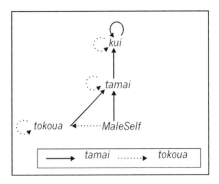

Figure 8.3 Kin term map from Figure 8.2 with sibling, reciprocals, and descending terms removed

remove the reciprocal attributes older/younger by removing the terms *ta'okete* 'older brother' and *tehina* 'younger brother' and replacing them with *tokoua* 'same sex sibling,' since *tokoua* does not have the older/younger attributes. Then we remove the reciprocal of *tamai* 'father,' namely *foha* 'son.' This has the effect of removing the descending structure from the kin term map. The simplified kin term map is shown in Figure 8.3.

8.5.2.2   Generating elements
We begin the algebraic construction by introducing an algebra symbol/element corresponding to each of the kin terms (which we will call generating kin terms) linked directly to the Self term in the simplified kin term map. Next, we add structural equation(s) that give an algebraic element the defining structural property of the kin term that we anticipate will correspond to the algebraic symbol. We then take all possible products using the algebraic symbol(s) that have been introduced and use the equations wherever possible to reduce products to simpler expressions. As the algebraic construction proceeds we introduce additional symbols and equations corresponding to reciprocals of the generating terms in the kin term map.

The structural equations are of two kinds. One set of structural equations is responsible for (1) giving each generating element its defining structural characteristics and (2) expressing the structural consequence of taking products of one generating element with another generating element. The other set of structural equations determines the overall form for the structure of the kinship terminology.

8.5.2.3   Ascending structure
For the TKT we begin with the symbols B, F and I, where I will be an identity element for the algebra, B will have the structural property of a sibling term, and F the structural property of an ascending kin term. The symbol B has

anticipated correspondence with the sibling kin term *tokoua*. A sibling term such as 'brother' satisfies the structural property that 'brother' of 'brother' is 'brother,' thus the first equation for the algebra will be:

$$BB = B \text{ (sibling structural equation).} \qquad (1)$$

The symbol F has anticipated correspondence with the kin term *tamai* 'father,' an ascending kin term. An *ascending term* satisfies, from a structural viewpoint, the property that products of the term with itself can be repeated to generate new kin terms. For the Tongan terminology we have the sequence *tamai*, *tamai* of *tamai* is *kui*, and the term *kui* is then repeated when taking additional products with the term *tamai*. Thus for the Tongan terminology we have the kin term computation: *tamai* of *tamai* of *tamai* is *tamai* of *tamai* is *kui*. We may express this equation algebraically as follows:

$$FFF = FF \text{ (ascending closure equation).} \qquad (2)$$

Note that Equations (1) and (2) structurally distinguish a sibling term from an ascending term.

We now need a structural equation to define the product between the symbols F and B. For a 'sibling' term and a 'father' term we have the structural property that

'father' of 'brother' is 'father.'

Corresponding to this kin term equation we have the algebraic structural equation:

$$FB = F \text{ (cross product equation).} \qquad (3)$$

At this stage the algebraic product, BF (read: 'brother' of 'father') is still a new, compound algebra symbol since there is, as yet, no equation in the algebra that would reduce this product to a simpler form. The structure produced by the generating elements B and F and equations (1)–(3) is shown in Figure 8.4. We will interpret this structure as representing the structure for the ascending male terms in the Tongan terminology.

8.5.2.4 Descending structure

We construct the descending structure by making an isomorphic copy of the ascending structure. The descending structure initially has the same morphological form as the ascending structure. In the isomorphic copy we introduce an element S to be the element isomorphic to F. The elements I and B will be the same in both structures. The element I will thus be the identity element for both the ascending structure and the descending structure.

We introduce equations isomorphic to equations (2) and (3):

$$SSS = SS \text{ (descending closure equation)} \qquad (2')$$

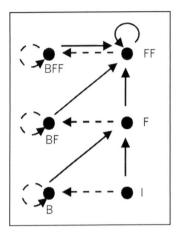

Figure 8.4 Algebra with sibling and father generating elements

and

$$SB = S \text{ (cross product equation).} \tag{3'}$$

We now have a structure of ascending elements and a structure of descending elements 'linked' by the identity symbol, I, and with the sibling element, B, common to both the ascending and the descending structures.

8.5.2.5 Combined ascending and descending structure
Next we consider all possible products using the symbols F, B, and S. For these symbols we have the equation:

$$SF = B \tag{4}$$

by virtue of the notion that the kin term product 'son' of 'father' yields a sibling kin term, namely B. Equation (4) implies that SFF = BF.
The product SBF = (SB)F = SF = B, thus we also have the derived equation:

$$SBF = B. \tag{5}$$

By a similar argument, we derive the equation SBFF = BF.

8.5.2.5.1 Reciprocal elements: F and S
We want the elements F and S to be reciprocal elements. In general, structural equations that make the algebra symbols X and Y into reciprocal elements are of the form XY = I. This equation is motivated by the observation that if a male ego refers to a male alter by the kin term K, then the kin term K' used by alter to refer to ego is the reciprocal of the kin term K, hence KK' = MaleSelf since a male ego would refer to

himself as MaleSelf. For the terms 'father' and 'son' we have 'father' of 'son' is MaleSelf, so we introduce the equation:

$$FS = I \text{ (reciprocal structural equation)}. \tag{6}$$

8.5.2.5.2 Reciprocal sibling elements: $B \rightarrow B+$ and $B-$ The reciprocal of the element B should be a symbol X with the property that either $BX = I$ or $XB = I$. This poses a logical dilemma as a candidate reciprocal for B is B since 'brother' is a self-reciprocal concept, hence at first glance it appears that we should introduce the equation $BB = I$. But from equation (1), $BB = B$, and so this would imply $B = BB = I$. The Tongan terminological solution to the dilemma (and the solution of other classificatory terminologies) is to bifurcate the symbol B into the pair of symbols, B+ and B−, and to introduce the sibling equations

$$B+B+ = B+ \tag{7}$$

and

$$B-B- = B- \tag{7'}$$

and the reciprocal equations

$$B+B- = I \tag{8}$$

and

$$B-B+ = I. \tag{8'}$$

The symbols B+ and B− correspond to the terms *ta'okete* and *tehina*, respectively.

   Equation (8) implies:

$$FB- = F \text{ (father structural equation)} \tag{3A}$$

since $B+B- = I$ implies $F = FI = F(B+B-) = (FB+)B- = FB-$. Similarly, equation (8′) implies:

$$FB+ = F \text{ (father structural equation)}. \tag{3B}$$

Equation (3′) has two isomorphs:

$$SB- = S \tag{9}$$

and

$$SB+ = S. \tag{9'}$$

Equation (4) ($SF = B$) and the bifurcation of B into B− and B+ imply the equations:

$$SF = B- \tag{10}$$

and

$$SF = B+ \tag{10'}$$

(that is, SF can either be B– or B+, but this potential ambiguity will be resolved in the next section). The algebraic structure corresponding to the combined ascending and descending structure is shown in Figure 8.5.

8.5.2.6 Reciprocal equations

A general property of reciprocal kin terms is that if $XY = Z$ is a structural equation for the terminology, then the reciprocal equation $(XY)^r = Y^r X^r = Z^r$ is a structural equation for the terminology, where X^r is the reciprocal term for the kin term X (and similarly for Y and Z). For the equations in Section 8.5.2.4, the reciprocal equations for equations (2), (3), (7), (8) are equations (2'), (3'), (7'), (8'), respectively, and (4), (5), (6) are self-reciprocal equations. Equations (3A) and (3B) have for their reciprocal equations:

$$B–S = S \tag{4A}$$
$$B+S = S, \tag{4B}$$

respectively.

These equations have a genealogical interpretation: genealogical younger brother of genealogical son is genealogical son and genealogical older brother of genealogical son is genealogical son. Finally we include the reciprocal equations for the remaining two equations, SB+=S and SB–=S:

$$B–F = F \tag{9*}$$
$$B+F = F. \tag{9'*}$$

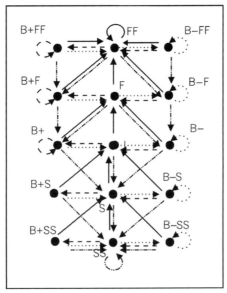

Figure 8.5 Ascending and descending algebraic structure

Remarkably, we have now introduced precisely the fundamental equations for a classificatory terminology simply by following a general procedure for the construction of an ascending and descending structure for a kinship terminology when a sibling term is a generating element. The general procedure for generating an ascending and descending structure for a terminology underlies both descriptive and classificatory terminologies (see Read and Behrens, 1990; Read, 2005). The construction thus implies that the classificatory aspect of the Tongan terminology (and for other classificatory terminologies) derives logically from a general ontology for the construction of a kinship terminology and the fact that a sibling term is one of the atomic terms in the kinship terminology. This contrasts sharply with the construction of a descriptive terminology where the construction is based on a single ascending term and a sibling term such as Brother in the American kinship terminology is a compound term constructed from taking products of the Mother or Father term with the Son term (Read and Behrens, 1990; Read, 2005).

We cannot emphasize too strongly the importance of this result for understanding not only the structure of terminologies such as the Tongan terminology, but also the implications it has for the centrality of the sibling relation in Tongan behavior and cultural representations. The centrality of the sibling relation in Tongan life reflects the centrality of the sibling element as an atomic element in the construction of the Tongan terminology.

The construction also removes the potential ambiguity of equation $(10')$ $SF = B+$ and equation (10) $SF = B-$ via the fact these two products imply, respectively, $I = B - B + = B - SF = (B - S)F = SF$ and $I = B + B - = B + SF = (B + S)F = SF$ and so we now have $SF = I$. The results in this section modify Figure 8.5 to yield the male structure for the TKT shown in Figure 8.6, which is isomorphic to Figure 8.2.

8.5.2.7   Male structure

We have now generated the structure for the male marked kin terms. The salient features are:

Generating elements: F, B+
Reciprocal elements: S, B–
Identity element: I
Structural equations:

$$B + B + = B+, \quad B - B - = B-$$
$$FB+ = F$$
$$FB- = F$$
$$FFF = FF$$

Isomorphic structural equations:

$$SB- = S$$
$$SB+ = S$$
$$SSS = SS$$

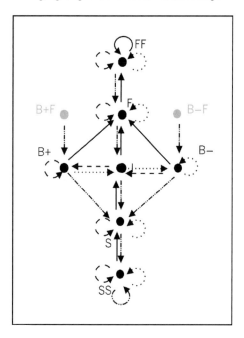

Figure 8.6 Algebraic structure for male elements

Reciprocal definition equations:

$$FS = I$$
$$SF = I$$
$$B+B- = I$$
$$B-B+ = I$$

Reciprocal equations (not already included above):

$$B-S = S$$
$$B+S = S$$

Classificatory equations:

$$B+F = F$$
$$B-F = F$$

The structure corresponding to these generating elements and equations is shown in Figure 8.6.

8.5.2.8   Female structure

We introduce female marked elements by making an isomorphic copy of the male structure summarized in Section 8.5.2.7. Under this isomorphism new female marked symbols, M, Z+, Z–, D, and i, are introduced corresponding to each of the male marked symbols: M ↔ F, Z+ ↔ B+, Z– ↔ B–, D ↔ S, and i ↔ I. This yields a structure of female marked elements (see right side of Figure 8.7) defined by the same equations as for the male marked elements but with the male marked elements replaced by their corresponding female marked elements.

8.5.2.9   Ethnographic implications

Note in Figure 8.6 the two nodes, B+F and B–F, in gray (and similarly the nodes for Z+M and Z–M in the isomorphic structure for female marked algebraic elements). These two nodes have been transformed into the "F" node since B+F=F=B–F. But the S arrows from these two nodes to B+ and B–, respectively, have not been transformed. Hence it follows that B+F and B–F are unlabeled, implicit nodes, yet their mapping to B+ and B– is still part of the structure. Consequently the algebraic structure implies that the genealogical instantiation B+F → {genealogical father's genealogical older brother} should have the property that (genealogical father's genealogical older brother)'s genealogical son will be genealogical older brother (since SB+F=B+) and similarly (genealogical mother's genealogical older sister)'s genealogical son will be genealogical older brother. Similar arguments apply to B–F.

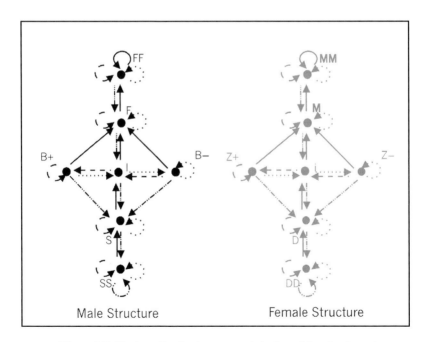

Figure 8.7 Algebra of male elements and algebra of female elements

Table 8.3 *'Older' 'younger' sibling terms*

	Man speaking	Woman speaking
Ta'okete	B+FB+S, MZ+S	Z+, FB+D, MZ+D
Tehina	B–FB–S, MZ–S	Z–, FB–D, MZ–D

Modified from Table 1 (Biersack, 1982).

This interpretation is ethnographically valid (Table 8.3) and so the algebraic construction makes evident the structural basis for the factual information provided in Table 8.3 and thereby accounts for the different behavior ego has towards genealogical older/younger siblings versus genealogical parallel cousins even though these two sets of genealogical relations are not differentiated terminologically as discussed previously.

8.5.2.10   Joint male structure and female structure
At this point we have two unconnected structures since we have introduced new elements {M, Z+, Z–, D, i} for the isomorphic copy of Figure 8.6 without any overlap with the generating elements {F, B+, B–, S, I} for the male marked elements (see Figure 8.7). We now consider how the male structure and the female structure are linked conceptually and structurally to make a single structure.

8.5.2.10.1   Conceptual linkage: sex marked identity elements   The culturally formulated means for conceptually connecting the two structures together is ingenious. Consider the two symbols, I (MaleSelf) and i (FemaleSelf). If I is instantiated with a male person, then what female should be used to instantiate the i symbol? That is, who should be a female ego corresponding to a male ego? The cultural solution that has been introduced into many of the classificatory terminologies is to instantiate female ego with male ego's genealogical sister and if i has been instantiated with female ego, then instantiate I with female ego's genealogical brother. Under this instantiation it follows that the symbol I corresponds to a kin term from the perspective of a female ego, namely I corresponds to the kin term 'brother (f.s.)', and similarly from the perspective of a male ego the symbol i corresponds to the kin term 'sister (m.s.)'! And we find in the Tongan terminology the terms *tuonga'ane* 'brother' used by a female speaker and *tuofefine* 'sister' used by a male speaker (see left and right sides of Figure 8.8).

Thus the I and i nodes in the structure labeled with the two terms, *tuonga'ane* and *tuofefine*, play a dual role: on the one hand, they mark the position at which an ego will be located (male ego at the *tuonga'ane* position, female ego at the *tuofefine* position) and on the other hand they determine the structural nodes for the kin terms to be used by a male ego for a female ego who is his

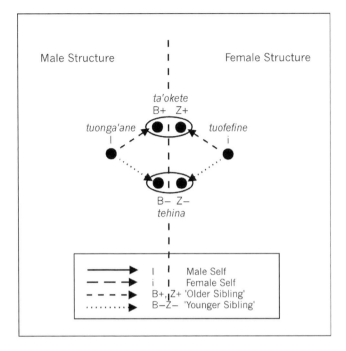

Figure 8.8 Structure for 'older sibling' and 'younger sibling' elements

genealogical sister, and vice versa. Consequently, a male speaker has a *ta'okete* 'older brother' or a *tehina* 'younger brother' and he has a *tuofefine* 'sister' but he does not have a *tuonga'ane* 'brother;' similarly for a female speaker, she has a *ta'okete* 'older sister,' a *tehina* 'younger sister' and a *tuonga'ane* 'brother' but she does not have a *tuofefine* 'sister.' This is structurally a very ingenious solution to conceptually integrating together the structure of male terms and the structure of female terms. It also accounts for the pattern in which it is only the 'same sex sibling' term that has the attributes older and younger.

Although the element I is an identity element in the structure of male terms (left side of Figure 8.7) and the element i is an identity element in the structure of female terms (right side of Figure 8.7), these elements lose their status as identity elements when we form the structure containing both the male and the female structures.[13] Hence products using elements I and i with elements that have the opposite sex marking, including the products Ii or iI, will not

---

[13] An algebra can contain at most one identity element. If I and i are both identity elements, then I = Ii = i.

simplify according to the equations for identity elements. Instead, products such as Ii and iI become new elements in the algebra. These two products correspond to *tuonga'ane* (f.s.) and *tuofefine* (m.s.) with instantiations 'brother of a female self' and 'sister of a male self,' respectively. Thus the algebraic structure accounts not only for the terms *tuonga'ane* (= I) and *tuofefine* (= i), but also for the usage of these kin terms according to sex of speaker, namely Ii = *tuonga'ange* (f.s.) and iI = *tuofefine* (m.s.). In other words, for the algebraic product Ii we have the interpretation that "i" is the algebraic element mapped to a female ego and for the algebraic product iI we have the interpretation that "I" is the algebraic element mapped to a male ego.

8.5.2.10.2 Structural linkage: 'older sibling' and 'younger sibling'   Consider the algebra symbols I, B+ and B– from the male structure and the elements i, Z+ and Z– from the female structure. If the two algebra symbols B+ and Z+ are made equivalent (see oval in upper part of Figure 8.8), and similarly B– and Z– are made equivalent, then we have a single older node and a single 'younger' node (see oval in lower part of Figure 8.8). These two combined nodes are not sex marked and structurally link further the male and the female structures. One combined node, call it B+&Z+, is labeled with the kin term *ta'okete* ('older same sex sibling') and the other combined node, B–&Z-, is labeled with the kin term *tehina* ('younger same sex sibling') under the isomorphism between the atomic algebra symbols and atomic kin terms.

8.5.2.11 Implications of the structural linkage for products
with 'son' and 'daughter'

A number of important structural consequences for the Tongan terminology with regard to terms for genealogical children of ego and ego's genealogical sibling arise from the fact that I, i, Ii, and iI are distinct elements (see top part of Figure 8.9, expanded from Figure 8.8). Consider the products with S ('son') and D ('daughter') in the algebraic structure. For the nodes iI and Ii these products yield the nodes (1) SiI and DiI (that is, algebra symbols corresponding to the kin terms for the genealogical son or daughter of a woman who is the genealogical sister of a male ego) and (2) SIi and DIi (that is, algebra symbols corresponding to the kin terms for the genealogical son or daughter of a man who is the genealogical brother of a female ego), respectively. Products of S and D with the two nodes, I and i, yield the nodes (3) SI and DI (that is, algebra symbols corresponding to kin terms for the genealogical son or daughter of a male ego) and (4) Si and Di (that is, algebra symbols corresponding to kin terms for the genealogical son or daughter of a female ego) as new, distinct nodes in the algebra.

Of these four pairs of products using S and D, each of the pairs except SI and DI becomes a single node without sex marking and each of these nodes is mapped to a different kin term (see Figure 8.9, bottom part of graph). Thus, the

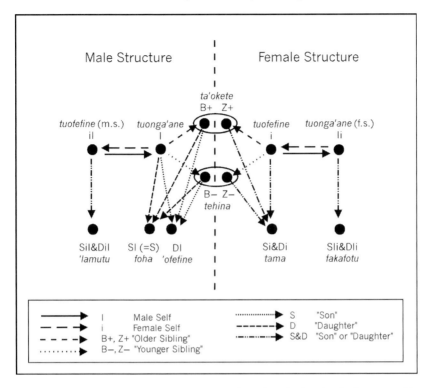

Figure 8.9 Structure for products of 'son' and 'daughter' elements with 'sibling' elements

kin terms *'ilamutu* and *fakafotu* correspond to the products SiI&DiI ('child' of 'sister' of MaleSelf) and SIi&DIi ('child' of 'brother' of FemaleSelf), respectively (see Figure 8.9) and the kin term, *tama* ('child' of FemaleSelf) corresponds to the products Si&Di ('child' of FemaleSelf).

In contrast, the nodes SI (= S) and DI ('son' of MaleSelf and 'daughter' of MaleSelf) correspond to different kin terms; namely, *foha* (with instantiation genealogical son, m.s.) and *'ofefine* (with instantiation genealogical daughter, m.s.). Keeping the terms SI and DI distinct appears to be a way to explicitly imbed the generating elements S and D into the kin term structure and has implications for the pattern of inheritance in Tongan society (discussed below). As a consequence, the Tongan terminology has the kin terms *foha* and *'ofefine* – but only for a male ego. In contrast a female has only the kin term *tama* ('child' of FemaleSelf).[14]

---

[14] Biersack (1982) lists *fefine* as an alternative term for *tama*, the term used by female ego for her child, regardless of sex. Hence the terminology appears to be symmetrical with respect to keeping

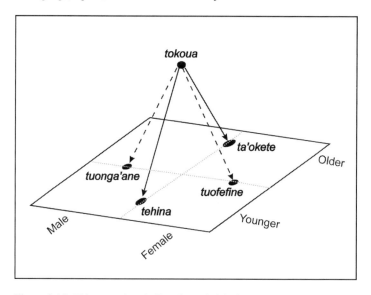

Figure 8.10 *Tokoua* and male/female and older/younger attributes

8.5.2.12 Structural implications of the term tokoua

In Bennardo and Read (2005: 13–16), we presented an attribute analysis of TKT in which *tokoua* 'same sex sibling' appeared to be a central term in the kinship terminology, yet in the final algebraic structure there is no element corresponding to this term. Rather than arising from the algebraic construction, the term *tokoua* with its transliteration 'same sex sibling' appears to play an ontologically prior role as the label for the concept of a sibling relation fundamental to the Tongan terminology as discussed above in Sections 8.5.2.1 and 8.5.2.2.

We can illustrate the structural position of *tokoua* by considering it to be a concept lying above the sibling plane as shown in Figure 8.10. Within the plane we have two divisions: horizontally male/female and vertically older/younger. The horizontal division arises from the pair of algebra symbols I and i that correspond to the terms *tuonga'ane* and *tuofefine*, respectively. The vertical division arises from the bifurcation of *tokoua* into two sibling terms, *ta'okete* and *tehina*, with attributes that can be transliterated as older/younger.

Thus structurally the term *tokoua* represents a primitive concept ('sibling') to which the pair of 'opposite sex sibling' terms *tuonga'ane* and *tuofefine* are linked through the associated identity symbols, MaleSelf and FemaleSelf (see Figure 8.7), that are initially unlabeled and then become labeled when they

the products SI, Si, DI and Di distinct, but asymmetrical with the property that the term *tama* is also used as a cover term for both Si and Di but no term is used as a cover term for SI and DI.

conceptually join together to form the male and female structures (see Figure 8.8). The derived sibling concepts *ta'okete* 'older (same sex) sibling'/*tehina* 'younger (same sex) sibling' also arise from the term *tokoua*. *Tokoua* has the structural property of first giving rise to a pair of 'same sex sibling terms' with +/– marking in the structure of male terms (see Figure 8.6) and then to an isomorphic pair of 'same sex sibling terms' with +/– marking in the structure of female terms (see Figure 8.7), and finally to identification of the two + marked terms and of the two – marked terms so as to form a single pair of 'same sex' terms *ta'okete*/*tehina* with +/– marking (see Figure 8.9). *Tokoua* thus has structural status as the non-sex marked and non-relative age marked sibling term for the terminology as a whole from which one arrives at the two relative age marked terms and the two gender marked terms in the sibling plane. The English word 'sibling,' however, has connotations that are not applicable to the Tongan concept of *tokoua*, hence the transliteration 'same sex sibling,' which reflects the manner in which the pair of terms *ta'okete*/*tehina* are constructed from the term *tokoua*.

8.5.2.13 Cross products of male marked and female marked algebra symbols
The remaining part of the algebraic construction consists of working out the cross products between the elements in the male structure and the elements in the female structure. This entails adding equations that take into account the sex marking of algebra symbols. The diagram at this point becomes overwhelmed with arrows due to the fact that there are ten generating elements: F, M, B+, B–, Z+, Z–, S, D, I, and i. The structure of the algebra is displayed, instead, in the form of an algebra Cayley table in parallel with the kin term Cayley table used to display the structure of kin term products (see Table 8.2). When these two Cayley tables are compared we find that they are isomorphic.[15] The isomorphism is shown in Table 8.2 (see Bennardo and Read, 2005, for a more detailed discussion regarding Table 8.2).

8.6   Tongan social life and kinship terminology revisited

Various puzzling issues were raised about TKT in Sections 8.2–8.4. We can now attempt to clarify some of them using the results of the algebraic analysis just introduced. We do not claim that all features of a terminology arise from the logic of how a kinship terminology is generated. Rather, the algebraic analysis permits us to determine whether a feature arises from the internal logic of how the structure is generated or whether the feature arises from reasons extrinsic to the logic of how the terminology is generated. We need then to look

---

[15] All of the algebraic calculations, production of structures, and testing for isomorphism have been done with the computer program Kinship Algebra Expert System (KAES) (Read and Fischer 2004).

for cultural interventions in order to account for the presence of those features in the terminology.

Here is a short list of the issues:

1. Siblings are distinguished only according to gender and age: (1) a Tongan female sibling is always higher in rank than her brother; (2) an older same sex sibling is always higher in rank than a younger one.
2. The linguistic distinction between *fa'etangata* 'older maternal uncle' and *tu'asina* 'younger maternal uncle' is not present in the otherwise symmetrical relationship, *mehekitanga* 'paternal aunts.'
3. The general tendency of the terminology at generation 1 down is not to mark for gender (e.g., *tama*, *fakafotu*, *'ilamutu*), but oddly gender is used when reference is made to a male's offspring (i.e., *foha* or *'ofefine*).
4. *Fahu*, where one is *'eiki* 'high' to one's 'mother's brother's children' and is *tu'a* 'low' to one's 'father's sister's children,' is not a kinship term.
5. At a Tongan funeral, in the generation 1 up, the father's side is *'eiki* 'high' and the mother's side is *tu'a* 'low;' in the generation 1 down, children are *tu'a* if the deceased is male and *'eiki* if the deceased is female.
6. There is a term for 'same sex sibling,' *tokoua*, but no corresponding term for 'opposite sex sibling.'

Regarding issue 1, the participation of the two concepts of gender and age in the structural generation of the terminology has become clear after the algebraic analysis. Two structures are independently constructed for male and female members and later joined. We did the construction starting from terms with male attributes, but it was an arbitrary decision and one could start from either a male or a female structure without affecting the results of the process. It is relevant that two gender-biased structures need to be independently posited to arrive at an elucidation of the internal logic of the whole TKT. This supports the conclusion we reached that the concept of gender plays a fundamental role in TKT, also preceding age.

These conclusions amend the picture of TKT we delineated in our attribute analysis in Bennardo and Read (2005: 13–16). The terminology is inherently gendered and aged. The gender neutral terms *kui* 'grandparent,' *motu'a* 'parent,' *tokoua* 'same sex sibling,' *tama* 'child,' and *mokopuna* 'grandchild,' while they may still be considered the backbone of TKT, are not its starting point. They are a set of specific terms that perform an important role during the genesis of the terminology. They are the 'structural glue' that keeps together the two male and female structures shown in Figure 8.7 to obtain the TKT in its entirety.

Age difference for 'same sex sibling' terms is introduced as a necessary feature in order for there to be consistency with defining reciprocal terms for the sibling terms. Age distinctions are consequently expected to appear and play determinant roles in the final terminology structure through the logic of the terminology. For siblings, we find two gender-neutral terms for older and younger by virtue of the logic of the construction and similarly for the child of same sex siblings of parent. For same sex siblings of parents the logic of the construction implies that an older/younger distinction will not be made.

Issues 2 and 3 therefore relate to an application of gender and age distinctions at junctures in the terminology that are not required by its internal logic. Algebraically, the age distinction at the mother's brother level (and not at the father's sister level where there is only one term, *mehekitanga*) realized in the two terms *fa'etangata* 'older MB' and *tu'asina* 'younger MB' is not necessary even though possible. In the same way, the distinction between male and female offspring of a male individual, *foha* and *'ofefine* (a distinction not present for children of a female where there is only one term, *tama*), is not logically necessary even though possible. This double (gendered and aged) asymmetry points again towards a cultural intervention external to the terminology. Notice, however, that the two asymmetries are obtained by using two basic concepts inherent in the logic of the terminology, thus supporting further our axiomatic choices.

Issue 6 about the centrality of *tokoua* 'same sex sibling' in the terminology (also suggested in the attribute analysis in Bennardo and Read, 2005: 13–16) has been confirmed and clarified by the algebraic analysis. We concluded that *tokoua* is a term that stands outside the logical plane of TKT and is situated in an ontologically prior level. It plays a central role and it functions as the basis from which age but not gender marked sibling terms are constructed. It also provides a contrast for the gender but not age marked sibling terms. This finding highlights the essential participation and central role played by siblinghood in the genesis of TKT and in Tongan kinship relations in general. Significantly, the structural starting point for all the terms is a term for an individual other-than-ego, namely *tokoua*, and from there the terminology is allowed to "grow" and be realized. This finding is congruent with the proposal under investigation of the primacy of radiality in the representation of spatial relationships and in other domains of Tongan knowledge.

The algebraic analysis, however, does not explain why a female sibling is always considered superior to a male sibling. This is a fundamental parameter that regulates several cultural behaviors (e.g., brother/sister avoidance practices) and is at the root of the *fahu* practice as elucidated in issues 4 and 5. The logic of the terminology only points to the fundamental role that gender plays in the genesis of TKT, but does not indicate any necessity of superiority of one gender over the other. We are then confident in asserting that this parameter has been introduced by cultural considerations external to the terminology itself. Finding a possible cultural explanation would clarify the practice of *fahu* as well as the other two asymmetrical uses of gender and age indicated in issues 2 and 3.

Several authors have pointed out the centrality of the group over the individual in Tongan culture (see Gifford, 1929; Beaglehole and Beaglehole, 1941;

Maude, 1971; Korn, 1974, 1978; Marcus, 1977, 1978, 1980; Kaeppler, 1978a, 1978b; Gailey, 1987; van der Grijp, 1993; James, 1995; Small, 1997; Helu, 1999; Evans, 2001; Morton, 2003). A comprehensive treatment of the various basic social units or groups of Tongan social organization and their historical and contemporary dynamics can be found in Evans (2001). Without going into unnecessary details, we will focus on a couple of important points he makes in his discussion.

All groups described, including *ha'a* 'patrilineage,' *fa'ahinga/kāinga* 'localized kin group, bilateral kindred, kin people,' and *fāmili* 'members of an individual's natal household,'[16] are essentially based on bilateral kinship relationships. *Kāinga*, however, "was central to both political and social organization at the local level" (Evans, 2001: 37). Moreover, "Title and thus political rank generally passed through men; 'blood' or social rank was passed through both men and women, and in this the rank of the women was more significant" (Evans, 2001: 34). In "title" one needs to read rights to land use by the titleholder's group and distribution to the individuals making up the group. A male primogeniture principle is also in place, thus reiterating the use of age as a constituting and salient part of Tongan social fabric.[17]

Being that this is the case, then why elevate one's sister status to create the *fahu* relationship wherein one's sister/s and one's sister/s' children have open access to one's property? From the point of view of the individual, this is not a positive outcome. From the point of view of a group, however, these children belong to one's lineal group and property is with this group after all, specifically and according to Evans the *fa'ahinga* (2001: 40). Furthermore, because of the *fahu* relationship, children have open access to their mother's brother's property, who belongs to a different group (affinal) from one's own. One's group, then, is economically and eventually politically strengthened by this possibility.

Another possible factor can be found in the attempt to maintain a balance between males and females. Since political power was "passed through men," it was made sure, in a complementary sense, that social power lay with women by making them superior to their siblings (with consequences at every generation level). The algebraic analysis of the terminology clearly indicates that such balancing processes are logically inherent in the genesis of TKT. Specifically, it occurs when the horizontal isomorphism joins the two gendered structures. In addition, the balance created goes beyond the two basic groups of males and females, and creates a new subtle balance between lineal and affinal groups. Then, in the final analysis we find two gender and bilateral groups that are sewn together by the threading role of the *fahu* relationships.

---

[16] The two terms *fāmili* and *kāinga* often overlap in usage (Evans, 2001: 62).

[17] When no male was present, the title was passed down to a female child.

Three factors, keeping property in the lineage, acquiring property from another lineage, and balancing power between gender groups and lineages, all concur in creating the asymmetries of the TKT we have highlighted in issues 2 and 3. It is necessary for a male individual to distinguish between male and female children because inheritance practices demand that male children inherit title and land. Thus, the TKT includes two gendered terms for children of a male. Primogeniture also participates in the inheritance process, hence it is important to know not only the gender but also the relative age of an individual. This is especially true when exercising one's privileges over *fahu* individuals. It is really important to know who is the heir to the property if a male wants to take the best advantage of his privileged position as *fahu* towards one's mother's brothers. Hence, the TKT distinguishes between older and younger mother's brothers as a cultural modification of the basic kinship structure

We started this section by indicating a number of issues that our discussion of TKT in Sections 8.2–8.4 had raised. With the help of the algebraic analysis of TKT we were able to resolve these issues. Issue 6, about the centrality of *tok-oua* 'same sex sibling,' has been confirmed and further clarified. Issue 1 is not directly resolved by the results of the algebraic analysis, but the same algebraic analysis makes apparent that a resolution is to be found in a cultural intervention. A centripetal process (inheritance) toward a basic social group (lineage) was suggested as a possible motivator. Inheritance practices were also suggested as possible causes for the asymmetries in TKT indicated in issues 2 and 3. Finally, issues 4 and 5 were found to be related to a basic social stance seen at work in the genesis of the TKT, namely, threading together centrifugal forces inherent in different gender and social groups (e.g., lineages). Both directly and indirectly, then, the algebraic analysis of the TKT provides needed clarifications and insights for the exploration of an unfamiliar social world.

8.7   Conclusion

We presented an algebraic account of the Tongan kinship terminology (TKT) that provided an insightful journey into the fabric of Tongan culture. We began with the ethnographic account of a social event. The account provided us with the activities of that day and the centrality of kin relations in the event, but it did not inform us of the conceptual system that the participants brought with them. Rather, it was a slice in time of an ongoing dynamic process that linked behavior with a conceptual system of kin relations and a conceptual system of kin relations with behavior. To understand this interplay we needed an account of the underlying conceptual system that is being activated during the event. Thus, we introduced a formal, algebraically based account of TKT. This account brought to the fore the underlying logic of TKT and allowed us to distinguish between features of the kinship system that arose from the logic of TKT as a generative structure and features that must have arisen through cultural intervention. Finally, we revisited the ethnographic account and we considered those aspects whose explication must lie in cultural interventions thus linking the kinship conceptual systems to other domains such as ranking and inheritance.

Moreover, one fundamental aspect of the Tongan kinship terminology is relevant to the current attempt to find support and evidence for radiality as a Tongan foundational cultural model, namely, the centrality of the sibling relation. In a descriptive terminology a sibling is a compound term constructed from taking products of the Mother or Father term with the Son term (Read and Behrens, 1990; Read, 2005), that is, it is constructed starting from ego. In a classificatory terminology like Tongan, the sibling term is one of the atomic terms. It is from there that the terminology springs out, generates. And this is more so when we look at the term *tokoua* 'same sex sibling' (see Figure 8.10). *Tokoua* had to be posited as lying in a different conceptual plane from the other four sibling terms, a generative first step toward the construction of the whole terminology rooted on siblinghood.

Fundamentally, then, we see the working of the radiality foundational model at play in the kinship terminology. A not-gendered, not-aged individual, other-than-ego individual, *tokoua*, is conceived first as the starting point of the terminology (conceptual radiality). The participation of gender and age contribute to the construction of four sibling terms, *tuonga'ane* and *tuofefine* (gender), *ta'okete* and *tehina* (age). A variety of operations between these terms and terms in other generations, i.e., father, continue the generative process.

Loisi, the child whose first birthday celebration was described at the opening of this work, is a teenager now and moved with her family to New Zealand and then Australia a few years ago. She is bilingual, fluent in Tongan and English. I don't know about the extent of her biculturalism, but I know for sure that she is competent in using the appropriate Tongan terms for her siblings, her parents and grandparents, her maternal and paternal relatives. Most likely she is capable of understanding who a *fahu* is and who can claim that position in a funeral. In other words, she is a competent TKT user.

Tongans very rarely live in isolation when abroad (Small, 1997; Morton, 2003). They tend to live in communities that attempt to replicate the structure, feel, and pace of a Tongan community. This simple fact assures Loisi a life full of Tongan events (typically, first birthdays, marriages, and funerals) many of which are constructed around the kinship relationships expressed in the TKT.

Very likely Loisi is not aware of the generating logic of TKT that the algebraic analyses presented have brought to the fore. She is not aware of the struggle that her predecessors went through to knead together a single bi-gender structure from two gendered ones. The ingenious solutions they implemented to obtain gender equality while preserving differences, as well as the skillful way in which group welfare was given priority over individual interests, are not much of her concern. She probably needs to decide how much of what she unconsciously knows about Tongan kinship can be preserved in the face of a different kinship system she is being exposed to and learning about in the new 'place' in which she is now living. The solutions for her are not yet available, but she stands tall on the shoulders of her ancestors whose exquisite reasoning and logic is partly inscribed in the kinship terminology they left behind.

Part III

Radiality in social relationships

9   Radiality and speech about social relationships

9.1   Introduction

The finding of radiality at the conceptual roots of the Tongan kinship terminology convinced me that the domain of social relationships needed to be the
next step in my investigation. Kinship is fundamental to the establishment of
a multitude of types of social relationships. Sometimes, in many cultures, it
is kinship exclusively that provides the necessary and sufficient reasons to
engage in any type of social relationships. Besides, a good number of ethnographic observations had already attracted my attention to this vital aspect of
the Tongan cultural milieu.[1]

Tongans position themselves socially in a distinctive way. In everyday conversations when trying to define their position in the social hierarchy, Tongans
often make initial reference to a high status person as a fixed point of reference.
They then trace their personal position from that person/point. Similarly, in a
fono 'official meeting,' an individual's status is indicated and determined by the
'distance' – calculated in units represented by intervening individuals – from
the highest status person present, for example, the local village chief, a noble,
or the king (Bott, 1972; Marcus, 1980). This is true at the village, island, and
national levels.

This conceptualization of social hierarchy and social relationships is remin-
iscent of the foundational cultural model I termed 'radiality.' Thinking radially
to locate objects in space – in this case, a social space – implies looking for
a fixed point of reference and describing the object to be identified, e.g., ego,
as positioned from/toward that point. It must be noticed that the specific way
in which Tongans position themselves socially and the official arrangement of
people in the *fono* would represent a sub-case of radiality as instantiated in a
single vector, away from one point or toward it.

The decision to investigate the domain of social relationships was also
influenced by two other bodies of literature: one about a number of proposals

---

[1] 'Relation' is another of the fundamental ontological categories as in Aristotle and Kant.

suggesting radiality in many aspects of Eastern[2] (e.g., Nisbett, 2003), South-East Asian (e.g., Kuipers, 1998), Micronesian (e.g., Ross, 1973), and other Polynesian societies (e.g., Shore, 1996; Herdrich and Lehman, 2002); and one containing current ideas about the content of a 'cultural' component-module of the mind (e.g., Jackendoff, 1992a, 1999, 2007; Pinker, 1997; Talmy, 2000b; Levinson, 2006) that is orchestrated around the mental representations of social relationships (i.e., kinship, group membership, dominance).

9.2   Investigating social relationships

What are social relationships? Granted that finding a satisfactory answer to this question is well beyond the scope of this work, I provide the guidelines I followed in thinking about social relationships and in preparing the tools to investigate them. In my definition of social relationships, I include the following: first and foremost kinship relationships; second, relationships regarding group membership, including social groups (e.g., in Tonga, married vs. not married, elders, etc.), religious groups, and geographical-residential ones such as being neighbors, co-villagers; third, dominance/power relationships, that is, those relationships that characterize a specific cultural milieu (local and as large as the specific cultural distribution is, i.e., in Tonga, national) due to rules that regulate who produces goods, who has privileged access to resources, and who establishes the rules/laws (social, political, economic) that the majority of the population abides by.

The specific focus of my investigation is not to arrive at the description of a typology of social relationships Tongans may engage in, but to explore a possible core and implicit structural organization Tongans might use in representing those relationships mentally. Then, the question arises, how does one go about investigating possible mental representations of social relationships? For example, one can ask people to talk about social relationships, i.e., their own and others'. Specific linguistic features, either lexical, syntactic, semantic, and/or pragmatic/discursive, may emerge that would provide some clues about the structural organization of the domain. But, how would one control for the difference in dimensionality between language and cognition, that is, one dimension versus many, respectively? Aren't linguistic data necessarily affected by the unidimensionality of the medium? One must conclude, then, that linguistic data, while enormously useful, are not sufficient.

---

[2] "Their universe was a continuous medium or matrix within which interactions of things took place, not by the clash of atoms, but by radiating influences" (Needham, 1962: 14, cited in Nisbett, 2003: 18). This quote by Needham is about China and it is generally accepted that the migration of the people who became Polynesian started from south-east China (Groube, 1971; Green and Pawley, 1973; Howe, 1984; Terrell, 1986; Kirch, 1990).

One may then be inclined to conduct some experimental data acquisition in which language would be kept as distinct as possible or even completely absent. For example, one could start with the administering of tasks requiring a minimal linguistic response such as a memory task eliciting a lexical list, e.g., free listing (Weller and Romney, 1988; Ross, 2004; see also Chapter 5). Or administer tasks that require no linguistic output, e.g., sorting, drawing (Bennardo, 2002a; see also Chapter 5). Certainly, the majority of investigations within cognitive science fall under these categories and a tremendous amount of knowledge about the human mind is being accumulated by using them. On the other hand, any experimental result, while it can be thought to be plausible in a variety of non-experimental situations, still leaves the doubt of being circumstantial to the experimental context. That is, how can one convincingly relate the results of the experiments to behavior in real life, to what people actually do? It must be concluded that also experimental data alone, notwithstanding their considerable efficaciousness, are not by themselves sufficient.

A way out of this methodological conundrum is provided by examples found in tasks involving the use of maps as done in the research on spatial representations (see Gould and White, 1974; Downs and Stea, 1977; Tversky, 1981, 1993, 1996; Golledge, 1999; Bennardo, 2002a). During these tasks subjects are asked to either draw a map, follow a map to reach a place, or talk about the relationships between maps and real places. The discrepancies and/or distortions of the geographical world produced in the maps drawn, or the places reached, or in the speech elicited are used to hypothesize specific mental representations of spatial relationships in those individuals. Fundamentally, real maps and real places provide the parameters to discover mental representations of those maps and/or places. Subjects' performance is matched with geographical reality to obtain information-rich data about mental representations of space.

I became convinced that if I could find a sufficiently equivalent substitute for geographical space in the domain of social relationships/space, I would be able to validate findings obtained by means of linguistic analyses and/or experimental tasks. It is at this juncture that social network analysis came to mind. Social network analysis can provide a similar accuracy about social relationships/reality to that found in maps about geographical relationships/reality (Wasserman and Faust, 1994). Both maps and social networks are simply a representation of the reality to which they refer. As such, they are not exhaustive, complete repetition of that reality. They leave something out in their representing effort. Nonetheless, they are types of representation that are the closest to the reality of the geographical world and of the social relationships world, respectively.

Once one has obtained a social network map of the social relationships world/space, results from linguistic and experimental data about the same world/space can be compared or, more precisely, correlated with it. This would allow one to discover those similarities, discrepancies, and/or distortions that are telling about specific ways of mentally representing significant aspects of the social world. Besides, social network analysis can be revealing regarding a preference for ego-centered or other-than-ego-centered networks, a fundamental issue for the present investigation.

What then are social network data? Social network data consist of information collected by means of questionnaires (for an example see Burkett, 1998), interviews (for an example see Wellman and Wortley, 1990), and/or structured observations (for an example see Bernard, Killworth, and Sailer, 1980, 1982; Freeman and Romney, 1987) about individuals' perceived and actual frequency of interactions with other individuals. The analyses of the social network data (e.g., density, symmetry, and centrality measures) highlight the nature (e.g., star graph, circle graph), structure, and composition of these imagined and actual social interactions in public arenas (Freeman, White, and Romney, 1989; Scott, 1992; Wasserman and Faust, 1994; McCarty, 2002). Radial organizations (star graphs) or vectorial subtypes (line graphs) – always centered on an individual different from the one providing the information – can be detected. The finding of circle graphs, graphs with low and uniform measures of centrality for all members, would undermine my radiality hypothesis. However, any network structure found contributes to the overall project of testing the social environment represented by the networks against linguistic and cognitive data about these same networks (Krackhardt, 1987).

9.2.1   Data collected about social relationships

To investigate the mental representations of social relationships a variety of data was collected: ethnographic data, experimental (cognitive) data, social network data, and linguistic data. The ethnographic data collected consist of detailed information about the village of Houma, which constitutes my main field site. For example, gender, age, occupation, subsistence plot owned or used, membership in one or more of the traditional village groups (based on age, marital status, or activity, e.g., weaving), religious affiliation, kinship relationship to other villagers, residential location (house occupied), recent or past history of emigration (personal or within family and/or extended family). Most of the data are stored in the Digitized Tonga Database described in Chapter 5, Section 5.2.2.

Besides, in the last fifteen years, I spent two thirds of my more-than-two-year-long residence in Tonga in the village of Houma. Consequently, I acquired by personal participation and observation a sufficient knowledge of the life of the village and its people. This knowledge was continuously revived by keeping frequently in contact with my host family even when I was forced to stay away from Tonga for two years because of lack of funds. Personal histories and public events are inscribed in my memory and written down in my extensive field notes. All these ethnographic materials, in addition to the available literature, constitute a fundamental foundation to all the quantitative analyses conducted. As a matter of fact, most of the data acquisition and analysis that is part and parcel of this book could not have been conducted in any meaningful way without it. A careful reading of the book should convince any reader of the indisputable character of this statement.

The experimental (cognitive) data consist of a set of cognitive tasks administered to adult (18+) villagers (the village of Houma mentioned above). The first task is a memory task, or free listing (see Weller and Romney, 1988; Ross, 2004), and involved asking adult individuals to remember their co-villagers. Typically, this task is used to find the extension of a domain and was supposed to obtain subjects' recall skewed toward those few who occupy central or apical positions in the social networks to which the subjects belong. This was not the case; nonetheless, valuable and supportive information was gathered toward the hypothesized radiality foundational cultural model (see Chapter 10).

The second task involved using knowledge about social space – kinship, social relationships, and social networks – while sorting a deck of photos of all the adult villagers.[3] This activity is called pile sort (see Weller and Romney, 1988; Ross, 2004). The concepts used during the sorting activity are revealing of essential parameters used to organize one's social relationship world. The third task, called the drawing task, involved using knowledge about social space while rendering that same space in a drawing (see Bennardo, 2002a). The only guidance provided was to use circles to represent women and triangles to represent men. These last two tasks differ from the oral interviews about the social fabric of the village (see below) because no linguistic coding was involved in performing the tasks. Thus, the results provide access to mental representations without the overt interference of language. Fuller descriptions of these three tasks together with the results of their analyses are presented in Chapter 10.

The social network data were also collected in the village of Houma and concerned all the adult villagers. I employed three data collection strategies: two questionnaires, five types of interview, and what I termed indirect observations. Since I could not observe the total interactions occurring among all villagers at any one time, I conducted repeated interviews (once a week for three weeks) with villagers about people they interacted with during the previous day (indirect observations). The interviewees were also asked about the reason and length of the interactions. The two questionnaires I administered asked questions about influence and about social support in the village. The interviews were about various types of social relationships (see below, linguistic

---

[3] I took photos, close-ups, of all the adult villagers, numbered them, printed them, and constructed a laminated deck to be safely used as many times as needed in the field.

data). I used the same protocol (a specific set of questions) in all the interviews, but each interview was left to grow in the direction that the interviewees felt comfortable to go. Also for these data, fuller descriptions and the results of their analyses are presented later, specifically, in Chapter 11.

Linguistic data have typically been assigned a privileged place when inquiring into the mind, that is, mental representations (Chomsky, 1972; Miller and Johnson-Laird, 1976; Dougherty, 1985; Lakoff, 1987; Pinker, 1997; Olivier and Gapp, 1998; Bowerman and Levinson, 2001). The way in which meaning is organized and expressed linguistically is regarded as a reflection of mental organization of knowledge (see, for example, Talmy, 2000a and 2000b; Strauss and Quinn, 1997; Quinn, 2005). For this reason, I conducted semi-structured interviews in which I inquired about and discussed social relationships. The interviews were all conducted in Tongan, videotaped, and transcribed in the field with the help of local assistants. The first group of interviews (18) was collected in 2002 and was about what I termed 'personal' relationships. In other words, interviewees were asked questions about 'their' relationships to other people in the village. At the end of the interviewing session, they were asked to read a list of all the adults in the village (95) and check if they had forgotten to mention anybody.

These are the questions asked during the 'personal relationships' interviews:

1. Who are your best friends? List
2. Who are the people of Houma you think you spend more time with? List
3. How much do you hang around with _____? Often – Sometimes – Rarely
4. Who are the people you respect most? List
5. Who are the most important people in the village? List
6. Who do you think will be the next *ofisa kolo* 'town officer'?
7. Who are the people you consult with before a *fono* 'village meeting'? List
8. Who do you ask for help to prepare a *pola* 'tray of food for special occasions'? List
9. Do you do *fatongia* 'duties'? No/yes (if yes)
10. Who do you do *fatongia* for? Church/*Kāinga* 'extended family' – Chief/ Noble – Other (List)
11. How often do you do it for _____? Often – Sometimes – Rarely
12. Do you work in a subsistence plot? No/yes (if yes)
13. Who do you ask for help for working in the subsistence plot? List
14. How often do you ask _____? Often – Sometimes – Rarely
15. Do you go to *faikava* 'drink *kava*'? No/yes (if yes)
16. Who do you like to go to *faikava* with? List
17. How often do you go with _____? Often – Sometimes – Rarely
18. You go to town: Often – Sometimes – Rarely
19. Who do you go to town with? List

20. How often do you go with _____? Often – Sometimes – Rarely
21. Whose car do you use when you go to town? Own – Other (specify)
22. How often do you use the car of _____? Often – Sometimes – Rarely
23. Who do you give food/money to when they need it? List
24. Who do you ask for money/food from when you need it? List
25. Who do you hang around with when you have time to kill? List
26. How often do you hang around with _____? Often – Sometimes – Rarely
27. Do you belong to a weaving group? No/yes (if yes)
28. Who are the members of your weaving group? List
29. Who do you prepare food with when there is a church gathering? List
30. Who do you exchange mats and *tapa* 'barkcloth' with? List

The second group of interviews (18) was collected in 2004 and was about what I termed 'perceived' social relationships of others. In other words, interviewees were asked questions about the existence and composition of groups in their village. In the same interviews they were also asked about their ideas, but especially knowledge, and also opinions about the current Tongan political situation. I also inquired about the monarchy versus democracy controversy that has characterized Tonga in the last decade. Basically, this section of the interview was about social relationships at a larger level, i.e., national, than those characterizing the daily life in the village.

These are the questions asked during the 'perceived' social relationships interview:

Local level:

1. There are people in the village that spend more time together than others. Besides spending more time together, they form groups of people that depend on each other. Do you know of any such group?
2. How many?
3. Do you know the names of the members?
4. Is there a person in these groups that is more important than the other members?
5. Do you belong to any of these groups?
6. If yes, which one?
7. Who are the members?
8. Which one do you think is the most important group in Houma? (Who are the members?)
9. Who do you think is the most important person in this group? (Why?)

Island–nation level:

1. The king represents Tonga. He is the descendant of a line of kings that goes back at least a thousand years. What do you think about him?

2. The king also represents the monarchy and all the nobles. What do you think about them?

3. The king is also the head of the state and he is ultimately responsible for what the government does or does not do. What do you know/think about the current political system (cabinet, nobles, parliament)?

4. Who is privileged by the current political system at the national level and at the local level (your village)?

5. In the last ten years, a democratic movement has started in Tonga; do you know anything about it?

6. Do you know who they are?

7. Do you know what kind of changes they want?

8. What do you think about the changes they are proposing?

9. If there were to be a change in Tonga toward a democratic government, who do you think will take advantage of this change at the national level and at the local level (your village)?

While in most cases the questions were phrased as indicated above, other times they only represented a reminder to me of what to ask and, when a specific subtopic was exhausted, what to ask next. In other words, this second type of interview was less structured than the list of questions might make it appear, and often I followed the lead of the interviewee to explore certain issues deemed pertinent. Both in 2002 and in 2004, the 18 people interviewed were 9 women and 9 men, of which 3 were younger adults (18+), 3 mature adults (30+), and 3 older adults (50+). Groups of six were selected from each of the three larger extended families (*kāinga*) in the village. I also considered their residential distribution over the village, their social status, and their religious affiliation.[4]

The third group of interviews (24) was collected in 2005 and was about what I termed 'indirect' social relationships. That is, interviewees were asked to tell a story that occurred in their village that they regarded as representative of village life. This time, it was the type of story, the people remembered as participating, and the expressed relationships among these latter that represented the relevant data. The interviewees were chosen among the clusters of villagers obtained (six clusters with distinctly different profiles of villager's influence over other villagers) by a preliminary analysis conducted on the questions about influence administered in 2004.

In July–August 2007, I conducted further interviews with individuals representing the top echelon of the Tongan population, such as nobles, ministers,

---

[4] This sample represents a good picture of a typical Tongan village structure (including commoners, chief, and elected officials); thus, the results are representative of the village population in Tonga. Residents in small villages represent more than 65% of the total population. Besides, the urbanity of the rest of the population closely resembles Tongan village life. In fact, the capital town of Nuku'alofa (pop. 20,000) is an assemblage of a number of small villages with their specific names and identities.

and top government, religious, and political figures. I labeled these interviews 'view from above' and they provide a necessary different point of view about the perceived social relationships at the national level. These are the questions I used (a slightly revised version of the questions for the perceived social relationships at the island–nation level above):

Democracy vs. monarchy interview protocol:

1. The king is the head of the government and he is responsible for what the government does, or does not do. Could you explain to me the current political structure (like the roles of the cabinet, the nobles, and the parliament)?
2. The king of Tonga is the descendant of a line of kings that goes back at least a thousand years. What do you think is the relationship between the king and his people?
3. The king represents the monarchy and all the nobles. What do you think of the relationship between the nobles and their people?
4. Who is privileged by the current political system at the national level?
5. In the last ten years, a democratic movement has started in Tonga. Do you know what kind of changes they want?
6. What do you think about the changes they are proposing?
7. What are the changes that have already occurred in Tonga?
8. What are the changes that are likely to occur in the future?
9. If there were to be a change in Tonga toward a democratic government, who do you think will benefit from this change?

In the same way as for the other questions, the ones listed above were used liberally during the interviews. Basically they represent the backbone used for the interviews – all interviews are comparable in content because they all contain the same questions – at the same time, each interview represents a unique speech event. With the addition of these interviews, the linguistic data collected represent a good sample of Tongan speech production about social relationships. Consequently, results of the analyses conducted on these data are considered appropriate for all of Tonga.

All the interviews conducted come to a total of around 45 hours of speech production about social relationships. I analyzed this linguistic corpus with two goals in mind: first, I wanted to see if I could obtain clues toward a salient presence of radiality in the structure of the mental representations of social relationships; second, data from this corpus, such as people (e.g., heads of families, government or religious officials, and chiefs) mentioned and groups (e.g., families, extended families, and cultural groups) mentioned could be later compared/correlated to the results of the analyses of the complete social network survey. The results of the analyses of the experimental (cognitive) tasks would also become part of this final comparison/correlation.

Partial homologies (e.g., radial and vectorial organization with other-than-ego as center or apex) between these three types of data are hypothesized as specific (e.g., 'radial') mental representations of social relationships. Only a few centers/apexes may exist embedded in individuals around which and out of which social relationships are organized and represented mentally. Thus, Johnson-Laird's statement: "A crucial feature [of mental models, in our case a 'foundational cultural model'] is that their structure corresponds to the structure of what they represent" (1999: p. 525), would be supported.

9.2.1.1 Analyses conducted on the linguistic data

In order to discover if the linguistic data about social relationships collected contained an indication of the use of the hypothesized foundational cultural model, I ran several analyses on the texts at an increasing level of complexity. The lexical frequencies analyses were at the word level. The metaphor analyses were at the sentence level. And finally, the discourse organization analyses were at the level of discourse, that is, stories/narratives. First, I conducted a frequency count of lexical items expressing radiality. The two lexemes focused on are two Tongan directionals, *mai* 'toward center' and *atu* 'away from center' (see Chapter 6, Section 6.2.1). The results of these counts in the interviews were compared with similar counts about other types of Tongan texts (written and oral). A higher incidence of occurrence (than in discourse about other topics) of the two directionals with a specific meaning (either toward or away from other-than-ego) was hypothesized and found.

Second, the metaphors used during the interviews were recorded, counted, and classified in types (see Strauss and Quinn, 1997: 144, for the role of metaphors in pointing to cultural models, but see also Lakoff and Johnson, 1980). The metaphor analysis reveals a Tongan model for social relationships whose core part is summarized by the following sentence: '*ofa* is giving, either giving help (up–down) or giving duty/respect (down–up) (Bennardo, forthcoming). Fundamentally, on a background of hierarchically arranged social positions, Tongans label many of the actions that characterize social relationships as a form of '*ofa* 'love' (Kavaliku, 1977). The directionality of the action (from agent to recipient) is essential in determining what type of action is envisaged: help, from up to down; duty/respect, from down to up. The preferred agent for the action, as hypothesized, is an individual other-than-ego and ego is kept as much as possible uninvolved. The opposite result, ego as preferred agent, would have undermined my radiality hypothesis.

Third, the discourse structure/organization of the content of the stories narrated during the interviews in 2005 was highlighted (both types and frequencies). I found, as hypothesized, a discourse radiality that implies narratives organized around what are termed 'referential nodes.' A referential node can be an actor (other-than-ego) or an event from which other actors or events are represented. The finding of narratives preferentially orchestrated around ego would have undermined my hypothesis.

9.3   The lexical frequency analysis (*mai–atu*)

The Tongan language differs substantially from Indo-European languages, including English, in the way in which spatial relationships are expressed. Instead of the eighty spatial prepositions used by English (Jackendoff, 1992b: 108), for example, Tongan uses only three spatial prepositions. In addition, Tongan has five post-verbal directionals that express vertical movement (up and down) and radial movement from or toward a specified center/point (Bennardo, 1999). These latter three (*mai, atu, ange*) are monolexemic examples of the closed class type (grammatical) whose meanings are expressed by a whole prepositional phrase in English (e.g., *mai* 'toward a center/point'). The focus of the lexical frequencies analyses is on two of the directionals expressing radial movement, that is, *mai* and *atu*.

9.3.1   Tongan directionals and the radiality foundational cultural model

In Bennardo (1999),[5] I assigned the meaning of 'toward a center' to *mai* and 'away from a center' to *atu* (see Figure 6.2, repeated here as Figure 9.1). These two directionals are typically used with the following two meanings (included in the conceptual content glossed):

Mai means 'toward speaker' and 'toward other-than-speaker' (see Figure 6.3, repeated here as Figure 9.2);

Atu means 'away from speaker/to addressee' and 'away from other-than-speaker' (see Figure 6.3, repeated here as Figure 9.2).

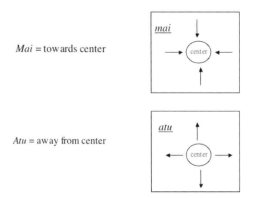

Figure 9.1 Basic meanings of *mai* and *atu*

[5] See also Churchward (1953) and Tchekhoff (1990).

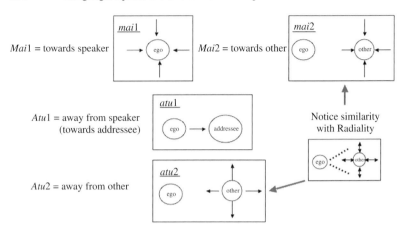

Figure 9.2 Two meanings for *mai* and *atu*

In (1)–(4), I provide examples of all four uses. These examples come from the interviews about social relationships.

(1) Example of *mai*1 (no. 3, 2002)
    a. *pea ko e kole pé ia ke nau tokoni **mai**…*
       then pr* the ask just it so they help **to me**…
       Then I ask so that they help me…
       *Presentational preposition (it introduces a noun, an event, etc.).

The *mai* in this sentence modifies the meaning of the verb to indicate direction toward speaker.

(2) Example of *mai*2 (no. 15, 2005)
    b. *na'e tanaki katoa **mai** ki 'api siasi ki hé*
       past* gather all **to them** to house church to there
       all of them gathered in the church there
       *Past tense is introduced by this particle.

The *mai* in this sentence also modifies the verb and it refers to direction toward 'them.'

(3) Example of *atu*1 (no. 1, 2005)
    c. *'io, lahi pé 'u me'a tonu ke tala **atu**…*
       yes, big just plural* thing right that told **you**…
       yes, I told you many right things…
       *Tongan has four classifiers that precede nouns to make them plural.

The *atu* in this sentence modifies the verb and indicates movement toward addressee, away from center/speaker.

(4) Example of *atu*2 (no. 20, 2005)
 d. *Maile, na'e … 'ohovale pé, 'alu **atu** mo e fanau pé heni ki ai, nau 'alu **atu** ki Tonga.*
    Maile, past … surprise just, go **forward** with the children just here to there, they go **forward** to Tonga.
    Maile was surprised, he went with the children there, they went to Tonga.

The two *atu* in these joined sentences modify the same verb, *'alu* 'go': the first *atu* indicates movement away from other-than-ego 'Maile;' the second *atu* indicates movement away from other-than-ego 'them.'

Given the similarity of the semantic content of *mai*2 and *atu*2 with the concept of radiality as proposed in this work (cf. Figure 9.2), I hypothesized that when compared to other texts (both oral and written) about any other topic, a higher incidence of use of *mai*2 and *atu*2 would be found in the interviews about social relationships. Thus, a preference to think radially about social relationships could be inferred. In other words, the use of the hypothesized radiality foundational cultural model could be induced by engaging interviewees on a specific topic such as social relationships (see D'Andrade, 2005: 90, on a similar strategy to investigate cultural models). The instantiation of the foundational cultural model would be supported by the quality of the linguistic production, specifically by a higher use of the two directionals *mai*2 and *atu*2.

Aspects of this hypothesis need to be clarified. What is meant by 'higher' incidence of use? The canonical use of *mai* and *atu* is the one in which they mean 'toward speaker' and 'toward addressee,' respectively (Shumway, 1988; Broschart, 1995). In his *Tongan Grammar*, Churchward (1953) defines *mai* and *atu* in the following way:

(a) *Mai*: hither, to or towards me or us, or to or towards the place or the time in which we or our thoughts are.
(b) *Atu*: hence: onward or away from the place or the time in which we or our thoughts are; to or towards you, to or towards the place in which you or your thoughts are; thither, to the place aimed at or journeyed towards. (Churchward, 1953: 193)

These definitions are trying to capture not only the meaning of the two directionals, but also most of their uses. In recent studies, two more concise definitions can be found that need to be looked at carefully. The first definition is:

Basically, the three are directional adverbs and indicate a movement: mai towards the centre; atu away from it; and ange to and from a place that is not the centre of interest, leaving the centre uninvolved. Thus it may apply to a place where the speaker has been, or will be, but where he is not at the time of speaking. (Tchekhoff, 1990: 105)

The second definition is:

Most commonly, *mai* is glossed as 'towards the speaker', *atu* as 'away from the speaker/ towards the hearer', and *ange* as 'across to somebody other than speaker or hearer'. (Broschart, 1995: 446)

The goal of both Tchekhoff's and Broschart's work is to demonstrate how social factors participate heavily in the construction of certain uses of the three directionals. What must be pointed out, however, is that the meanings from which they start are not as rich as the meanings suggested by Churchward, and this is more so for Broschart than for Tchekhoff. Tchekhoff left out from the meaning of *atu* the 'towards the hearer' part, while Broschart left out many of their meanings except for the basic deictic ones.

Both authors later deal with many of the uses of these directionals and show how social and cultural factors contribute to these uses. I subscribe to some of their conclusions, but am compelled to suggest that if we start from a limited meaning of these directionals, our findings may be derived from inappropriate premises. My proposal (Bennardo, 1999) tries to do justice to the ones previously mentioned and introduces the concept of Center, out of which (*mai*) or toward which (*atu*) movement is conceptualized and expressed linguistically.

The fact remains, though, that canonical uses of *mai* and *atu* as 'away from speaker' and 'toward addressee' respectively, are the most common. It is impossible to quantify such 'commonality,' but I would heuristically propose to treat a canonical use to be at or above 75% of occurrences, that is three in four uses.[6] Thus, making the non-canonical use range between 0% and 25%, basically, at a maximum of one every four uses and at an average of 12.50% or one of every eight uses. I consider the definition I am adopting for non-canonical use to be set at a high level, but I would rather err in the direction of overestimating its incidence than underestimating its incidence.

9.3.2   Types of texts analyzed

Before running the frequency analyses on the interviews about social relationships, my speech was erased from the texts, so that only the interviewees' speech would be counted and analyzed. The first group of interviews (2002) totaled 19,599 words, the second (2004) 17,046 words, the third (2005) 18,812, and the fourth (2007) 30,733. The overall total was 86,190 words.

The written texts analyzed came from different types of printed sources like newspapers, a book about Tongan mythology, a high school textbook, and a conference proceedings. The intention was to put together as varied a group of written sources as possible about an assortment of topics. It needs to be considered that not too many written sources in Tongan are available to allow a systematic sampling of written Tongan. I believe though that the texts collected represent a good and varied sample of what is available. These are the written texts analyzed:

- six newspaper articles about a variety of topics including current political situation, visiting officials to the kingdom, and letters to the editor;

---

[6] See a similar statistical reasoning in Chapter 4, Section 4.3.

- four myths selected from a book on Tongan mythology;
- four texts from a high school textbook about a variety of topics including Tongan etiquette, traditional marriage, and the life of Queen Salote;
- four texts from the proceedings of a conference on the political situation in Tonga and the possibility of the introduction of democracy.

The total words counted in these texts amounted to 28,748.

In my previous fieldwork, I had conducted a number of interviews about a number of subjects including traditional Tongan farming, vanilla farming, funeral, marriage, weaving, a traditional game (*lafo*), and various rituals. I had also collected narratives (nine) about old local and national myths as well as speeches (twelve) in salient cultural events such as *fono* 'village meeting,' *fakaafe* 'meal/feast invitation,' and *misinale* 'yearly donation to church.' All these oral texts had already been transcribed in the field with the help of local native assistants and I named them 'oral' texts so as to contrast them in one way with the written texts and on the other with the interviews focused specifically on social relationships. After I had erased my speech in the same way as I had done with the interviews, the total number of words for these texts was 38,997.

I am perfectly aware that some (or all) of the texts I labeled 'oral' do contain implicitly or explicitly speech about social relationships. I am thinking especially of the texts about the Tongan funeral and the wedding ritual. Nonetheless, the focus of those interviews was not on the social relationships involved, but more on the number, sequence, and type of events that each 'ritual' entails. In many cases, clarifying the social relationships (either kinship or power based) among individuals was essential to the presentation of some events (e.g., presents brought by the bride's family or who can come into contact with the body of a deceased person). However, these social facts would be supporting the main narrative, not motivating it.

The total corpus consisted of 153,935 words. The final set of texts onto which the frequency analyses were conducted consisted of three subsets, written texts, oral texts, and interviews about social relationships. In this way I was able to compare results across modes – written vs. oral – and also across topics – social relationships vs. other. I expected to find a higher frequency of *mai*2 and *atu*2 in the interviews about social relationships, higher than the typical more formal language of written texts – in which detachment from an ego-centered position is characteristically employed – and definitely higher than the other types of oral texts about a variety of other topics.

9.3.3   Results and discussion of the frequency analyses

Before analyzing the frequencies obtained, a loglinear analysis and a Poisson regression analysis were conducted on the data. The intention was to find out if there existed a significant relationship between types of texts and use of directionals. The results were encouraging. In fact, it was found that:

- there is an overall statistical association between the different types of Tongan directionals and the different types of texts in which they occur;
- the overall test of independence between types of texts and use of directionals was rejected (χ^2 = 90.8, 16 df, p value <0.0001).

In other words, the Tongan directionals and the texts in which they occur are significantly related. A discussion and interpretation of this relationship is now introduced.

Figure 9.3 shows the frequency of use of *mai* and *atu* in all three types of texts. The first significant difference to be noted in Figure 9.3 is the one between written texts (0.48% and 0.50%) and oral texts (0.67% and 0.72%): higher frequency of both *mai* and *atu* in oral texts. Second, oral texts (0.67% and 0.72%) differ from interviews (0.51% and 0.18%): less frequency of both *mai* and *atu* in interviews. Third, there is a similarity in the occurrence of *mai* between written texts and interviews (0.48% in written texts and 0.51% in interviews): the frequency of *mai* is almost the same. Finally, there is a significant difference in the occurrence of *atu* in interviews: less frequency of *atu* in interviews (0.18% vs. 0.50% in written texts and 0.72% in interviews).

Interviews about social relationships are, then, similar to written texts in the use of *mai* (but less than oral) and different from written and oral texts (less than both) in the use of *atu*. It can be stated that speakers behave in a distinctive way in interviews about social relationships. That is, it appears that speakers highlight less movement toward ego and/or other-than-ego than they do in other oral texts (less use of *mai*) while at the same time they exercise caution in addressing and/or referring to other-than-ego (lowest use of *atu* than in other types of texts).

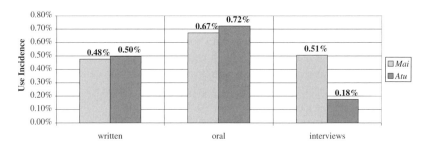

Figure 9.3 Frequencies of use of *mai* and *atu*

An explanation for this phenomenon could be found in the cultural ecology of interviews that Tongans may hold, one that could be termed pan-Polynesian (see Duranti, 1997). In other words, the low use of *atu* can be explained by the way in which Tongans conceptualize interviews. That is, since a powerful (for Tongans) American professor is interviewing them, it is appropriate not to address this person directly by limiting the use of *atu* (see Keenan, 1974; Ochs, 1988; Duranti, 1994). However, the oral texts were conducted by myself as well, so since the interviewer variable was kept constant, it cannot be used to fully explain the phenomenon. It is more likely, then, that it is the subject matter, social relationships – together with the interviewer's attributed status – that may be conducive to such a conceptual-linguistic posture. Yet the major hypothesis to be tested by the frequency counts discussed here does not address the issue of less or more occurrence/use of *mai* and *atu*, but it specifically states that it would be forms of *mai*2 and *atu*2 that are expected to be found as more frequently used (above an average of 12.50%). In Figure 9.4, I present the results about the frequency count regarding *mai*1 and *mai*2.

Figure 9.4 shows a higher use of *mai*1 in all three types of texts. A significant difference between interviews and other types of texts (written and oral) is also indicated. The use of *mai*1 is higher in interviews (73.85% vs. 63.50% in written texts and 67.56% in oral texts) and the use of *mai*2 is lower (25.46% vs. 35.77% in written texts and 32.06% in oral texts). The higher incidence of *mai*1 could be expected, since it is typically described as the most common usage of the term. What is surprising is the relative high usages of *mai*2 (25.46%), that are at a minimum of 1 out 4 times in the interviews (in all three cases it is much higher than the canonical average of 12.50%). On the other hand, a higher use of *mai*2 than in the other two types of texts was not found in the interviews. In addition, fewer uses of *mai*2 were also found in oral texts (32.06%) than in written texts (35.77%).

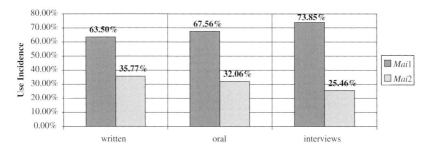

Figure 9.4 Frequencies of use of *mai*1 and *mai*2

I propose three possible explanations for the findings about *mai*2: (a) written texts typically require more caution about self-expression, less focus on the individual (writer/ego), and more attention to other (both point of view and events centered on other), thus less use of *mai*1 and more use of *mai*2 (highest percentage of *mai*2, 35.77%); (b) oral texts, and especially interviews, may typically require more focus on the individual (speaker/ego), thus more use of *mai*1 and less use of *mai*2 (higher percentages of *mai*1, 67.56% and 73.85%); (c) focusing on an other-than-ego individual's inner mental life is not a typical stance in Tongan and in Polynesian discourse at large (see Levy, 1973; Ochs, 1984, 1988; Schieffelin, 1990; Duranti, 1988; Morton, 1996; Mageo, 1998), especially for speech in which a relationship is described as toward this person, thus intruding on somebody's social identity, social space, and social status. Then, less use of *mai*2 and more uses of *mai*1. These explanations may provide some needed clarification toward the overall higher use of *mai*1, but do not account fully for the higher use of *mai*2 (much above canonical average of 12.50%). I discuss these results in more detail when a clearer global picture is obtained.

In Figure 9.5, I present the results of the frequency counts for *atu*1 and *atu*2. It is evident from this figure that high frequencies of *atu*2 were detected. Besides, there is a marked difference in the frequency of use of *atu*2 between the three types of texts. In written texts *atu*2 is used a little less than two thirds of the times (62.24%), while it is used one third of the times in oral texts (33.33%) and almost half of the times in interviews (44.37%). The canonical use of *atu* as expressed in *atu*1 usages is completely inverted in the written texts, 62.24% vs. 28.67%. Again this may be due to the nature of written communication. More surprisingly, though, also in oral texts and in interviews the use of *atu*2 reaches a considerable incidence, 33.33% in oral texts and 44.37% in interviews, clearly supporting the present working hypothesis. Considering that uses of *atu*2 are considered not canonical (e.g., Shumway, 1988; Broschart, 1995), these results are unique indeed.

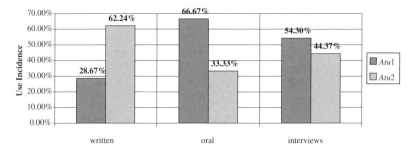

Figure 9.5 Frequencies of *atu*1 and *atu*2

The main hypothesis that was conducive to the lexical frequency analyses conducted was that a higher (than canonical average 12.50%) occurrence of *mai*2 and *atu*2 would be found in the linguistic production about social relationships. It can be stated that the main hypothesis was substantially confirmed by the analyses. That is, much higher than canonical average 12.50% uses of *mai*2 (25.46%) and *atu*2 (44.37%) were clearly found in the interviews; thus it appears that speakers may be using the hypothesized 'radiality' cultural model when thinking and expressing linguistically social relationships. However, four types of interviews were included under the rubric 'interviews' (personal, perceived, indirect, and view from above), and while they were all about social relationships, each of them may have required a different approach to the topic. I decided, then, to conduct some further analyses on the available data.

In the first additional analysis, I wanted to see if the four different types of interviews showed similar uses of *mai*1, *mai*2, *atu*1, and *atu*2. The expectation was to find more use (above canonical 75%) of *mai*1 in the so-called personal interviews about social relationships conducted in 2002, and more use (above canonical average 12.50%) of *mai*2 in the 'perceived' social relationships interviews (2004) and in the 'view from above' interviews about social relationships conducted in 2007. In fact, the questions in the personal interviews (see Section 9.2.1) should be conducive to a more frequent focus on ego and the questions in the 'perceived' and 'view from above' interviews should cause a more frequent focus on other-than-ego. No specific expectation existed about uses of *mai*1 and *mai*2 in the indirect social relationships interviews conducted in 2005. Uses of *atu*2 were expected to be high (above canonical average 12.50%) in all four types of interviews as in the previous analyses.

The results in Figure 9.6 show that both expectations for uses of *mai*1 and *mai*2 were confirmed: high use of *mai*1 (85.51%) in 2002 'personal' interviews and high use of *mai*2 in 2004 'perceived' interviews (27.17%) and in 2007 'view from above' interviews (36.20%). The results concerning the 2005 'indirect' interviews (83.93% use of *mai*1 and 16.07% use of *mai*2) are a little surprising, and I discuss them below when looking at the global results for uses of *mai*2.

The results in Figure 9.7 about the frequency of use of *atu*1 and *atu*2 confirm what was expected and had already been observed in the previous counts (see Figure 9.5). That is, a high incidence of use of *atu*2 was generally found in all four types of interviews (26.67% in 2002, 31.25% in 2004, 45.83% in 2005, and 53.09% in 2007). It seems, then, that the results of these more detailed analyses about the four types of interviews do not change the usage picture already obtained by the general comparison between different types of texts introduced above (Figure 9.4 and Figure 9.5). A general high use of *atu*2 is observed and not a corresponding general high use of *mai*2. I consider the 'average' frequencies of *mai*2 results in the interviews about personal social

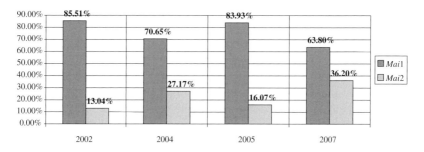

Figure 9.6 Frequencies of use of *mai*1 and *mai*2 in interviews

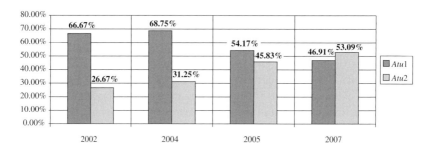

Figure 9.7 Frequencies of *atu*1 and *atu*2 in interviews[7]

relationships conducted in 2002 and those in the interviews about perceived social relationships conducted in 2004 to be in need of further discussion.

I advocate caution in drawing conclusions, i.e., negative, from these results. The inconsistency between uses of *mai2* and *atu2* needs to be evaluated by considering that their use took place within two specific speech events, in our case an interview about personal social relationships (2002) and an interview in which an exemplary story about village life was elicited (2005). The use of *mai2* (toward a center other-than-ego) implies a focus on an individual by taking his/her perspective. The questions in the interview about personal social relationships were asking the interviewee to focus on himself/herself and his/her social life. Thus the maximum use of *mai*1 is registered and an average use of *mai2*. As a matter of fact, it should be surprising that uses of *mai2* still remained slightly above average (13.04%, more than once in eight times). The

---

[7] The sum of all frequencies comes to 100%, except for 2002 interviews where there are also some *atu* used to express time.

higher use of *atu*2 (26.67%) in these same interviews becomes even more important in supporting the working hypothesis.

There were no hypotheses offered about the second speech event, an interview in which an exemplary story about village life was elicited (2005). However, following what I said about speech event one, it could have been possible to expect a higher use of *mai*2 because the interviews elicited narratives. These latter typically contain descriptions of actions of the main character/s that may be reported followed by *mai*2 or *atu*2. *Atu*2 frequencies were definitely high (45.83%, almost one in every two times), but use of *mai*2 was just slightly above average (16.07%). In other words, while the focus on other-than-ego can be generally confirmed by the two results combined, it did not take place in a significant manner for *mai*2. Again, I want to point out that focusing on an other-than-ego individual is not a typical stance in Tongan and in Polynesian discourse at large, especially for speech in which a relationship is described as toward this person (use of *mai*2), thus intruding on somebody's social identity, social space, and social status. On the other hand, relationships radiating out of an individual (other-than-ego) are typically addressed and talked about profusely in the slow-paced and mostly uneventful life of a Tongan village. Then, it is very likely that the nature of the speech event combined with the two cultural traits mentioned had relevant roles to play in determining some of the results obtained.

In conclusion, the main hypothesis was partially supported by the lexical frequencies analyses. Thus, it appears that Tongans use the hypothesized 'radiality' cultural model in mentally representing social relationships as well as in instantiating them linguistically. However, other cultural norms such as the ecology of interviews and appropriateness or inappropriateness of taking someone else's perspective in reporting on events about other-than-ego individuals were also invoked as possible factors in explaining some of the data.

9.4   The metaphor analysis[8]

In an excellent article published in 1977, Kavaliku defines the Tongan term *'ofa* 'love' as the "treasure of Tonga" (p. 47), and then he adds "It seems to me that *'ofa*, to Tongans, is the philosophy behind their way of life" (p. 67). Kavaliku discusses several meanings of the term including: care, concern, gift, help, hope, kindness, sadness, sexual love, and sharing. He later reaches two relevant conclusions: first, "The usages of *'ofa* [love] show the kind of relationships between members using the term" (p. 67); and second, "… we could not comprehend or understand *faka'apa'apa* [respect] unless we understand *'ofa* [love]" (p. 50).

---

[8] This section is a slightly revised version of Bennardo (forthcoming).

Three important lessons can be learned from Kavaliku's article: (1) the concept of *'ofa* plays a crucial role in the construction of the way in which Tongans think about their social world; (2) the term *'ofa* 'love' itself expresses social relationships; (3) an understanding of *'ofa* gives insight into the meaning of other salient social terms such as, for example, *faka'apa'apa* 'respect.' Nonetheless, the author left unexplored the possibility of finding a unified account of the various meanings of *'ofa* 'love.' Can a metaphor analysis account for such a diverse usage of *'ofa* 'love'? Or at least, part of this usage? Furthermore, is there a common cultural model about social relationships that generates metaphors including *'ofa* 'love' and thus contributes to its various meanings?

In this section, I present an analysis of metaphors used by Tongans when talking about the domain of social relationships. The intention is to use metaphors as a privileged entry into the mental representation of social relationships (see Strauss and Quinn, 1997; Quinn, 2005). A number of types of metaphors are identified and their source domains highlighted. Many of these metaphors involve the concept of *'ofa* 'love' and related concepts like *faka'apa'apa* 'respect.' The metaphor analysis reveals a comprehensive organizational structure for the domain of social relationships, a cultural model. This structure replicates the organization present in other domains of Tongan knowledge.

9.4.1   Metaphor analysis: methodology

In *Metaphors We Live By*, Lakoff and Johnson (1980) presented a systematic analysis of the salient role played by metaphors in organizing individual knowledge (see also Lakoff, 1987; Johnson, 1987). In 1997, Strauss and Quinn used metaphor analysis to arrive at forms of collective knowledge they called "cultural models" (see also Holland and Quinn, 1987; D'Andrade and Strauss, 1992; Shore, 1996; and especially Quinn, 2005). While I do not believe that metaphors are the exclusive way in which knowledge is generated, I agree with Lakoff and Johnson that they are a relevant way in which individual knowledge is organized. Similarly, though I define a 'foundational' cultural model as an internal homology between domains of knowledge in a number of mental modules that are also partially shared among the members of a socio-ethnic group, I agree with Strauss and Quinn that a metaphor analysis can provide essential insights into the collective mental organization of knowledge.

I consider the two reasons just stated sufficient grounds to justify the extensive metaphor analyses conducted over the linguistic data collected. These data, as mentioned above, consist of the transcriptions of 60 interviews I conducted about various forms of social relationships, "personal," "perceived" (either at the village or at the nation level), and "indirect" with 47 individuals (eleven people were interviewed twice and one person three times). Each interview lasts between 25 and 35 minutes, thus making the corpus analyzed around

24 hours long. A conservative word count which excluded my speech[9] gave a total of 55,457 words.[10]

The first analysis performed on the data was the identification of metaphors themselves. This took the repeated careful reading of the texts by both myself and my Tongan graduate assistant. Informed by Lakoff and Johnson's (1980) suggested typology we read the texts several times both individually and together and identified what we think is the total metaphorical corpus present in the data. Then we proceeded to transfer the metaphors onto cards (see Quinn, 2005 for a similar procedure) and sorted them by type. This analysis took several tries and long discussions. In addition, we later identified the source domain for each metaphor. During these first stages of the analysis we also wrote down key words that appeared to be being used often enough to attract our attention. This whole procedure was first applied to the 2004 texts and later expanded to the other two groups of data as well.

Once the list of metaphors, their typology, a list of their source domains, and a number of key words were obtained, I proceeded to analyze these data further and to try to find out if there was an organizing principle, a threading system that would provide some coherence to the data. My intention was threefold: first, to see if the metaphoric use of 'ofa 'love' could help explain some of the various meanings indicated by Kavaliku (1977); second, to see if some form of radiality, the hypothesized foundational cultural model, would be a salient participant in the production of the metaphors used; third, to see if the use of this foundational cultural model could be the explanatory force behind several forms of reasoning embedded in the texts and specifically in the metaphor usage.

9.4.2   Metaphor analysis: results

9.4.2.1   Metaphors: general frequencies

After several careful readings of the texts of the 2002, 2004, and 2005 interviews,[11] a good number of metaphors were found, exactly 650, of which 211 (32.46%) were in the texts collected in 2002, 319 (49.07%) were in the texts of 2004, and 120 (18.46%) were in those of 2005. In the texts of 2004,

---

[9] Estimated at around 30% of the total interview time.
[10] The count could have been much higher had I:
   separated the articles in the texts that usually appear attached to preceding particles or prepositions;
   counted the constitutive elements of contracted forms;
   or included typical omission of many grammatical features (e.g., temporal marker) in oral speech production.
[11] Crucial for this analytic stage was the help provided by my Tongan graduate assistant, Lisita Taufa.

Table 9.1 *Metaphor frequencies*

Type of text	Length of texts (words)	%	Metaphors	%	Frequency index
Personal [2002]	19,599	35.34%	211	32.46%	0.92
Perceived (local) [2004]	4,867	8.78%	74	11.38%	1.30
Perceived (national) [2004]	12,179	21.96%	245	37.69%	1.72
Indirect [2005]	18,812	33.92%	120	18.46%	0.54
Total	55,457	100.00%	650	100.00%	

74 (23.19%, or 11.38% of total) were found in the section about local 'perceived' social relationships, and 245 (76.80%, or 37.69% of total) in the section about national 'perceived' social relationships, or interviews about "monarchy versus democracy." In other words, 37.69% (245) of all metaphors were found in 21.96% (12,179 words) of the total of texts, the highest frequency index (1.72) in all the four types of texts (interviews) collected. Table 9.1 shows all the frequencies for all the types of texts. It also contains a column in which the frequency index (obtained by dividing metaphor percentages by length of texts percentages) of metaphors in each type of text is indicated.

Table 9.1 shows that the most use of metaphorical forms (245 with 1.72 frequency index) occurs in speech about a specific subtopic, that is, talking about the major features of the present monarchy and the changes advocated by the democratic movement or 'perceived social relationships' at the island and national level. Explanatory reasons for this usage could possibly be found in the inherently difficult task of speaking about highly complex forms of social organizations beyond the immediate village environment and the likely lack of adequate language (i.e., vocabulary) to express those relationships. In addition, in the texts about 'perceived' social relationships at the local level (i.e., village), metaphors show the second highest frequency index (1.30). Thus, it can be deduced that whenever speech is not about 'personal' or 'indirect' (i.e., village life stories) social relationships, that is, it is about other-than-ego, the use of metaphors increases substantially.[12]

This finding can be interpreted either as a tendency to favor talk that is not about ego, thus increasing the chances of metaphorical usage in those texts that are longer and more frequent. Or it may be interpreted as related to the nature of the metaphors used that are centered on other-than-ego and not on ego, thus fitting better the speech produced about texts in which other-than-ego is discussed. We may be able to propose a suggestion in either direction once

---

[12] Notice that while the "indirect" texts are also predominantly about other-than-ego (see Bennardo, in press), the explicit topic is not social relationships but stories about the village life.

we find out what type of metaphors are used and which type are used most both generally in all texts and in particular in 2004 texts, especially in the 'perceived' social relationships texts.

9.4.2.2 Metaphor types

Informed by Lakoff and Johnson's (1980) typology, the metaphors found were classified into orientational and ontological. For this latter, four subcategories were used: personification, entity and substance, container, and state as action. Metaphors of state as action were divided into two types: love is giving help (typically, from social superior to inferior), and love is giving respect and doing your duty (typically, from social inferior to superior). This is the typology used:

1. orientational (e.g., social stratification or being up or down);
2. ontological: personification (e.g., an institution/social group/event is a person);
3. ontological: entity and substance (e.g., an individual/social group/event is like something in nature, e.g., tree);
4. ontological: container (e.g., an individual/social group/event is a place);
5. ontological: state as action (e.g., love is giving help);
6. ontological: state as action (e.g., love is giving respect, doing your duty).

It should be stressed in anticipation of much discussion that follows, that the last two types of metaphors are peculiar to the Tongan cultural milieu and represent one of the major findings of the analyses conducted (but see Kavaliku, 1977). Above, for each of the types of metaphor identified a typical exemplification from the texts is indicated in parenthesis. I introduce below some linguistic examples from the texts for those exemplifications.[13]

I need to point out that Tongan does not have a verb to be and among other grammatical ways to express existence, one way is by vicinity, that is, if two nominal phrases are produced in a sequence (with a short pause dividing them) it is often implied that the first 'is' the second. I am pointing out this phenomenon because it will help the reading of some of the examples that follow.

1. <u>Social stratification or being up or down</u>: … *kae kei fiefia pé kakai Tonga ke kei fakalangilangi'i pé 'a e Tu'i* [*ooh*] *'uhinga pé kei **ma'olunga** pé kae kei **ma'ulalo** pé e kakai …*
    "… but still happy Tongan people that still shines the King [ooh] because still **high** but still **low** the people …"
    '… Tongan people are happy that the King still shines because the King is **high** and the people are **low** …'
    [13K, June 11, 2004].

---

[13] The information in square brackets refers to the interview transcript out of which the quote is taken.

This metaphor of "society being like a vertical axis/ladder" where people are located either in the upper or lower part is ubiquitous in Tongan talk about many social aspects of their world. This phenomenon is understandable in a society where stratification and hierarchy are a constitutive part of its structure, i.e., monarchy.

2. A social/abstract group is a person: ... *pau ke tokoni'i kinautolu he* **Pule'anga** ...
    "... must help them the **Government** ..."
    '... the **Government** must help them ...'
    [17K, June 3, 2002].

Social groups (e.g., family, extended family, and village), cultural groups (e.g., elders, unmarried people, and weaving women[14]), and political groups (e.g., nobles, government, and democratic party) are typically attributed features of an individual. Thus, they think, speak, help, or do whatever else a person can do.

3.   An individual/social group is an entity/substance: ... *ka 'e nofo e Tu'í 'o fakalangilangi* ...
    "... but will stay the King **to shine** ..."
    '... the King will still be the King and **shine** ...'
    [12S, June 10, 2004];

3a. ... *ko e **kakai** ko é ko e **me'a** vale* ...
    "... those **people** are a **thing** insignificant ..."
    '... those **people** are an insignificant **thing** ...'
    [5S, June 9, 2005].

The king or the nobles or the chiefs are traditionally attributed object-like features, the most paramount being the capacity to shine that is interpreted as a sign of being the location of positive forces or *mana*. The phenomenon of attributing object-like features to persons is also present in expressions referring to commoners (see 3a above).

4. A social group is a place: ... *ko e kaume'a 'i tu'a fāmili* ...
    "... the friends **outside the family** ..."
    [12M, May 29, 2002].

Spatial expression are commonly used accompanying terms referring to social groups (e.g., family, extended family, village). Thus, these abstract social concepts are treated as if they were places/containers which enter into spatial relationships.

---

[14] Women in a village get together in specific locations (typically a hall) to weave mats. This activity that produces one of the objects (the other is *ngatu* 'tapa cloth') regarded as the 'wealth' of an individual or group (*kāinga* 'extended family') is linguistically labeled (*fefine lalanga* 'women weaving') and saliently recognized by villagers.

5. Love is giving help: … *kapau ko e* ***'ofa mai pé***, ***tokoni mai*** *eh* …
    "… if they **love me**, they **help me**, eh …"
    [11U, May 5, 2002].

It is transparent in the above statement that the concepts of love and help are supposed to go together. Actually, the presence of love implies that of help. In other words, love is giving help.

6.   Love is giving respect/doing your duty:
    G: *Ko e há 'a e fekau'aki mo e Tu'i mo e kakai Tonga?*
    K: *Ko e fekau'aki ko e Tu'i Tonga, Tu'i 'o Tonga ['io] eh? ['io, Tu'i pé, ka ko e fekau'aki lelei pé mahalo pé kovi? ke 'ofa 'a e kakai ki he Tu'í] 'io, ['io]* ***'ofa lahi 'a e kakai ki he Tu'i***, *pea pehé pé mo e Tu'i ki he kakai [ko e 'uhinga ko e Tu'i pé] ki he Tu'i pé, oh, oh, 'io,* ***'ofa 'a e kakai***, *['ofa 'a e kakai]* ***faka'apa'apa***, *eh ['io] ki he Tu'i.*
    "G: What is the relationship between the King and the people of Tonga?
    K: The relationship with the King, he is the King of Tonga [yes] eh? [yes, King, but it is a good or maybe a bad relationship? So that the people love the King] yes [yes **the people love the King a lot**, and the same the King loves the people [only because he is the King?] the King, oh, oh, yes, **the people love**, [the people love] **respect** eh? [yes] the King."
    [4K, June 7, 2004];

6a. G: *'Io, pea ko e há e me'a 'uhinga ke 'ofa ki ai? Ki he Tu'i … kapau 'a koe eh, 'oku ke 'ofa ki he Tu'i? ['io] 'io, ko e há 'a e 'uhinga 'oku 'ofa ki ai?*
    S: *'E tauhi e fonua mo e … ['io, …] …* ***fatongia***.
    "G: Yes, then what is the reason they love him? The King … if you eh, do you love the King? [yes] yes, why do you love him?
    S: He looks after the land and … [yes, …] … **duty**."
    [8S, June 7, 2004];

6b. G: *Pea ko e Tu'i eh, ko e kakai 'i Tonga ni 'ofa lahi ki ai, ko e há 'a e uhinga 'oku nau 'ofa ki he Tu'i 'a e kakai?*
    S: *Nau 'ofa ai koe'uhí [mo'oni? Ke 'ofa lahi ki he Tu'i pé 'ikai] 'io [he'ilo] 'ofa pé [mo'oni?] 'io, 'ofa 'a e kakai,* ***tauhi e lao*** *['io] konisitutone, tauhi e kakai, 'i ai p*é *'e taha 'oku maumau,* ***'ikai ke ne tauhi 'e ia***, *'ofa,* ***'ikai ke 'ofa*** *ki he Tu'í.*
    "G: Then the King eh, the people of Tonga love him, why do they, the people, love the King?
    S: They love him because [true? They love the King or not?] yes [I don't know] they just love [true?] yes, the people love, **they obey the law** [yes] the constitution, the people obey, there is somebody who breaks the law, **he doesn't obey**, **love**, **he doesn't love** the King."
    [5S, June 7, 2004].

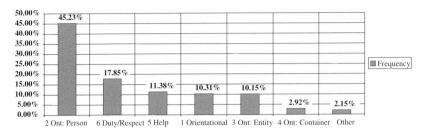

Figure 9.8 Frequency of types of metaphors

In the three examples in 6, 6a, and 6b, speakers clearly indicate an equivalence between the concept of *'ofa* 'love' and that of *faka'apa'apa* 'respect' and *fatongia* 'duty.' In 6b, the speaker explicitly states that loving the king is the same as "obeying the law." And he adds that those who break the law, hence don't love, don't love the King.

9.4.2.3   Frequency of the six types of metaphors

In Figure 9.8, the occurrence of the six types of metaphors in the texts is shown. Almost half of the metaphors (294 or 45.23%) are type 2, that is, "person," where an abstract entity, a social group, an event or an object is attributed person-like features. This is not surprising since this type of metaphor is very common worldwide. What is noticeable is the fact that it does not co-occur with other types of metaphor in which abstract ideas and other concepts are likened to a machine, e.g., the body as a machine, the mind as a computer, etc. Although this type of metaphor is extremely common in Western cultures, none of the Tongan metaphors recorded are of this latter type.[15]

A third of the metaphors (190 or 29.23%) or more than half (53.37%) of the remaining 54.77% are made up of the sum of type 6, love is giving "duty/respect" (116 or 17.85%), and type 5, love is giving "help" (74 or 11.38%). Within the domain under investigation, social relationships, these types of metaphors are very salient. Besides they are relational in nature. That is, a social relationship is elucidated as a specific type of connection among individuals differentially located on the social ladder, i.e., giving. This latter activity is codified by giving help on one side (up–down) and giving respect/doing your duty (down–up) on the other. Moreover, both activities are often covered by the same lexical term, *'ofa* 'love.' Later, I discuss the meaning and implications of such a finding.

---

[15] Another contrasting finding is the extremely low frequency of the 'container' metaphor (19 or 2.92%).

The frequency of type 1, "orientational" (67 or 10.31%), and type 3, "entity" (66 or 10.15%), metaphors is relatively low, but the nature of these metaphors is very relevant. Orientational metaphors are predominantly of the up–down type, thus highlighting the prevailing concern and ubiquity of social hierarchy. Entity metaphors are almost exclusively of the type in which an individual/social group is likened to an object found in nature, especially regarding the capacity to reflect light or shining property of such objects. This preoccupation with shining located in a few individuals as a sign of contact with or presence of divinity, i.e., *mana* 'force, power,' is widely documented in Polynesian societies (Shore, 1989).

The concept of *mana* 'power' is at the core of traditional Polynesian and Tongan religion (Handy, 1927; Gifford, 1929; Williamson, 1933). Described either as substance or process (Keesing, 1984; Valeri, 1985), as cause or effect (Hogbin, 1936; Firth, 1940), *mana* always implies coming into contact with supernatural forces by means of another human being – usually a chief – who acts as mediator. The supernatural 'power' radiates out of this person and brings good to individuals, to the land, and to crops if a number of procedures are followed, otherwise misfortune results. Thus the practice of 'binding' and its relationship with the concept of *tapu* 'taboo' can be understood (see Gifford, 1929; but also Shore, 1989). One of the physical manifestations or explicit signs of *mana* is typically the fact that the body of the individual 'shines' as it 'radiates' power. Thus, the practice of oiling one's body so that it shines in contemporary Polynesian (and Tongan) dancing and rituals partially derives from this belief.

The frequency of occurrence of the two types of giving expressed by metaphors type 5 (love) and type 6 (duty/respect) in the various types of texts (interviews) reveals that their uses are linked to the specific contexts – at the personal or island/national levels – in which the social relationships are conceptualized and linguistically expressed.

Figure 9.9 shows a different distribution for love as giving help and love as giving duty/respect. The former is much more frequent in interviews about

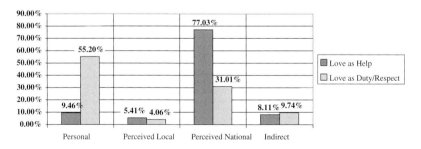

Figure 9.9 Frequency of type 5 (love) and type 6 (duty/respect) metaphors

perceived social relationships at the island and national level (77.03%); this frequency is more than twice as much as the general frequency of any metaphor in the same type of texts (37.69%, see Table 9.1). The latter is more frequent in interviews about personal relationships (55.20%), almost twice as much as the frequency of any metaphors in the same type of texts (32.46%, see Table 9.1). It appears that behavior in personal relationships is conceived as giving duty/respect to others, while behavior in wider social relationships is conceived as giving help.

9.4.3   Reasoning with the model

The types and frequencies of metaphors discussed so far have highlighted a fundamental model that Tongans use in mentally representing and speaking about social relationships. I summarize the model in this way:

society is hierarchical, ladder like; individuals are located at different levels of the society's ladder; *'ofa* 'love' links these individuals to make them a whole; *'ofa* is giving, either giving help (up–down) or giving duty/respect (down–up); few higher people (especially one, the king) are in contact with divinity and a physical feature of this property is their bodily shining.

The model is composed of a 'core' part and a 'periphery' that is not expressed as often. The core is: *'ofa is giving, either giving help (up–down) or giving duty/respect (down–up)*. People utilize this model (especially the 'core') in their thinking and reasoning about social relationships, either consciously or unconsciously. The following are three examples from the texts in which the model, better, its 'core,' explicitly transpires in what individuals are saying:

7.   … **'ofa** 'a e kakai ['ofa 'a e kakai] **faka'apa'apa**, eh ['io] ki he Tu'i [ki he Tu'i] …

      "… **love** the people [love the people] **respect**, eh [yes] to the King [to the King] …"

      '… the people love [the people love], respect, eh, [yes] the King [the King] …'

      [4K, June 7, 2004].

8.   … *'Ofa lahi 'a e kakai ki he Tu'í* ['io] *koe'uhí lahi ange* **'ofa 'a e Tu'í ki he kakai**, *tufa 'a e kelekele ta'e totongi, tukufakaholo pé kelekele he fāmili 'o a'u ki he ngata'anga 'o mamani, ha'ele pé Tu'i ki muli feinga ha me'a ke mo'ui ai 'a e kakai, ko e kakai 'i Tonga ni nau nofo pé 'i Tonga ni, ko e Tu'í pé 'oku 'alu 'o feinga* ['o, 'io hoko atu] *ki he ngaahi Pule'anga, ki ha fa'ahinga me'a 'ofa **ke tokoni ki he kakai katoa**, 'o e fonua* …

      "… people love a lot the King [yes] because **the King loves the people** more, he divides out the land without pay, the family inherit the land till the end of the world, the King goes abroad to get things for the life of the people, the

people of Tonga just stay in Tonga, the King goes to try [yes, go on] with many Governments, to get presents **to help all the people**, of the country …"
[16S, June 12, 2004].

9. … *'ofa pé nautolu ki he Tu'i, koe'uhi pé ko e Tu'i ia 'o Tonga, 'ikai lava ke liliu e Tu'í ia, kuo pau pé ia ke nofo hono tu'unga fakaTu'i, ['io] pea ko e Tu'i 'oku **tokoni** pé ia ki he kakai 'o Tonga …*
"… they [people] **love** the King, because he is the King of Tonga, you can't change the King, he must stay in his royal place [yes] then the King **helps** the people of Tonga …"
[17M, June 18, 2004].

In the first example, *'ofa* 'love' for the king is explicitly equivalent to *faka'apa'apa* 'respect.' In the other two examples, the *'ofa* 'love' of the king for the people of Tonga is explicitly equivalent to his helping the people and the country. In the first case, the state of love is equivalent to the act of giving respect in a social down–up direction, from the people to the king. In the second case, the state of love is equivalent to the act of giving help in a social up–down direction, from the king to the people. What is left implicit in both cases is the hierarchical nature of society. Notice also that in these examples the 'shining' of the king does not appear either, even though it is very common and frequent throughout the texts.

The model works well in elucidating a variety of Tongan reasoning about daily or exceptional behavior and social relationships. I personally checked this model extensively both in Tonga with a variety of individuals in a number of social events and in the US with my Tongan assistants. Basically, the reasoning employs both *modus ponens* and *modus tollens* in this way:

Modus ponens:	*Modus tollens:*
If love, then help	If love, then help
Help, therefore love	Not help, therefore not love
If love, then duty/respect	If love, then duty/respect
Duty/respect, therefore love	Not duty/respect, therefore not love

Examples of the use of these two types of reasoning are abundant in my field notes and my memory. A typical problem with villages that are supposed to have a resident noble is that contemporary nobles prefer to reside in the capital town of Nuku'alofa instead of their native villages. Villagers complain about the *fatongia* 'duty'[16] they have to give to the noble in spite of the explicit

---

[16] *Fatongia* 'duty' includes the donation of produce, animals (typically pigs), and services to the noble.

lack of love on the noble's side who chose to reside in town. The lack of love by residing elsewhere is explained by the impossibility of the noble helping villagers when need might occur. Besides, they add, the unwillingness to be helpful may be due to lack of contact and familiarity with villagers' problems. Clearly, the *modus tollens* introduced above is at work in these situations (if love, then help; not help, therefore, not love; if love then duty/respect; not duty/ respect, therefore not love).

Tongan diaspora has been the subject of several publications recently (Small, 1997; Morton, 2003) and I was able to witness the impact it is having even in the daily life of small and remote villages. Fundamentally, villagers talk about relatives who live abroad as full of love if they receive help from them whenever they ask for it, especially via phone and about monetary issues. In contrast, they talk about lack of love when the opposite is true, or at least, when not all the salient requests advanced are satisfied. Here we witness a clear use of the *modus ponens* introduced above (if love, then help; help, therefore love; if love, then duty/respect; duty/respect, therefore love). As I already mentioned, examples of these two types of reasoning are abundant. This is especially true in the days following Tongan events like funerals or first year birthdays where a lot of exchange and giving is expected on the side of culturally established donors and receivers. The presence or lack of the appropriate amount and quantity of receiving/giving acts of exchange triggers the two types of reasoning.

In the following section I investigate salient key words linked to the 'giving' metaphors. Key words provide the possibility of discovering the origin of the 'giving' activity, that is, does it originate from ego or other-than-ego? The results of this latter investigation are extremely significant. In fact, possible indications are obtained as to the effective use of 'radiality' in the generation of metaphors when thinking and talking about social relationships.

9.4.4   The key word 'ofa 'love'

Once the saliency of the model introduced after the metaphor analysis was established, it became clear that I needed to look into what Quinn (2005: 71–2) calls "key words." A key word refers to the global cultural model speakers are employing in constructing their linguistic production about a specific domain, in our case social relationships. A key word is also part of a local model of its own and this model as well is likely to be intrinsically related to the global model to which the word refers (see Minsky, 1975; Fillmore, 1982; Brewer, 1984). An analysis of key words, then, may illuminate both the local and the global model that generate them. Thus, this analysis may provide further insight and support into the cultural model, eventually the foundational cultural model already highlighted in other domains of knowledge, and currently being elicited from the metaphor analysis.

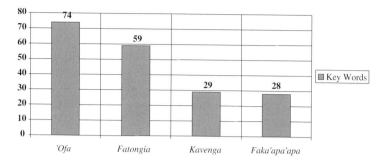

Figure 9.10 Frequency of key words

Key words that emerged from my further analysis of the texts were the following: *'ofa* 'love,' *fatongia* 'duty,' *kavenga* 'lighter duty,' and *faka'apa'apa* 'respect.' All four words are subsumed under the model just elucidated above and used to instantiate the model. Since *fatongia, kavenga,* and *faka'apa'apa* are considered by the model as forms of *'ofa*, it was expected that a frequency count for the four words would privilege *'ofa*.

Figure 9.10 shows that the prediction was correct. There were 74 instances of *'ofa* and fewer instances for the other three words (59, 29, and 28, respectively). Furthermore, I checked for the frequency of the four key words in the different types of texts.

Figure 9.11[17] shows that *'ofa* 'love' was used prevalently in texts about perceived social relationships at the national level (77.03%), while *fatongia* 'duty,' *kavenga* 'lighter duty,' and *faka'apa'apa* 'respect' combined were used mostly in texts about personal social relationships (55.20%). Thus, it appears as if *'ofa* is linguistically realized/instantiated as duty/respect when talking about personal relationships, and it is explicitly instantiated as love when talking about wider webs of social interactions, mainly at the national level. In Tonga, these latter mean relationships between the king and the nobles and between both of them and commoners. It appears that *'ofa* may be the suggested thread stitching together the various hierarchically organized layers of Tongan society.

What is then the model for *'ofa*? We have already seen that *'ofa* as state is metaphorically conceptualized as an action, the specific action being that of giving. When using *'ofa* in speech, then, there are three possible choices the speaker can make (horizontal direction): express a giving from ego to other;

---

[17] The data in this figure are the same as those in Figure 9.9 because the key words considered were a necessary pointer to the presence of metaphor type 5 and 6 (i.e., *'ofa* is help, *'ofa* is duty/ respect).

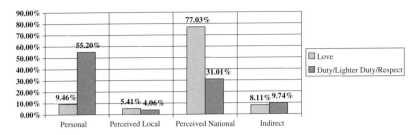

Figure 9.11 Frequency of key words in types of texts

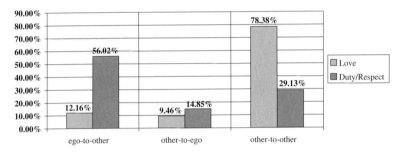

Figure 9.12 Direction (horizontal) of the two types of love

express a giving from other to ego, or express a giving from other to other. Besides, the hierarchical reality of Tongan society (typically implied) provides the possibility of making three further choices (vertical direction): express a giving from an upper layer of society to a lower layer; express a giving from a lower layer of society to an upper layer; or express a giving taking place at the same layer of society. Figures 9.12, 9.13, and 9.14 contain data about these possibilities.

The data in Figure 9.12 show that '*ofa* 'love' is conceptualized more often as other-to-other (78.38%), rarely as ego-to-other (12.16%), and even less as other-to-ego (9.46%). Thus ego is kept as much as possible out of the picture. However, when '*ofa* is conceptualized as duty/respect, then, it appears more frequently as ego-to-other (56.02%), frequently as other-to-other (29.13%), and less frequently as other-to-ego (14.85%).

It transpires from these results that interviewees are willing (at least 56.02% of the time) to express linguistically forms of '*ofa* 'love' which start from their ego only in the form of duty/respect to others, while they are prone to express

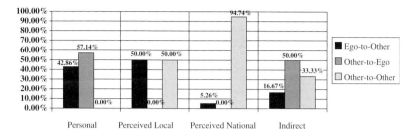

Figure 9.13 Horizontal direction of love in various types of texts

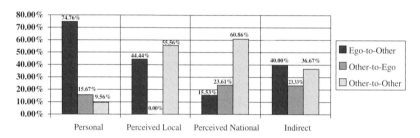

Figure 9.14 Horizontal direction of duty/respect in various types of texts

very frequently (78.38% of the time) another form of *'ofa* (very likely, as 'help') only as a relationship linking a person other-than-ego to another person also other-than-ego. Then, looking/talking at/about others involved in social relationships, interviewees instantiate *'ofa* as the stitching thread among them (others-to-others). Talking about their own social relationships, they instantiate *'ofa* as duty/respect (ego-to-others).

When we look at the horizontal direction of the distribution of *'ofa* as love and *'ofa* as duty/respect in the various types of texts, we see that the former (Figure 9.13) is most frequently (94.74%) used in the other-to-other mode especially in the texts in which perceived social relationships at the national level are discussed. The latter (Figure 9.14) instead, *'ofa* as duty/respect, is more frequently (74.76%) used in the ego-to-other mode especially in the texts in which personal social relationships are discussed.

These two distributions support what is stated above regarding the results in Figure 9.10. That is, individuals are likely to conceptualize *'ofa* as duty/respect when talking about personal social relationships, thus including ego. And they

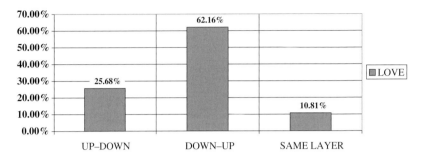

Figure 9.15 Direction of love (vertical)

are more likely to conceptualize *'ofa* as love (help) when talking about social relationships at a wider level of inclusion (island and nation), thus excluding ego. Notice, however, that the frequency of the former (love, 94.74%) is much higher than that of the latter (duty/respect, 74.76%).

Figure 9.15 shows that the preferred vertical direction for the uses of *'ofa* is down–up (62.16%). Furthermore, Figure 9.16 shows that this preference is more frequent in both types of 'perceived' social relationships texts (75.00% for local and 75.00% for national). The up–down direction (Figure 9.16) is noticeably used in the personal texts (42.86%) and the indirect texts (33.33%), relevantly used in the national texts (24.56%) and completely absent in the local texts (0.00%).

Summing up our current discussion of the frequencies of the four key words investigated, I can state that there is a preference for conceptualizing *'ofa* as love especially in talking about social relationships between other-than-ego individuals, thus excluding ego. This preference goes hand in hand with a preference for a down–up direction, thus originating in other individuals at a lower level of society, including ego, and going up to other individuals. When *'ofa* is conceptualized as duty/respect, then ego is included and the direction is frequently (42.86%) up–down,[18] that is, from an upper level of society to a lower one, where ego belongs.

It appears then, that the model obtained by the metaphor analysis and introduced in the previous section finds some significant support in the analysis of the reasoning practice by Tongans and in the key words analysis just concluded, especially the core part: *'ofa is giving, either giving help (up–down) or giving duty/respect (down–up).* Furthermore, the analysis of the key words adds a couple of important pieces to the picture introduced so far. Individuals

---

[18] Exactly the same frequency is noted in the same-layer strategy (42.86%).

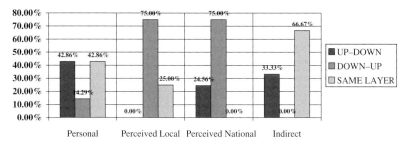

Figure 9.16 Detailed direction of love (vertical)

prefer to talk about social relationships among other individuals, thus excluding themselves. And when they do so, they assign a specific direction to these social relationships, down–up, that is, from a lower level of society (where they belong) to a higher one. However, when the focus shifts to personal relationships, the preferred direction is up–down or same layer (see Figure 9.16).

It seems like a collective stance is chosen (that includes ego) and social relationships are conceptualized as upward. When focus gets too close to ego as in personal social relationships, then the direction shifts to either same layer or up–down. Since radiality implies the highlighting of other-than-ego instead of focusing on ego, we can deduce that radiality appears to be the cognitive engine behind the Tongan metaphor construction of, reasoning about, and talking about social relationships.

9.4.5   Source domains and metaphors about the king

As stated in Section 9.4.1, the metaphor analysis conducted includes retrieving the source domains of the various metaphors found. Surprisingly enough, only three major source domains are found for all the metaphors:

1. the domain of 'human beings' with all the body features they display, the activity they can conduct, and the emotions, feelings, thoughts they can have;
2. the domain of 'nature' and all the things/objects it contains (including vegetation);
3. the domain of 'space' and spatial relationships.

Again to be noticed is the fact that no metaphor is derived from the domain of modern (e.g., industrial machines, motor boats, engines) and/or contemporary (e.g., radio, television, computers) technology. It must be pointed out that this phenomenon is not due to the absence of such technology in contemporary Tongan life in which both types are widely present and color daily life. Nonetheless, when conceptualizing and talking about social relationships, technology of any type is not used as source for metaphors. This is also true for traditional technology, such as that used in house building, canoe building, agriculture, fishing and the like. The absence of this latter type of source domains is peculiar to metaphors about social relationships. In fact, they are found in Tongan talk (and written texts) about other domains.

All three domains used, human beings, nature, and space, are very common sources for metaphors in cultures and languages throughout the world. Human characteristics are typically assigned to institutions, social groups, and events, in the same way as human beings are assigned characteristics of natural entities (animals, vegetation, geographical features, e.g., mountains) or forces. The domain of space and spatial relationships is also very frequently used as a source for metaphor construction. Besides, the axis that Tongans privilege is the vertical axis and it was to be expected in a very stratified society such as the Kingdom of Tonga (Gifford, 1929; Lātūkefu, 1974; Marcus, 1980; Gailey, 1987; Helu, 1999; Evans, 2001).

The salience of the domain of space as a source for Tongan metaphors when talking about social relationships takes a greater meaning in the light of two related phenomena:

- the Tongan preferred way to represent spatial relationships mentally and linguistically;
- the results obtained from the 'metaphors about the king' activity.

The first phenomenon was pointed out in Chapters 3 and 5. Tongans prefer a radial form of representing spatial relationships both linguistically and mentally, especially in short-term and long-term memory about large-scale space. This phenomenon implies choosing a fixed point of reference in the field of the speaker and representing objects as from or toward that point. We saw in the same chapters that different linguistic and mental representations of spatial relationships (e.g., uses of the translation subtype of the relative frame of reference) share fundamental characteristics that led me to hypothesize 'radiality' as a basic representational strategy for various Tongan domains of knowledge.

Once confronted with the finding of space as a salient source domain for metaphors about social relationships, I expected a similar bias for representing these latter as that found in space. The results of the metaphor analysis presented so far support my expectations. Ego is kept as far as possible out of focus, other-than-ego is highlighted, and relationships are conceptualized and talked about as toward or away from the focalized other-than-ego.

In a small country like Tonga (around 100,000 people), the figure of the king dominates the social, political, and imaginative daily life of any individual, either resident in a major town, or in a remote village. It is for this reason that I developed a protocol in which I asked all the adult residents of the village that is my regular fieldwork site to fill in the blank of this sentence three times:

Ko e Tu'í, ko e .... 'o Tonga
'The King is the .... of Tonga.'

The intention was to obtain as many metaphors as possible about the king and at least three from each individual. The expected responses were that individuals would focus on the king, his qualities, and what he does for Tongans, while whatever people do for him (thus involving ego as generator) would be much less frequent. For example, metaphors like "the king is the source of happiness" would be more common than metaphors like "the king is the one who deserves first consideration." In the former type, other/king is the focus and action originates from there. In the latter type, the focus is the king, but action generates from ego.

Out of the possible 95 adults living in the village, 87 were interviewed because 8 were not resident at the time of the administration of the activity. Altogether I collected 247 acceptable responses that were divided into 39 types (plus one 'don't know' type including one response). These latter were further aggregated into six groups labeled as follows: ruler, source, king's action, kinship, center/essence, and miscellaneous. These groupings are presented in Table 9.2 in decreasing order (except for 'miscellaneous') of frequency of types (and not of number of instances in the group).

The analysis of these words/metaphors for the king reveals that 24 types/words are focused on the king's qualities and on what he is/does for Tongans. That is, types/words 4, 5, 6, 7, 9, 10, 11, 12, and 13 are about qualities of the king (I include 32 and 33 also in this group for a total of 42 responses out of 247, 17.00%). I interpret this group of metaphors as focusing on or choosing the center, in this case the king. This focus is not surprising and was expected, actually motivated by the protocol.

Types/words 16, 17, 18, 19, 20, 21, 22, 23, and 24 (a total of 17 responses, 6.88%) explicitly define the king as source. Here the focused-on king (the center) is metaphorically indicated as the source of life and of a variety of relevant aspects of life such as beauty, happiness, and peace. Finally, types/words 1, 2, 3, 8, 25, 26, 27, and 28 (I include 29, 30, and 31 also in this group for a total of 175 responses, 70.85%) are about the king's actions that are directed to any Tongan. Thus, the source of the action is the king, or other-than-ego, and the recipient is ego (i.e., Tongans). Only 2 types/words (14 and 15), and possibly another 2 (34 and 39) for a total of 7 responses, 2.83%, are about Tongans doing things for the king. That is, the source of the action is ego and the direction is to other-than-ego or the king.

The focus on the king was expected and induced by the nature of the activity. The focus on the qualities of the king and how his actions affect people was

Table 9.2 *Metaphors about the king*

Group	Types/Words	No. of instances
Ruler:		
	1. pule 'ruler'	64
	2. taki/tataki/takimu'a 'leader'	59
	3. hau 'champion'	37
	4. aoniu 'supreme'	12
	5. tu'i 'king'	10
	6. kalauni 'crown'	7
	7. mafi 'power'	5
	8. hia 'Robin Hood type'	3
	9. ulu 'head'	1
	10. kanokato 'outstanding value'	1
	11. fakaleveleva 'supreme over all'	1
	12. poto taha 'smartest'	1
	13. taloni 'throne'	1
	14. fakamu'omu'a 'to give first consideration'	1
	15. faka'uto'uta 'given careful consideration'	1
Source:		
	16. to'a 'source of peace'	5
	17. mo'ui'anga 'source of life'	3
	18. hoifua/hoifua'anga 'source of beauty'	2
	19. fiefia'anga 'source of happiness'	2
	20. taukapo 'source of happiness'	1
	21. malu'i 'source of life'	1
	22. fakahela 'cause of tiredness'	1
	23. muimui 'lower part of bunch of bananas'	1
	24. melino'anga 'source of peace'	1
King's actions:		
	25. fakafofonga 'representative'	2
	26. sevaaniti 'servant'	1
	27. tokoni ofi ki he kakai 'helps people'	1
	28. fakalaloa 'intercessor'	1
Kinship:		
	29. tamai 'father'	3
	30. tangata 'father/man'	3
	31. kāinga 'extended family'	1
Center/Essence:		
	32. uho 'core/center'	2
	33. elito 'essence'	1
Miscellaneous:		
	34. manako/mokoi 'liking/desire'	4
	35. huelo 'ray of light'	2
	36. palataisi 'paradise'	1
	37. ma'olunga 'height/importance'	1
	38. tofi'a 'heritage'	1
	39. fili 'choice'	1

hypothesized and confirmed by the findings. Significantly, also the prediction that the majority of the actions expressed or alluded to would not be generated from ego was clearly and distinctly supported (70.85% vs. 2.83%).

These findings as well as those about metaphor types and frequencies in Tongan linguistic productions about social relationships provide evidence that the domain of social relationships is structured in a radial fashion. That is, individuals are selected in ego's field of social relationships and conceptualizations of actions follow in which the focus is one of those individuals, either toward or away from them. Ego is kept as much out of the picture as possible. Thus, more support to the general hypothesis of radiality as a Tongan foundational cultural model is added.

9.5   The discourse structure analysis

The lexical frequencies analyses conducted on the linguistic data provide strong evidence for the high use of *atu2* and mild evidence of an increased use of *mai2*, thus partially supporting the hypothesis of radiality as instantiated in a higher number of uses of *mai2* and *atu2* in speech about social relationships. The metaphor analyses – in general at the sentence level, when we do not take into consideration the analyses of key words – also provide strong support for the general hypothesis of radiality as a Tongan foundational cultural model. The combined results already provide clear support for the hypothesis of radiality in the mental representation of social relationships when expressed in speech about them.

However, I deemed it necessary to look into the discourse organization of some texts, specifically the stories elicited in 2005. That is, instead of focusing exclusively on the lexical level (frequencies) and the sentence level (metaphors), I thought it would be worthwhile to investigate the overall discourse organization of the narrative texts as a possible indication of mental organization of knowledge. Specifically, I looked for traces of the radiality foundational cultural model (i.e., focus on other-than-ego) here hypothesized as the generative root for the representations of social relationships (see Quinn, 2005 for a variety of similar strategies).

After a long and careful examination of the 2005 interviews, 73 stories were found in the 24 transcriptions. These stories were later arranged in the following typology:

1. "personal" (7 stories, 9.59%), where ego is mentioned as main participating character;
2. "*kāinga*" 'extended family' (15 stories, 20.55%), where the focus is on the *kāinga* and ego is excluded (40% of times);

3. "small group" (21 stories, 28.77%), where the focus is on a small group of people from the village and ego is excluded (38.10% of times); and
4. "whole village," (30 stories, 41.10%) where the focus is on the whole village and ego is excluded (53.33% of times).

Considering that these results refer to a population of 95 adults (87 present during the collection of the data), the number of times (almost nine out of ten times) that ego is put in the background of these narratives assumes a saliency worthy of notice.

The results in Figure 9.17 show a strong preference (41.10%) for the "whole village" type of story. Moreover, almost all interviewees, 21 out of the 24 individuals (87.50%), narrated "whole village" stories, while only 15 people (62.50%) narrated "small group" stories, 12 people (50.00%) narrated "*kāinga*" stories, and only 7 people (29.17%) narrated "personal" stories. None of the seven people who narrated "personal" stories did so in isolation, but narrated also either "whole village" stories, or "small group" stories, or a combination of the other three types.

I interpret these last findings and the ones about types of stories in Figure 9.17 as an indication of a preference to organize the narrative discourse around other-than-ego individuals. As a matter of fact, when the three social story categories of "*kāinga*," "small group," and "whole village" are combined, we obtain a total of 90.41% of the stories narrated not centered on ego. Thus, it is clear that the interviewees were carefully conceptualizing narratives as not centered on ego or without a relevant ego participation.

Furthermore, a plausible explanation is found for the high use of *atu*2 in these texts (see Figure 9.7). In fact, narratives centered on other-than-ego individuals would tend to increase the description of events with real or metaphoric movement away from that individual (thus, higher use of *atu*2). The focus on

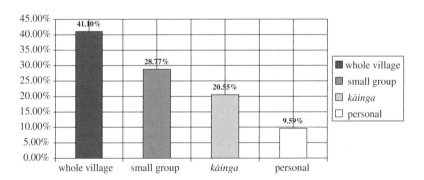

Figure 9.17 Types of stories in 2005 interviews

other-than-ego in narratives, however, does not explain the low use of *mai*2 in those same narratives. As I have already suggested, the real or metaphoric movement of objects and/or events toward the other-than-ego individual (use of *mai*2) appears to be culturally constrained. In other words, while it appears appropriate to center one's thought on other-than-ego (e.g., narratives not centered on ego), only movement away from the latter is typically expressed (high use of *atu*2), and movement toward other-than-ego is not commonly addressed (low use of *mai*2).

These findings are in line with Duranti's (1994) statements about Samoans' dislike of making direct accusations of any wrongdoing, and his documentation of a high use of subjectless and/or agentless transitive constructions (both in *fono* '[village] meetings' and in everyday conversations) consisting of only a verb and an object. Uses of transitive and ergative constructions with fully expressed subjects/agents are reserved for specific and rare occasions/narratives like blaming/accusing and/or praising. Tongans' high use of *atu*2 appears to be another way to express an action initiated by a non-specified other-than-ego, but affecting or ending on a specified object. The Tongan low use of *mai*2, instead, would be another way to avoid addressing a specified other-than-ego individual. In fact, if the sentence expresses movement/action directed toward a specific individual, the identity of the target of the action would become apparent.

Both grammatical devices, use of subjectless transitive and/or fully subjected and ergative sentences in Samoan and high use of *atu*2 and low use of *mai*2 in Tonga, seem to be the result of a specific cultural way (pan-Polynesian) of thinking about social relationships. Cultural rules and restrictions apply to the production of linguistic expressions addressing social relationships. Parts of these rules and restrictions are generated by a specific way of representing mentally the social relationships addressed. And this organization may be shared by other domains of knowledge within and among mental modules. In other words, the Tongan foundational cultural model labeled 'radiality' could be the co-generator of those cultural restrictions on the production of linguistic expressions about social relationships. How far such a cultural model is shared in Polynesia remains to be seen.

9.6   Conclusion

As stated at the beginning of this chapter, linguistic data are an invaluable source when trying to look into mental representations of knowledge. Consequently, the investigation of the domain of social relationships included a number of interviews about the domain from a variety of perspectives. The first group of interviews were about social relationships at the personal level. The second group inquired about perceived social relationships in one's village, island,

and national territory. The third group required participants to tell a story about their village life, thus indirectly addressing social relationships. The final group of interviews were conducted with the top echelon of society – nobles, ministers, and high government and church officials – and they were about social relationships at the national level.

This linguistic corpus was then analyzed at the lexical level (frequencies), the sentence level (metaphor), and at the discourse structure level. Each analysis added some supporting evidence toward the hypothesis, that is, it appears that Tongans use the 'radiality' foundational cultural model in mentally representing social relationships as well as in instantiating them linguistically. In other words, individuals are selected in ego's field of social relationships and conceptualizations of actions follow in which the focus is one of those individuals, either toward or away from them. Ego is kept as much as possible out of the picture.

Such a state of affairs is predicted to have some influence on the quality of the performance obtained during the cognitive tasks administered whose topic is one's social relationships. The role of language is kept to a minimum in these tasks and consequently mental representations of social relationships are more likely to be directly instantiated in the behavioral output required by the fulfilling of the tasks at hand. In the following chapter, I present the results of the analyses of the data obtained with the administering of the memory task (free listing), the sorting task, and the drawing task.

10 Radiality and mental representations of social relationships

10.1 Introduction

In the investigation of spatial relationships presented in Chapters 3–5, the linguistic data was deemed insufficient to provide an adequate picture of the mental representation of those same relationships and a set of psychological tasks was also administered. It was the results of these latter tasks, together with crucial ethnographic data, that provided the most enlightening information about the structure and format of the mental representation of spatial relationships (see Chapter 4). Similarly, when investigating the mental representations of social relationships it is not sufficient to collect and analyze only linguistic data. Consequently, I decided to administer a battery of three cognitive tasks in which the topic was kept constant, social relationships, and the participation/interference of language was kept to a minimum.

The first task administered was the memory task or free listing. In this task participants were asked to name all the adult co-villagers they could remember. Thus, their mental coverage of a significant part, their co-villagers, of the domain of social relationships was obtained. It is obvious that their social world extends well beyond the boundaries of their village; nonetheless, it is their co-villagers that represent the most salient component of their daily social lives. The second task was a pile sort task. During this task, individuals were asked to sort a deck of cards containing the photos of all their adult co-villagers. After the first sort, they were invited to sort their piles again, if they saw that as a possible task (half of them did not).

Finally, I administered a drawing task. In this task, participants were asked to draw on a provided sheet of paper a number of people they considered as the ones they interact most with during their daily lives. The only other relevant instruction given was to use squares for males and circles for females. All three activities were videotaped. I now discuss in length the rationale for the administering of the three tasks and the results obtained.

10.2   The memory task (free listing)[1]

In 1988, Weller and Romney suggested the use of free-listing activities as one of the ways to isolate a domain as well as discover its defining boundaries (1988: 9–10). Besides, Ross (2004) adds that a free-listing activity can primarily obtain "a list of culturally relevant items on which most of the informants agree" (2004: 90). In other words, when investigating a domain of knowledge, by using a free-listing activity one can discover if the domain is culturally salient, what its linguistic and cognitive boundaries are, and which units/members are themselves more salient than others. Inspired by Weller and Romney (1988) and Ross (2004), I decided to use a free-listing activity to isolate the domain of social relationships and to discover its inherent structure and boundaries. Basically, I was interested in finding out what are the fundamental principles underlying the mental representations of social relationships in Tongan. My current hypothesis is that radiality is the most salient structural characteristic of these representations.

Since my field site consists of a small village whose population is limited to 95 adult individuals, I decided to ask all the villagers about everybody else. In other words, I asked all the adult villagers to tell me the names of the residents of the village they could remember. In such a way, a consistent part of their social world would be touched upon by this memory task. Of course, other individuals residing in other places could be part of their social world, as I know they are. Nonetheless, for the majority of them the village is the social and spatial unit within which most of their social life unfolds.

In this section, I report on the results of the free-listing activity. None of the socially prominent individuals such as the local chief, the town officer, and many elders appeared in a salient position, i.e., at the top of the list, when the lists were aggregated. This led me to look elsewhere to extract the meanings that those lists may have encoded. I noticed that the majority of people that appeared to be remembered first where also residing in the same part of the village, i.e., the front. I then produced memory routes for each list obtained and aggregated these results. The results of the analyses conducted on these newly obtained data show that a spatial bias congruent with that already documented for spatial relationships (Bennardo, 2000a, 2002a) is also present in these data about social relationships. The consequences of such a finding for a preferential way of representing knowledge by Tongans (i.e., the radiality foundational cultural model) are discussed in closing the section.

10.2.1   Methodology

Faced with the task of investigating the way in which social relationships are mentally represented by Tongans, I decided to use a free-listing activity.

---

[1] This section is a reduced version of Bennardo (2008).

Basically, I asked individuals to list the number of co-villagers they could remember. The lists provided were written down while being produced. The main hypothesis was that people first mentioned would be the more salient, and consequently, those better remembered by all interviewees would be the most salient individuals in the domain of social relationships.

The activity was conducted in a small village in the northern Tongan archipelago of Vava'u. Due to the size of the village, 172 residents, I decided to administer the activity to the whole adult population, 95 villagers, instead of a random sample of that same adult population. Moreover, this strategy allowed me to obtain a complete picture of a local community wherein social relationships are typically established in Tonga. I am perfectly aware that the villagers' social lives are not limited by the boundary of the village where they reside. Kinship, social, and religious ties often exist with a variety of places, including neighboring villages, other islands, archipelagoes, the capital town (locus of a constant migration flux in the last three decades), and abroad, including New Zealand, Australia, and the United States. However, life in a village is still the typical life experience that the majority of Tongans have. Thus, I can also claim that the picture obtained represents a sample of the total population of Tonga. The only exception to village residence is represented by three towns, including the capital town, in three different archipelagoes whose populations range between a few thousands and around twenty thousand for the capital (the total population of the kingdom is around 100,000).

With the help of assistants, I interviewed all the adults of the village: eighty-eight individuals out of ninety-five possible ones (seven individuals were not in the village when the task was administered). The interviews were conducted in the house of residence of each interviewee to avoid a 'space' bias (the place of the interview and its neighboring residents) in the lists produced. Each individual in a list was ranked and a value for each person remembered was calculated using the following formula:

(number of people – memory rank) + 1/number of people remembered

This formula produced standardized values from 0.01 to 1.00 for all people ranked. Aggregate numbers (sum of all values) for each individual were also calculated and a final rank was determined using the following formula:

aggregate/total number of people

Then, a lower rank meant 'less remembered' (less salient) and a higher rank meant 'better remembered' (more salient). Since I administered the activity to the village where I have conducted extensive fieldwork during the last fifteen years, I already had a clear picture of the social structure/composition of the population involved. The most salient individuals in the village are the local chief, the *matāpule* 'talking chief,' the *ofisa kolo* 'town officer,' several *'ulumotu'a* 'head of extended family and/or household,' and elders (both female and male). Then, my working hypothesis was that these individuals would be found at the top of the list.

10.2.2   The first results

On average people remembered 51/95 co-villagers (seven individuals were not in the village the day the memory task was administered and were not interviewed), ranging from 18 to 86. This high average bears witness to the very close-knit type of social life typical of a small village the size of the one involved. After applying the two formulas introduced in Section 10.2.1, I obtained a ranked list of all the people remembered. The results were quite surprising and did not confirm the hypothesis (see Figure 10.1 for the results regarding the top 35 individuals in the list).

First, there was no evident gender bias in the results: in the top ten individuals, five were female and five were male. Second, the local chief, expected to rank very high in the list, ranked only 35th. Third, the *ofisa kolo* 'town officer' was the only one ranked according to the hypothesis; in fact, he stands 2nd in the list. Fourth, the first *'ulumotu'a* 'head of extended family and/or household' was ranked 8th, and there were only four of them in the first top 27 individuals, out of a possible 14 *'ulumotu'a* present in the village. Fifth, four unmarried individuals, expected to rank very low in the list because of their known low position in the local village structure, were found in the top 14, with the first of them ranked 5th. Sixth, while the top six individuals belong to the same *kāinga* 'extended family,' this *kāinga* is the one with the most members, 31 adult members (1 in every 3 adult villagers), and so the result is not surprising nor unexpected. Besides, when I checked if a specific *kāinga* 'extended family' would appear to be more prominent than others, I found that at least five *kāinga* 'extended family' were present in the top 13 individuals. Thus, I could not assign any special value to *kāinga* membership.

10.2.3   The memory routes and the second results

Puzzled by the results, I continued to examine the data and noticed that the people that were at the top of the list all lived in a specific area of the village. It appeared as if proximity of residence had triggered closeness of recall. Consequently, I decided to check if a 'spatial' strategy and/or other strategies – and how frequently each of them – had been employed in producing the memory list. This analysis involved the production of what I called 'memory routes.' That is, each individual's list was transposed onto the map of the village, so that I could determine where the list started, how it went along the village space (i.e., from which house to which house), and where it ended.

The map of the village (Figure 10.2) I used to produce the memory routes came from the Digitized Tonga database (see a full description of the database

	Social Status	NAME	Code #	RANK
1	elder	Lea	68	0.46
2	town officer	Kaliti	64	0.42
3	elder	Feliuaki	62	0.42
4	elder	Tumoe	69	0.42
5	unmarried	Vika	70	0.41
6	elder	Fine	63	0.39
7	elder	Laluini	67	0.39
8	ulumotu'a	Samisoni	66	0.38
9	young married	Malia	65	0.38
10	unmarried	Maluhola	71	0.38
11	elder	Nusi	57	0.37
12	young married	Isileli	24	0.37
13	ulumotu'a	Sunia	29	0.37
14	young married	Ungatea	23	0.36
15	ulumotu'a	Sipe	79	0.36
16	elder	Saane	58	0.36
17	elder	Salote	49	0.35
18	elder	Tevita-Muau	72	0.35
19	elder	Ana	30	0.33
20	elder	Mula	85	0.33
21	young married	Afa	59	0.32
22	unmarried	Keasi	31	0.32
23	elder	Ana	80	0.32
24	unmarried	Aiona	44	0.31
25	elder	Siale	20	0.30
26	unmarried	Tupou	86	0.29
27	ulumotu'a	Sione	1	0.28
28	young married	Maletá	56	0.28
29	young married	Taufa	40	0.28
30	elder	Ane	34	0.28
31	young married	Tupou	25	0.27
32	married	Lisiate	51	0.27
33	young married	Lose	36	0.27
34	unmarried	Ulaiasi	78	0.27
35	CHIEF	Hala'api'api	89	0.27

Figure 10.1 Top part of ranking list

in Chapter 5, Section 5.2.2). In this map, I indicate how the village is conceived by the villagers as composed of three parts: a 'front,' the north-western part also called *Holani*,[2] a 'middle,' called *Faleono*,[3] and a 'back,' the south-eastern part also called *Selusalema*.[4] This information plays an important role in the analyses that follow.

[2] *Holani* glosses as 'Holland' and villagers state that it received that name because at the beginning of the twentieth century a person from Holland resided in that part of town for some time. But not all villagers agree on this etymology.

[3] *Faleono* glosses as 'six houses.' This name is strictly related to the origin myth about the village that states that only six houses inhabited by six brothers were once the root nucleus of the village.

[4] *Selusalema* glosses as 'Jerusalem' and it was named in this way because it hosted the first Wesleyan church of the village. The current church building is now in a different part of the village (i.e., the middle or *Faleono*) and there are no remains of the old church except in people's memory.

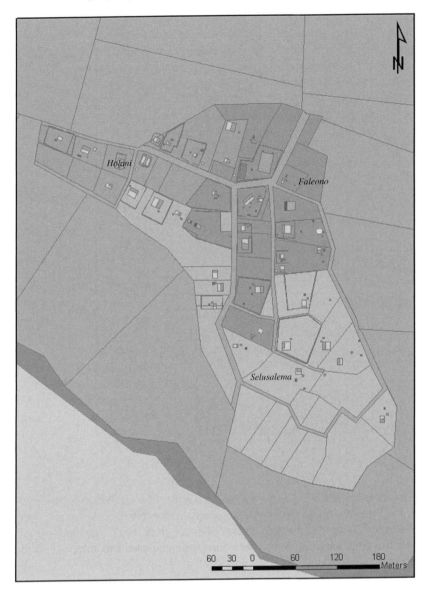

Figure 10.2 Map of the village

While transferring the memory lists of the various individuals interviewed onto the map, the ethnographic information in the database was also used, e.g., sometimes a change in direction (from front-back to front-side) could be explained by noticing the kinship relation between the people living in the

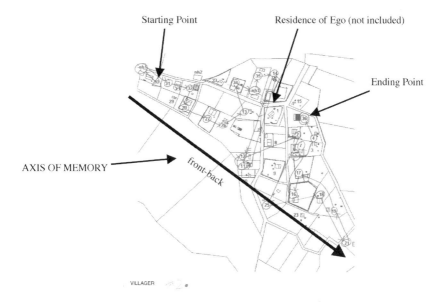

Figure 10.3 Example of a 'memory route'

places involved. In the end, while some 'cultural' strategies were also employed, e.g., kinship, age group,[5] and religion,[6] the strategy that was employed by all individuals was a spatial one. Using this strategy means to start listing people from a specific area of the village and then move to other areas in a sequential and typically directional (e.g., from front to back) fashion (Figure 10.3).

By comparing the part of the village from where individuals started their list with the actual residence distribution of all the individuals interviewed, a salient bias toward the 'front' of the village became noticeable (Figure 10.4). In fact, while only 34.74% of the villagers reside in the front, 56.18% of them started their lists from the front. At the same time, while the same percentage of people live in the middle (34.74%), only 23.60% started from the middle. And, finally, while 25.26% live in the back, only 20.22% started from the back. It is apparent that a significant part of the village population not living in the front still chose to start their lists with individuals residing in the front of the village.

[5] There are minimally three age groups in a Tongan village: unmarried, married, elders.
[6] There are three major religious groups in the village: Wesleyan (majority) and Mormon (minority), plus an individual who belongs to the Tokaikolo Christian Church (a branch of the Wesleyan Church).

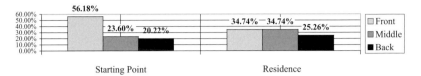

Figure 10.4 Comparing starting point of memory route and residence

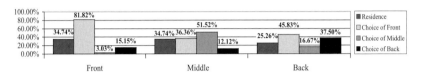

Figure 10.5 Detailed comparison of starting point and residence

The fact that it is people not residing in the front who privilege that part of town in their memory list becomes clearer when we examine the results about choice of starting point for each group of individuals residing in the three parts of the village (Figure 10.5). The content of Figure 10.5 shows how 81.82% of people residing in the front chose the front as their starting point. This contrasts with the 51.52% of people residing in the middle who started from the middle and even more significantly with the 37.50% of people residing in the back who started from the back, clearly privileging (45.83%) the front over the choice of back.

These results need to be added to those of the analyses I conducted on the data about the inclusion or not of the self in the lists and about the nature of the individuals with whom people chose to start their lists. Both analyses intended to find out how salient was the inclusion of the self in the lists and how it compared to the choice of other-than-ego.

Only 18.18% (16/88 individuals) included self in their lists; thus, the remaining 81.82% (72/88 individuals) did not do so. And, more significantly, only 6.82% (6/88 individuals) started their lists with themselves (Figure 10.6). A good percentage of interviewees started their lists with members of their household (46.49%, 41/88 individuals), but more importantly, 55.68% (49/88 individuals) started their lists with a member of a household different from their own.

In conclusion, these are the fundamental findings obtained by the analyses conducted on the memory lists:

1. a variety of cultural strategies were employed, e.g., kinship, religion, age group;

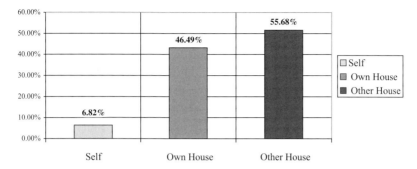

Figure 10.6 Self/Other starting points

2. the most common strategy was the 'spatial' strategy, wherein interviewees chose a specific part of the village (either front, middle, or back) to start their list and continued by moving in a specific direction to other parts;
3. within the 'spatial' strategy, the front of the village was privileged as the starting point of the list;
4. very few individuals included self in their lists;
5. of those individuals who included self, very few started their lists with self;
6. the great majority of the interviewees started their lists with other-than-ego members within their own household and/or other-than-ego members of another household.

How do these results relate to the hypothesis of radiality as a Tongan foundational cultural model? An essential feature of that hypothesis is the choosing of a point in the field of ego and the representing/expressing of relationships as away-from/toward that point. This mental process, if present in the representation of social relationships, would result in a backgrounding of ego/self and a foregrounding of other-than-ego individuals. Results 4, 5, and 6 just introduced appear to strongly support the hypothesis. In addition, the privileging of the front of the village reflects perfectly the preference for the translation subtype of the relative frame of reference and for the radial subtype of the absolute frame of reference already indicated in Chapter 3 and Chapter 6, Section 6.2.1. I used both these preferences to formulate the radiality hypothesis. Thus, at the end of this discussion of the results of the memory task, I consider my hypothesis substantially corroborated.

10.3   The pile sort task

Pile sort tasks are regarded as extremely informative about categorization processes (Weller and Romney, 1988; Ross, 2004). Specifically, they reveal which categories are employed to perform the task and which of these categories are more salient. Thus, they make it possible to obtain insights into the internal organization – such as the presence of specific categories and of a particular relationship among them – of the mental domain under investigation.

As pointed out in the previous section, co-villagers represent an extensive part of the social world typically inhabited by Tongans. The content of the pile sort task was then the 95 adult co-villagers already targeted by the memory task. Differently than what I did with the memory task, I administered the pile sort task to a sample of the adult population. The twenty-four individuals (fourteen female and ten male) who participated were randomly selected from six clusters (four individuals from each cluster) obtained by the social network data (see Chapter 11). The intention was to administer the task to the same number of people for each elicited cluster of individuals sharing similar social network characteristics. Since the task is intended to provide insights into the mental representation of social relationships, this sampling technique attains a crucial significance.

I personally took close-up photos of all the adult villagers and had the printed version of these photos laminated to make up a smooth and durable deck of photo cards. This visual stimulus allowed the task to be performed with minimal interference from language. Participants, in fact, could perform the task without naming other individuals or having to either read or write any text. This prevented problems that might have arisen from a lack of minimal literacy skill while keeping language interference to an absolute minimum. Of course, I used language to give the instructions on how to perform the task. At the end of the task, after the first and possibly second sorting, I also asked the participants to explain their sorting criteria. These explanations were intended to help in disambiguating what might have been sorting criteria difficult to elucidate relying only on my interpretation.

10.3.1   Results of the pile sort task

From the analyses of the sorting results, I was able to identify eleven strategies that the participants used during the performance of the task: (1) cultural group; (2) *kāinga* 'extended family;' (3) *fāmili* 'family;' (4) gender; (5) religion; (6) political group; (7) *kaunga'api* 'neighborhood;' (8) religious stage; (9) same ranking stage; (10) *kaungame'a* 'friends;' and (11) house. All of these strategies need some clarification.

In Tongan villages, the adult population is divided into cultural groups such as *fine mui* 'unmarried female,' *talavou* 'unmarried male,' *to'utupu* 'not married,' *tangata 'eiki* 'married males,' *fefine 'eiki* 'married females,' *tangata matua* 'old males,' and *fefine matua* 'old females.' It is these groups that were used to sort the photo cards with the strategy labeled 'cultural group.' The strategy *kāinga* 'extended family' refers to a group of people living in different households, mostly in the same village. They are related to one another by a bilateral relationship of consanguinity (cognatic system or kindred). The strategy *fāmili* 'family' corresponds to a nuclear family. 'Gender' is here intended to mean only male and female. The strategy 'religion' refers to the presence in the village of three religious group, Wesleyan, Mormon, and Tokaikolo Christian Church (a branch of the Wesleyan Church).[7] 'Political group' refers to a number of committees in the village who look after issues such as water supply, electricity, and scholarship fund to help needy children in the village to pay their school fees.

After analyzing a variety of interviews explicitly conducted about the concept of *kaunga'api* 'neighborhood,' I reached the conclusion that a Tongan *kaunga'api* 'neighborhood' includes on average 4.6 houses. All these houses are very close and must be visible (see Bennardo and Schultz, 2004). It is this version of the concept that was used when the strategy is labeled '*kaunga'api.*' The strategy named 'religious stage' refers to the various stages an individual goes through as a member of the Wesleyan Church. Similar to the last one, the 'same ranking stage' strategy refers to a sorting in which individuals at the same stage within the Wesleyan Church were grouped together. The strategy 'friends' is self-evident and the one labeled 'house' was used to group together individuals living in the same house. These individuals typically include a *fāmili* 'family' and also a few collaterals, and/or affinals, and/or consanguineals.

The types of strategy employed already give some indications about the preferred criteria used to sort the co-villagers that appear in the deck of cards. Seven strategies (63.64%) refer to membership in a group (cultural group, *kāinga*, *fāmili*, political group, neighborhood, friends, and house), while only four strategies (36.36%) refer to qualities of an individual (gender, religion, religious stage, and same ranking stage). Belonging to a group is more salient than individual characteristics.

I detected a total of seventy occurrences of use of the eleven strategies employed by the participants during the sorting task. The top three strategies used are 'cultural group' (18/25.71%), '*kāinga*' (15/21.43%), and '*fāmili*' (10/14.29%). Together they represent 61.43% of the strategies employed. They are all strategies about groups and the first one about a characteristic of an individual is 'gender' (8/11.43%), immediately followed by 'religion' (6/8.57%). Moreover, other group strategies follow like 'political group' (4/5.71%), 'neighborhood' (4/5.71%), thus bringing the total to 72.85% (Figure 10.7). It appears as if membership in a group such as a cultural one, a

---

[7] Only one individual in the village belongs to this latter.

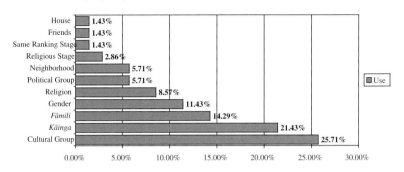

Figure 10.7 Frequency of sorting strategies

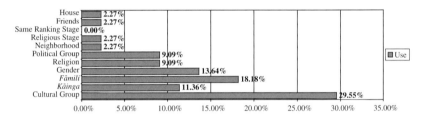

Figure 10.8 Frequency of strategies in first sort

kāinga, a *fāmili*, a political one, and neighborhood is the predominant criterion in sorting the individuals in the deck of cards.

Looking at the frequency of occurrence of the strategies employed in the first sorting only, the results do substantially confirm the ones discussed above (Figure 10.8). The 'cultural group' strategy is the top one used (13/29.55%), followed by '*fāmili*' (8/18.18%) and by 'gender' (6/13.64%). The strategy '*kāinga*' is now in fourth place (5/11.36%). The 'cultural group,' the '*kāinga*,' and the '*fāmili*' strategies still represent 59.09% of the total. And to this figure one needs to add the increased incidence of use of 'political group' (4/9.09%) and 'neighborhood' (4/9.09%), thus reaching a total of 77.27%.

How do these results relate to the current working hypothesis of radiality? The relationship is not straightforward but it can be safely arrived at in only a few steps. The results introduced clearly indicate that when engaged in sorting co-villagers a number of strategies were preferentially used. These strategies highlight the fact that it is not characteristics of an individual, e.g., gender, religion, friendship, but characteristics of groups to which individuals belong that are predominantly and more saliently considered while sorting, e.g., cultural group, *kāinga*, *fāmili*, and political group. The preference then is to think about groups and their characteristics over thinking about individuals and their characteristics.

To accomplish this, one needs to focus on other-than-ego over ego. In other words, ego's features as possibly matching other individuals' features are not the major conceptual focus. It is features of groups that represent the principal concern, and a group by definition supersedes the individual, either ego or other-than-ego. A group, though, in itself is an other-than-ego for a thinking individual. Thus, the conceptual focus highlighted by the sorting activity is other-than-ego, that is, a fundamental aspect of the hypothesized radiality foundational cultural model.

10.4   The drawing task

In Chapter 5, Section 5.5 (see also Bennardo, 2002a), I presented an analysis of two drawing tasks I administered to a number of Tongan individuals. The results of that task provided crucial insights into their mental representation of spatial relationships. The common structural organization of those representations I termed 'radial.' A center, other-than-ego, is chosen and then other elements/parts of the representation are radially, either centrifugally or centripetally, related to it.

Encouraged and inspired by those results, I used a similar task in order to obtain insights into the mental representation of social relationships. The drawing task was administered to the same sample of the adult population I had chosen for the pile sort task. Thus, twenty-four individuals (fourteen female and ten male) were randomly selected from six clusters (four individuals from each cluster) obtained by the social network data (see Chapter 11). Again and similarly to the pile sort task, since also this task is intended to obtain insights into the mental representation of social relationships, I regard the sampling technique used appropriate to the domain under investigation.

I asked the participants to think carefully about the people they interact most with during their daily lives. Then, I instructed them to 'draw' this group of people on a provided sheet of paper by using circles for women and squares for men – participants were invited to write the names of those individuals inside or next to those circles and squares. I also told them that they could distribute those drawings/people over the sheet as they liked. Finally, I checked if they were ready to start and then let them start their drawings. When they finished, I asked them to explain the content of the drawings by mentioning if there were any grouping strategies they had used. The activity was videotaped so that later I would have access to the sequence in which the drawing was constructed, their comments while drawing, and the final discussion at the end.

The major hypothesis was that the drawings would reflect the structural organization of their mental representation of social relationships by being organized in a radial way. Mainly, the drawings would

- be started from the center of the sheet of paper;
- not contain ego;
- show clusters of people made on the basis of characteristics of a group (e.g., *fāmili*, *kāinga*) and not of individuals (e.g., gender).

This drawing behavior would partially resemble that already elicited in the drawing tasks about the village and the island (see Chapter 5, Section 5.5), that is, choosing a specific 'center' (either a place in the village or on the island) to start the drawing or start the drawing from the center of the sheet of paper. At the same time, it would also replicate the findings from the pile sort task just introduced in Section 10.3, that is, grouping people according to characteristics of a group and not of individuals.

10.4.1   Results of the drawing task

The first analysis I conducted on the drawings was to see where the activity had initiated, that is, where the participants started to draw on the sheet of paper. This analysis was made possible by the availability of the sessions in videotapes, later digitized and made into DVDs. As shown in Table 10.1, only 7 individuals, that is, 29.16% or almost 1 every 3, started their drawing from a 'central' place of the paper. The remaining participants drew by starting on the top-left (13/54.16%) or bottom-left (4/16.66%) corner of the paper.

For the second analysis, I looked at the shape of the drawings. Three formats were identified, radial, column, and left-to-right writing style (Figure 10.9). In the radial format, the drawer started from the center of the sheet of paper and proceeded to add other individuals radially from that center. In the column format, the drawer started typically from the top-left and proceeded down as making a list. In the left-to-right writing style, the drawer started from the top-left (and sometimes from the bottom-left) and proceeded to the right as if in writing.

I discovered a fourth and final format once I was able to add to the drawings the sequence in which people had been inserted. This final format I called 'radial from corner.' When using this format, an individual would draw the first person in a corner of the paper and then proceed by adding other people randomly toward the right, or left, or center of the paper (see Figure 10.10 for an example with starting point from the bottom-left of the paper).

When I finished counting the frequency of use of the two formats including radiality, 'radial' and 'radial from corner,' I found out that they were used by 54.16% of the participants (Table 10.2). This finding is relevant since literacy

Table 10.1 *Starting point of the drawing on the sheet of paper*

Subject	Center	Center-right	Center-top	Top-left	Bottom-left
1	X				
2	X				
3				X	
4					X
5				X	
6				X	
7				X	
8			X		
9			X		
10				X	
11				X	
12				X	
13				X	
14				X	
15		X			
16					X
17				X	
18				X	
19					X
20	X				
21	X				
22					X
23				X	
24				X	
Total	4	1	2	13	4
%	16.66%	4.16%	8.33%	54.16%	16.66%

is almost universal in Tonga. Nonetheless, only 16.66% of the participants used a writing style drawing format and only 29.16% used a column style drawing format. Both of these latter two styles are commonly associated with literacy.

Once I had distributed the drawers who used radial formats within three age groups (6/18–30, 9/31–50, and 9/51 – above), it turned out that only 3/23.07% belonged to the younger groups, and the remaining drawers belonged in equal numbers (5/38.46% and 5/38.46%) to the other two groups. However, the frequency (of radial format) in each category was slightly higher for the older two groups (55.55%) as compared to the young group (50.00%). It appears as if older individuals prefer a 'radial' strategy more often than younger ones. This makes a lot of sense when we consider that the population of Tongan villages is mostly engaged in subsistence, thus, having very little occasion to exercise their literacy skills, and occasionally returning to illiteracy with old age.

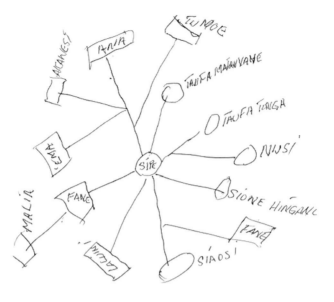

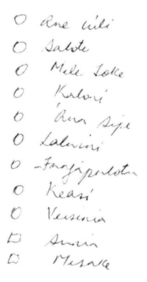

Figure 10.9 Examples of shapes of drawings

Figure 10.9 (*Cont.*)

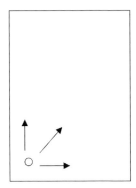

Figure 10.10   Radial from corner

The third analysis I conducted regarded the first person that was inserted in the drawing. A variety of situations occurred, and they are summarized in Table 10.3.

The first important finding regards the number of people that inserted ego in the drawing. Only three individuals (12.50%) did insert ego and they also began the drawing with it. All of the other drawings did not have ego in them. Another three individuals (12.50%) started their drawings with a *kaungame'a* 'friend.' These two choices indicate a focus on the individual, that is, ego and a person freely 'chosen' to associate with regardless of kinship, religion, or other sociocultural grouping. The great majority of the drawings (18/75.00%) were started with people belonging to specific sociocultural groups, like *fāmili* 'family,' *kāinga* 'extended family,' *lalanga* 'mat weaving group,' church, and *komiti* 'village committee.'[8]

---

[8] These village committees take care of village needs like water, electricity, scholarship funds for children's school fees, and others.

Table 10.2 *Format of drawing*

Subject	Radial	Radial from corner	Column	LR-writing
1	X			
2	X			
3				Xdown
4		X		
5	X			
6		X		
7		X		
8		X		
9			X	
10			X	
11				Xdown
12			X	
13		X		
14		X		
15	X			
16		X		
17			X	
18			X	
19				Xup
20	X			
21	X			
22				Xup
23			X	
24			X	
Total	6	7	7	4
%	25.00%	29.16%	29.16%	16.66%

The final analysis I conducted regards the clustering of people in the draw-ing. In order to arrive at the set of strategies in Table 10.4, I used the sequence of individuals inserted in the drawing, the final description of the drawing by the drawers, and my detailed knowledge of each of the participants' status, age, kinship relations, and residential place in the village (besides the knowledge of the place of the interview I had recorded). The Tongan Digitized database (see Chapter 5, Section 5.2.2) was extensively used during all these analyses and its availability turned out to be crucial in many instances to reach empirical conclusions about the data under analysis.

I detected nine clustering strategies (for a total of 75 uses) employed by the participants in producing their drawings: *fāmili* 'family,' *kāinga* 'extended family,' *kaunga'api* 'neighborhood,' gender, *lalanga* 'mat weaving group,' age group, church, *komiti* 'village committee,' and friends. Individuals used

Table 10.3 *First person in the drawing*

Subject	Self	*Kaungame'a*	*Fāmili*	*Kāinga*	*Lalanga*	Church	*Komiti*
1			X				
2	X						
3		X					
4		X					
5					X		
6			X				
7			X				
8						X	
9	X						
10					X		
11			X				
12				X			
13				X			
14			X				
15						X	
16		X					
17			X				
18							X
19					X		
20						X	
21	X						
22			X				
23			X				
24				X			
Total	3	3	8	3	3	3	1
%	12.50%	12.50%	33.33%	12.50%	12.50%	12.50%	4.16%

a variety of combinations of some of these strategies in their drawings, and each person often used some of the strategies more than once. The strategies associated with the characteristics of an individual, such as gender, friends, and church,[9] represent only 14 of all the strategies used, that is, 18.66%. Besides, the most used strategy of the three mentioned, gender, was only used by 8 people, that is, 33.33%. In contrast, the strategies associated with sociocultural groups, such as *fāmili*, *kāinga*, *kaunga'api*, *lalanga*, age group, and *komiti*, represent 61 of all the strategies used, that is, 81.33%. Similarly, the most used strategy of these just mentioned, *fāmili*, was used by 19 people, that is, 79.16%.

[9] I decided here to group the strategy 'church' as an individual characteristic to follow a similar choice I made before in Section 10.3.1 about 'religion.' I am convinced though that the strategy 'church' here was used as a social group and not as an individual characteristic. However, the significance of the results does not change very much either way.

Table 10.4 *Clustering strategy/ies in the drawing*

Subject	Fāmili	Kāinga	Kaunga'api	Gender	Lalanga	Age group	Church	Komiti	Friends
1	X	X	X	X		X			
2	X							X	
3						X			
4	X	X							
5	X	X	X	X	X		X		
6	X	X	X		X				
7	X		X						
8	X	X	X	X			X		
9		X	X						
10	X				X				
11	X	X	X				X		
12	X	X	X	X		X			
13	X	X	X	X					
14	X	X	X		X				
15	X	X	X	X			X		
16	X		X			X			
17	X		X		X				
18								X	
19	X								
20			X		X	X	X		
21	X	X	X	X					X
22	X	X		X		X			
23	X				X				
24		X	X						
Total (75)	19	14	14	8	7	5	5	2	1
% out of 24	79.16%	58.33%	58.33%	33.33%	29.16%	20.83%	20.83%	8.33%	4.16%
% out of 75	25.33%	18.66%	18.66%	10.66%	9.33%	6.66%	6.66%	2.66%	1.33%

How do the results of the above analyses on the drawing task data relate to the local task hypotheses? The first hypothesis – drawers would start their drawings from the middle of the sheet of paper – was not supported by the results. In fact, only 29.16% of the participants adopted this strategy. On the other hand, the shape of the drawing adopted by the majority of the participants showed a clear preference for some form of radiality, and this was more so with older individuals.

The second hypothesis – the drawings would not contain ego – was definitely supported. Only three individuals chose to insert ego in the drawing. Thus, the remaining 21 (87.50%), a substantial number of people, did not do so. This focus on other-than-ego was also substantiated by 75.50% of people starting their drawing with somebody belonging to a sociocultural group. This preference was also repeated in their choices of strategies for clustering the people drawn. Here the strategies using sociocultural groups represent 81.33% of the total strategies used. Therefore, the third hypothesis – the drawings would show clusters of people made on the basis of characteristics of a group (e.g., *fāmili*, *kāinga*) and not of individuals (e.g., gender) – was also fully supported by the results.

Confronted with the request to 'draw' the people they interacted most with, the participants made a variety of decisions that activated mental representations of social relationships. Some of the characteristics of these mental representations found their way into the characteristics of the drawings produced. In spite of being explicitly asked to think about the people they most interacted with, the participants did not regard it as necessary to insert ego in their drawings. Thus, ego must be backgrounded in their representations of social relationships as compared to other-than-ego. Besides, the groupings of the people they thought of as the ones they most interacted with were obtained by thinking of characteristics of groups and not of individuals. Then, the salience of the group, as compared to the individual, in their mental representations of social relationships is shown to be very robust. In other words, two fundamental organizing principles emerge for those representations of social relationships: (a) the backgrounding of ego and the foregrounding of other-than-ego, and (b) the consequent relevance of the group over the individual.

10.5   Conclusion

In this chapter, I presented the rationale, hypotheses, and results of three cognitive tasks about social relationships. The intention was to explore mental representations of social relationships for the presence of 'radiality,' the hypothesized Tongan foundational cultural model, without the mediating role of language. The results of the first task, memory list or free listing, pointed toward a preference for the backgrounding of ego and the foregrounding of other-than-ego. The results of the second task, pile sort, also pointed to a similar preference connected to a focus on the group over the individual. The findings of the analyses conducted on the third task, drawing task, pointed again in the same directions, backgrounding of ego and focus on group.

All the above findings are congruent with the general hypothesis of radiality as a foundational cultural model. Essential to radiality, as defined in Chapter 6, is the backgrounding of ego and the foregrounding of other-than-ego. The focus on a group entails that this generative process was already activated and instantiated by choosing an other-than-ego. Thus, in their own particular way, the mental representations of social relationships are fundamentally structured in a way similar to the mental representations of spatial relationships. That is, non ego-centered foci are used to organize the constituting elements, places and things for space, and individuals and groups for social relationships.

Social relationships as the main domain in the social cognition module (see Chapter 1, Section 1.3), then, seem to be structured similarly to the content of the spatial relationships module, to some of the content of the action module (exchange patterns), and to other domains in the conceptual structures module: religion, navigation, kinship, and possession. I suggest that the inter- and intra-modular regularity observed represents a relevant Tongan cognitive phenomenon. I labeled this phenomenon "radiality" and I conceive it as a generative process underlying the organization of Tongan knowledge in general. I call it a foundational "cultural" model because it is replicated across individuals, thus shared by a culturally similar population, and because it is at the root of various domains of knowledge (foundational). So, it represents an internal model for knowledge construction, storing, and retrieving and at the same time an external model shared and taken for granted by a culturally homogeneous group.

11   Radiality in social networks[1]

11.1   Introduction: why social networks?

When one investigates the mental representation of spatial relationships, a very common methodology includes the use of maps. Subjects are asked to draw maps, to transfer information from or to maps, to talk about maps, and so on (see Gould and White, 1974; Downs and Stea, 1977; Tversky, 1981, 1993, 1996; Golledge, 1999; Bennardo, 2002a). The discrepancies and/or distortions of the geographical world produced in the maps drawn, or the places reached, or in the speech elicited are used to hypothesize specific mental representations of spatial relationships in those individuals. Subjects' performance is matched with geographical reality to obtain information-rich data about mental representations of space.

A map, however, is only one of the many ways in which we represent reality, a reduction of the almost infinite details that characterize the world around us. Nonetheless, working with maps gives us a good insight into the way spatial relationships are represented in the mind and the way in which one works with these mental representations to navigate in the world. In short, we use maps to understand how we represent the world and how we further process these representations in reasoning about and acting in the world.

When it comes to social relationships, researchers are typically amazed at their intricacies and complexity. However, as complicated as they are, they cannot surpass in number and structure the complexity of the spatial world surrounding us. What is missing in the research about social relationships is an intermediate representational stage as that held by maps in the investigation of spatial representations. I believe that this intermediate level of representations can be provided by social network data.

Social network analysis can obtain a similar accuracy about social relationships/reality as that found in maps about geographical relationships/reality (Wasserman and Faust, 1994). Both maps and social networks are simply a representation of the reality to which they refer. As such, they are not an

---

[1] With the collaboration of Charles Cappell.

exhaustive, complete repetition of that reality. They leave something out in their representing effort. Nonetheless, they are types of representation that are the closest to the reality of the geographical world and of the social relationships world, respectively.

Once one obtains a social network map of the social relationships world/ space, results from linguistic and experimental data about the same world/ space can be compared or, more precisely, correlated with it. This procedure allows one to discover those similarities, discrepancies, and/or distortions that are telling about specific ways of mentally representing significant aspects of the social world. Besides, social network analysis can be revealing regarding a preference for ego-centered or other-than-ego-centered networks, a fundamental issue for the present investigation.

What then are social network data? Social network data consist of information collected by means of questionnaires (for an example see Burkett, 1998), interviews (for an example see Wellman and Wortley, 1990), and/or structured observations (for an example see Bernard, Killworth, and Sailer, 1980, 1982; Freeman and Romney, 1987) about individuals' perceived and actual frequency of interactions with other individuals. The analyses of the social network data (e.g., estimating centrality, outcloseness, and betweenness measures) highlight the nature (e.g., radial), structure, and composition of these imagined and actual social interactions in public and private arenas (Freeman, White, and Romney, 1989; Scott, 1992; Wasserman and Faust, 1994; McCarty, 2002). Radial organizations (star graphs) or vectorial subtypes (line graphs) – always centered on an individual different from the one providing the information – can be detected. The finding of circle graphs, graphs with low and uniform measures of centrality for all members, would undermine my radiality hypothesis. However, any network structure found contributes to the overall project of testing the social environment represented by the networks against linguistic and cognitive data about these same networks (Krackhardt, 1987).

11.2   The social structure of a Tongan village

The linguistic and cognitive data about local social relationships were all collected in the village of Houma, Vava'u, one the major three field sites for the research presented in this book (see Chapter 2, Section 2.4). Consequently, I decided it was appropriate and necessary to collect the data for the social network analysis in the same village. I have already described this village in Chapter 2, Section 2.4. However, I briefly reintroduce here its major characteristics.

The village is small, even in Tongan terms, with only 172 residents, comprising 95 adults (i.e., 18 years and up). This small number made possible complete social network surveys of the adult population. The village is located in the northern Tongan archipelago of Vava'u on a government estate. While the village lacks a residing noble, the residing chief is directly descended from a well-established line of chiefs – one of his ancestors sat in the council of chiefs that approved the first set of Tongan laws (the Vava'u Code) in 1839, several years before the 1875 Constitution (Lātūkefu, 1974). However, he cannot claim full inheritance to nobility because one individual in his line of descent was conceived out of wedlock.

Besides the chief, a *mātāpule*, a ceremonial leader, is also in residence, but his saliency to the life of the village seems even less recognized and very few elderly people ever mention his existing title. Much more visible is the local Wesleyan minister.[2] Ministers, however, are rotated every four years, and while they may appear very prominent during their appointment, neither they nor their role become part of the long-lasting social fabric of the village.

Another prominent figure is the *ofisa kolo* (town officer). This town officer is elected every three years. Thus, the formal social structure suggests three formal positions with some formally recognized authority: a chief with quasi-noble links, a ceremonial officer, and an elected town officer. Other occupational roles may account for variable degrees of influence as well. In a village whose main income comes from subsistence, it is crucial to point out the presence of wage laborers earning cash and to note that the cash economy has become more significant in the last few decades. I classified villagers into six occupational categories:

- 'subsistence workers and homemakers' (58);
- 'public employees' (2): the town official and a police officer;
- 'professionals' (11): 3 high school teachers (commute daily to Neiafu, the main town on the island), 3 nurses (commute daily to Neiafu), an elementary school teacher, a school principal, 2 bank employees, and a retired minister;
- 'wage workers' (13): 2 shop assistants (commute daily to Neiafu), 2 furniture factory workers (in the capital town of Nuku'alofa), 1 security guard (commutes daily to Neiafu), 1 taxi driver (commutes daily to Neiafu), 1 at a car dealer (commutes daily to Neiafu), 1 as a cleaner at the market (commutes daily to Neiafu), 1 at the telephone office (commutes daily to Mangia, a very close neighboring village), 1 at the Ha'apai airport (in the Ha'apai archipelago, the middle archipelago of the three making up the kingdom), 1 at a gas station (commutes daily to Neiafu), 1 food distributor for *falekoloa*s throughout the island of Vava'u,[3] 1 unspecified;
- 'entrepreneur-shop owners' (4): 2 grocery store co-owners, a food stand owner at the market in Neiafu, a mechanic (commutes daily to Neiafu);
- 'not working' (5).

---

[2] There are also a few individuals of Mormon faith in the village. However, they do not have a residing minister, probably because their number is small.
[3] This information is updated to July 2005.

The development of cash commodity markets introduces the possibility of additional resources that organize the structure of social networks in the village. I hypothesize that the distribution of symbolic skills associated with market-based jobs and income will correlate with the distribution of influence.

Kinship ties are of paramount importance to the life of a Tongan village. The two major kin groups are *fāmili* 'family' or household and *kāinga* 'extended family.' A *fāmili* consists of a married couple and their children living in the same house and usually includes male and/or female collaterals and affinals. The *'ulumotu'a* 'head of the family' presides over this group. A *kāinga* consists of relatives living in different households in the same village or in several villages. They are related by bilateral relationships of consanguinity in a cognatic system. A specific *'ulumotu'a* 'head of the *kāinga*' presides over this group besides his own family. Thus, we hypothesize that *kāinga* is a factor in organizing social networks in the village, an attribute representing traditional village structure, to the extent that the differing *kāingas* vary in cultural status or access to resources. The head of each *kāinga* also, hypothetically, possesses a traditional basis of authority. Thus, Tongan social structure contains a priori 'authority ranking' relations available for social influence (Fiske, 1991).

Two prominent parameters in establishing hierarchy in all societies are gender and age. In Tongan culture, a female (sister) is always considered higher in rank than a male even though inheritance of land and titles goes through the male line and primogeniture usually is enforced. Because of traditional brother–sister avoidance, from around the age of ten, boys sleep in a separate house. Though avoidance is less strictly enforced now, it still affects daily life. Brothers and sisters do not discuss sex nor share certain activities, such as watching videos. Gender and age should, therefore, be additional characteristics that determine the structure of social influence.

Four further groups are recognized in the village: *to'u tupu* 'unmarried individuals,' *kau matu'a* 'male elders'/*fine matu'a* 'female elders,' and the *lalanga* 'weaving group.' The first one is usually composed of young individuals, but it may contain members of any age, if they never married. Interestingly, the elders group is explicitly labeled as male or female, reflecting the gender divide already highlighted. The weaving group is composed only of women of various ages with different individual skills, even though typically a minimum level of competency is expected.

In conclusion, the village has a traditional, kin-based and monarchical social structure, i.e., an 'authority ranking' type (Fiske, 1991). Recently, 'communal sharing' norms of equality (Fiske, 1991), also present in the traditional fabric of the village social life, have been embedded in the rhetoric of an emerging democratic political movement emphasizing equality. Alongside these two set of norms, i.e., monarchical/authority ranking and democratic/communal sharing, a small-scale, modern economic activity – a cash economy with a degree of occupational differentiation – is developing alongside the traditional sub-sistence farming and craft production.

11.3   Methodology

The social network data were collected using the following strategies: two questionnaires, three types of interviews (see Chapter 9, Section 9.2.1),[4] and what I termed indirect observations. Since I could not observe the total inter-actions occurring among all villagers at any one time, I conducted repeated interviews (once a week for three weeks) with villagers about people they had interacted with during the previous day (indirect observations). The interview-ees were also asked about the reason and length of the interactions.

11.3.1   Two questionnaires

The two questionnaires I administered contained questions about influence and about social support in the village. In the first questionnaire, I asked all avail-able adult villagers about people they could influence and about people that could influence them. In total, there were four questions about three different scenarios. The scenarios I devised were about a real situation (see question 1a) and two hypothetical ones (see questions 1b, 2a, and 2b). The two imagined scenarios were very ecologically motivated and I arrived at their composition after a lengthy selection process in cooperation with several villagers (not cur-rent residents). The four questions posed were as follows:

Questionnaire about social networks: influence (SNI)
To influence and being influenced: four questions to all villagers (95)

(1a) I have donated $1,000 to spend for Houma.
       If you propose to buy oil for the water pump:
       Who could you persuade to vote for/support you?
       SHOW LIST + OTHER

(1b) The town officer assigned you to prepare two *pola* 'trays of food' for the next visit by the king. You said yes at first, but now realize that you cannot afford to prepare two, but only one.
       Who do you think you can persuade to support your change?
       SHOW LIST + OTHER

(2a) You are having a dispute with a kin member about a border of a lot (or about some crop use, or about the assignment of *fahu*[5] for a funeral).

---

[4] These are the same interviews that were used to collect the linguistic data.
[5] The deceased's *fahu* is typically one's father's sister.

Who can come in and make you change your mind/convince/persuade you to compromise?
SHOW LIST + OTHER

(2b) You are having a dispute with a non-kin member about a border of a lot (or about some crop use, or about the assignment of *fahu* for a funeral). Who can come in and make you change your mind/convince/persuade you to compromise?
SHOW LIST + OTHER

In the second questionnaire, I asked all available adult villagers about people they would support/help if needed and about people who would support/help them if needed. In total, there were four questions about two different scenarios. In this case, the scenarios devised were both about hypothetical situations. The four questions posed were as follows:

Questionnaire about social networks: social support (SNS)
To give or receive support: four questions to all villagers (95)

(1a) If you must give a *fakaafe* 'meal invitation', who could you count on for help?
SHOW LIST + OTHER

(1b) If X (name from list) gives a *fakaafe* 'meal invitation', could s/he count on your help?
SHOW LIST+ OTHER

(2a) A typhoon has damaged your house/property: Who will you ask for help to repair/fix/get place back in shape?
SHOW LIST+ OTHER

(2b) A typhoon has damaged X's (name from list) house/property: Can s/he count on you for help to repair/fix/get place back in shape?
SHOW LIST+ OTHER

The two questionnaires were translated into Tongan and administered to the whole adult population of the village, that is, 95 individuals. After each question, the list of the 95 villagers was read to the interviewees in order to help them remember the current adults in the village. The list ends with 'other' to allow interviewees to add any individual not listed.

The administering of the questionnaire was done over a three week period with the help of five local assistants whom I personally trained by administering the questionnaires to them in an exemplary fashion. Each evening they reported back to me about their daily activities and any problems they encountered. Thus corrective actions were taken in some cases, such as a second administering of the questionnaire. Six people in the list were not residing in the village during the administering of the questionnaires and three individuals not on the list had taken up residence. I eliminated from the data absent villagers as well as new residents.

11.3.2   Types of analyses[6]

All the data obtained were organized into sociometric form. A wide range of procedures was used to uncover the structure of the social networks by using *Ucinet 6*, a social network analysis application (Borgatti, Everett, and Freeman, 2002). Other programs were also used like NETDRAW, PAJEK (Batagelj and Mrvar, 1996), and SAS. The first group of analyses included measures of density, symmetry, and transitivity of the networks. The density measure tells us what percentage of the potential relations were activated by the question. Symmetry tells us the proportion of relations that were reciprocated, thus a measure of symmetric relation. And the transitivity measure reveals the extent to which groups of three villagers have at least one set of closed relations, such that if villager A is related to villager B, and villager B is related to villager C, it is also the case that villager A is related to villager C. The transitivity measure indicates the extent to which intermediaries are not important and can be thought of as highlighting a more developed hierarchical structure.

The second group of analyses conducted included four measures of centrality. The rationale was that variations in the villagers' centrality measures would stand for a type of radiality (or star graph) for the social networks elicited, thus allowing one to examine and/or test the principal hypothesis. The four measurements were: outdegree, outcloseness, betweenness, and network constraint. Outdegree represents the number of villagers each ego mentioned as someone they would be able to relate to directly (indegree represents the opposite measure, that is, the number of villagers that nominate ego as someone they could relate to directly). Outcloseness takes into account the ability of ego to extend relations throughout the network and measures how close or proximate that extended sphere of relationships is (Wasserman and Faust, 1994: 183–8). A higher number indicates that more villagers can be reached in fewer steps. This is a measure of the extent of the relationship across the entire network, through intermediary links as well as direct links.

Betweenness is a measure of the network's dependence on the ability of a villager to link other villagers in the network (Wasserman and Faust, 1994: 188–92). Betweenness measures of centrality thus describes the degree to

[6] All the analyses presented in this chapter were conducted with the collaboration of Charles Cappell, Department of Sociology, Northern Illinois University. The sociomatrices were prepared with the help of Jeff Wagley, Nathan Walters, Tony Robertson, all Undergraduate Research Apprentice Program (URAP) students to myself at Northern Illinois University. A longer and more in-depth discussion of the results can be found in Bennardo and Cappell (2008) and Bennardo and Cappell (in preparation).

which the network is characterized by how much the connections between villagers are dependent upon a link to a third party. This can be thought of as a form of brokerage relationship. Constraint is a measure of the 'redundancy' in the network, a measure of how interconnected one's alters are with one another. In establishing relationships broadly within a social group, it appears that closed, constrained, network-based positions reflect closer relationships.

Various mechanisms are found to generate variance in centrality, a form of status in social networks. In practically all societies, control of valued resources, whether material or symbolic, differentiates members' network characteristics. Affiliation with kinship groups that have been afforded traditional status, as well as age and gender need to be considered. Modern society generates influence positions in networks based on market characteristics. For each centrality measure, several villager characteristics were used to predict the individual villager's relationship balance. Age and gender were examined, as well as the *kāinga* to which the villager belonged, to assess the influence of traditional status characteristics. Access to resources was measured by examining the following characteristics: income, owning an automobile, occupation, and control over land.

The distributions of these resources are highly skewed. For example, only 10 villagers own a plot of land, and only 2 own two plots. The vast majority of villagers (58/95) work as subsistence farmers or perform homework, 11/95 are classified as holding jobs that require some educational training, 4/95 are entrepreneurs operating small shops, and 2/95 are public employees. Sixty-eight percent (65/95) of the villagers report no earned income; a single villager reports T$600, the highest of any villager. Only 17/95 villagers own a car, with one villager owning two.

To examine the mechanisms that may be generating a villager's network position in terms of centrality measures, eight separate analyses were conducted. The four network-derived measures of influence for two of the influence questions (SNI1a and SNI1b) were analyzed: degree balance – the balance between the outdegree and indegree (a measure of direct asymmetric influence); the outcloseness measure (a measure of the global influence of a villager, the extensiveness of their influence); the normed betweenness measure (a measure of the bridging or linking influence a villager has); and the constraint measure (a measure of the social capital due to closure or redundancy in the villager's network). Regression analysis was used to model the variation in each of the eight network-based measures. Various models were specified, checking for stability and spurious effects.

Finally, the results from some linguistic data and some cognitive data were correlated with the results of some social network data. Two sets of linguistic data were used. The first consists of the lists of people mentioned in the first part (local level) of the 'perceived' social relationships interviews (see

Chapter 9, Section 9.2.1). The second set consists of the lists of people obtained in the 'indirect' social relationships interviews (see Chapter 9, Section 9.2.1). The reason these linguistic data were selected for correlation is the fact that both data, the linguistic and the social network, are directly related to the same social reality, the village of Houma. Besides, the narratives in the second sets were produced by a randomly selected sample of individuals from six clusters of villagers obtained by a preliminary analysis conducted on the social network questions about influence. In a similar fashion, the cognitive data chosen to be correlated with the social network data were the lists of villagers obtained by the memory task, free listing (see Chapter 10, Section 10.2).

11.4   Hypotheses about forms and types of social networks

Bennardo and Cappell (in press) start their work on the influence structure in a Tongan village in this way:

Tatau, tatau pé, katoa tatau 'the same, just the same, all the same,' this is what most Tongan villagers rushed to say when asked if any person within the village groups they had just mentioned was *mahu'inga taha* 'most important.' They produced very similar statements when asked if any of the groups they had identified within the village was more important than the others.

Given the very close-knit social life characterizing a Tongan small village, one can expect social networks to reflect communal sharing and equality matching relationships (Fiske, 1991). But one also needs to recognize that hierarchical structures and authority ranking are common to nearly all social groups as well (Chase, 1980; Fiske, 1991), even when individual differences in relevant resources and qualities are minimal (Gould, 2002; Webster and Hysom, 1998). Informal authority relations are likely to exist in the village under investigation, in combination with other forms, such as communal sharing, which may predominate superficially.

   A constitutional monarchy with a closed set of noble hereditary titles, and with a single villager representing the monarch, leads one to anticipate radial, asymmetric social networks, perhaps a star graph, in the extreme case (Wasserman and Faust, 1994: 171). But more generally, I predict that the measure of centrality in the social network structure is consistent with the hypothesized foundational cultural model of 'radiality.' I therefore hypothesize that social networks have appreciable variation in the degree of centrality realized by their members, and that the level of centrality derived for each villager is correlated to other radial social and cultural systems. The finding of circle graphs, graphs with low and uniform measures of centrality for all members, would undermine this hypothesis and support the villagers' claims as reported by Bennardo and Cappell (in press), "we are all the same."

A few individuals seem a priori to be well positioned to occupy central positions in the village's social network structure. First and foremost, the various *ulumotu'a* 'head' of any *kāinga* 'extended family' present in the village may be some of those individuals. Second, the town officer may occupy one of those positions. Elected individuals by definition are able to attract the favorable attention of a good number of villagers towards their person; thus, they may play central influential roles in the life of the village. Third, community elders are well positioned to occupy central roles in the village. I do not focus on the minister resident in the village because the time-limited appointment (four years) does not allow a minister to become an integral and lasting part of the social fabric of the village. Since power between genders is perceived overall as balanced by Tongans, although unevenly distributed in different contexts (e.g., rank and heredity), it is not expected to have an effect on the virtual positions of centrality. Kinship ties have traditionally played a relevant role in Tongan social life (Gifford, 1929; Lātūkefu, 1974; Helu, 1999). Kinship is expected to play an influential role in distributing the level of centrality across the influence network.

Finally, changes in the economic practices of Tongan villages have occurred in the past few decades (Gailey, 1987; Tupouniua, 1977; van der Grijp, 1993, 2004), including the formation of large communities overseas (Small, 1997; Evans, 2001; Morton, 2003; see also Modell, 2002). Principles of a cash economy have been introduced into a village life fundamentally based on subsistence, i.e., local wage jobs and economic activities like running small shops, and especially revenues from transnational relatives. These changes have had an impact on the villagers' social lives, in sum creating additional sources of human and social capital (Burt, 2000; Coleman, 1990). Therefore, it is possible that variation in the resources derived from the market economy may correspond to variations in the centrality measures.

11.5   *Kāinga* structures in the village

As explained in Chapter 2, Section 2.2, a fundamental social Tongan unit is the *kāinga* 'extended family.' A *kāinga* consists of relatives living in different households in the same village or in several villages. They are related by bilateral relationships of consanguinity in a cognatic system. A specific *'ulumotu'a* (head of the *kāinga*) presides over this group besides his own family. Knowledge of *kāinga* composition and boundaries is essential in the assignment of specific roles in funeral rituals (Kaeppler, 1971, 1978b) and in determining possible marriages (exogamy). This latter application, however, was in the past and it is nowadays dealt with lightheartedly by Tongans. Typically, a wife belongs to her husband's *kāinga*, but if the husband lives matrilocally (in wife's village), then he is considered part of the wife's *kāinga*. As importantly, *kāinga* knowledge

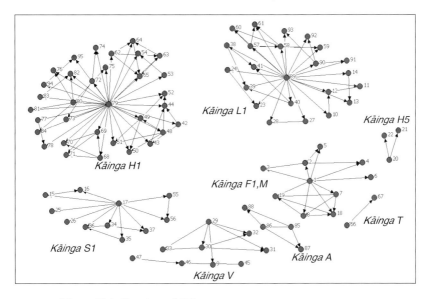

Figure 11.1 Structure of *kāingas*

is necessary to determine land inheritance, funeral proceedings, and the assignment of respect in special ceremonial events as well as in daily life.

I collected extensive data about *kāinga* compositions in the village and
then created a sociomatrix capturing the authority relations implied by the
practical kinship status-ranking in the village. The purely theoretical and
formal kinship structure identifies 21 distinct *kāingas*. The graphs in Figure
11.1 are instead based on my understanding of the actual day-to-day practices of authority relations based on *kāinga* structure. The relations graphed in
Figure 11.1 show only eight distinct subgraphs capturing the relation: villager
A has kinship rank-authority over villager B. The eight graphs in Figure 11.1
refer to the following *kāingas*:

H1: H1 represents the largest *kāinga* in the village. The village officer,
(villager 64) is a member of this *kāinga*.

L1: This subgraph labeled L1 consists of three branches and has encapsulated
members from two other *kāingas*. The village chief (89), easily visible
due to his centrality, and his wife (90) are in this *kāinga*.

H5: The members of this subgraph are not from the village under analysis.
They are the wife of a minister who decided to continue her residence
after her husband passed away while residing in the village, and two of
her children (adults).

F1, M: F1 is the group that hosted me during my fieldwork. Members of M are considered members of the F1 *kāinga* because their elder member was adopted into the F1 *kāinga*. F1 is also related to other *kāinga*s via female members. These relationships are not immediately acknowledged by the members of the other *kāinga*s. Many members of this group migrated to the capital town or abroad (e.g., New Zealand).

T: The subgraph labeled T is a small network whose *'ulumotu'a* (66) is the current holder of the title of *mātāpule* in the village: a rank below village chief but one with several privileges and ceremonial duties especially during noble or royal visits to the island.

A: The few members of this *kāinga* belong to an original founding group of the village. However, most members have migrated abroad, especially the US.

V: The previous town officer (29) belongs to this group. While separate from F1, strong ties exist between them.

S1:   Another *kāinga* descending from an original founding group. A police officer and a nurse are members of this group.

       This sociomatrix of *kāinga* authority-rank relations was used during the analyses of the social support data (see Section 11.6.2).

11.6   Results of the social network analyses

The network density for the social networks was very high, above and around 50%. Symmetry was found at around 40% (slightly higher, 47%, for social support networks). Then, given the high density, it is not surprising that most influence relations are transitively closed, over 75%. As a consequence of these properties, when graphs are produced for the networks, they reveal a dense cluster of points at the center and a peripheral ring (Figure 11.2).

The graphs were not helpful in displaying the structure of the various social networks, so from now on I rely mostly on subgraphs and the statistical results. These latter do provide clear indications toward the nature/structure of the networks.

11.6.1   Analysis of influence

In Bennardo and Cappell (2008), the authors reported on some analyses conducted on questions SNI1a and SNI1b about influence (see Section 11.3.1). The two questions are supposed to determine the structure of potential influence in the village. A measure of the asymmetrical degree of influence an actor has in a network is determined by obtaining the imbalance between outdegree and indegree. Computing the difference between outdegree and indegree gives a measure for each actor; the mean of this value for the entire village is zero by definition.

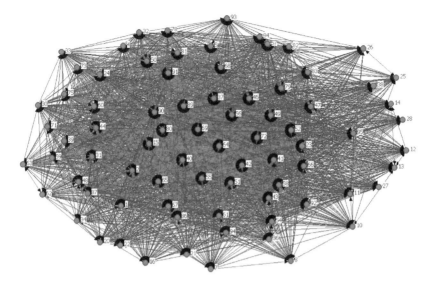

Figure 11.2 Example of graph obtained

Table 11.1 contains the top quarter of asymmetric influencers in the village, those who have a preponderance of outdegree compared to indegree nominations on both relations. The villagers' identification codes highlighted in bold print occur in both relations. These six villagers are the most asymmetrically influential in the village. They occupy positions where they are able to influence many more villagers than are able to influence them.

Based upon the imbalance between indegree and outdegree, these six villagers (47, 58, 67, 77, 80, 90), should be "referential nodes" in the cognitive imagery of villagers. They should be distinguished by their radiality in the cognitive descriptions of the important villagers, yet in the semi-structured ethnographic interview, no villagers were explicitly identified as exceptionally influential.

This group consists of one male (47) and five females (58, 67, 77, 80, 90). Three women (67, 80, 90) are wives of three *'ulumotu'a* (head of *kāinga* 'extended family'), one woman (58) is married to a prominent member of the *kāinga* of the local chief, and one woman (77) is the oldest female (still living in the village) in her *kāinga*. The only man (47) is married to a member of the oldest *kāinga* in the village, he resides matrilocally – thus, typically considered a member of his wife's *kāinga* and not his own – and is a major figure in the minority Mormon group. The majority of villagers belong to the local Wesleyan Church.

Table 11.1 *List of asymmetric influencers (from Bennardo and Cappell, 2008)*

RS code no	Degbal-SNI1a	RS code no	Degbal-SNI1b
46	45	**67**	52
90	44	**77**	51
56	39	**47**	45
41	38	93	45
42	38	48	44
37	37	95	43
40	37	24	42
58	37	32	41
23	36	**90**	40
51	36	83	40
55	36	44	40
64	36	50	34
80	36	11	33
15	35	63	33
69	35	9	33
72	35	34	32
49	34	70	30
77	34	**58**	29
47	33	**80**	28
43	32	33	27
52	32	35	26
65	30	8	25
66	25	88	24
67	25	92	22
86	24	94	22
87	24	49	21

The identities of these potential "referential nodes," while not activated in the open-ended questioning, reflect characteristics in synchrony with a number of cultural parameters contributing to the construction of the village social structure. In fact, since female siblings are always considered superior to male siblings, notwithstanding age differences (see Section 11.2, above), it is salient that five of the most asymmetrically influential are female. Similarly, while no *'ulumotu'a* appear in this group, three of the women are wives of *'ulumotu'a*. Thus it is likely that their asymmetric influence is the result of both their status as wives of *'ulumotu'a* and their gender.

A similar hypothesis can be examined by looking at the thirteen villagers that share the highest measures of "outcloseness" for the two relations: 15, 37, 41, 42, 49, 52, 55, 56, 58, 64, 65, 69, 72. Table 11.2 identifies the villagers with the highest ranking on outcloseness, a measure of global influence for the two

Table 11.2 *List of villagers with highest global influence measures (outcloseness) (from Bennardo and Cappell, in press)*

RS Code no	Outcloseness-SNI1a	RS Code no	Outcloseness-SNI1b
23	100.000	37	100.000
37	100.000	41	100.000
40	100.000	42	100.000
41	100.000	49	100.000
42	100.000	52	100.000
46	100.000	55	100.000
49	100.000	56	100.000
51	100.000	64	100.000
52	100.000	18	100.000
55	100.000	19	100.000
56	100.000	69	97.778
64	100.000	58	95.652
69	100.000	65	95.652
90	100.000	72	94.624
80	98.876	66	91.667
58	97.778	67	88.000
15	96.703	77	84.615
65	96.703	61	83.019
72	95.652	15	81.481
43	93.617	60	79.279

relations. Of these thirteen, six are female (49, 56, 58, 65, 69) and seven are male (15, 37, 41, 42, 52, 55, 64, 72), so gender appears to play no role in this measure of influence. These individuals belong to only four of the twenty-one *kāinga* present in the village: 15 and 37 to *kāinga* S1, 41 and 58 to *kāinga* L1, 55 and 56 to *kāinga* M, 42, 49, 52, 64, 65, 69, and 72 to *kāinga* H1. However, 56 is a female who belongs to *kāinga* S1 and since her husband resides matrilocally, they are both considered as belonging to *kāinga* S1 (see Figure 11.1). So, individuals from only three of the twenty-one *kāingas* appear to have the highest global influence. Noticeably, the *kāinga* of the local chief does not appear in this group, contrary to the hypothesis that traditional hierarchy is an important influence-generating mechanism.[7]

The town officer (64) appears in the list as expected. Interestingly, two couples (55, 56 and 64, 65) also appear in the list. It seems that their individual capacity of influencing others is enhanced by the corresponding capacity of their spouses. This is more so in the case of the town officer (64) and his

[7] Consider, though, that the local chief is not fully recognized in his line of descent and that chiefs' power was deeply undermined by the 1875 Constitution.

wife (65). And in the case of 55 and 56, they both have jobs that bring cash income, including the wife's nursing job in the local hospital (in the main town). Two other individuals are linked by a mother–daughter relationship (49 and 52). The mother is a prominent weaver in the village weaving group (all female) and the daughter is a wage laborer in the local town. Finally, female 58 appears as both asymmetrically influential and "globally influential." She is married to a prominent villager (second in line to be *'ulumotu'a*) of the *kāinga* of the local chief. This factor and her gender must be contributing to her centrality.

Besides the details about the various measures of asymmetricality and the people they yielded, the results so far indicate that the structures representing the networks of influence in the village are possibly star graphs. Thus, the local hypothesis is supported, where the village is hierarchically organized when influence is taken into consideration. A similar result was obtained by Bennardo and Cappell (2008) when a cluster analysis was performed on the four measures of influence, outdegree (local influence) and outcloseness (global influence) for the SNI1a and SNI1b questions.

The results of this analysis places villagers in increasingly heterogeneous clusters, and eventually into a single group. Since the method is variance based, one can use the proportion of variance in the four measures explained by the grouping as a diagnostic index for the most useful clustering. This produces clusters of villagers that have the most homogeneous distributions on the four measures of influence. The results indicate that six clusters can account for 80.9% of the variance in these four measures of the villager's influence. With ten clusters, 89.8% is accounted for. Below are the characterizations of the six clusters.

Cluster one (twenty-four members) is labeled "political influentials." Villagers in cluster one appear to be among the most politically influential with a notable exception: they lack direct administrative influence[8] over villagers with resources who could help them change the decision regarding the *pola*s 'tray of food.' Even though their global influence over others with these resources is extremely high, indicating they have influence over a few villagers who, in turn, have influence over a larger number of villagers, they lack direct influence. The village official, 64, who may be the target of influence, is a member of this cluster. The chief (89) and the ceremonial leader (66) are also in this cluster. Four *'ulumotu'a* 'heads of family' (55, 66, 79, and 89) are in this cluster as well.

Cluster two (ten members) is labeled "core influentials." Villagers in cluster two are the most pervasively influential villagers; they consistently are measured with high direct and global influence across both influence relations.

---

[8] Bennardo and Cappell (2008) define 'administrative' influence as that elicited by question SNI1b (finding people that can convince/influence an authority figure to change his/her mind) and 'voting' influence the one elicited by question SNI1a (directly convincing somebody to support/vote for you).

Cluster three (seventeen members) is called "moderate influentials." Villagers in cluster three have as much voting influence over others as those villagers in clusters one and two do, but they are differentiated from the "core influentials" in that they have less direct influence over those who may help alter an administrative decision. Their global influence over villagers with such resources, however, exceeds that of the "core influentials." This cluster is distinct because of its average discrepancies between direct influence (outdegree) and global (outcloseness) administrative influence.

Cluster four (twenty-four members) is named "moderate 'administrative' influentials." Villagers in cluster four have low to moderate levels of voting influence and moderate levels of administrative influence. Their global influence over villagers equals their direct influence. Cluster five (nine members) is called "administrative bounded influentials." Villagers in cluster five have moderate levels of administrative influence over those who could help change official decisions, but no voting influence. This again reinforces our earlier observation that different contents or contexts of influence are represented in distinct influence networks. Finally, cluster six (six members) is labeled "non-influentials." Villagers in cluster six are the least influential.

Again, the local hypothesis of a hierarchical structure characterizing village social life is supported by the results of the cluster analysis. What is the relevance of these local findings within the global hypothesis of radiality? Or better, can these data lead to supporting or undermining evidence of the global hypothesis? In order to answer these questions, it is necessary to find what parameter/s is/are causing the variance that leads to the formation of the groups just described above. In other words, when villagers are answering the two questions under analysis, they are shaping their answer according to specific organizing concepts. Such concepts can be revealing regarding their mental representation of social relationships. That is, they may be using individual characteristics of individuals (including themselves), such as gender, age, land ownership, income, and/or more collective features such as belonging to cultural groups like *kāinga* 'extended family,' thus either focusing on characteristics that ego and other-than-ego maximally share (e.g., gender, age, income), or focusing on collective entities that need to be conceived as other-than-ego (e.g., *kāinga*)

To examine the parameters that may be generating a villager's network position in terms of influence and centrality measures, eight separate analyses were conducted. The four network-derived measures of influence for each of the two influence questions (voting and administrative) were analyzed: degree balance – the balance between the outdegree and indegree; the outcloseness measure; the normed betweenness measure; and the constraint measure. Regression analysis was used to model the variation in each of the eight network-based measures. Various models were specified, checking for stability and spurious effects.

The only factor able to account for any substantial and statistically significant variation in asymmetric influence was *kāinga* membership (Bennardo and Cappell, 2008). While ownership of land, cars, and income explained no substantial variation when considered individually, income does explain a portion of the variance in vote influence balance when *kāinga* is controlled for; the more income the more the asymmetric voting influence of the villager. *Kāinga* membership continues to be the most important explanation of vote influence even when the resource variables are included in the same model. These results indicate that parameters based primarily in traditional village life (i.e., *kāinga* membership) and secondarily in the overlying market economy (i.e., income) operate side-by-side to generate influence and centrality.

These findings seem to indicate the presence and development of a recent, market-based set of resources that can generate different types of influence. Tonga, while a small and relatively isolated locale, appears to be in a transitional state from a traditional based system of village influence of perceived uniformity of influence based on shared subsistence farming and *kāinga* membership to one that is also responsive to market success via income and occupation. In other words, traditional collectivistic mental postures are being either accompanied by or replaced by a closer attention to more typically Western individualistic postures. Neither postures are exclusively present in Tonga or in any other place, but the balance between the two is slightly moving toward an increasing role of individualistic postures in Tonga.

Besides, the fact remains that in an attempt to explain salient parameters used by villagers to answer questions about social networks, it became clear that an other-than-ego parameter such as *kāinga* membership is found to have a large priority over any other parameter. Such a finding supports the radiality global hypothesis. However, it still needs to be seen what the findings about social support suggest. Furthermore, correlations between the social network data and the linguistic and cognitive data should also provide further insights.

11.6.2   Analysis of support

In Bennardo and Cappell (in preparation), an analysis of the second set of questions about social support (see Section 11.3.1 above) is presented. The focus is on the support network generated by SNS1a measures, who one could count on for help in giving a *fakaafe* 'invitation' (see Chapter 5, Section 5.7.1, for a description). For this question, outdegree represents a measure of the extent of social support. Indegree represents the extent of social obligations, the degree to which the villager is counted upon by others for social support.

Not much detail can be seen by inspecting the graph of all villagers, so Bennardo and Cappell (in preparation) present two graphs. In Figure 11.3, the ego-graph of the village chief showing his extensive social network is

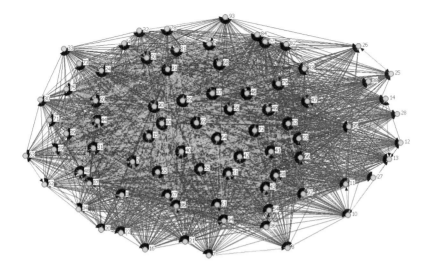

Figure 11.3 Ego network of village chief (node no. 89) (Note: lighter lines indicate reciprocal relation) (from Bennardo and Cappell, in preparation)

introduced. As one can see from his network, the chief (no. 89) is densely and centrally embedded in social support relations. While the average outdegree and indegree of the entire SNS1a network is 59.3, the chief's average value is 27.59. This value indicates that the village chief has more social obligations than sources of social support. As a matter of fact, he was the only one during the interview that mildly complained exactly about this situation and how he needs to rely on support from members of his *kāinga* residing in other places (both in Tonga and abroad) to fulfill his obligations.

In Figure 11.4, Bennardo and Cappell (in preparation) introduce a second graph that shrinks the relations only to those among *kāinga* groups. From this graph we learn that while *kāinga* social support from within the *kāinga* is extensive, so too are the social support relations that reach across *kāingas*. Each node in the Figure 11.4 represents a *kāinga* (the major *kāingas* are reduced to eleven groups).

In a small traditional village like Houma, one would expect social support to be mutual. That is, the giving and receiving of social support would be based on communal sharing and equality matching, not used to generate unequal exchanges that can generate hierarchy (Fisk, 1991). From the descriptive statistics in Table 11.3, one can see that across the types of social support and across the asking or giving of support, only about half of all relations are consistently reciprocated. Without comparative measures of reciprocated social

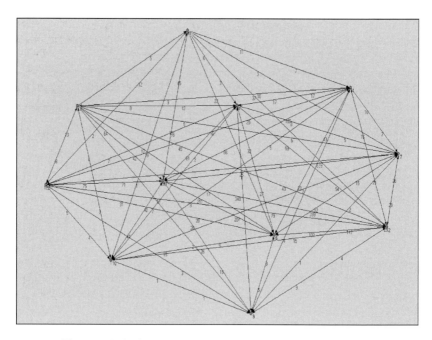

Figure 11.4 Social support relations (SNS1a) among *kāingas* (from Bennardo and Cappell, in preparation)

Table 11.3 *Descriptive statistics for level of symmetry (reciprocity of social support)*

Variable	Mean	Median	Standard deviation
Symmetric SNS1a	0.475	0.500	0.169
Non-symmetric SNS1a	0.525	0.500	0.169
Out non-symmetric SNS1a	0.525	0.528	0.305
In non-symmetric SNS1a	0.475	0.472	0.305
Symmetric SNS1b	0.460	0.523	0.204
Non-symmetric SNS1b	0.540	0.477	0.204
Out non-symmetric SNS1b	0.548	0.538	0.373
In non-symmetric SNS1b	0.452	0.462	0.373

support measures from other similar situations, one can only speculate whether this level is at, above, or below the norm. However, the fact that not an overwhelming majority of relations are reciprocated opens a line of inquiry regarding the extent to which unbalanced social support structures may contribute to generate hierarchy. Some supporting evidence is provided by the ego network of the chief presented in Figure 11.3, where the imbalance between receiving and giving support is documented both in the social network data and in the interview with him.

The two largest aggregated *kāingas* (see Section 11.5 above) are those designated as H1 (29 villagers, also the town officer's *kāinga*) and L1 (20 villagers, also the chief's *kāinga*). Bennardo and Cappell (in preparation) present the network graphs of these two *kāingas* just showing the smaller, most immediate *kāingas* involving these traditional and administrative leaders (Figure 11.5 and Figure 11.6).

From the two subgraphs it can be seen how social support relationships within a *kāinga* exponentially increase with the number of members. In fact, the subgraph in Figure 11.6 (the larger *kāinga* including the current town officer) is clearly denser than the one in Figure 11.5 (the smaller *kāinga* that includes the local chief). It appears as if within a *kāinga* reciprocity is largely practiced, but in a few cases, like that of the chief, one's position fosters unbalanced realizations of support, thus, possibly contributing to the establishing of hierarchy. These cases, however, are less clear than those documented for influence in Section 11.6.1.

Such a situation would be conducive to hypothesizing a larger incidence of outdegree (also indegree) measures for the social support networks than for the influence networks because villagers should mention a higher number of

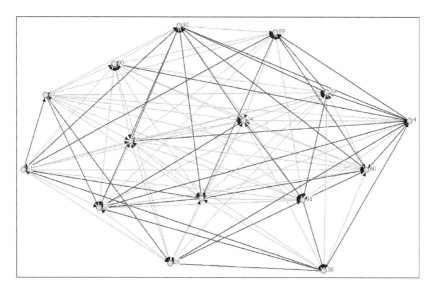

Figure 11.5 Subgraph of SNS1a relations within the village chief's (no. 89) *kāinga*. (Note: lighter lines indicate reciprocal relation) (from Bennardo and Cappell, in preparation)

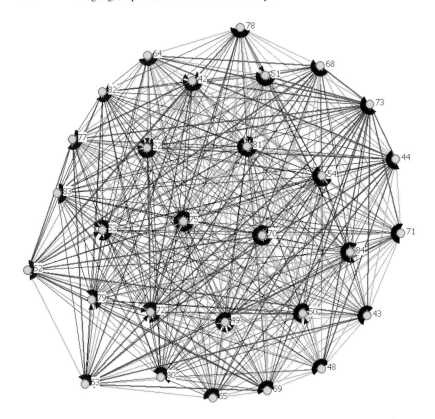

Figure 11.6 Subgraph of SNS1a relations within the village officer's (no. 64) *kāinga*. (Note: lighter lines indicate reciprocal relation) (from Bennardo and Cappell, in preparation)

others they rely upon. Similarly, outcloseness measures should be higher for social support than for influence because it is likely that villagers' support networks would extend wider than that of influence. Finally, betweenness for social support is expected to be lower than that for influence networks. In fact, direct reciprocity within and among *kāinga* members is more likely than use of third parties.

The results in Table 11.4 confirm all the three hypotheses about the possible differences between influence networks and social support networks. In fact, outdegree (54.373 vs. 33.093) and outcloseness (76.213 vs. 57.602) measures are higher and betweenness (31.922 vs. 62.275) measures are lower for social networks than for influence networks. It appears, then, that social support networks are indicating the existence of more circle graphs (see Wasserman and

Table 11.4 *Outdegree, betweenness, and outcloseness for influence and social support*

	Mean	Median	Standard deviation
OUTDEGREE			
Outdegree SNI1a-b	45.517	53	31.024
Outdegree SNI2a-b	20.668	16.5	21.776
Outdegree SNI1a-b, SNI2a-b	33.093	34.75	26.400
Outdegree SNS1a-b, SNS2a-b	**54.373**	**57.5**	**26.182**
BETWEENNESS			
Betweenness SNI1a-b	38.674	32.157	44.239
Betweenness SNI2a-b	85.876	47.234	162.681
Betweenness SNI1a-b, SNI2a-b	62.275	39.696	103.460
Betweenness SNS1a-b, SNS2a-b	**31.922**	**28.719**	**24.059**
OUTCLOSENESS			
Outcloseness SNI1a-b	65.450	71.715	27.892
Outcloseness SNI2a-b	49.755	53.827	20.225
Outcloseness SNI1a-b, SNI2a-b	57.602	62.771	24.059
Outcloseness SNS1a-b, SNS2a-b	**76.213**	**75.116**	**17.526**

Note: Results for SNI1a-b and SNI2a-b are presented separately because they differ.

Faust, 1994: 171) than star graphs as was the case for the influence networks. Direct reciprocity of social support is more common both within *kāingas* (see Figures 11.5 and 11.6) and between *kāingas* (see Figure 11.4). Thus, if one's position in a social support network is more on an equal footing with anybody else, then social networks take the shape of a circle graph.

However, there are two pieces of data that indicate the resilience of uneven, hierarchical relationships between individuals in the village. First, the high mean (54.373) and the high standard deviation in the outdegree measures (26.182) for a group of 95 villagers point to a wide spread of individual situations within the population. Thus, we may be possibly witnessing a hierarchical distribution of social obligations and social support. Second, the chief's social support network in Figure 11.3 confirms exactly this possibility. In conclusion, the differentiation found in the influence networks is not fully replicated in the social support networks, even though traces of a similar way in which networks configure were detected.

11.6.3   Analysis of indirect observations

The indirect observation data presented a challenge to the analysis because they differ substantially from the other two set of social network data. In fact, while recalling the previous day interaction can potentially provide a good snapshot of the social networks activated by individual villagers and collectively by all

Table 11.5 *Indegree for indirect observation (people mentioned)*

Indegree	Mean	Median	Standard deviation
Indirect observation (people mentioned)	12.095	12	9.820

villagers, the activity relies heavily on one's memory. Thus, the results maybe compared and/or be similar to those obtained by the memory cognitive task.

The indegree measure presented in Table 11.5 indicates a good level of interaction with other co-villagers (12.095 out of 95). When we consider the 9.8 standard deviation, we may conclude that some villagers interact daily with more than a fifth of their co-villagers. Once we take into account the high level of activity segregation between genders (see Chapter 2, Section 2.2), the results can be interpreted as many villagers interacting daily with almost half of the same gender co-villagers. If we add the ethnographic fact of age grouping within gender, then we can almost conclude that some villagers may interact daily with most of the other co-villagers of the same gender and age.

The bulk of the analyses of the indirect observation are still in progress with the collaboration of Charles Cappell. We are sure that these further analyses will yield more enlightening information about the status of the social networks in the village under investigation. The minimal results I just introduced must suffice for the time being. These results already allow me to expand the correlations run over most of the data collected. That is, the partial picture of the networks obtained by the influence data, the social support data, and minimally by the indirect observation data are now being compared to the results of the analyses conducted over the linguistic and cognitive data about social relationships.

11.7   Results of correlations[9]

As I stated in the introduction to this chapter, the results of the social network analyses provide a map of the social relationships world. As with any map, they are a partial picture of the 'world' they represent;[10] nonetheless, they represent a positive step toward an objective representation of that world. Furthermore, people use, either consciously or unconsciously, individual and collective mental representations of that world. The linguistic and the cognitive data collected about social relationships were analyzed (see Chapter 9 and Chapter 10) in an attempt to make the nature of those representations explicit.

---

[9] The correlations were run with the help of Charles Cappell.
[10] "All maps are spatial analogies in the sense that they preserve some of the spatial relationships of the world they depict" (Hutchins, 1995: 61).

The availability of the social network map of the social relationship world makes possible a comparison between the two sets of data. That is, centrality measures of influence, social support, and indirect observation social networks can be correlated with the results of some of the linguistic and cognitive data. The assumption is that mental representations of social relationships do participate in the construction of social networks in the social world. In other words, people's social behavior is generated by the way people think and organize their social relationships in their minds. A relevant feature regarding the nature of these mental constructions, i.e., radiality, is hypothesized to be reflected in the nature of people's social behavior or social networks, i.e., star graph networks.

The first measure of network centrality that is correlated is the indegree, that is, the number of times an individual is nominated by other co-villagers. The indegree measure for the influence, the social support, and the indirect observation networks is correlated with the results of three other analyses about the representations of social relationships. First, the results of the interview about social relationships, people mentioned in the first part (local level) of the 'perceived' social relationships interviews (see Chapter 9, Section 9.2.1). Second, the lists of people obtained in the 'indirect' social relationships interviews (see Chapter 9, Section 9.2.1). And third, the lists of villagers obtained by the memory task, free listing (see Chapter 10, Section 10.2).

Given the nature of the social networks presented in Section 11.6, I propose a number of local hypotheses. The star graph nature of influence networks should be conducive to higher correlations with the interview results. Villagers were asked after all to think of ways in which the social world of the village was structured. Questions about preferential traditional groups like *kāinga* were asked as well as information being requested about their internal structures. Similarly, in the narrative texts, choosing a co-villager as the center of a specific episode to be reported and narrated is expected to activate a parameter like *kāinga* membership. Thus, since *kāinga* is one of the generative forces for the influence social networks, the two sets of data are expected to show similarity, hence substantial correlations.

The cognitive data from the free-listing activity, i.e., memory based, are also expected to correlate well. In fact, though the main parameter used to create the lists is spatial, i.e., sequence of houses in a mental scanning of the village (see Chapter 10, Section 10.2), the organizing principle behind both data is hypothesized to be the same, radiality. Thus, both the influence social networks and the memory lists should reflect that shared structure.

In contrast to the influence networks, the tendency to obtain circle graphs for the social support networks makes it plausible that few or only marginal correlations would be found between the indegree centrality measure of the influence social networks and the linguistic data, the interview and the narrative

Table 11.6 *Correlations of influence, support, and indirect observation indegree with interview, memory, and narrative*

	Interview	Memory	Narrative	p value for H_0 that r=0
Influence indegree				
Indegree SNI1a (voting)	**0.322**	**0.336**	**0.274**	0.002/0.001/0.009
Indegree SNI1b (influence decision)	0.046	0.004	0.001	0.666/0.970/0.990
Indegree SNI2a (kin dispute mediator)	**0.693**	**0.311**	**0.610**	<0.0001/0.003/<0.0001
Indegree SNI2b (non-kin dispute mediator)	**0.772**	**0.342**	**0.628**	<0.0001/0.001/<0.0001
Social support indegree				
Indegree SNS1a (ask help *fakaafe*)	0.129	0.172	0.149	0.233/0.110/0.167
Indegree SNS1b (give help *fakaafe*)	0.185	0.172	0.150	0.087/0.110/0.165
Indegree SNS2a (ask help repairs)	0.102	0.123	**0.232**	0.344/0.254/0.030
Indegree SNS2b (give help repairs)	**0.224**	0.164	0.186	0.037/0.128/0.084
Indirect observation indegree				
Indegree (people mentioned)	-0.014	**0.221**	0.190	0.891/0.032/0.066

texts. The centrality measure of the independent observation social networks instead should correlate well with the results of the cognitive data. In fact, both required the use of memory about co-villagers, though in a different way.

The results of the first type of correlations (Pearson) between indegree centrality measures of influence, social support, and independent observation networks and the linguistic data (interview and narrative) and the cognitive data (free listing or memory) are contained in Table 11.6. The picture that emerges is very nuanced, and requires a finer description, a closer examination, and a lengthier discussion.

First, substantial correlations exist for the indegree measures of the influence networks, while the few correlations for the social support and the indirect observation networks are low if not very weak. These results are all in line with the local hypotheses just introduced. Second, the most positive correlations are between influence networks and interview and narrative data. Lower correlations exist between influence networks and the cognitive task, i.e., memory. Furthermore, the positive correlations are not replicated for question SNI1b. This question is about people that can act as intermediaries in influencing the town officer to change an assigned task and is labeled 'administrative' influence by Bennardo and Cappell (2008). Third, a low correlation exists between

Table 11.7 *Correlations of influence and support outdegree with interview, memory, and narrative*

	Interview	Memory	Narrative	p value for H_0 that r=0
Influence outdegree				
Outdegree SNI1a (voting)	0.073	0.068	0.055	0.493/0.528/0.611
Outdegree SNI1b (influence decision)	0.143	0.028	0.050	0.179/0.794/0.641
Outdegree SNI2a (kin dispute mediator)	0.0176	0.181	0.081	0.870/0.089/0.449
Outdegree SNI2b (non-kin dispute mediator)	0.109	0.077	0.044	0.310/0.473/0.678
Social support outdegree				
Outdegree SNS1a (ask help *fakaafe*)	0.114	0.067	0.003	0.293/0.537/0.976
Outdegree SNS1b (give help *fakaafe*)	0.130	0.085	0.172	0.228/0.432/0.110
Outdegree SNS2a (ask help repairs)	0.156	0.063	0.002	0.150/0.56/0.982
Outdegree SNS2b (give help repairs)	0.030	0.0283	0.041	0.780/0.795/0.708

social support networks and only two of the three data sets, namely, interview and narrative. A low correlation exists between indirect observation networks and the results of the memory cognitive task.

The results of the correlations between outdegree measures of the influence and social support networks do not replicate those just introduced for indegree measures (Table 11.7). No significant correlations are found. The correlation results between betweenness of the influence and social support networks (Table 11.8), instead, replicate in many respects those about indegree measures. That is, two questions (SNI2a and SNI2b) used to generate betweenness of influence networks correlate positively with interview data and in a lower manner with narrative data. One of the two questions (SNI2a) also correlates with the data of the memory cognitive task. Two modest correlations also exist between one question (SNS1a) used to generate betweenness for social support networks and the memory cognitive task and between another question (SNS1b) and the interview data.

How do these local results relate to the larger hypothesis of radiality as a foundational cultural model? First, the fact that features of social networks correlate with features of linguistic and cognitive representations of social relationships is remarkable all by itself. Besides, this significant finding validates the common untested assumption that mental representations of social relationships contribute to the generation of social behavior.

Table 11.8 *Correlations of influence and support normed betweenness scores with interview, memory, and narrative*

	Interview	Memory	Narrative
Influence betweenness			
NBetweenness SNI1a (voting)	0.047	0.105	–0.031
p value for H_0 that r=0	0.658	0.325	0.770
NBetweenness SNI1b (influence decision)	0.112	0.041	0.080
p value for H_0 that r=0	0.294	0.703	0.453
NBetweenness SNI2a (kin dispute mediator)	**0.404**	**0.303**	**0.292**
p value for H_0 that r=0	<0.0001	0.003	0.005
NBetweenness SNI2b (non-kin dispute mediator)	**0.403**	0.115	**0.249**
p value for H_0 that r=0	<0.0001	0.282	0.019
Social support betweenness			
NBetweenness SNS1a (ask help *fakaafe*)	0.059	**0.248**	0.113
p value for H_0 that r=0	0.583	0.020	0.298
NBetweenness SNS1b (give help *fakaafe*)	**0.265**	0.188	0.147
p value for H_0 that r=0	0.013	0.080	0.175
NBetweenness SNS2a (ask help repairs)	–0.091	0.185	0.059
p value for H_0 that r=0	0.340	0.086	0.585
NBetweenness SNS2b (give help repairs)	0.181	0.1201	0.111
p value for H_0 that r=0	0.093	0.266	0.307

Second, the three measures of centrality of networks – indegree, outdegree, and betweenness – that were correlated to the two linguistic data sets and to the memory cognitive data represent three different ways in which ego relates to other-than-ego in social networks. Indegree represents the number of villagers that nominate ego as someone they could relate to directly. Thus, it stands for an other-than-ego to ego type of relationship. Outdegree represents the number of villagers each ego mentioned as someone they would be able to relate to directly. Thus, it stands for an ego to other-than-ego type of relationship. Betweenness represents the network's dependence on the ability of a villager to link other villagers in the network. In other words, it describes the degree to which the network is characterized by how much the connections between villagers are dependent upon a link to a third party. Thus, it stands for an other-than-ego to other-than-ego type of relationship.

Third, one can further examine the results in two ways: (a) by looking at which networks produce the most extensive correlations, and (b) by looking at which network centrality measures correlate best. The correlation results clearly indicate that it is the influence networks that are the most extensively correlated with the two linguistic data sets and the cognitive data set. These networks are characterized by star graphs, thus composed of central individuals toward which and from which a number of relationships are established.

In other words, a hierarchical organization or 'authority ranking' (Fiske, 1991). The radial nature of these influence networks seems to correlate extensively with the way in which villagers speak about and think of, i.e., represent mentally, social relationships: those individuals with more influence centrality have higher levels of cognitive centrality. This result beautifully supports the global hypothesis of radiality.

The social support networks, on the other hand, do not correlate well with the other data sets. The nature of these networks is likely not star graphs but circle graphs, where equality is highlighted. It appears that collectivism (Triandis, 1995) or 'communal sharing' norms of equality (Fiske, 1991) characterize these networks (one must note, though, the moderate level of reciprocity in social support). Then, since the radiality hypothesis is about a mental organization of knowledge that may contribute to the generation of social behavior, these results open the discussion to a diversified participation of radiality in the contextual construction of one's behavior. Radiality does appear to contribute to the generation of influence networks, but is set aside when social support networks are constructed. In other words, villagers realize that social support networks in their small close-knit community could be a better living (and surviving) strategy to implement than that of always complying to the hierarchical dictates reverberating onto their village from the centralized monolithic monarchy that characterizes their society. My ethnographic experience amply supports this conclusion.

The extension of the correlation between each centrality measure of the networks and the other data can be used to rank the three ways in which these three measures stand for types of relationships between ego and other-than-ego. Since the indegree is the measure that correlates most extensively (see Table 11.6), it is the relationship 'from other-than-ego to ego' that is most salient, thus participating in the construction of both sets of data. The betweenness measure is the one that correlates less extensively than the indegree, but more than the outdegree (see Table 11.8). Then, the relationship 'other-than-ego to other-than-ego' is also less salient than the 'from other-than-ego to ego,' but more salient than 'from ego to other-than-ego.' Finally, the outdegree measure is the one that correlates least (see Table 11.7). Then, the relationship 'from ego to other-than-ego' is the least salient.

To summarize, the ranking of the three relationships between ego and other-than-ego as evinced from the correlation results stands in this way: first, from other-than-ego to ego; second, from other-than-ego to other-than-ego; third, from ego to other-than-ego. The foregrounding of other-than-ego and backgrounding of ego are constituent parts of the radiality foundational cultural model I hypothesized. The results of the correlations just introduced provide further additional supporting evidence towards my global hypothesis.

11.8   Conclusion

I started this chapter by presenting an innovative idea modeling some of the features of the research on spatial relationships and applying them to my research on social relationships. I obtained social networks and treated them as maps of the social world of a specific village population. The structures of the social networks were used to argue the possibility that the radiality foundational cultural model has reflexes in the social world constructed by individuals holding it. Besides, as a further and ultimate test of the radiality hypothesis, I correlated results from the social network analyses with the results of the analyses conducted on two sets of linguistic data, an interview and the narrative, and one set of cognitive data, free listing or memory.

The results of the correlations (see Tables 11.6, 11.7, and 11.8) speak to a contextually circumscribed relationship between mental representations of social relationships and social networks. The Tongan radiality foundational cultural model may be used to generate influence social networks, but the model is less present in the construction of social support networks. Considering that objective social data such as social networks were compared to subjective data like the linguistic and the cognitive data, it is very encouraging that some articulated but still positive correlations between the two sets of data emerged.

The long and painstaking process of social network data acquisition, preparation, and analysis has yielded three fundamental and crucial conclusions: first, social networks vary in their structure as a function of the role actors put them to play when they generate them; second, there is a close relationship between the mental representations of social relationships and the social networks that realize them (social networks also contribute to the construction of those mental representations); third, the radiality foundational cultural model is apparently used in the generation of some of those networks.

12   A radial mind

12.1   The Tongan radial mind

I started this book with an episode that illustrated the instantiation of the Tongan radiality foundational cultural model in the social relationships domain. The episode highlighted my assistant's preoccupation with others as the cause of her feeling *mā* 'shame' because of the particular event in which she could be participating. This explicitly stated and widely realized mental posture, primary focus on other-than-ego, resonated with a similar organization, i.e., radiality foundational cultural model, characteristic of a number of Tongan domains of knowledge.

First, I introduced extensive evidence about the way in which knowledge about spatial relationships in Tonga is preferentially organized in a radial manner. That is, a specific form of an absolute frame of reference. *A fixed point of reference in the field of ego is selected and objects are represented as from or toward that point.* The fixed points of reference used are contextually provided by cultural parameters. It is this non-ego based (other-based) mental organization of knowledge in the spatial relationships module (radiality) that is repeated in the preferential organization of other knowledge domains in other mental modules and as such it was eventually proposed as a foundational cultural model.

Second, I discussed exemplary salient Tongan actions and rituals, including meetings, invitations, and donations at the village level, and exchanges at various levels of complexity, village, inter-island, and national levels. I concluded that the mental representations of these events are organized radially like spatial relationships. I was capturing an initial glimpse of the existing homology between mental domains of knowledge, i.e., space and action. Third, I looked into a fundamental concept around which the traditional Tongan religious belief system was organized. Here too, I found a radial organization of knowledge as instantiated in the concept of *mana* 'force.' My brief excursion into the literature about traditional Oceanic (including Tongan) navigation yielded other evidence towards a mental organization of knowledge based on other-than-ego. It is at this juncture that my hypothesis of the radiality foundational cultural model clearly emerged.

Fourth, the peculiar features of the linguistic realizations of Polynesian possession attracted my attention to this domain. In line with space and action, my analyses of Tongan possession revealed a radial conceptualization of the relationship between the possessor and the possessed. Similarly, the preferences indicated for spatial relationships were found replicated by the investigation of the mental representations of temporal relationships. The extensive presence of what by now I labeled the radiality foundational cultural model became a compelling hypothesis to be further tested.

Fifth, as a universally salient domain, I chose kinship as another testing ground for my hypothesized foundational cultural model. I presented, then, the algebraic analysis conducted with Dwight Read on the Tongan kinship terminology. The results were encouraging. The terminology is conceptually centered on siblings and not on ego as in the American kinship terminology. The primary mental focus is on other-than-ego and the terminology is later generated from there. The radiality hypothesis was supported.

Finally, since kinship is an essential part of social cognition, I extended my hypothesis to the whole domain of social relationships. The discussion of the results of the analyses I conducted on the linguistic, cognitive, and social network data collected about this domain represents a convincing supporting argument for the general hypothesis. Radiality represents a fundamental principle of the mental representations of social relationships in the Tongan mind. I concluded my excursus by recognizing that this shared fundamental organization of knowledge, i.e., radiality as a foundational cultural model, is at the root of a number of Tongan domains of knowledge; a generative principle that participates in the construction of knowledge in each individual while being shared in the whole cultural milieu. As a matter of fact, it is this mental phenomenon that contributes substantially to molding that milieu. Thus, people sharing that milieu while experiencing it and developing in it, build in their turn a similar mind. A circular intimate relationship, characteristic of any cultural milieu, is established between minds and the milieu in which people develop and mature.

12.2   Three emerging proposals

Before starting the investigation of the Tongan mind reported in this work, I made explicit the theoretical landmarks that oriented and shaped the space of my research and within which I was able to generate both my general and local hypotheses. I adopted an intensional approach to cognition (Keller and Lehman, 1991) that can be exemplified as a way of thinking of the mind as working in the same fashion as a mathematical theory, rooted in axioms out of which theorems are logically derived. And I subscribed to an architecture of the mind as organized around specialized modules (Jackendoff, 1997, 2007) whose internal structure is computational, i.e., theory-like.

While the research unfolded, I defined key concepts like culture, cultural milieu, cultural model, foundational cultural model, social relationships, and social network as emerging from the interaction between the theoretical tools adopted and the large amount of data collected and analyzed. As a further fruitful result of this interaction, I am now in a position to advance three proposals: a revision of the architecture of the mind previously adopted, a minimal typology of cultural models and their place in this architecture, and a unit of analysis for research focusing on culture as a mental phenomenon.

12.2.1   A revision of the architecture of the mind

'Radiality' can be characterized as follows: a point in the field of ego, i.e., other-than-ego, is chosen to function as the source/goal of a number of relationships with other points in the same field, including ego. Essentially, this particular knowledge organization, a specific type of general radiality, stands for the foregrounding of other-than-ego while ego is relegated to the background. This minimal structural organization, a cognitive 'molecule,' is fundamental to human cognition and can be found in a variety of knowledge domains within and across linguistic and cultural boundaries. In Tongan cognition, this 'molecule' plays a fundamental role in the generation and organization of a variety of knowledge domains. It is, in other words, a cultural primitive, i.e., a distinctive feature of Tongan culture. Thus, the privileged role assigned to this cognitive molecule makes Tongans think – and eventually act – in a specific manner about the physical, human, and social world in which they live.

Where is this foundational cultural model localized within the architecture of the mind? First and fundamentally, it is found in the spatial representation module, as exemplified by the preferential use of the radial subtype of the absolute frame of reference. Second, it is replicated in the language module, as demonstrated by the meanings of the Tongan directionals, especially *mai*2 'toward other-than-ego' and *atu*2 'away from other-than-ego.' Third, the action module contains relevant and frequent radial organizations, especially regarding public actions such as *fono* 'village meeting,' *faikava* 'kava ceremony,' *fakaafe* 'invitation,' *misinale* 'yearly donation to church,' and official visit of the king. Fourth, the traditional religious belief system and traditional navigation knowledge as components of the conceptual structures module also reveal radial organizations.

Finally, kinship terminology and social relationships, as parts of the social cognition module (Jackendoff, 2007; Levinson, 2006; Talmy, 2000b), clearly indicate radiality as a fundamental organizing principle. Besides all these modules and the domains therein, I found radiality in two further domains of knowledge, namely, possession and time. These latter findings led me to rethink the architecture of cognition as presented in Chapter 1, Figure 1.2 (here reproduced as Figure 12.1).

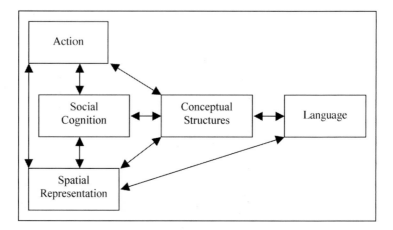

Figure 12.1 Jackendoff's revised architecture of cognition

I propose to put at the core of the architecture ontological domains such as the Aristotelian substance, quantity, quality, relation, place (space), time, possession, and action (see Westerhoff, 2005). Furthermore, the content of the spatial representation module, specifically frames of reference and in the Tongan case, the preferred radial subtype of the absolute frame of reference, needs to be considered at the root of the architecture. This is in line with proposals advanced regarding child cognitive development (Piaget and Inhelder, 1956; Pick, 1993; Mandler, 2004) where spatial concepts appear very early in cognition, and the extensive literature on the visual system (Marr, 1982; Tovée, 1996; Hayworth and Biederman, 2006) wherein the close link between our cognition of spatial relationships and the spatial organization in the brain of those same relationships is clearly established.

In Figure 12.2, I present a revised architecture of cognition that takes into account these proposals. The various mental modules are positioned developmentally from left to right. The ontological category of space (spatial representation module) stems from the human brain organization and feeds other categories/modules such as time, possession, and action (for this latter relationships, see Mandler, 2004). I did not include in the categories/modules proposed any one that I have not investigated, thus leaving open to further research the possibility of expanding and refining this proposal by eventually adding further foundational cultural models stemming from space or other ontological categories.

The output of the spatial representation module feeds into social cognition like the other ontological categories/modules do. All the categories are also directly connected with the conceptual structures module and eventually language,

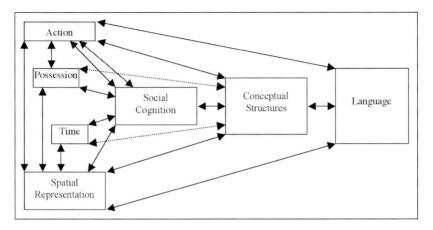

Figure 12.2 New proposed architecture of cognition

either directly or via conceptual structures. For example, on one hand, radiality, as a fundamental organization within the spatial representation module, is directly represented linguistically in the Tongan directional system. On the other hand, the output of the social cognition module arrives at language via the conceptual structures module. In fact, the Tongan kinship terminology, while starting from a sibling (instantiation of radiality), also takes into consideration gender and age (content of the conceptual structures module) at its very beginning. In English, instead, the system starts from ego and only gender is added (Bennardo and Read, 2007). All the indicated relationships between modules are reciprocal and loop back to cross-fertilize one another.

12.2.2 A minimal typology of cultural models

In the literature on cultural models, a distinction is made between two levels of molarity and two terms (among others) are used to distinguish them: schema and model. Typically, in cognitive psychology, cognitive science, cognitive linguistics, and cognitive anthropology, schemas (or schemata) are defined as more general (long-term memory) mental constructions and as such at a higher level of molarity, while models are defined as more particular (short-term memory) mental constructions and closer to perceptual input (see Brewer, 1987; Lakoff, 1987; Shore, 1996). D'Andrade (1995: 152), a cognitive anthropologist, uses the terms reversing the meaning, thus assigning to model the more abstract role and to schema the place closer to perception. In addition, cognitive anthropologists define a model as a cultural model when it is shared within a population/community (Casson, 1983; D'Andrade, 1989; Gatewood and Lowe, 2006).

While many authors explicitly state that some models and schemas are recursively employed to construct larger models (Brewer, 1999; Strauss and Quinn, 1997; D'Andrade, 2005), only Shore defines foundational schemas as those that "organize or link up a 'family' of related models" (1996: 53). In an attempt to clear the field of a confusing and unnecessary terminological conundrum, I propose to simplify the matter and use only two terms: foundational cultural model and cultural model. The former refers to simpler and more abstract models that organize only a few bits of knowledge during the earliest stage of cognitive development, such as those within ontological domains. They are out of awareness and it is very difficult to bring them to consciousness. The latter refer to larger and less abstract models that encompass knowledge from a variety of source domains. They are also out of awareness, but can be brought to consciousness either by others (researchers) or on occasion by oneself.

My proposed distinction between foundation cultural models and cultural models points attention to the fact that culture is found at various levels of molarity in the mind, and minimally two. Foundational cultural models are generated early (both synchronically and diachronically) and they are typically associated with ontological categories. Cultural models are constructed later (again, both synchronically and diachronically) and pull together knowledge from a variety of sources, such as the social cognition module (for Tongan examples see kinship terminology, social relationships, and hierarchy), the conceptual structures module (for Tongan examples see the traditional religious belief system and traditional navigation), the action module (for Tongan examples see social encounters and rituals), the proprioception module (for a Tongan example see the ethnographically established way of thinking and presenting oneself socially in Chapter 1, Section 1.1 and Chapter 9, Section 9.1), reasoning (for a Tongan example see reasoning with the cultural model highlighted by the metaphor analysis in Chapter 9, Section 9.4), emotions, values, and others (Figure 12.3).

The output of this mental organization may or may not be conducive to action or behavior. The action/behavioral output may be slightly different from what one represents mentally (see action module), but cannot be completely unrelated and/or independent from both foundational cultural models and cultural models. The results of the analyses of the social network data (see Chapter 11) demonstrated the existence of an articulated, nonetheless clear relationship between the cognition of social relationships and the actual social networks realized by the villagers.

12.2.3   A unit of analysis for culture in mind

In any scientific investigation, one of the fundamental questions that one needs to answer is to clearly define a unit of analysis. In linguistics, for example, the

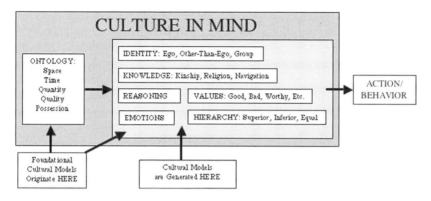

Figure 12.3 Culture in mind

phoneme is the unit of analysis for phonology, and the sentence is the unit of analysis for syntax. Within the investigation of culture as a mental phenomenon, or culture in mind, I propose to use the foundational cultural model as a unit of analysis. Generated early, synchronically and diachronically, foundational cultural models represent primary attempts at blending innate capacities and experiences in compact, simple, and long-lasting units. These units already possess meaningful internal structures. Later, they eventually participate in the construction of more complex units with emergent characteristics of their own, e.g., cultural models.

For example, the Tongan foundational cultural model of radiality that I proposed throughout this book has this internal structure: other-than-ego, vector, ego. Notice how other-than-ego is foregrounded and ego is backgrounded. It is possible to organize this content in a different manner, such as ego, vector, other-than-ego. And it is certain that this occurs within the Tongan or any human mind. However, the radiality organization is the one that is very likely constructed early, preferred over other configurations, and used in later organizations of knowledge. This syntactic organization, to use a linguistic metaphor, represents a generative cognitive 'molecule' or structure that has reverberating repercussions within the whole subsequent organization and construction of knowledge that occurs at later stages of development and experience. A number of foundational cultural models may be at the core of any culture. The findings about Tonga suggest a way in which these other units may be discovered. First, one needs to conceive of a specific way in which the architecture of the mind unfolds. The one adopted here was Jackendoff's representational modularity (see Chapter 1, Section 1.3), later slightly modified in Section 12.2.1 above. Second, one needs to decide about a way to think of the working of cognition. The one adopted here was a fully intensional and computational approach (see Chapter 1, Section 1.4). Third, one needs to arrive at an understanding of at least one of the ontological domains to enhance the chances of finding one of the potential foundational cultural models characterizing the culture under investigation.

As I have already stated in the previous section, cultural models represent organizations of knowledge at a different level of molarity than foundational cultural models and can be investigated in a variety of manners (see, for example, Strauss and Quinn, 1997; D'Andrade, 2005; Gatewood and Lowe, 2006). Research about foundational cultural models needs by definition a multi-domain investigation that is very likely to require interdisciplinary collaborations and approaches. The present work bears witness to this statement and I am convinced it can also provide a model for future research.

12.3   Final remarks

The first part of the investigation presented in this book was about the representation of spatial relationships in Tongan. Space is a fundamental ontological domain close to brain organization and clearly present and used to organize other domains of knowledge. It is here that a picture started to emerge of the radiality foundational cultural model later to be found in other ontological domains (e.g., possession, time) and also in other Tongan domains of knowledge (e.g., religion, navigation, kinship, social relationships).

Radiality, as a specific, simple, compact, and long-lasting structural organization of knowledge, emerges from the spatial representation module and spreads over a number of other modules and domains wherein. A related but important ancillary result is that one could in principle use findings about preferences in the spatial representation module to predict fundamental organizations of other modules and/or domains. The sophisticated methodology already available to investigate the domain of spatial relationships makes it likely that in the future attempts could be made to have the research on space precede the research of other domains. An attempt in this fashion is already under way within a collaborative research proposal currently being constructed by myself to examine the content of the proprioception module (identity construction) in many cultures including American, Chinese, Filipino, German, Italian, and Japanese cultures.

Finally, I want to point out that as much as the research I conducted was about the Tongan mind, the whole project would never have obtained the results it yielded without a keen attention and understanding of the Tongan cultural milieu. It was my long residence in the country and the close ties I established with a host family and a specific place, a village and its population, that brought about those insights into the Tongan mind I reported here. A detailed cross-disciplinary methodology helped in directing me toward the goal I had in mind by making it possible to collect a considerable quantity of data that were later rigorously analyzed. Nonetheless, it was my extensive and detailed ethnographic knowledge that allowed me to find insightful meanings in otherwise unenlightening data strings. For this, I want to close the book with a deeply felt and thankful thought for Tonga and its wonderfully hospitable and warm people.

References

Abelson, Robert and Roger Schank. (1977). *Scripts, Plans, Goals, and Understanding: An Inquiry into Human Knowledge Structures.* Hillsdale, NJ: Lawrence Erlbaum Associates, Publishers.

Allen, Anne E. Guernsey. (1993). Architecture as Social Expression in Western Samoa: Axioms and Models. *Traditional Dwellings and Settlements Review*, 5, 1: 33–45.

Aoyagi, M. (1966). Kinship Organisation and Behaviour in a Contemporary Tonga Village. *Journal of the Polynesian Society*, 75: 141–76.

Baayen, H. and E. Danziger (Eds.). (1994). *Max Planck Institute for Psycholinguistics: Annual Report 14, 1993*, Nijmegen, The Netherlands: Max Planck Institute for Psycholinguistics.

Ballim, A. and Y. Wilks. (1992). *Artificial Believers: The Ascription of Belief.* Hillsdale, NJ: Lawrence Erlbaum.

Barrow, John. (1993). *Captain Cook: Voyages of Discovery.* Chicago: Academy Chicago Publishers.

Bartlett, F. C. (1932). *Remembering.* London: Cambridge University Press.

Batagelj, Vladimir and Andrej Mrvar. (1996). *Pajek – Program for Large Network Analysis.* Home page http://vlado.fmf.uni-lj.si/pub/networks/pajek/

Bateson, Gregory. (1972). A Theory of Play and Fantasy. In G. Bateson, *Steps to an Ecology of Mind*, pp. 177–93. New York: Ballantine Books.

Beaglehole, E. and P. Beaglehole. (1941). *Pangai: Village in Tonga.* Wellington, New Zealand: Polynesian Society Memoir, 18.

Behrens, C. (1984). *Shipibo Ecology and Economy.* Doctoral dissertation, University of California, Los Angeles.

Bender, A., G. Bennardo, and S. Beller. (2005). Spatial Frames of Reference for Temporal Relations: A Conceptual Analysis in English, German, and Tongan. In Bruno G. Bara, Lawrence Barsalou, and Monica Bucciarelli (Eds.), *Proceedings of the 27th Annual Conference of the Cognitive Science Society*, pp. 220–5. New York: Lawrence Erlbaum.

Bender, A., S. Beller, and G. Bennardo (forthcoming). Temporal Frames of Reference: A Conceptual Analysis and Empirical Evidence from English, German, and Tongan. *Cognitive Science.*

Bennardo, G. (1993). Towards a Computational Approach to Spatial Cognition: An Investigation of Relevant Computations in the Visual System and the Linguistic System. *Cognitive Science Technical Report*, University of Illinois at Urbana-Champaign, Beckman Institute.

(1996). *A Computational Approach to Spatial Cognition: Representing Spatial Relationships in Tongan Language and Culture*. Doctoral dissertation, University of Illinois at Urbana-Champaign, Urbana, Illinois.

(1998). Conceptual Semantics and Linguistic Knowledge, Cognitive Anthropology and Cultural Knowledge: A Common Enterprise? Paper read at *The 97th Annual Meeting of the American Anthropological Association*, Philadelphia , PA. December 5, 1998.

(1999). The Conceptual Content of Tongan Directionals: Mental Representations of Space in Tongan. *Rongorongo Studies*, 9, 2: 39–61. Auckland, New Zealand: The Institute of Polynesian Languages and Literatures.

(2000a). Language and Space in Tonga: 'The Front of the House is Where the Chief Sits!' *Anthropological Linguistics*, 42, 4: 499–544.

(2000b). A Conceptual Analysis of Tongan Spatial Nouns: From Grammar to Mind. *Languages of the World*, 12. Münich, Germany: Lincom Europa.

(2000c). Possessive Markers in Tongan: A Conceptual Approach. In Steven R. Fischer (Ed.), *Possessive Markers in Central Pacific Languages*, special issue of *Language Typology and Universals*, Berlin 53 (2000) 3/4: 269–80.

(2002a). Map Drawing in Tonga, Polynesia: Accessing Mental Representations of Space. *Field Methods*, 14, 4: 390–417.

(2002b). Mental Images of the Familiar: Cultural Strategies of Spatial Representations in Tonga. In G. Bennardo (Ed.), *Representing Space in Oceania: Culture in Language and Mind*. Canberra: Pacific Linguistics.

Bennardo, G. (Ed.). (2002c). *Representing Space in Oceania: Culture in Language and Mind*. Canberra, Australia: Pacific Linguistics, Research School of Pacific and Asian Studies, The Australian National University.

Bennardo, G. (2003). Language, Mind, and Culture: From Linguistic Relativity to Representational Modularity. In Marie Banich and Molly A. Mack (Eds.), *Mind, Brain, and Language: Multidisciplinary Perspectives*, pp. 23–60. New York: Lawrence Erlbaum Associates, Publishers.

(2004). Linguistic Untranslatability vs. Conceptual Nesting of Frames of Reference. In K. Forbus, D. Gentner, and T. Regier (Eds.), *Proceedings of the 26th Annual Conference of the Cognitive Science Society*, pp. 102–7. New York: Lawrence Erlbaum.

(2008). Familiar Space in Social Memory. *Social Structure and Dynamics*, 3, 1: 7–23.

Bennardo, G. Metaphors in Tongan Linguistic Production about Social Relationships: 'Ofa 'Love' is Giving. *Anthropological Linguistics*.

Bennardo, G. and Charles Cappell. (2008). Influence Structures in a Tongan Village: "Every Villager is not the Same!" *Social Structure and Dynamics*, 3, 1.

Bennardo, G. and Charles Cappell. (in preparation). Social Support in Tonga.

Bennardo, G. and D. W. Read. (2005). The Tongan Kinship Terminology: Insights from an Algebraic Analysis. *Mathematical Anthropology and Cultural Theory*, 2, 1: 1–51. http://www.mathematicalanthropology.org/.

Bennardo, G. and Kurt Schultz. (2003). Constructing the 3-D World of Speech Events. *Journal of Linguistic Anthropology*, 13, 1: 98–119.

(2004). Three Innovative Research Tools to Store, Visualize, and Analyze Data in and from the Field. *Field Methods*, 16, 4: 396–413.

Bennardo, G., Kelly Hattman, and Jennifer Testa. (2001). Digitizing a Polynesian Village: In Search of Inter-Modular Relationships. Invited presentation at the *Cognitive Studies Brown Bags*, Northern Illinois University, March 23, 2001.

(2007). Cognition, Algebra, and Culture in the Tongan Kinship Terminology. *Journal of Cognition and Culture*, 7, 2: 49–88.

Bernard, H. R., P. D. Killworth, and L. Sailer. (1980). Informant Accuracy in Social Network Data IV: A Comparison of Clique-Level in Behavioral and Cognitive Network Data. *Social Science Research*, 11: 30–66.

(1982). Informant Accuracy in Social Network Data V: An Experimental Attempt to Predict Actual Communication from Recall Data. *Social Networks*, 2: 191–218.

Besnier, N. (1992). Polynesian Languages. In W. Bright (Ed.), *International Encyclopedia of Linguistics*, pp. 245–51. Oxford: Oxford University Press.

Biederman, I. (1988). Aspects and Extensions of a Theory of Human Understanding. In Z. Pylyshyn (Ed.), *Computational Processes in Human Vision: An Interdisciplinary Perspective*, pp. 370–428. Norwood, NJ: Ablex.

Biersack, A. (1982). Tongan Exchange Structures: Beyond Descent and Alliance. *The Journal of the Polynesian Society*, 91, 2: 181–212.

Biggs, B. (1969). *Let's Learn Maori: A Guide to the Study of the Maori Language*. Auckland: Auckland University Press.

Boas, F. (1911). Introduction. *Handbook of American Indian Languages*. Bulletin 40, Part I, Bureau of American Ethnology, pp. 1–83. Washington, DC: Government Printing Office.

Borgatti, S. P., M. G. Everett, and L. C. Freeman. (2002). *Ucinet 6 for Windows*. Harvard: Analytic Technologies.

Boroditsky, L. (2000). Metaphoric Structuring: Understanding Time through Spatial Metaphors. *Cognition*, 75: 1–28.

(2001). Does Language Shape Thought? English and Mandarin Speakers' Conceptions of Time. *Cognitive Psychology*, 43: 1–22.

Boroditsky, L. and M. Ramscar. (2002). The Roles of Mind and Body in Abstract Thought. *Psychological Science*, 13: 185–88.

Bott, E. (1972). Psychoanalysis and Ceremony. In J. S. L. Fontaine (Ed.), *The Interpretation of Ritual*, pp. 205–37. London: Tavistock.

Bott, Elizabeth (1981). Power and Rank in the Kingdom of Tonga. *The Journal of the Polynesian Society*, 90, 1: 7–82.

Bott, E. (1982). *Tongan Society at the Time of Captain Cook's Visit*. Wellington: The Polynesian Society

Bowerman, Melissa. (1996). Learning How to Structure Space for Language: A Crosslinguistic Perspective. In P. Bloom, M. A. Peterson, L. Nadel, and M. F. Garrett (Eds.), *Language and Space*, pp. 385–436. Cambridge, MA: The MIT Press.

Bowerman, Melissa and S. C. Levinson. (2001). *Language Acquisition and Conceptual Development*. Cambridge: Cambridge University Press.

Brewer, B. and Julian Pears. (1993). Introduction: Frames of Reference. In N. Eilan, R. McCarthy, and B. Brewer (Eds.), *Spatial Representation: Problems in Philosophy and Psychology*, pp. 25–30. Cambridge, MA: Blackwell.

Brewer, W. (1984). The Nature and Functions of Schemas. In *Handbook of Social Cognition*, Vol. I, pp. 119–60. Hillsdale, NJ: Lawrence Erlbaum Associates, Publishers.

(1987). Schemas versus Mental Models in Human Memory. In P. Morris (Ed.), *Modelling Cognition*, pp. 187–97. New York: John Wiley & Sons Ltd.

(1999). Schemata. In R. A. Wilson and F. C. Keil (Eds.), *The MIT Encyclopedia of the Cognitive Sciences*, pp. 729–30. Cambridge, MA: The MIT Press.

Brewer, W. F. and G. V. Nakamura. (1984). The Nature and Functions of Schemas. In R. S. Wyer and T. K. Srull (Eds.), *Handbook of Social Cognition*, Vol. 1, pp. 119–60. Hillsdale, NJ: Erlbaum.

Broschart, J. (1986). Remarks on Tongan Grammar. Mimeo, 'Atenisi University, Nuku'alofa, Tonga.

(1995). The Social Perception of Space. Non-spatial Determinants of the Use of Directionals in Tongan (Polynesia). In A. Frank and W. Kuhn (Eds.), *Spatial Information Theory*, pp. 443–462. Berlin: Springer.

(1997a). Locative Classifiers in Tongan. In G. Senft (Ed.), *Referring to Space: Studies in Austronesian and Papuan Languages*, pp. 287–35. Oxford: Clarendon.

(1997b). Why Tongan Does it Differently: Categorial Distinctions in a Language without Nouns and Verbs, *Linguistic Typology*, 1, 2.

Brown, Penelope, Günter Senft, and L. Wheeldon (Eds.). (1993). *Max-Planck Institute for Psycholinguistics: Annual Report 13, 1992*, Nijmegen, The Netherlands: Max-Planck Institute for Psycholinguistics.

Buck, Peter H. (1938). *Vikings of The Sunrise*. Philadelphia: J. P. Lippincott Company.

Burkett, Tracy Lynn. (1998). *Co-sponsorship in the United States Senate: A Network Analysis of Senate Communication and Leadership, 1973–1990*. Unpublished Dissertation, University of South Carolina, Columbia.

Burt, Ronald. (2000). The Network Structure of Social Capital. *Research in Organizational Behavior*, 22: 345–423.

Cablitz, Gabriele H. (2006). *Marquesan: A Grammar of Space*. Berlin: Mouton de Gruyter.

CARG [Cognitive Anthropology Research Group]. (1992). *Manual for the Space Stimuli Kit 1.1*. Nijmegen, The Netherlands: Max-Planck Institute for Psycholinguistics.

Carlson-Radvansky, Laura and D. Irwin. (1993). Frames of Reference in Vision and Language: Where is Above? *Cognition* 46: 223–44.

Casasanto, D. and L. Boroditsky. (2003). Do we Think about Time in Terms of Space? *Proceedings of the 25th Annual Conference of the Cognitive Science Society*, pp. 216–21. Boston, MA: Lawrence Erlbaum.

Casson, Ronald. (1983). Schemata in Cognitive Anthropology. *Annual Review of Anthropology*, 12: 429–62.

Chase, Ivan. (1980). Social Process and Hierarchy Formation in Small Groups: A Comparative Perspective. *American Sociological Review*, 45: 905–24.

Christopher, B. (1994). *The Kingdom of Tonga: A Geography Resource for Teachers*. Nuku'alofa, Tonga: Friendly Islands Bookshop.

Chomsky, N. (1957). *Syntactic Structures*. The Hague: Mouton.

(1972). *Language and Mind*. New York: Harcourt Brace Jovanovich.

(1986). *Knowledge of Language*. New York: Praeger.

(1995). *The Minimalist Program*. Cambridge, MA: The MIT Press.

Chung, S. (1978). *Case Marking and Grammatical Relations in Polynesian*. Austin, TX: University of Texas Press.

Churchward, C. M. (1953). *Tongan grammar*. Nuku'alofa, Tonga: Vava'u Press.

Clark, H. Herbert. (1970). The Primitive Nature of Children's Relational Concepts. In John R. Hayes, *Cognition and Development of Language*, pp. 269–78. New York: John Wiley & Sons, Inc.

Clark, R. (1973). Transitivity and Case in Eastern Oceanic Languages. *Oceanic Linguistics*, 12, 2: 559–607.

Cohen, Robert (Ed.). (1985). *The Development of Spatial Cognition*. London: Lawrence Erlbaum Associates, Publishers.

Coleman, James S. (1990). *Foundations of Social Theory*. Ch. 12: Social Capital, pp. 300–21. Cambridge, MA: Belknap Press of Harvard University Press.

Collocott, E. E. V. (1924). Marriage in Tonga. *Journal of the Polynesian Society*, 33: 166–84.

(1927). Kava Ceremonial in Tonga. *Journal of the Polynesian Society*, 36: 21–47.

Craik, K. (1943). *The Nature of Explanation*. Cambridge: Cambridge University Press.

Crane, A. E. (1991). *Geography of the Tropical Pacific*. Nuku'alofa, Tonga: Friendly Islands Bookshop.

D'Andrade, Roy. (1987). A Folk Model of the Mind. In Dorothy Holland and Naomi Quinn (Eds.), *Cultural Models in Language and Thought*, pp. 112–48. Cambridge: Cambridge University Press.

D'Andrade, Roy G. (1989). Cultural Cognition. In M. I. Posner (Ed.), *Foundations of Cognitive Science*, pp. 795–830. Cambridge, MA: MIT Press

(1995). *The Development of Cognitive Anthropology*. Cambridge: Cambridge University Press.

(2005). Some Methods for Studying Cultural Cognitive Structures. In Naomi Quinn (Ed.), *Finding Culture in Talk: A Collections of Methods*, pp. 83–104. New York: Palgrave Macmillan.

D'Andrade, Roy G. and Claudia Strauss (Eds.). (1992). *Human Motives and Cultural Models*. Cambridge: Cambridge University Press.

Danzinger, Eve (Ed.) (1993). *Cognition and Space Kit Version 1.0*. Nijmegen, The Netherlands: Max-Planck Institute for Psycholinguistics.

Danziger, Eve and Susanne Gaskins. (1993). Exploring the Intrinsic Frame of Reference. Mimeo, Nijmegen, The Netherlands: Cognitive Anthropology Research Group at the Max-Planck Institute for Psycholinguistics.

Dougherty, Janet D. W. (Ed.). (1985). *Directions in Cognitive Anthropology*. Urbana, IL: University of Illinois Press.

Dougherty, J. D. and C. M. Keller. (1985). Taskonomy: A Practical Approach to Knowledge Structures. In Janet D. W. Dougherty (Ed.), *Directions in Cognitive Anthropology*, pp. 161–74. Urbana, IL: University of Illinois Press.

Downs, Roger M. and David Stea. (1977). *Maps in Minds: Reflections on Cognitive Mapping*. New York: Harper and Row Publishers.

Duranti, Alessandro. (1988). Intentions, Language, and Social Action in a Samoan Context. *Journal of Pragmatics*, 12: 13–33.

(1994). *From Grammar to Politics: Linguistic Anthropology in a Western Samoan Village*. Los Angeles: University of California Press.

(1997). *Linguistic Anthropology*. Cambridge: Cambridge University Press.

Dyen, I. (1981). The Subgrouping of the Polynesian Languages. In J. Hollyman, and A. Pawley (Eds.), *Studies in Pacific Languages and Cultures*, pp. 83–100. Auckland: Linguistic Society of New Zealand.

Elbert, S. H. (1953). Internal Relationships of Polynesian Languages and Dialects. *Southwestern Journal of Anthropology*, 9: 147–73.

Ellen, P. and C. Thinus-Blanc (Eds.). (1987). *Cognitive Processes and Spatial Orientation in Animal and Man*. Boston: Martinus Nijhoff Publishers.

Evans, Mike. (2001). *Persistence of the Gift: Tongan Tradition and Transnational Context*. Waterloo, Ontario: Wilfrid Laurier University Press.

Evans, V. (2003). *The Structure of Time*. Amsterdam: John Benjamins.

Feinberg, Richard. (1988). *Polynesian Seafaring and Navigation: Ocean Travel in Anutan Culture and Society*. Kent, OH: The Kent State University Press.

Ferdon, E. N. (1987). *Early Tonga: As the Explorers Saw it 1616–1810*. Tucson, AZ: The University of Arizona Press.

Fillmore, J. Charles. (1975). *Santa Cruz Lectures on Deixis*. Bloomington, IN: Indiana University Linguistics Club.

   (1982). Frame Semantics. In The LSOK (Ed.), *Linguistics in the Morning Calm*, pp. 111–37. Seoul, Korea: Hanshin Publishing Company.

Finney, Ben R. (Ed.). (1976). *Pacific Navigation and Voyaging*. Wellington, New Zealand: The Polynesian Society Inc.

Firth, Raymond. (1940). The Analysis of Mana: An Empirical Approach. *Journal of the Polynesian Society*, 49: 483–510.

Fiske, Alan P. (1991). *Structures of Social Life: The Four Elementary Forms of Human Relations*. New York: The Free Press.

Fodor, J. (1983). *Modularity of Mind*. Cambridge, MA: MIT Press.

   (1998). *In Critical Condition: Polemical Essays on Cognitive Science and the Philosophy of Mind*. Cambridge, MA: MIT Press.

Freeman, L. C. and A. K. Romney. (1987). Words, Deeds, and Social Structure: A Preliminary Study of the Reliability of Informants. *Human Organization*, 46: 330–4.

Freeman, L. C., D. R. White, and A. K. Romney (Eds.). (1989). *Research Methods in Social Network Analysis*. Fairfax, VA: George Mason University Press.

Frege, G. (1975). On Sense and Reference. In D. Davidson and G. Harman (Eds.), *The Logic of Grammar*, pp. 116–28. Encino, CA: Dickenson.

Gailey, C. W. (1987*). Kinship to Kinship: Gender Hierarchy and State Formation in the Tongan Islands*. Austin, TX: University of Texas Press.

Gallistel, C. R. (1993). *The Organization of Learning*. Cambridge, MA: The MIT Press.

Gatewood, J. B. and J. W. G. Lowe. (2006). *Employee Perceptions of Credit Unions: A Pilot Study*. Madison, WI: Filene Research Institute Monograph #1752–113.

Geertz, Clifford. (1973). *Interpretations of Culture*. New York: Basic Books.

   (1980). *Negara: The Theater State in Nineteenth-Century Bali*. Princeton, NJ: Princeton University Press.

   (1984). From the Natives' Point of View: On the Nature of Anthropological Understanding. In R. A. Shweder and R. A. LeVine (Eds.), *Culture Theory*, pp. 123–136. Cambridge: Cambridge University Press.

Gelman, Susan A., J. D. Coley, and G. M. Gottfried. (1994). Essentialist Beliefs in Children: The Acquisition of Concepts and Theories. In Lawrence A. Hirschfeld and Susan A. Gelman (Eds.), *Mapping the Mind: Domain Specificity in Cognition and Culture*, pp. 341–65. Cambridge: Cambridge University Press.

Gentner, D. (Ed.). (2001). *Spatial Metaphors in Temporal Reasoning*. Cambridge, MA: MIT Press.

Gentner, D. and A. L. Stevens (Eds.). (1983). *Mental Models*. Hillsdale, NJ: Erlbaum.

Gentner, D., M. Imai, and L. Boroditsky. (2002). As Time Goes by: Evidence for Two Systems in Processing Space Time Metaphors. *Language and Cognitive Processes*, 17: 537–65.

Gifford, E. W. (1929). *Tongan Society*. Honolulu, HI: Bernice P. Bishop Museum.

Gladwin, Thomas. (1970). *East is a Big Bird: Navigation and Logic on Puluwat Atoll*. Cambridge, MA: Harvard University Press.

Goldman, I. (1970). *Ancient Polynesian Society*. Chicago, IL: The University of Chicago Press.

Golledge, R. G. (1999). *Wayfinding Behavior: Cognitive Mapping and Other Spatial Processes*. Baltimore, MD: The Johns Hopkins University Press.

Golson, Jack (Ed.). (1963). *Polynesian Navigation: A Symposium on Andrew Sharp's Theory of Accidental Voyages*. Wellington, New Zealand: The Polynesian Society Inc.

Goodale, J. (1971). *Tiwi Wives*. Seattle, WA: University of Washington Press.

Goodenough, W. (1957). Cultural Anthropology and Linguistics. Reprinted in Dell Hymes (Ed.) (1964), *Language in Culture and Society: A Reader in Linguistic Anthropology*, pp. 36–9. New York: Harper & Row Publishers.

Gopnik, A. (1988). Conceptual and Semantic Development as Theory Change. *Mind and Language*, 3: 197–216.

Gould, Peter and Rodney White. (1974, reprinted 1986). *Mental Maps*. New York: Routledge.

Gould, Roger V. (2002). The Origins of Status Hierarchies: A Formal Theory and Empirical Test. *American Journal of Sociology*, 107: 1143–78.

Grace, G. W. (1968). Classification of the Languages of the Pacific. In A. P. Vayda (Ed.), *Peoples and Cultures of the Pacific*, pp. 63–79. Garden City, NY: The Natural History Press.

Green, R. (1966). Linguistic Subgrouping within Polynesia: The Implications for Prehistoric Settlement. *The Journal of the Polynesian Society*, 75, 1: 6–38.

(1979). Lapita. In J. D. Jennings (Ed.), *The Prehistory of Polynesia*, pp. 27–60. Cambridge, MA: Harvard University Press.

Green, R. and A. Pawley. (1973). Dating the Dispersal of the Oceanic Languages. *Oceanic Linguistics*, 12, 1: 1–68.

Greenfield, Patricia M. (2005). Paradigms of Cultural Thought. In K. J. Holyoak and R. G. Morrison (Eds.), *Cambridge Handbook of Thinking and Reasoning*, pp. 663–82. Cambridge: Cambridge University Press.

Groube, L. M. (1971). Tonga, Lapita Pottery, and Polynesian Origins. *The Journal of the Polynesian Society*, 80, 3: 278–316.

Handy, C. E. S. (1927). *Polynesian Religion*. Honolulu, HI: Bernice P. Bishop Museum.

Haugen, Einar. (1957). The Semantics of Icelandic Orientation. *Word*, 13: 447–60.

Haviland, J. B. (2000). Pointing, Gesture Spaces, and Mental Maps. In D. McNeill (Ed.), *Language and Gesture*, pp. 13–46. Cambridge: Cambridge University Press.

Hayworth, K. and I. Biederman. (2006). Neural Evidence for Intermediate Representations in Object Recognition, *Vision Research*, 46: 4024–31.

Heelan, Patrick A. (1988). *Space, Perception, and the Philosophy of Science*. Berkeley, CA: University of California Press.

Helu, Futa (1979). Tongan Poetry III: The Fakatangi (Part 2). *Faikava*, 3: 18–20.

(1999). *Critical Essays: Cultural Perspectives from the South Seas*. Canberra, ACT: The Journal of Pacific History (RSPAS, Australian National University).

Herdrich, David J. and F. K. Lehman. (2002). On the Relevance of Point Field for Spatiality in Oceania. In G. Bennardo (Ed.), *Representing Space in Oceania: Culture in Language and Mind*, pp. 179–97. Canberra, Australia: Pacific Linguistics, Research School of Pacific and Asian Studies, The Australian National University.

Hilder, Brett. (1965). Kau Moala the Tongan Navigator. *The Journal of the Institute of Navigation*, 18: 246–9.

Hill, Clifford. (1982). Up/Down, Front/Back, Left/Right. A Contrastive Study of Hausa and English. In J. Weissenborn and W. Klein (Eds.), *Here and There: Cross-Linguistic Studies on Deixis and Demonstration*, pp. 13–42. Amsterdam: John Benjamins.

Hill, Deborah. (1997). Finding your Way in Longgu: Geographical Reference in Solomon Islands' Language. In Gunter Senft (Ed.), *Referring to Space: Studies in Austronesian and Papuan Languages*, pp. 101–26. Oxford: Oxford University Press.

Hirschfeld, Lawrence A. and Susan A. Gelman (Eds.). (1994). *Mapping the Mind: Domain Specificity in Cognition and Culture*. Cambridge: Cambridge University Press.

Hofstede, Geert. (1991). *Cultures and Organizations: Software of the Mind*. London: McGraw-Hill.

Hogbin, H. I. (1936). Mana. *Oceania*, 6, 3: 241–74.

Hohepa, P. W. (1969). The Accusative-to-Ergative Drift in Polynesian Languages. *The Journal of the Polynesian Society*, 78: 295–329.

Holland, Dorothy. (1992). How Cultural Systems Become Desire. In R. D'Andrade and C. Strauss (Eds.), *Human Motives and Cultural Models*, pp. 61–89. Cambridge: Cambridge University Press.

Holland, Dorothy and Naomi Quinn (Eds.). (1987). *Cultural Models in Language and Thought*. Cambridge: Cambridge University Press.

Hoponoa, Leonaitasi. (1992). Pro-Democratic Movement in Tonga: The Case of Samiuela 'Akilisi Pohiva. In Donald H. Rubinstein (Ed.), *Pacific History: Papers from the 8th Pacific History Association Conference*, pp. 97–100. Mangilao, Guam: University of Guam Press.

Howe, K. R. (1984). *Where the Waves Fall*. Honolulu, HI: University of Hawaii Press.

Hubel, H. David. (1988). *Eye, Brain, and Vision*, New York: Scientific American Library.

Hutchins, E. (1983). Understanding Micronesian Navigation. In D. Gentner and A. L. Stevens (Eds.), *Mental Models*, pp. 191–225. Hillsdale, NJ: Lawrence Erlbaum.

(1995). *Cognition in the Wild*. Cambridge, MA: The MIT Press.

Ito, Karen L. (1985). Affective Bonds: Hawaiian Interrelationships of Self. In Geoffrey M. White and John Kirkpatrick (Eds.), *Person, Self, and Experience: Exploring Pacific Ethnopsychologies*, pp. 301–27. Berkeley, CA: University of California Press.

Jackendoff, R. (1983). *Semantics and Cognition*. Cambridge, MA: The MIT Press.

(1990). *Semantic Structures*. Cambridge, MA: The MIT Press.

(1992a). Is There a Faculty of Social Cognition? In Ray Jackendoff, *Language of the Mind: Essays on Mental Representation*, pp. 69–82. Cambridge, MA: The MIT Press.

(1992b). *Languages of the Mind: Essays on Mental Representation*. Cambridge, MA: The MIT Press.

(1997). *The Architecture of the Language Faculty*. Cambridge, MA: The MIT Press.

(1999). The Natural Logic of Rights and Obligations. In Ray Jackendoff, Paul Bloom, and Karen Wynn (Eds.), *Language, Logic, and Concepts*, pp. 67–95. Cambridge, MA: The MIT Press.

(2002). *Foundations of Language: Brain, Meaning, Grammar, and Evolution*. Oxford: Oxford University Press.

(2007). *Language, Consciousness, Culture: Essays on Mental Structure*. Cambridge, MA: The MIT Press.

Jackendoff, R. and B. Landau. (1992). Spatial Language and Spatial Cognition. In Ray Jackendoff, *Languages of the Mind: Essays on Mental Representation*, pp. 99–124. Cambridge, MA: The MIT Press.

James, K. (1991). Regeneration in Heaven. *History and Anthropology*, 5, 2: 259–67.

(1994). Tonga's Pro-Democracy Movement. *Pacific Affairs*, 67, 2: 242–63.

(1995). Right and Privilege in Tongan Land Tenure. In R. Gerard Ward, and Elizabeth Kingdon (Eds.), *Land, Custom and Practice in The South Pacific*, pp. 157–97. Cambridge: Cambridge University Press.

(2002). The Recent Elections in Tonga: Democratic Supporters Win but Does Democracy Follow? *Journal of Pacific History*, 37, 3: 313–22.

(2003). Is There a Tongan Middle Class? Hierarchy and Protest in Contemporary Tonga. *The Contemporary Pacific*, 15, 2: 309–36.

Johnson, Mark. (1987). *The Body in the Mind: The Bodily Basis of Meaning, Imagination, and Reason*. Chicago, IL: University of Chicago Press.

Johnson-Laird, P. N. (1980). Mental Models in Cognitive Science. *Cognitive Science*, 4: 71–115.

(1983). *Mental Models: Towards a Cognitive Science of Language, Inference, and Consciousness*. Cambridge: Cambridge University Press.

(1999). Mental Models. In R. A. Wilson and F. C. Keil (Eds.), *The MIT Encyclopedia of the Cognitive Sciences*, pp. 525–7. Cambridge, MA: The MIT Press.

Kaeppler, A. L. (1971). Rank in Tonga. *Ethnology*, 10, 2: 174–93.

(1978a). Melody, Drone, and Decoration: Underlying Structures and Surface Manifestations in Tongan Art and Society. In M. Greenhalgh and V. Megaw (Eds.), *Art in Society: Studies in Styles, Culture and Aesthetics*, pp. 261–274. Washington, DC: National Gallery of Art.

(1978b). Me'a Faka'eiki: Tongan Funerals in a Changing Society. In Niel Gunson (Ed.), *The Changing Pacific: Essays in Honour of H. E. Maude*, pp. 174–202. Oxford: Oxford University Press.

(1978c). Exchange Patterns in Goods and Spouses: Fiji, Tonga and Samoa. *Mankind*, 11, 3: 246–52.

Kavaliku, Sione Langi. (1977). 'Ofa! The Treasure of Tonga. *South Pacific Social Science*, 6: 47–67.

Keenan, Elinor Ochs. (1974). *Conversation and Oratory in Vakinankaratra, Madagascar*. Ph.D. dissertation, University of Pennsylvania.

Keesing, R. (1984). Rethinking Mana. *Journal of Anthropological Research*, 40, 1: 137–56.

Keller, Janet D. (1992). Schemas for Schemata. In Theodore Schwartz, G. M. White, and Catherine A. Lutz (Eds.), *New Directions in Psychological Anthropology*, pp. 59–67. Cambridge: Cambridge University Press.

Keller, J. D. and C. M. Keller. (1993). Thinking and Acting with Iron. In S. Chaiklin and J. Lave (Eds.), *Understanding Practice: Perspectives on Activity and Context*, pp. 125–43. Cambridge: Cambridge University Press.

(1996a). Imaging in Iron, or Thought is not Inner Speech. In J. J. Gumperz and S. C. Levinson (Eds.), *Rethinking Linguistic Relativity*, pp. 115–29. Cambridge: Cambridge University Press.

(1996b). *Cognition and Tool Use: The Blacksmith at Work.* Cambridge: Cambridge University Press.

Keller, J. D. and F. K. Lehman. (1991). Complex Concepts. *Cognitive Science*, 15, 2: 271–92.

(1993). Computational Complexity in the Cognitive Modeling of Cosmological Ideas. In Pascal Boyer (Ed.), *Cognitive Aspects of Religious Symbolism*, pp. 74–92. Cambridge: Cambridge University Press.

Kingdom of Tonga. (2007). *Preliminary Results: Population Census 2006.* Nuku'alofa: Statistics Department.

Kirch, P. V. (1988). A Brief History of Lapita Archaeology. In P. V. Kirch and T. L. Hunt (Eds.), *Archaeology of the Lapita Cultural Complex: A Critical Review*, pp. 1–8. Seattle, WA: Burke Museum.

Kirch, V. Patrick. (1990). *The Evolution of the Polynesian Chiefdoms.* Cambridge: Cambridge University Press.

Kirk, J. and P. J. Epling. (1973). Taxonomy of the Polynesian Languages. *Anthropological Linguistics*, 15, 1: 42–70.

Kirkpatrick, John. (1985). Some Marquesan Understanding of Actions and Identity. In Geoffrey M. White and John Kirkpatrick (Eds.), *Person, Self, and Experience: Exploring Pacific Ethnopsychologies*, pp. 80–120. Berkeley, CA: University of California Press.

Kita, S., E. Danziger, and C. Stolz. (2001). Cultural Specificity of Spatial Schemas, as Manifested in Spontaneous Gestures. In M. Gattis (Ed.), *Spatial Schemas and Abstract Thought*, pp. 115–46. Cambridge: MIT Press.

Korn, Shumalit R. Deckter. (1974). Tonga Kin Groups: The Noble and the Common View. *Journal of the Polynesian Society*, 83: 5–13.

(1978). Hunting the Ramage: Kinship and the Organization of Political Authority in Aboriginal Tonga. *Journal of Pacific History*, 13, 1: 107–13.

Krackhardt, D. (1987). Cognitive Social Structures. *Social Networks*, 9: 109–34.

Kranjec, A. (2006). Extending Spatial Frames of Reference to Temporal Concepts. In R. Sun and N. Miyake (Eds.), *Proceedings of the 28th Annual Conference of the Cognitive Science Society*, pp. 447–52. Mahwah, NJ: Lawrence Erlbaum.

Kronenfeld, David. (1973). Fanti Kinship: The Structure of Terminology and Behaviour. *American Anthropologist*, 75: 1577–95.

(1996). *Plastic Glasses and Church Fathers.* Oxford: Oxford University Press.

(2008). Cultural Models. *Intercultural Pragmatics*, 5, 1: 67–74.

Kuipers, Joel C. (1998). *Language, Identity, and Marginality in Indonesia: The Changing Nature of Ritual Speech on the Island of Sumba.* Cambridge: Cambridge University Press.

Kusserow, A. (2004). *American Individualisms: Child Rearing and Social Class in Three Neighbourhoods.* New York: Palgrave Macmillan.

Kyselka, Will. (1987). *An Ocean in Mind.* Honolulu, HI: University of Hawai'i Press.

Lakoff, G. (1987). *Women, Fire, and Dangerous Things: What Categories Reveal about the Mind.* Chicago, IL: The University of Chicago Press.

Lakoff, G. and M. Johnson. (1980). *Metaphors We Live By.* Chicago, IL: University of Chicago Press.

Landau, B. and R. Jackendoff. (1993). "What" and "Where" in Spatial Language and Spatial Cognition. *Behavioral and Brain Sciences*, 16, 2: 17–38.

Lātūkefu, S. (1974). *Church and State in Tonga*. Honolulu, HI: The University of Hawai'i Press.

Lawry, William. (1852). *Missions in the Tonga and Feejee Islands*. New York: Lane and Scott.

Leach, Edmund. (1974). *Claude Lévi-Strauss*. Chicago, IL: The University of Chicago Press.

Leaf, Murray. (1971). The Punjabi Kinship Terminology as a Semantic System. *American Anthropologist*, 73: 545–54.

Lehman, F. K. (1985). Cognition and Computation: On Being Sufficiently Abstract. In Janet D. W. Dougherty (Ed.), *Directions in Cognitive Anthropology*, pp. 19–48. Urbana, IL: University of Illinois Press.

Lehman, F. K. and G. Bennardo. (2003). A Computational Approach to the Cognition of Space and its Linguistic Expression. *Mathematical Anthropology and Cultural Theory*, 1, 2: 1–83.

Lehman, F. K. and K. Witz. (1974). Prolegomena to a Formal Theory of Kinship. In P. Ballanoff (Ed.), *Genealogical Mathematics*, pp. 111–34. The Hague: Mouton.

(1979). A Formal Theory of Kinship: The Transformational Component. *Report #11, Committee on Culture and Cognition*. University of Illinois at Urbana-Champaign.

Levelt, W. J. M. (1982). Cognitive Styles in the Use of Spatial Direction Terms. In R. J. Jarvella and W. Klein (Eds.), *Speech, Place, and Action: Studies in Deixis and Related Topics*, pp. 251–70. New York: John Wiley & Sons Ltd.

Levelt, J. M. William. (1984). Some Perceptual Limitations on Talking About Space. In A. J. van Doorn, W. A. van de Grind, and J. Koenderink (Eds.), *Limits in Perception*, pp. 323–58. Utrecht: VNU Science Press.

(1989). *Speaking: From Intention to Articulation*. Cambridge, MA: The MIT Press.

Levinson, S. C. (1996a). Frames of Reference and Molyneaux's Question: Cross-Linguistic Evidence. In P. Bloom, M. A. Peterson, L. Nadel, and M. F. Garrett (Eds.), *Language and Space*, pp. 109–70. Cambridge, MA: The MIT Press.

(1996b). Language and Space. *Annual Review of Anthropology*, 25: 353–82.

(2003). *Space in Language and Cognition*. Cambridge: Cambridge University Press.

(2006). On the Human "Interaction Engine." In N. J. Enfield and Stephen C. Levinson (Eds.), *Roots of Human Sociality: Culture, Cognition, and Interaction*, pp. 39–69. Oxford: Berg.

Levi-Strauss, Claude. (1952). *Structural Anthropology*. New York: Basic Books.

Levy, Robert I. (1973). *Tahitians: Mind and Experience in the Society Islands*. Chicago, IL: University of Chicago Press.

Lewis, David. (1964). Polynesian Navigational Methods. *Journal of the Polynesian Society*, 73, 4: 364–74.

(1972). *We, the Navigators*. Honolulu, HI: The University of Hawai'i Press.

(1974). Voyaging Stars: Aspects of Polynesian and Micronesian Astronomy. In *The Place of Astronomy in the Ancient World*. A Joint Symposium of the Royal Society and The British Academy. London: Oxford University Press.

Liben, L. S., A. H. Patterson, and N. Newcombe (Eds.). (1981). *Spatial Representation and Behavior Across the Life Span*. New York: Academic Press.

Lichtenberk, Frantisek. (1985). Possessive Constructions in Oceanic Languages and in Proto-Oceanic. In Andrew Pawley and Lois Carrington (Eds.), *Austronesian Linguistics at the 15th Pacific Studies Science Congress*, pp. 93–140. Pacific Linguistics, C-88.

Linkels, Ad. (1992). *Sounds of Change in Tonga*. Nuku'alofa, Tonga: Friendly Islands Book Shop.

Lloyd, R. (1997). *Spatial Cognition: Geographic Environments*. Boston, MA: Kluwer Academic Publishers.

Lynch, J. (1972). Passives and Statives in Tongan. *The Journal of the Polynesian Society*, 81, 1: 5–18.

  (1982). Towards a Theory of the Origin of the Oceanic Possessive Constructions. In Amran Halim, Lois Carrington, and S. A. Wurm (Eds.), *Papers from the Third International Conference on Austronesian Linguistics*, Vol. 1, *Pacific Linguistics*, Series C-74, pp. 243–68.

Lyons, J. (1977). *Semantics*. Cambridge: Cambridge University Press.

Mackey, M. C. (2003). *Time's Arrow: The Origins of Thermodynamic Behavior*. Mineola, NY: Dover.

Mageo, Jeannette M. (1998). *Theorizing Self in Samoa: Emotions, Genders, and Sexualities*. Ann Arbor, MI: The University of Michigan Press.

Magnon, A. (1997). *Arrow of Time and Reality: In Search of a Conciliation*. Singapore: World Scientific.

Malinowsky, Bronislaw K. (1922). *Argonauts of the Western Pacific*. New York: E. P. Dutton.

Mandler, Jean M. (1984). *Stories, Scripts, and Scenes: Aspect of Schema Theory*. Hillsdale, NJ: Lawrence Erlbaum Associates.

  (2004). *The Foundations of Mind: Origins of Conceptual Thought*. Oxford: Oxford University Press.

Marcus, G. E. (1977). Succession Disputes and the Position of the Nobility in Modern Tonga. *Oceania*, 47: 220–41.

  (1978). Status Rivalry in a Polynesia Steady-State Society. *Ethos*, 6: 242–69.

  (1980). *The Nobility and the Chiefly Tradition in the Modern Kingdom of Tonga*. Wellington: The Polynesian Society, Inc.

Marr, David. (1982). *Vision*. New York: W. H. Freeman and Company.

Marshall, L. (1976). *The !Kung of Nyae Nyae*. Cambridge, MA: Harvard University Press.

Martin, J. (1818). *The Natives of the Tongan Islands*. London: John Murray.

Maude, Alaric. (1971). Tonga: Equality Overtaking Privilege. In Ron Crocombe (Ed.), *Land Tenure in the Pacific*, pp. 106–28. Oxford: Oxford University Press.

McCarty, C. (2002). Measuring Structure in Personal Networks. *Journal of Social Structure*, 3, 1.

McGlone, M. S. and J. L. Harding. (1998). Back (or Forward?) to the Future: The Role of Perspective in Temporal Language Comprehension. *Journal of Experimental Psychology: Learning, Memory, and Cognition*, 24: 1211–23.

Mead, G. H. 1967[1934]. *Mind, Self and Society*. Chicago, IL: The University of Chicago Press.

Medin, D. L. (1989). Concepts and Conceptual Structure. *American Psychologist*, 44, 12: 1469–81.

Miller, G. A. and P. N. Johnson-Laird. (1976). *Language and Perception*. Cambridge, MA: The Belknap Press of Harvard University Press.

Milner, G. (1973). It is Aspect (not Voice) Which is Marked in Samoan. *Oceanic Linguistics*, 12, 2: 621–40.

(1976). Ergative and Passive in Basque and Polynesian. *Oceanic Linguistics*, 15, 1: 93–106.

Minsky, M. (1975). A Framework for Representing Knowledge. In P. H. Winston (Ed.), *The Psychology of Computer Vision*, pp. 211–77. New York: McGraw-Hill.

Modell, Judith S. (Ed.). (2002). Constructing Moral Communities: Pacific Islander Strategies for Settling in New Places. Special issue of *Pacific Studies*, 25: 1–2.

Moore, E. Timothy. (Ed.). (1973). *Cognitive Development and the Acquisition of Language*. New York: Academic Press.

Morton, Helen. (1996). *Becoming Tongan: An Ethnography of Childhood*. Honolulu, HI: University of Hawai'i Press.

(2003). *Tongan Overseas: Between Two Shores*. Honolulu, HI: University of Hawai'i Press.

Morton, K. L. (1972). *Kinship, Economics, and Exchange in a Tongan Village*. Ph.D. Dissertation, University of Oregon.

Murphy, G. L. and D. Medin. (1985). The Role of Theories in Conceptual Coherence. *Psychological Review*, 92, 3: 289–316.

Nisbett, Richard E. (2003). *The Geography of Thought: How Asians and Westerners Think Differently … and Why*. New York: The Free Press.

Núñez, R. E. and E. Sweetser. (2006). With the Future behind them. Convergent Evidence from Aymara Language and Gesture in the Crosslinguistic Comparison of Spatial Construals of Time. *Cognitive Science*, 30, 401–50.

Núñez, R. E., B. A. Motz, and U. Teuscher. (2006). Time after Time: The Psychological Reality of the Ego- and Time-Reference-Point Distinction in Metaphorical Construals of Time. *Metaphor and Symbol*, 21, 133–46.

Ochs, Elinor. (1984). Clarification and Culture. In D. Shiffrin (Ed.), *Georgetown University Round Table in Languages and Linguistics*, pp. 325–41. Washington, DC: Georgetown University Press.

(1988). *Culture and Language Development: Language Acquisition and Language Socialization in a Samoan Village*. Cambridge: Cambridge University Press.

Olivier, Patrick and Klaus-Peter Gapp. (1998). *Representation and Processing of Spatial Expressions*. Mahwah, NJ: Lawrence Erlbaum Associates, Publishers.

Ozanne-Rivierre, F. (1997). Spatial References in New Caledonian Languages. In Gunter Senft (Ed.), *Referring to Space: Studies in Austronesian and Papuan Languages*, pp. 83–100. Oxford: Oxford University Press.

Palmer, Bill. (2002). Absolute Spatial Reference and the Grammaticalisation of Perceptually Salient Phenomena. In G. Bennardo (Ed.), *Representing Space in Oceania: Culture in Language and Mind*, pp. 107–57. Canberra, Australia: Pacific Linguistics, Research School of Pacific and Asian Studies, The Australian National University.

Pawley, A. (1966). Polynesian Languages: A Subgrouping Based on Shared Innovations in Morphology. *The Journal of the Polynesian Society*, 75, 1: 39–64.

(1973). Some Problems in Proto-Oceanic Grammar. *Oceanic Linguistics*, 12: 103–88.

(1974) Austronesian Languages, *Encyclopedia Britannica*, 13th Edition, pp. 484–93.

Pederson, Eric. (1993). Geographic and Manipulable Space in Two Tamil Linguistic Systems. In Andrew U. Frank and Irene Campari (Eds.), *Spatial Information Theory: A Theoretical Basis for GIS*, pp. 294–311. Berlin: Springer.

(1995). Language as Context, Language as Means: Spatial Cognition and Habitual Language Use. *Cognitive Linguistics*, 6, 1: 33–62.

Pederson, Eric and Ardi Roelofs (Eds.). (1995). *Max-Planck Institute for Psycholinguistics: Annual Report 15, 1994*. Nijmegen, The Netherlands: Max-Planck Institute for Psycholinguistics.

Pederson, Eric, Eve Danziger, David Wilkins, Stephen Levinson, Sotaro Kita, and Gunter Senft. (1998). Semantic Typology and Spatial Conceptualization. *Language*, 74: 557–89.

Piaget, Jean and Barbel Inhelder. (1956). *The Child's Conception of Space*. New York: The Humanities Press Inc.

Pick, L. Herbert. (1993). Organization of Spatial Knowledge in Children. In N. Eilan, R. McCarthy, and B. Brewer (Eds.), *Spatial Representation: Problems in Philosophy and Psychology*, pp. 31–42. Oxford: Basil Blackwell Ltd.

Pinker, S. (1994). *The Language Instinct*. New York: HarperCollins.

   (1997). *How the Mind Works*. New York: W. W. Norton & Company.

   (1999). *Words and Rules*. New York: Basic Books.

Quinn, Naomi. (2005). *Finding Culture in Talk: A Collections of Methods*. New York: Palgrave Macmillan.

Read, D. W. (1984) An Algebraic Account of the American Kinship Terminology. *Current Anthropology*, 25: 417–440.

   (1997). Kinship Algebra Expert System: A Software Program for Modeling the Logic of Kinship Terminologies. Unpublished manuscript. UCLA.

   (2000). Formal Analysis of Kinship Terminologies and its Relationship to What Constitutes Kinship. *Mathematical Anthropology and Cultural Theory*, 1, 1: 1–46. See http://www.mathematicalanthropology.org/

   (2001a). Formal Analysis of Kinship Terminologies and its Relationship to What Constitutes Kinship. [In special issue 'Kinship'] *Anthropological Theory*, 1, 2: 239–67.

   (2001b) What is Kinship? In R. Feinberg and M. Ottenheimer (Eds.), *The Cultural Analysis of Kinship: The Legacy of David Schneider and Its Implications for Anthropological Relativism*, pp. 78–117. Urbana, IL: University of Illinois Press.

   (2005) Kinship Algebra Expert System (KAES): A Software Implementation of a Cultural Theory. *Social Science Computer Review*, 24, 1: 43–67.

Read, D. W. and C. A. Behrens. (1990). KAES, an Expert System for the Algebraic Analysis of Kinship Terminologies. *Journal of Quantitative Anthropology*, 2: 353–93.

Read, D. W. and M. D. Fischer. (2004). Kinship Algebra Expert System (KAES). See http://kaes.anthrosciences.net/

Rivers, W. H. R. (1916). The Father's Sister in Oceania. *Folk-Lore*, 21: 42–59.

Rogers, G. (1977). 'The Father's Sister is Black': A Consideration of Female Rank and Powers in Tonga. *Journal of the Polynesian Society*, 86: 157–82.

Romney, A. K. (1989). Quantitative Models, Science and Cumulative Knowledge. *Journal of Quantitative Research*, 1: 153–223.

Ross, H. M. (1973). *Baegu: Social and Ecological Organization in Malaita, Solomon Islands*. Urbana, IL: University of Illinois Press.

Ross, Norbert. (2004). *Culture and Cognition: Implications for Theory and Method*. London: Sage Publications.

Rumelhart, David. (1980). Schemata: The Building Block of Cognition. In R. Spiro (Ed.), *Theoretical Issues in Reading Comprehension*, pp. 33–58. Hillsdale, NJ: Lawrence Erlbaum Associates, Publishers.

Sahlins, M. D. (1958). *Social Stratification in Polynesia*. Seattle, WA: University of Washington Press.

  (1962). *Moala: Culture and Nature on a Fijian Island*. Englewood Cliffs, NJ: Prentice-Hall.

Schieffelin, Bambi B. (1990). *The Give and Take of Everyday Life: Language Socialization of Kaluli Children*. Cambridge: Cambridge University Press.

Scott, J. (1992). *Social Network Analysis*. Newbury Park, CA: Sage.

Senft, Gunter. (1994). Spatial Reference in Kilivila: The Tinkertoy Matching Game – A Case Study. *Language and Linguistics in Melanesia*, 25: 55–93.

Senft, G. (Ed.). (1997). *Referring to Space: Studies in Austronesian and Papuan Languages*. Oxford: Oxford University Press.

Shapiro, Warren. (1982). The Place of Cognitive Extensionism in the History of Anthropological Thought. *Journal of the Polynesian Society*, 91: 257–97.

Sharp, Andrew. (1964a). Polynesian Navigation. *The Journal of the Institute of Navigation*, 11, 1: 75–6.

  (1964b). *Ancient Voyagers in Polynesia*. Berkeley, CA: University of California Press.

Shore, Bradd. (1989). Mana and Tapu. In Alan Howard and Robert Borofsky (Eds.), *Developments in Polynesian Ethnology*, pp. 137–73. Honolulu, HI: University of Hawai'i Press.

  (1996). *Culture in Mind: Cognition, Culture, and the Problem of Meaning*. Oxford: Oxford University Press.

Shumway, B. Eric. (1988). *Intensive Course in Tongan*. Laie, HI: The Institute for Polynesian Studies.

Small, Cathy. (1997). *Voyages: From Tongan Villages to American Suburbs*. Ithaca, NY: Cornell University Press.

Stiles-Davis, Joan, Mark Kritchevsky, and Ursula Bellugi (Eds.). (1988). *Spatial Cognition: Brain Bases and Development*. London: Lawrence Erlbaum Associates, Publishers.

Strauss, Claudia and Naomi Quinn. (1997). *A Cognitive Theory of Cultural Meaning*. Cambridge: Cambridge University Press.

Talmy, Leonard. (1983). How Language Structures Space. In H. L. Pick and L. P. Acredolo (Eds.), *Spatial Orientation: Theory, Research, and Application*, pp. 225–82. New York: Plenum Press.

  (2000a). *Toward a Cognitive Semantics, Volume 1: Concept Structuring Systems*. Cambridge, MA: The MIT Press.

  (2000b). *Toward a Cognitive Semantics, Volume 2: Typology and Process in Concept Structuring*. Cambridge, MA: The MIT Press.

Taumoefolau, Melenaite. (1996). Nominal Possessive Classification in Tongan. In John Lynch and Fa'afo Pat (Eds.), *Oceanic Studies: Proceedings of the First International Conference on Oceanic Linguistics*, pp. 295–306. Pacific Linguistics, C-133.

Tchekhoff, C. (1973a). Some Verbal Patterns in Tongan. *The Journal of the Polynesian Society*, 82, 3: 281–92.

  (1973b). Verbal Aspects in an Ergative Construction: An Example in Tongan. *Oceanic Linguistics*, 12, 2: 607–20.

(1981). *Simple Sentences in Tongan*. Canberra: Department of Linguistics, Research School of Pacific Studies, The Australian National University.

(1990). Discourse and Tongan mai, atu, ange : Scratching the Surface. in J. H. C. S. Davidson (Ed.), *Pacific Island Languages*, pp. 105–10. Honolulu, HI: University of Hawai'i Press.

Terrell, J. (1986). *Prehistory in the Pacific Islands*. Cambridge: Cambridge University Press.

Tovée, Martin, J. (1996). *An Introduction to the Visual System*. Cambridge: Cambridge University Press.

Triandis, Harry C. (1995). *Individualism and Collectivism*. Boulder, CO: Westview Press.

Tuan, Yi-Fu. (1974). *Topophilia: A Study of Environmental Perception, Attitudes, and Values*. Englewood Cliffs, NJ: Prentice-Hall, Inc.

Tupouniua, P. (1977). *A Polynesian Village: The Process of Change*. Suva, Fiji: South Pacific Social Sciences Association.

Turnbull, David. (1994). Comparing Knowledge Systems: Pacific Navigation and Western Science. In J. Morrison, P. Gerarthy, and L. Crowl. (Eds.), *Science of Pacific Island People: Ocean and Coastal Studies. Vol. 1*, pp. 129–44. Institute of Pacific Studies.

Tversky, Barbara. (1981). Distortions in Memory for Maps. *Cognitive Psychology*, 13: 407–33.

(1993). Cognitive Maps, Cognitive Collages, and Spatial Mental Models. In Andrew U. Frank and Irene Campari (Eds.), *Spatial Information Theory: A Theoretical Basis for GIS*, pp. 14–24. Berlin: Springer.

(1996). Spatial Perspective in Descriptions. In P. Bloom, M. A. Peterson, L. Nadel, and M. F. Garrett (Eds.), *Language and Space*, pp. 463–529. Cambridge, MA: The MIT Press.

Valeri, Valerio. (1985). *Kinship and Sacrifice: Ritual and Society in Ancient Hawai'i*. Chicago, IL: University of Chicago Press.

van der Grijp, P. (1993). *Islanders of the South*. Leiden: KITLV Press.

(2004). *Identity and Development: Tongan Culture, Agriculture, and the Perenniality of the Gift*. Leiden: KITLV Press.

Wasserman, Stanley and Katherine Faust. (1994). *Social Network Analysis: Methods and Applications*. Cambridge: Cambridge University Press.

Wassmann, J. (1994). The Yupno as post-Newtonian Scientists: The Question of What is 'Natural' in Spatial Description. *Man*, 29: 645–66.

Wassmann, Jürg and Pierre R. Dasen. (1998). Balinese Spatial Orientation: Some Empirical Evidence of Moderate Linguistic Relativity. *Journal of the Royal Anthropological Institute (incorp. Man)*, 4: 689–711.

Webster, Murray, Jr. and Stuart J. Hysom. (1998). Creating Status Characteristics. *American Sociological Review*, 63: 351–78.

Weiner, Annette B. (1976). *Women of Value, Men of Renown, New Perspectives in Trobriand Exchange*. Austin, TX: University of Texas Press.

Weissenborn, Jürgen. (1986). Learning How to Become an Interlocutor: The Verbal Negotiation of Common Frames of Reference and Actions in Dyads of 7–14 Year Old Children. In Jenny Cook-Gumperz, William A. Corsaro, and Juergen Streeck (Eds.), *Children's Worlds and Children's Language*, pp. 377–404. Berlin: Mouton de Gruyter.

Weller, Susan C. and A. Kimball Romney. (1988). *Systematic Data Collection*. Newbury Park, CA: Sage Publications.

Wellman, B. and S. Wortley. (1990). Different Strokes from Different Folks: Community Ties and Social Support. *American Journal of Sociology*, 96: 558–688.

Westerhoff, Jan. (2005). *Ontological Categories: Their Nature and Significance*. Oxford: Clarendon Press.

White, Geoffrey M. and John Kirkpatrick (Eds.). (1985). *Person, Self, and Experience: Exploring Pacific Ethnopsychologies*. Berkeley, CA: University of California Press.

Williams, David W. and James D. Hollan. (1981). The Process of Retrieval from Very Long-Term Memory. *Cognitive Science*, 5: 87–119.

Williamson, R. W. (1933). *Religious and Cosmic Beliefs of Central Polynesia*. Vols. I and II. Cambridge: Cambridge University Press.

Wilson, William H. (1976). The o/a Distinction in Hawaiian Possessives. *Oceanic Linguistics*, 15, 1: 39–50.

(1982). *Proto-Polynesian Possessive Marking*. Pacific Linguistics, B-85.

Author Index

Subject Index

absolute FoR, 124, 168, 177
  cardinal points subtype, 61
  radial subtype, 61, 124, 130, 146, 154, 182
  single-axis subtype, 61, 86
  uses of, 65, 70–75
approach to cognition, 4
  blended, 8
  radically intensional, 4, 8, 340
architecture of human cognition, 3, 340
  revision of, 341, 342
atu 'away from center', 175, 252
*atu*1 'away from speaker/to addressee', 253
*atu*2 'away from other-than-speaker', 253
authority ranking, 312, 317, 337
axioms of space, 179–180
axis bias, 100

Cayley product table, 215, 233
centrality of the sibling relation, 238
circle graphs, 317, 330, 333, 337
classificatory terminology, 208, 225
closeness of recall, 290
cluster analysis, 324, 325
clustering strategies, 304
cognitive preferences, 106
cognitive tasks, 16, 178
  drawing task, 247, 287
  free listing, 247, 287
  pile sort, 247, 287
collectivism, 14
communal sharing, 312, 317, 337
compositionality, 179
constellations of knowledge, 7
correlation, 333, 334, 337
  rationale, 317
cultural milieu, 106, 186, 341, 346
  as a behavioral place, 106
  as a human place, 106
  as a physical place, 106
cultural model, 10, 12, 174, 243, 263, 341, 343, 346
  definition of, 11, 174

location in mind, 11, 341
  minimal typology, 341, 344
cultural strategies, 293, 294
cultural tasks, 88, 116
  drawing, 116, 117, 169
  memory, 116, 131, 169
culture in mind, 10, 13, 341

deck of photo cards, 296
Digitized Tonga database, 107, 290
discourse organization analysis, 252, 283
domains of knowledge, 2, 187
drawing strategies, 122, 126

ego, 1, 212, 260, 276, 279, 280, 299, 303, 336, 341
  field of, 2, 3, 177
ego-centered networks, 246
egocentric selves, 13
ego-to-other, 276
equality matching, 317
ethnographic data, 16, 243, 246, 287
exchanges, 110, 155, 186
experimental data, 245, 246

faka'apa'apa 'respect', 264
fakaafe 'invitation', 110, 155
fala 'mat', 26, 163
fale 'house', 36
fale papa 'European house', 78
fale Tonga 'oval thatched houses', 78
fāmili 'family', 25, 156, 297
fetongi 'exchange', 110, 155
field sites, 31
  Hihifo, 36
  Houma, 32
  Ngele'ia, 34
fono 'meeting', 27, 110, 131, 186
FoR cognitive tasks, 88, 104
  Animals in a Row, 89, 90, 98
  Red and Blue Chips, 89, 92, 98, 99, 102
  Transitivity, 89, 93, 102

368

spatial nouns, 28, 52, 56
spatial prepositions, 3, 29, 48
typology of FoRs, 43, 182, 184, 186

untranslatability, 178, 182
uses of FoR in Tongan

in large-scale space, 62, 70, 75
in small-scale space, 62, 70

variance, 325
visibility, 66, 76, 77, 82, 86, 103, 180
lack of, 66